ITEMS:

ITEMS: Is Fashion Modern?

Paola Antonelli
and Michelle Millar Fisher

THE MUSEUM OF MODERN ART, NEW YORK

Published in conjunction with the exhibition *Items: Is Fashion Modern?*, organized by Paola Antonelli, Senior Curator, and Michelle Millar Fisher, Curatorial Assistant, Department of Architecture and Design, at The Museum of Modern Art, New York, October 1, 2017–January 28, 2018

Hyundai Card

The exhibition is made possible by Hyundai Card.

WGSN

Major support is provided by WGSN.

Sincere thanks to the members of Friends of *Items*, a special patron group generously supporting the Museum in celebration of the exhibition.

Paint provided by Farrow & Ball.

Additional support is provided by the Annual Exhibition Fund.

Produced by the
Department of Publications,
The Museum of Modern Art, New York
Christopher Hudson —*Publisher*
Chul R. Kim —*Associate Publisher*
Don McMahon —*Editorial Director*
Marc Sapir —*Production Director*

Edited by Rebecca Roberts with Stephanie Emerson, Emily Hall, Tanya Heinrich, Libby Hruska, Maria Marchenkova, and Don McMahon
Image consultancy by Sarah Rafson, Point Line Projects
Book concept and design by Lana Cavar and Natasha Chandani, Clanada
Illustrations by Narcisa Vukojevic
Production by Hannah Kim
Printed and bound by Gorenjski Tisk Storitve, Slovenia

This book is typeset in Circular Pro and Burgess. The paper is 100 gsm Munken Polar Rough and 135 gsm Magno Starr

Published by
The Museum of Modern Art
11 West 53 Street
New York, New York 10019-5497
www.moma.org

Library of Congress Control Number: 2017952659

ISBN: 978-1-63345-036-3

Distributed in the United States and Canada by Artbook | D.A.P.
75 Broad Street, Suite 630
New York, New York 10004
www.artbook.com

Distributed outside the United States and Canada by Thames & Hudson Ltd
181A High Holborn, London WC1V 7QX
www.thamesandhudson.com

Front cover: Ben Westwood, *Carry On Kilts* (detail), promotional image for Worlds End Boutique, London, 2016. See p. 153

Back cover: Kabelo Kungwane, a member of the South African design collective Sartists, 2015. Photograph by Keagan Kingsley Carlin. See p. 93

Printed in Slovenia

093

019

017

Hyundai Card

Hyundai Card is proud to sponsor *Items: Is Fashion Modern?* at The Museum of Modern Art, New York. This trailblazing exhibition provides a first-of-its-kind opportunity to understand fashion within the wider field of design.

As MoMA's first exhibition on fashion in many decades, *Items* examines fashion in the context of society, culture, and technology rather than through the typical lens of mass consumption. The exhibition challenges existing ideas about fashion's role in contemporary culture and reconsiders fashion as a catalyst for social change. By tracing the history of each item's design and offering visions of its future, *Items* both reflects on today and helps us speculate about tomorrow.

Hyundai Card is committed to creating and promoting the kind of forward-thinking vision that is exemplified in *Items*. As Korea's foremost issuer of credit cards, Hyundai Card seeks to identify changes in culture, society, and technology and to utilize them to enrich lives. Whether we're hosting tomorrow's cultural pioneers at our stages and art spaces, building libraries devoted to design, travel, music, and cooking for our members, or designing credit cards and digital services that are as beautiful as they are functional, Hyundai Card's most inventive endeavors all draw from the creative well that the arts provide.

A nine-year sponsor of The Museum of Modern Art, Hyundai Card is delighted to make *Items: Is Fashion Modern?* possible.

CORE EXHIBITION TEAM

Department of Architecture and Design
Paola Antonelli —*Senior Curator*
Michelle Millar Fisher —*Curatorial Assistant*

Stephanie Kramer —*Research Assistant*
Anna Burckhardt —*Twelve-Month Intern*
Kristina Parsons —*Project Curatorial Assistant*
Margot Drayson, Alice Gong, Oliver Graney,
and Maria McLintock —*Seasonal Interns*

Department of Exhibition Planning
Rachel Kim —*Exhibition Manager*

Department of Exhibition Design
Betty Fisher —*Senior Manager*
Aaron Harrow—*AV Design Manager*
Mike Gibbons—*AV Exhibitions Foreperson*

Department of Graphic Design
Elle Kim —*Senior Art Director*
Kevin Ballon —*Graphic Designer*
Claire Corey —*Production Manager*

Department of Education
Sara Bodinson —*Director, Interpretation*
Jenna Madison —*Assistant Director,
Interpretation*

Department of Registration
Jennifer Wolfe —*Associate Registrar*
Regan Hillman —*Senior Assistant Registrar*

Department of Art Preparation
Tom Krueger —*Assistant Manager,
Art Handling and Preparation*

Department of Conservation
Lynda Zycherman —*Sculpture Conservator*
Megan Randall —*David Booth Fellow in
Sculpture Conservation*

Master Dresser
Tae Smith

Department of Publications
Rebecca Roberts —*Editor*
Hannah Kim —*Senior Marketing and
Production Coordinator*
Maria Marchenkova —*Assistant Editor*

Department of Communications
Meg Montgoris —*Publicist*

Department of Development
Bobby Kean —*Associate Director,
Exhibition Funding*
Jessica Smith —*Development Officer*

074

033

WGSN

We believe that we are all citizens of the world and members of communities.

We believe that geographical coordinates are figments of the imagination.

We believe that inspiration comes from the monumental and the mundane.

We believe that good design can and has changed the world.

Which is why we are proud to be major supporters of *Items: Is Fashion Modern?* at The Museum of Modern Art, New York.

We are WGSN, and with you we create tomorrow.

WGSN is the world's leading trend authority for creative thinkers. Our global trend forecasters and data scientists obsessively decode the future to provide the authoritative view on tomorrow.

095

111 items, with texts by Luke Baker (LB), Anna Burckhardt (AB), Michelle Millar Fisher (MMF), Stephanie Kramer (SK), Mei Mei Rado (MMR), and Jennifer Tobias (JT)

051

047

104

053

070

064

FOREWORD   As exhibitions at The Museum of Modern Art have demonstrated time and again, design shapes us all and a rigorous and considered design history must be expansive. Yet historically the Museum has not engaged with one particular area of design: fashion. *Items: Is Fashion Modern?* persuasively argues that a robust and complete design canon must include the kind of design that we wear. Six or seven years ago, Paola Antonelli and I began a conversation about the place of fashion within the institution's larger commitment to design, and now she has brought to life the brave, experimental, and soundly researched *Items*. The goal of the exhibition and catalogue is to help bring into focus our relationship to a ubiquitous, aspirational, and complex design field. The title of the exhibition simultaneously gestures to the quotidian nature of fashion—we all purchase, sport, and treasure items of clothing—and serves up a question that is open-ended and deliberately difficult to answer.

When the guest curator Bernard Rudofsky organized the first exhibition of fashion at the Museum, *Are Clothes Modern?*, in 1944, he unabashedly promised "an entirely new and fresh approach to the subject of clothes," and his well-received project remains a flash point in the history of exhibiting fashion. More than seven decades later, *Items*, MoMA's second fashion exhibition, recalibrates Rudofsky's inquiry to consider the whole ecosystem of fashion through a selection of the garments and accessories—from precious jewels to mass-produced staples—that have had a strong influence on the world in the past century. Humble masterpieces like clogs and chinos are displayed alongside high-fashion ensembles from Comme des Garçons and Pierre Cardin; other pieces were crafted specifically for this presentation. The 111 items in this volume, arranged alphabetically, represent the most ubiquitous or iconic form of their respective typologies. In the exhibition, these stereotypes are complemented by painstakingly gathered materials that contextualize each item and trace its history back to its archetype. In twenty-eight cases, the item has been reimagined by a contemporary designer in response to the social, political, technological, and cultural landscape of the twenty-first century.

Items brings together more than 350 works from storied museums, private collections, and backs of closets. The result is an incisive and engaging reflection on the past, present, and future of a field that touches us all in myriad ways. On a daily basis, clothing constitutes the first interface between us and the world; it is at once a deeply embodied form of design, intimately bound to psychology and identity, and part of a set of systems that exploit labor and greedily strip the environment. *Items* suggests that we dismiss this field of design at our peril. I am grateful to Paola Antonelli, Senior Curator, and Michelle Millar Fisher, Curatorial Assistant, Department of Architecture and Design, for conceiving the exhibition with perserverance and skill, and to the many colleagues who have collaborated with them during their sartorial odyssey. On behalf of the staff and trustees of the Museum, I would also like to thank Hyundai Card and WGSN for their generous support of this milestone exhibition.

— Glenn D. Lowry
Director, The Museum of The Modern Art

Pockets

Buttons

Fully clothed man carries seventy or more buttons, most of them useless. He has at his disposal two dozen pockets.

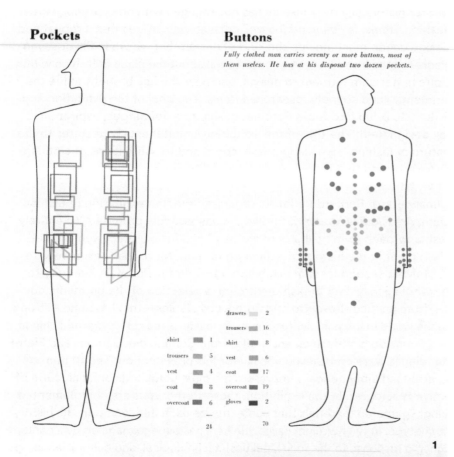

	drawers	2
	trousers	16
shirt ▮ 1	shirt	8
trousers ▮ 5	vest	6
vest ▮ 4	coat	17
coat ▮ 8	overcoat	19
overcoat ▮ 6	gloves	2
⎯		⎯
24		70

WHO'S AFRAID OF FASHION? — Paola Antonelli

Items: Is Fashion Modern? is the first exhibition on fashion at The Museum of Modern Art since 1944. Although the Museum was established in 1929 for the express purpose of "encouraging and developing the study of modern arts and the application of such arts to manufacture and practical life,"[1] and indeed has included architecture and design since its founding, the only fashion item in the collection when I began my career at MoMA in 1994 was an early-twentieth-century Delphos dress by Mariano Fortuny, acquired in 1987.[2] Ever since, the Museum's acquisitions of clothing and accessories have been sporadic: a few garments here and there, injected into wider conversations on technology (digital production, for instance) or functional typologies (such as the sports hijab or parkas for the homeless). Today the design collection includes four dresses, one coat, one shirt, and four head coverings.[3] Incremental progress has been made, but there is still a long way to go. Our collection must encompass fashion if it is to complete the circle that connects all forms of design—from architecture to textiles, from manufactured objects to digital artifacts—in the fertile dialogue at the root of the diverse and open-ended contemporary incarnation of the modern.

Fashion is unquestionably a form of design. As with other types of design, its pitch is struck in the mediation between form and function, means and goals, automation and craftsmanship, standardization and customization, universality and self-expression, and pragmatism and vision. In other words, fashion partakes in all the existential dilemmas of design, and since its involvement in our lives is so intimate and intrinsic, it is an especially agile mediator between the universal and the personal, capable of magnifying our rawest emotions. Like other physical and digital forms of design, it moves on a spectrum ranging from postindustrial seriality (from ready-to-wear to fast fashion) to precious, hand-crafted uniqueness (haute couture). Like all design, it exists in the service of others. In most cases, it is conceived by an individual to dress others—sometimes many, many others—so that they can function in the world, in different arenas, and not only cover but also express themselves. Moreover, like all design, fashion has consequences— social, political, cultural, and environmental. And the influence works both ways: military research, for example, has long pioneered new, wearable materials and technologies that have been incorporated into the clothing of private citizens. Culture wars and political protests continue to be waged through garments. Today fashion is produced *en masse* and distributed on a global scale. An increase in customers with disposable income and the advent of e-commerce have drastically altered buying behaviors, eliciting demand for up-to-the-minute choices and the expectation of both affordable pricing and on-demand luxury. Fast fashion, in particular, is an arena for social, political, economic, and environmental conflict. The death of more than 1,100 workers in 2013

Left:
1— "Pockets" and "Buttons," from the 1947 book Bernard Rudofsky produced in conjunction with his exhibition *Are Clothes Modern?* (MoMA, 1944). The caption reads, "Fully clothed man carries seventy or more buttons, most of them useless. He has at his disposal two dozen pockets."

2— Brandon Wen and Laura Zwanziger's half-scale plus-size dress form Tolula, designed at Cornell University's 3-D body-scan lab in 2013. Photograph by the designers. Like the other new designs illustrated in this essay, this prototype was presented in the *Items* exhibition (corresponding in this case to Comme des Garçons's Body Meets Dress—Dress Meets Body)

3— *Are Clothes Modern?* exhibition at The Museum of Modern Art, 1944. View of the entrance. Unknown photographer

4— Jumpsuit prototype designed by Richard Malone for *Items: Is Fashion Modern?*, 2017. Photograph by the designer

when a garment factory in Dhaka, Bangladesh, collapsed catalyzed public consciousness of how complexly entwined the fashion system is in our social and personal economies. Fashion is a design field of enormous impact. Still, like other forms of design, it often does not get the wider critical consideration or respect it is due.

When design curators try to explain the importance of their field, often they simply point to objects closeby—a purse, the kitchen shelf, a vending machine interface—and say, "Design is all around us." Fashion design is even closer; it is literally all over us—and throughout us, as it turns out, since we use it to project, aspire, express, and redesign ourselves, and to size up and judge others. For this reason, a history of modern design that excludes fashion hardly seems plausible. So in 1995 I asked the formidable first director of MoMA's Department of Architecture, Philip Johnson, why the Museum had not given fashion the time of day. Johnson had started his career at MoMA in 1932, and in 1995 he was a trustee and the chairman of the Acquisitions Committee of the Department of Architecture and Design. His exhibitions and books had created the official narrative of twentieth-century modernity in these fields, without including garments. He explained to me that fashion, bound as it was to seasonal rhythms and compulsory stylistic rebirths, was considered ephemeral and thus antithetical to the ideals of modernism—timelessness above all. Johnson's argument was unconvincing, coming from a keen observer of the latest trends in architecture and art and a famed curator who had coined several new movements "of the moment," Deconstructivism being only the most recent.[4] Interestingly, he never mentioned the Museum's one previous foray into fashion—*Are Clothes Modern?*, a 1944 exhibition by the architect and curator Bernard Rudofsky. Had MoMA been afraid of fashion? Although Rudofsky's exhibition might seem to suggest the contrary, it was an outlier—just as Rudofsky was. Two decades later, in 1964, he returned to the Museum and cemented his position as MoMA's (and Johnson's) resident thorn-in-the-side with the exhibition *Architecture Without Architects: A Short Introduction to Non-Pedigreed Architecture*, which, with its earnest celebration of vernacular constructions, is considered to be neither the first nor the last, but definitely one of the sharpest nails in the coffin of modernist architecture.

What was—and is—the issue with fashion? Perceived frivolity? Codependency—the idea that we always dress for others, a fluid form of relational aesthetics that would be anathema in modernist design? Its association with the feminine and consequent dismissal by the largely patriarchal powers that be in museums, in academia, and pretty much everywhere else? Its slow rate of absorption by major fine arts institutions, even while artists—from Louise Bourgeois and Joseph Beuys to Andrea Zittel and Yinka Shonibare—have recognized and deployed clothing's considerable power of expression? Or perhaps its immediate digestibility by the popular market and its excessive commercialism, which contribute to the taint of "vulgarity" often cited to support an artificial separation between design and the fine arts (which are famously devoid of commercial value)? Generally speaking, art museums have treated fashion with various measures of ambivalence and longing, trying to absorb it into the realm of art while at the same time keeping their distance—sometimes marking this separation with the term "costume," perhaps to lift clothing design above the populist fray and treat it as an applied art, keeping it in the same limbo reserved for glass arts and ceramics. That said, some institutions have adopted fashion with enthusiasm, the best-known example being the Metropolitan Museum of Art's venerated Costume Institute, inaugurated in 1946.[5] In 2011, Suzy Menkes, then the fashion editor of the *International Herald Tribune*, took notice of a slew of fashion exhibitions happening around the world—from the blockbuster

Alexander McQueen: Savage Beauty at the Met in New York to monographic exhibitions on Madame Grès in Paris, Jean Paul Gaultier in Montreal (the first stop in a long tour), Chanel in Shanghai, and Dior at the Pushkin State Museum of Fine Arts in Moscow, among others. In an article devoted to the phenomenon, she traced the history of fashion exhibitions in museums and spoke to curators and critics in an attempt to outline the criteria by which such projects are conceived and could be critiqued.[6] In the same essay, Menkes concluded that "fashion has developed from being a passion for a few to a fascination—and an entertainment—for everybody." And therein lies another conundrum: most forms of design, but especially fashion design, are too often considered "lesser" disciplines in the art world (much the way film is), because no matter how extensive the scholarly literature they engender, they still manage to immediately connect and inspire—and usually delight—at levels that are accessible by the many as well as by the few.

I am embarrassed to admit that at first I felt anxiety about using "fashion" in the title of this exhibition. In the end, I was encouraged to do so by two great colleagues, MoMA's director, Glenn Lowry, and distinguished design curator Glenn Adamson. Both advised that no good curatorial strategy ever came from being afraid of the central terms of the dialogue to which one is hoping to contribute, and so the word *fashion* stayed and was embraced (guardedly, then with abandon) and interrogated—in the title itself, and throughout the essays, exhibition wall texts, and public programs associated with this project. Recently I was able to reflect upon this process of weaving fashion into MoMA's interdisciplinary museum context as part of a discussion hosted by *The Brooklyn Rail*, which asked various contributors—including esteemed fashion curator Valerie Steele and historian Rhonda Garelick—to consider fashion's relationship to fine art.[7] It is a project that Rudofsky kick-started with his 1944 exhibition, in which he attempted to (re)locate fashion within wider discourses of art, society, and culture—his traditionalist paragon of dignity being not design (as it is here), but art. With the dispassionate gaze of an anthropologist, he explored individual and collective relationships with mid-century clothing in the waning moments of World War II, when conventions were being questioned but old attitudes still prevailed: women continued to pour their bodies into uncompromising silhouettes, and menswear still demanded superfluous pockets, buttons, cuffs, and collars.[8] "It will not be a style or fashion show; it will not display costumes; it will not offer specific dress reforms," reads *Are Clothes Modern?*'s 1944 press release. "The purpose of the exhibition is to bring about an entirely new and fresh approach to the subject of clothes."[9] Rudofsky's provocative exhibition was a prompt for the public of its day to reconsider their relationship with the clothes they wore, and with the designers and systems that produced those clothes.

Further along in the press release, Rudofsky railed against the peripheral role that fashion had been given in the allied scholarship of the visual arts and culture, lamenting:

> It is strange that dress has been generally denied the status of art, when it is actually a most happy summation of aesthetic, philosophic and psychological components. . . . [Its] intimate relation to the very source and standard of all aesthetic evaluations, the human body, should make it the supreme achievement among the arts.

Little seems to have changed in the past seven decades. In an article on the musician and fashion muse Lady Gaga in March 2016, *New York Times* fashion critic Vanessa Friedman wrote, "For while fashion may be famous for its elitism, it has long been seen,

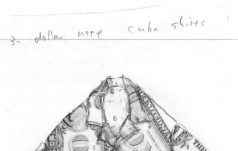

dollar note cuba shirts

5

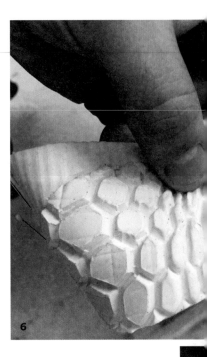

6

7

LUCY JONES

ADJUSTABILITY
Almost like shape wear, or a 'waist-trainer' the legs can be dressed separately, and then wrapped to close with elastic and velcro.

ADDED CUSHION/ THICKNESS
Since this area will have most contact with chair, I would like to play with the thickness/yarn weight to ensure more comfort and/or practicality due to friction and fragility of sheer portions of tights.

FINAL DESIGN 1a - standing view

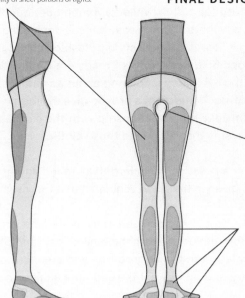

CLOSED BUTTOCK REGION
The buttock area is closed off to prevent any skin breakdown caused if this area was left open like the front view/open crotch design. The edges will be reinforced by thicker yarn and binding.

COMPRESSION
To promote stabilized blood circulation, these areas will have compressed yarn.

8

and often sees itself, as the stepchild of the art world; the less worthy creative form. We all have our complexes."[10] Like many fields of creative endeavor, fashion—as a place of research and a professional landscape—still needs validation. At the same time, however, fashion is now being recognized by curators, writers, and researchers outside its very core—as well as by designers and by the people who Instagram it, dream of it, borrow it, buy it, wear it, and monetize it—as the gold mine it has always been: an intersectional, global, cultural, social, and political phenomenon.

This exhibition's subtitle, *Is Fashion Modern?*, reprises the question that titled Rudofsky's first show, while *Items* indicates an object-centered, design-led investigation. Rudofsky's broad approach provided a springboard from which to consider the ways in which fashion items are designed, manufactured, distributed, and worn today. Here "modern" still maintains many of the positive nuances that have made it a core tenet of MoMA's mission since 1929, indicating a constructive attitude toward the future based on the unity of the arts, working together on society's current needs and priorities, and privileging a departure from tradition that is not based on rejection of the past but rather on respect and reinvention. Yet the question that Rudofsky posed in 1944 still bears repeating in 2017 precisely because of the disconnect between what we wear and who we are, between the ways in which clothing is made and the ways in which it *might* be made. Every single item in the exhibition and in this book represents a key to the complexities of such a system, a lens with which to magnify its inner workings and understand its impact.

Most fashion exhibitions in art museums follow straightforward and traditional modes of art-historical investigation, privileging either the personality of a creator or focusing on moments in history or regions of the world. They produce important scholarship, but often curators sweep process and context—fashion's more mundane, contaminated, gloriously designlike sides—under a dazzlingly beautiful carpet. I have learned important lessons from wholly predictable exhibitions that fit this description, but there are exceptions that pierced the veil of genius or truly addressed and explained a particular ecosystem of fashion, and are thus profoundly memorable. One was *Juste des vêtements* (Just Some Garments), an exhibition on the work of Japanese designer Yohji Yamamoto curated by Pamela Golbin at the Musée de la Mode et du Textile in Paris in 2005, for which the designer's Tokyo atelier was reconstructed in the galleries on rue de Rivoli to show how fashion really/mythologically happens.[11] Another is the 1998 exhibition on the great protagonist of American fashion, visionary designer Claire McCardell, at The Museum at FIT (Fashion Institute of Technology) in New York.[12] When it comes to contextualization, a striking example was the 2015 show in Stockholm *Utopian Bodies*, by curatorial duo Sofia Hedman and Serge Martynov, which contemplated fashion

Left:
5— Development sketches for a new guayabera concept designed by Ryohei Kawanishi for *Items: Is Fashion Modern?*, 2017
6, 7— Materials testing for the biker jacket prototype designed by Asher Levine for *Items: Is Fashion Modern?*, 2017. Photograph by the designer

8— Development sketches for the tights prototype designed by Lucy Jones for *Items: Is Fashion Modern?*, 2017

in relationship to different urgent and timely issues—such as sustainability, gender, and memory—within an arresting installation design.[13] Although monographic shows exist also in design, MoMA curators have traditionally privileged thematic exhibitions, in which objects become portals to a deeper understanding of the world in all its political, technological, sociological, cultural, economic, philosophical—in other words, in all its systemic—complexity, without sacrificing aesthetic consideration. Clothes are especially profound and charged examples of design that allow us to explore these knotty realms.

Items was born around 2011, initially emerging as a list of "garments that changed the world," and it encompassed clothes and accessories that have had a profound impact during the time range covered by MoMA's collection. It was originally an exploration of potential acquisitions that seemed necessary to tell a more accurate history of modern design. This volume and the related exhibition explore a small slice of such canonical and noncanonical garments from all over the world through the nexus of their complex and dynamic production, allowing readers and audiences to understand the larger implications of—and their own participation in—the systems that govern and produce this design field. The list is hardly exhaustive, either in terms of cultural and geographic reach or in number (arbitrarily, 111 objects, a ceiling that purposely provokes others into highlighting omissions and proposing additions). The *Items* curatorial team has chosen to celebrate our center of gravity, New York, by using the city as an observatory, albeit one equipped with a particularly powerful and inquisitive telescope. New York's diversity and density, and its inhabitants' penchant for intense conversations—for instance, about contamination or appropriation—have taught us that while you cannot write somebody else's story or compile somebody else's list, it does not take much to trigger a vivacious and productive response. Our list of 111 items is, thus, like any abbreviated compilation, particular, filled with this team's soul and personalities, and also inductive, crafted to distill a common experience and inspire a reaction. The goal of the exhibition is to stimulate curiosity and focus attention so that everyone who passes through it might look at fashion in a different way, with more awareness, agency, and respect. Throughout the gestation of this project, the public—from third graders to seasoned scholars—felt inspired to suggest, comment on, approve, decry, or amend both the choice of items and the way each was represented.

In the exhibition and in this catalogue, garments created for the benefit of many (such as the white T-shirt or the dashiki) coexist with rarefied fashion episodes for the delight of a few (Martin Margiela's Tabi footwear series, for instance, or Yves Saint Laurent's Le Smoking). What they have in common is their influence on the world, whether direct and immediate, as evidenced by millions of purchases, or mediated and metabolized at first by institutional and financial elites. Thanks to the cross-pollination made possible by physical and cultural migrations, rampant appropriation, and the disseminating power of media both old and new, nowhere do high and low engage in so productive a conversation as in fashion.

In the Museum galleries, we examine these items in three tiers: archetype, stereotype, and prototype. Presented first in the incarnation that made it significant in the last one hundred (or so) years—the stereotype—each item is then accompanied by contextual material that traces its origins back to historical archetypes. Our method for defining a design's stereotype was necessarily subjective but drew on the collective consciousness: when you close your eyes and think of a sari, or a pair of chinos, or a pearl necklace, what do you see? *That* is the item's stereotype. In our constructive stereotyping, we were helped by a diverse, international advisory committee (see p. 282) and by the impressive roster of speakers who participated in a two-day colloquium at the Museum in May 2016[14]; our efforts were further buttressed by research, interviews, and extensive travels—to India and Bangladesh, Nigeria and South Africa, and many other places in Asia, Europe, and the US. Finally, for about a third of the pieces, when advancements in technology, social dynamics, visual culture, or political awareness warranted it, we complemented the item with a newly commissioned design—a prototype to jump-start a new life cycle for the garment with pioneering materials, more sustainable approaches, or novel design techniques. (The preparatory drawings for some of these commissions illustrate this essay.)

The exhibition is laid out so as to provide both deliberate and serendipitous adjacencies. From an area devoted to mutating ideas of the body and silhouette, spanning issues of size, image, and gender—this space presents, among many other items, the little black dress, the Wonderbra, the sari, and Rudi Gernreich's Unisex Project—the exhibition segues into a zone devoted to new technologies and visions of the future, bringing experiments such as Issey Miyake's A-POC (A Piece of Cloth) and Pierre Cardin's Cosmoscorps collection into conversation with Gore-Tex, sunscreen, and the Moon Boot. The fascinating relationship between emancipation, modesty, introversion, and rebellion—concepts that paradoxically share many common traits, in fashion and beyond—is introduced by the hoodie and the turtleneck, and this portion of the show includes items as diverse as leather pants, the cheongsam, the slip dress, the bikini, the hijab, and kente cloth, all connected by a thread of alternately muted or roaring subversion. Next comes a section devoted to items whose foremost function is to deliver a message, sometimes explicit (a graphic T-shirt, a tattoo, a particular use of a bandanna) and other times implicit (a Birkin bag or a diamond engagement ring). Sports—often a source not only of technological but also of stylistic innovation and the basis of contemporary casual wear and street wear—inspired a section charting the myriad ways in which fashion and athleticism have met over the past century, whether in the form of sports jerseys and other street-wear staples like the polo shirt and the Converse All-Star, or revered high-fashion collaborations such as Yamamoto's Y-3. A section dedicated to everyday uniforms features humble masterpieces such as the Breton shirt and Levi's 501s, professional attire such as the pencil skirt and loafers, and the ubiquitous, multipurpose Dutch wax textiles—indispensable staples that are all but invisible, so entrenched are they in our habits and behaviors. The exhibition concludes with a study of power—hard and soft—embodied by, among other garments and accessories, a selection of men's suits, Donna Karan's Seven Easy Pieces, the stiletto heel, and the pearl necklace. In order to make our inquiry's shift to a global scale clearer, we commissioned information designer Giorgia Lupi to create a mural that places the 111 items within larger systems—for instance, the United Nations' sustainability protocol, adapted for the future of fashion.

Each of the items in the exhibition engages many intersectional themes and could therefore be positioned usefully in any number of constellations. This catalogue, however, takes a different tack, presenting the material alphabetically, for ease of reference. A short essay on each of the 111 items in the exhibition appears in the order suggested by the first letter of its name, though we have in some cases decided to take certain license—for example, opening the sequence with 501s, omitting their maker's well-known name in order for them to lead the pack as harbingers of modernity, fashion, and design's interdependency. We have relied on primary sources from the past century, including material-culture references such as *Vogue*, *Harper's Bazaar*, and the *New York Times*, to describe particular cultural moments, and have, of course, drawn heavily on available scholarship, archival materials, and interviews. Novel visual interpretations of the items in the show were solicited from five photographers: Omar Victor Diop, Bobby Doherty, Catherine Losing (in collaboration with stylist Anna Lomax), Monika Mogi, and Kristin-Lee Moolman (with longtime collaborator Ibrahim Kamara), and those stellar images are among the many hundreds included here.

In this project, high fashion lives comfortably alongside the white T-shirt and jeans and other familiar items whose histories we are not so well-acquainted with (perhaps the true definition of a "humble masterpiece").[15] Equally, in a protomodern approach that emphasizes the interrelationship and continuity between all forms of culture, fashion items of all sorts can exist alongside the architectural models, chairs, posters, and video games that constitute this Museum's design history. Making these connections has always been part of MoMA's mission—at least in the Department of Architecture and Design, where we get to place highly diverse objects side by side in considered juxtapositions that allow our audiences to bring their own experiences to bear, too. It is plain that what we wear informs our everyday experience of self and society. The foundational clothing designs included here allow us to talk rightfully about fashion as a salient area of design—one that should not and cannot be ignored. I believe that the writers, curators, students, and members of the general public who recognize and embrace this show's approach can help locate a new center of gravity for the field of fashion and generate their own provocative questions for further exhibitions, books, public discussions, and personal reflections—at least some of which, I trust, will happen at MoMA. No modern design history is complete without fashion.

Right:
9, 10— Breton sweater prototype designed by Unmade for *Items: Is Fashion Modern?*, 2017. Photograph by Luke Bennett
11— Still from a video produced in conjunction with the little black dress prototype designed by Pia Interlandi for *Items: Is Fashion Modern?*, 2017

12— Development sketches for the harem pants prototype designed by Miguel Mesa Posada for *Items: Is Fashion Modern?*, 2017

9

10

11

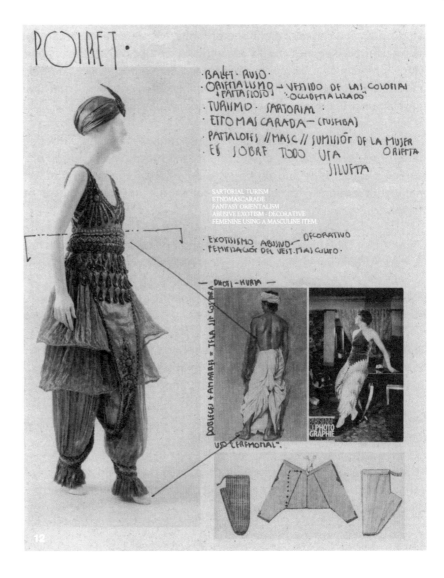

12

ABOUT THE PHOTO ESSAYS   For this catalogue, a novel interpretation of each of the 111 checklist items was entrusted to one of five photographers chosen for their idiosyncratic talents and distinctive points of view: Omar Victor Diop, Bobby Doherty, Catherine Losing (in collaboration with stylist Anna Lomax), Monika Mogi, and Kristin-Lee Moolman (with longtime collaborator Ibrahim Kamara). Each photographer was given eight pages in which to present a roughly equal share of the items from the checklist, arranged in alphabetical order. Losing was assigned Air Force 1 through Bucket Hat; Mogi, Burkini through Fur Coat; Diop, Gore-Tex through Monogram; Doherty, Moon Boot through Snugli; and Moolman, Space Age through YSL Touche Éclat. Given free rein, some chose to shoot the exact objects on the checklist while others took the items as prompts from which they abstracted. The results speak to five very different strategies of documentation that are as much still life as fashion photography, and mine the histories of advertising and graphic design as well as conventional modes of sartorial presentation.

Diop created a set of twenty-one playing cards, silhouetting doppelgänger items framed by boldly colored and patterned edges. Doherty employed jewel-toned colors, shooting, among other vignettes, a ripe watermelon bursting a two-piece maternity outfit at its seams. Losing imaged, among other pieces on her list, balaclavas haunting a shop window. Over a series of eight photographs, Moolman and Kamara synthesized wholly new ensembles gleaned from a secondhand clothes market in Johannesburg's city center. Mogi homed in on a *kawaii* teen decorating her Converse kicks, kitted out in Capri pants and a Fitbit—checking off three items on her list in one shot. Each individual intervention plays against the denser heterogeneity of figures illustrating the alphabetic texts.

The photographers have used the 111 items on the list as lenses through which to investigate form, color, gesture, environment, and more. The resulting pictures embrace fashion photography and yet carry us beyond fashion into the realm of design and its many intersections with culture, technology, art, anthropology—in other words, with the world.

Omar Victor Diop uses photography as primary medium to capture the diversity of modern African societies and lifestyles. He was born in 1980, in Dakar, Senegal.

Bobby Doherty is an American photographer born in 1989 in Brewster, New York. He currently lives in Brooklyn.

Catherine Losing is a British photographer and film director based in London. She was born in 1985 in Doncaster, U.K. Anna Lomax is an artist and designer. Born and bred in South London, she currently works in London and New York.

Monika Mogi is a photographer and director born in 1992. She grew up in Japan and the United States and lives in Tokyo.

Kristin-Lee Moolman is a photographic artist and filmmaker currently working in Johannesburg. Ibrahim Kamara is a London-based stylist of Sierra Leonean origin.

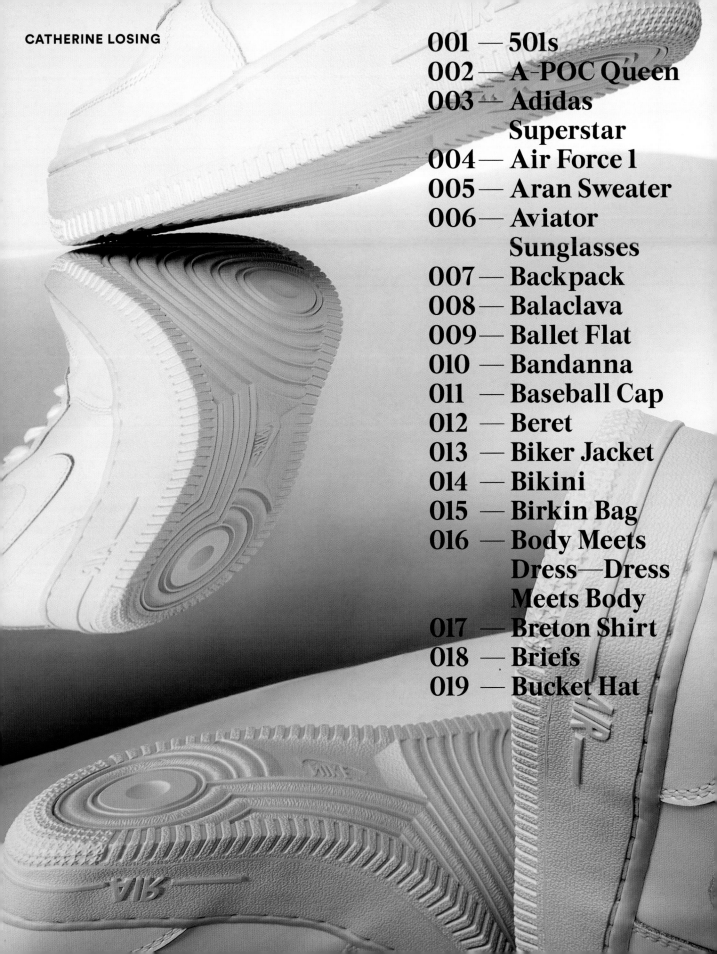

CATHERINE LOSING

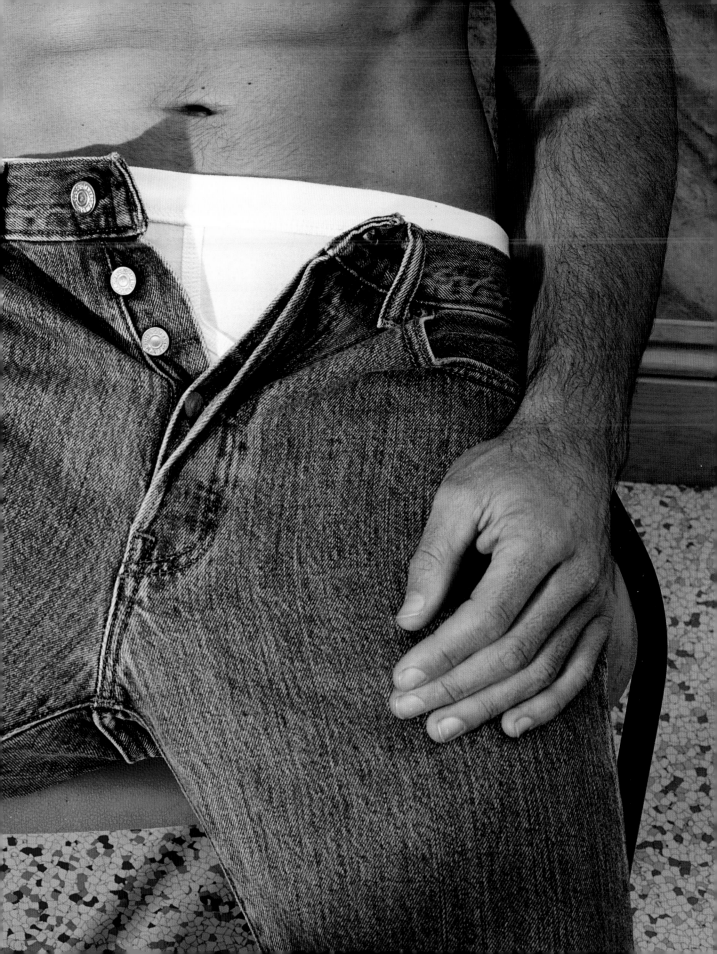

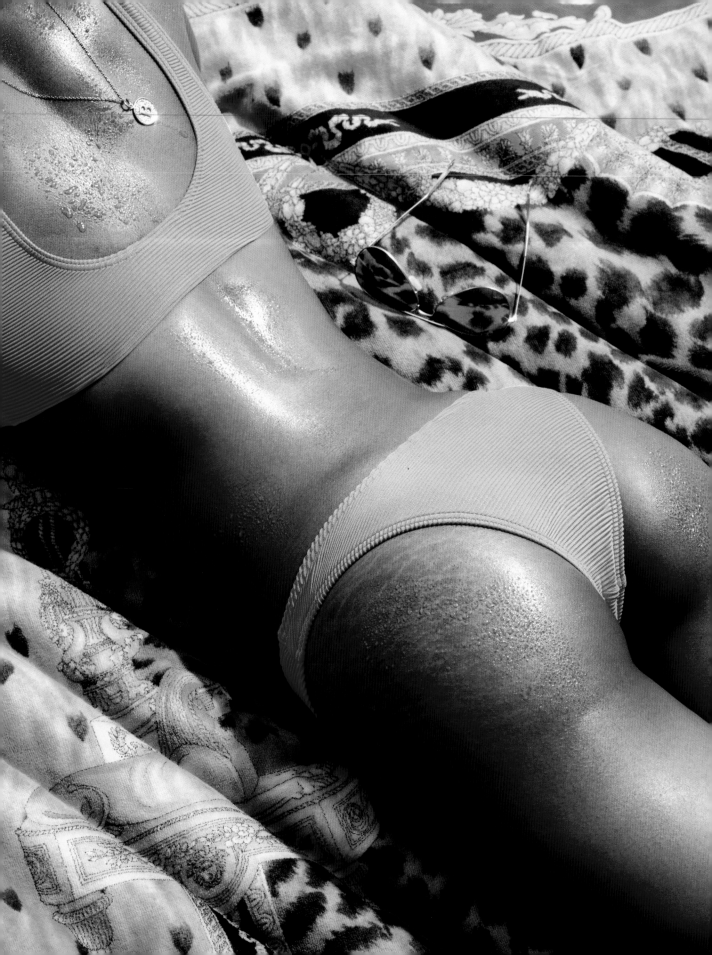

1

2

501s Jeans are a fashion paradox. At once universal and highly personal, they reflect our anxiety about both fitting in and standing out. Levi Strauss & Co.'s 501 jeans are the most famous and most popular; in fact, they are "the best selling garment of all time," according to cultural critic James Sullivan.[1] They hark back to 1873, when Bavarian immigrant Levi Strauss and Nevada tailor Jacob Davis patented a process for using copper rivets to strengthen the corners of pants pockets. Their "waist overalls" (worn by California's gold miners and laborers) featured a single back pocket with Levi's iconic arcuate stitching design, a front watch pocket, a cinch at the back waist, suspender buttons, and an additional rivet at the crotch. Named 501s for a production lot number, they were cut from nine-ounce XX blue denim, a warp-faced twill textile woven from indigo-dyed and white (or undyed) cotton thread. In 1901 an additional back pocket was added, and belt loops were incorporated in 1922. The suspender buttons were removed in 1937, and the back cinch strap and crotch rivet were eliminated during World War II in response to materials rationing under the U.S. government's Limitation Order L-85.

501s were not the first denim pants, as the durable material was already in use for men's and women's work wear and prison and naval uniforms, but they were the first to use the rivets that have become a defining feature of jeans.[2] Following the iconic 501s, other American denim brands emerged at the turn of the twentieth century, including OshKosh B'Gosh, Blue Bell (later Wrangler), and H. D. Lee Mercantile Company. Jeans received a boost of glamour from the Hollywood cowboy movies of the 1920s and 1930s, and as the garment's silhouette became more streamlined, women began wearing them, too. Publicity photographs of actresses Ginger Rogers and Carole Lombard wearing jeans while camping and fishing helped associate the garment with leisure and individualism. In 1934 Lady Levi's were introduced, the first branded jeans marketed exclusively to women; they resembled 501s but emphasized the waist.[3] Young people embraced jeans wholeheartedly around the middle of the century, inspired by film idols like Marlon Brando and James Dean and electrified by rock-and-roll heroes like Eddie Cochran. During World War II, American GIs wore jeans overseas while off duty, and in war-devastated countries like Japan they became symbols of freedom and wealth.[4] In the latter half of the century, jeans' connotations oscillated between the countercultural and the commercial. They were a back-to-nature retort to postwar consumer culture in the 1960s (particularly for the hippie movement), but by the 1970s the phenomenon of designer jeans had elevated the garment to a status symbol.[5]

The twenty-first-century denim universe is fluid and fragmented, encompassing no-frills oversize jeans sold by street-wear and work-wear labels such as like Fubu and Carhartt, designer-enhanced distressed jeans, and retro-inspired jeans, which have spawned a submarket for vintage Levi's 501s. Although (or because) the garment is a conformist choice in both high fashion and the mass market, the demand for eccentric variation is extreme: in 2017 the American brand Prps introduced a pair of mud-stained jeans, touted by the retailer Nordstrom as "rugged, Americana workwear that's seen some hard-working action with a crackled, caked-on muddy coating that shows you're not afraid to get down and dirty."[6]

An estimated 1.2 billion pairs of jeans were sold worldwide in 2016.[7] It takes a little over a thousand gallons of water to produce a single pair,[8] and the life cycle of a pair of jeans emits more than 73 pounds of carbon, while the runoff from dyeing and finishing chemicals has polluted countless bodies of water, most notably the Pearl River in the Chinese industrial city Xintang.[9] In response, Levi's has brought its 501s full circle, aiming to cultivate a "consumer who values durability and demonstrates a real attachment to an object," Levi's global product innovation director, Paul Dillinger, has said. "What we're trying to do is encourage our consumer to be conscious

that when they purchase a pair of jeans, that is not an isolated event."[10] Cotton Inc., another American company, has instituted Blue Jeans Go Green, a program that collects discarded jeans for use as insulation in new homes for needy families.

The Global Denim Project, a multidisciplinary research project established in 2007 by London-based scholars Daniel Miller and Sophie Woodward, features research ranging from the anthropological to the sociological, including an exploration of jeans' contribution "to the everyday sexualization of the body" in Milan and their role as "an important mode of objectification of inequalities and social differences" in Brazil.[11] The project is premised on the notion that the garment expresses "something about the changing world that no other clothing could achieve."[12] On both a micro and a macro level, jeans—and their most popular iteration, Levi's 501s—embody both timelessness and temporality: though constantly evolving and proliferating, in their essentials they have remained unchanged for more than a century. —SK

Previous page:
1— Indians Motorcycle Club, Tokyo, from the documentary film *The 501® Jean: Stories of an Original*, 2016
2— Levi Strauss & Co. waist overalls, 1890

Right:
3— Advertisement for Levi's Lot 701 jeans, 1951
4— Cowboys working for the Dangberg Land & Live Stock Co., Nevada, c. 1930. Unknown photographer

Get that WESTERN feeling

WAY BACK IN THE GOLD-DIGGING DAYS OF THE '49ERS, CALIFORNIA STAKED ITS ORIGINAL CLAIM TO BEING THE SPORTSWEAR CENTER OF THE WORLD . . . WHEN A MAN NAMED LEVI STRAUSS MADE THE FIRST WORKING PANTS FOR MINERS AND THEREBY CREATED THE PATTERN OF A CENTURY. FOR NOW, A HUNDRED YEARS LATER, THESE SAME STURDY RIVETED DENIMS STILL ARE STANDARD GEAR FOR AMERICA'S WORKING MEN. MORE THAN THAT, THEY'VE BEEN ADAPTED FOR AND ADOPTED BY THE WOMEN. "LADY LEVI'S" LIKE THESE YOU SEE ON THIS PAGE . . . ARE JUST THE THING FOR ROUGHING IT, FOR RIDING. IN FACT, THEY'RE RESPONSIBLE FOR CHANGING THE RIDING HABITS OF A NATION, MORE WOMEN VOTING FOR THE ROUGH-N-READY COWBOY EASE OF DENIMS IN PREFERENCE TO SINGLE-PURPOSE FORMAL EQUESTRIAN ATTIRE. LEVI'S AND PLAID COTTON WESTERN SHIRTS MADE BY LEVI STRAUSS AND COMPANY ARE REGULATION GARB FOR THE THOUSANDS OF DUDE RANCHES SPRINGING UP ALL OVER THE COUNTRY . . . EVEN WITHIN SPITTING DISTANCE OF NEW YORK CITY! YES, LEVI'S ARE A SYMBOL OF THE GROWING POPULARITY OF WESTERN WEAR FOR THE REAL RANCHER OR THE DUDE . . . AND FOR THE STUDENT, TOO! (THEY'RE THE RAGE OF MANY A CAMPUS WHERE THE IDENTIFYING RED TAG IS A BADGE OF MERIT.) IT'S THAT WESTERN FEELING WORKING OVER-TIME, CREATING SALES IMPETUS FOR YOU! AND SO, WE BRING YOU A WESTERN ISSUE WITH SLACKS AND SHORTS AND THE TWEEDSY-WEEDSY SPORTSWEAR CALIFORNIA MAKES FOR ACTIVE AND SPECTATOR SPORTS. AND WE SUGGEST THAT YOU GET . . . AND SELL . . . THAT WESTERN FEELING, FOR THERE'S NO RESISTING IT!—V. S.

As appearing in the
CALIFORNIA STYLIST,
July, 1951, issue

3

4

A — 002

A-POC QUEEN   Beginning in 1971 with his first women's wear collection, the Japanese designer Issey Miyake has probed the relationship between two-dimensional cloth and the three-dimensional human body, taking the space between them as the focus of his design. Miyake began developing his A-POC knitting technique in collaboration with textile engineer Dai Fujiwara in 1997, a continuation of his ongoing experimentation with the materiality of textiles, including, for example, his 1993 Pleats Please project. In that earlier work, Miyake made a case for pleating as a distinctive single-process method of transforming two-dimensional fabric into a three-dimensional garment. With A-POC (also a single-process method), he and Fujiwara focus on the economy of material and of design during the fabrication process.

Officially debuting in the Issey Miyake spring/summer 1999 collection, the A-POC Queen is a raschel-knit tube textile generated from a single, continuous thread by a computer-programmed industrial knitting machine. An intricate system of links and holes creates sections in the fabric that can be cut out with scissors into a range of finished garments —no sewing required. Variations are possible, allowing the wearer to be the final arbiter of the design. A dress, for example, can be full or three-quarter length, and its sleeves can range in length or even extend into mittens. Comprising a complete outfit, including socks and a bag, the A-POC Queen not only provides a total system of dress for its wearer but also maximizes the output of a single piece of cloth: very little waste is created. A-POC, an acronym for "A Piece of Cloth," is also a play on the word *epoch,* a call for

those in the field of design to look to the next century with a sense of responsibility. Of the project, Fujiwara has written, "'A Piece of Cloth' is a constantly evolving concept that will translate into different forms from this epoch to the next. . . . The process of making things advances but never severs its ties with the knowledge of the age that preceded it."[1]

The A-POC Queen draws on the history of garment patternmaking, a skill codified early on in the Spanish volume *Libro de geometría, práctica y traça* (Book of the practice of tailoring, measuring, and marking out), published in 1589. Its author, Juan de Alcega, describes his instructions for minimizing waste and maximizing efficiency in pattern cutting as "something quite new and never before seen in Spain."[2] Patternmaking was definitively elevated a century and a half later by its inclusion as a trade in the dictionary of sciences, arts, and crafts compiled by Denis Diderot, published beginning in 1751. Miyake has directly alluded to this long history when contextualizing A-POC, citing advancements made during the Industrial Revolution as integral to the birth of ready-to-wear fashion and foundational to the system of production that sustains its growth and diversification today: "The latter half of the eighteenth century saw the Industrial Revolution, spurred on greatly by the inventions of the spinning machine and the steam engine. This in turn gave birth to a new middle class, particularly after the French Revolution. These social and industrial upheavals changed the history of clothing and popularized fashion, which had hitherto been only for the privileged aristocracy. From these beginnings eventually came haute couture, with a host of new creative ideas; in time, prêt-à-porter (ready-to-wear) was derived from that. Fashion, ever since, has been diversifying as the world around it changes."[3]

While technology has democratized fashion production, perhaps most notably with the emergence of commercial patterns for the home sewer (the Butterick pattern company's Walkaway dress of 1952 was so named for one's ability to "sit down at a sewing machine in the morning and walk away wearing it to lunch"),[4] the advancements in mass production that began with the Industrial Revolution now enable ever-rising levels of consumption and waste. Recently, the New Zealand designer Holly McQuillan proposed a solution to this problem. Her TWINSET: Embedded Zero Waste of 2010 is a suite of patterns that create multiple garments with no fabric waste at all, featuring, for example, hoodie/T-shirt, pant/jacket, and dress/vest/pant combination patterns. Like McQuillan's project, the A-POC Queen provokes a reevaluation of the relationship between cloth and the body within the larger context of the global economy, the environment, and our technological milieu. "Will fashion be able to afford to keep the same old methodology?" Miyake has asked. "I have endeavored to experiment to make fundamental changes to the system of making clothes."[5] —SK

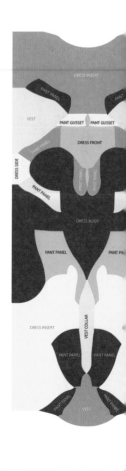

Right:
1— **A-POC Queen Textile, by Issey Mikaye and Dai Fujiwara, from the Issey Miyake spring/summer 1999 collection. Photograph by Hiroshi Iwasaki**
2— **Patterns from TWINSET: Embedded Zero Waste, by Holly McQuillan, 2010**
3— **A-POC Le Feu, by Issey Miyake and Dai Fujiwara, from the Issey Miyake spring/summer 1999 collection. Photograph by Yasuaki Yoshinaga**
4— **Cassock pattern from *Libro de geometría, práctica y traça* (Book of the practice of tailoring, measuring, and marking out), by Juan de Alcega, 1589**

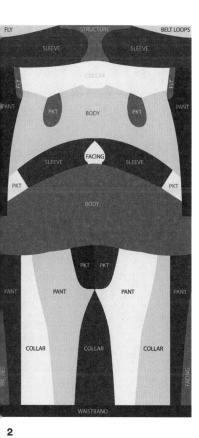

2

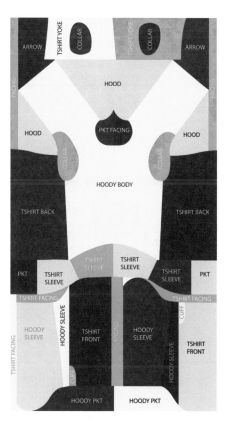

4

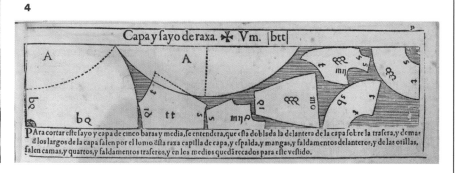

Capa y ſayo de raxa. ✳ Vm. |btt|

PAra cortar eſte ſayo y capa de cinco baras y media, ſe entendera, que eſta doblada la delantera de la capa ſobre la traſera, y demas d los largos de la capa ſalen por el lomo dſta raxa capilla de capa, y eſpalda, y mangas, y faldamentos delanteros, y de las orillas, ſalen camas, y quartos, y faldamentos traſeros, y en los medios quedã recados para eſte veſtido.

ADIDAS SUPERSTAR The Superstar is one of the world's most iconic and influential sneakers. Conceived specifically for basketball, it was issued in 1969 by Adidas, the company founded in 1924 by the German brothers Adolf (Adi) and Rudolph (Rudi) Dassler. Having previously produced footwear for soccer, tennis, and track and field, Adidas had recently entered the basketball market, and the Superstar was an alternative to the 1965 high-top Adidas Pro Model already worn by professional basketball players. It was also an improved and updated version of the low-top Supergrip basketball shoe the company had released six years earlier, in 1963. The strength of the Supergrip's elasticated midsole destroyed the cementing on its outsole and vamp (across the top of the foot), but the Superstar's sturdy ridged rubber toe cap, or "shell toe," was adhered to the vamp, reinforcing it and thus mitigating the problem.

The shoe was specifically tailored to reflect the increasing levels of skill within the sport and to take advantage of basketball's growing popularity globally. The Superstar shared the cushioned heel, arch support, felt insole, padded ankle, and extremely soft cowhide leather of the Supergrip, with the addition of an adjustable arch support, an extra-large heel counter (the heel support inside the shoe), and the rubber toe cap. Toe coverage had long been a feature of canvas-and-rubber basketball shoes; adding a toe cap to the already resistant leather provided a whole new level of protection from injury and the wear and tear associated with running and pivoting. The Superstar also featured the three signature side stripes, designed for midfoot support, that Adi Dassler had trademarked in 1949.[1] By 1970 the Superstar was the shoe of choice for professional basketball players, including, most famously, Kareem Abdul-Jabbar.

While the Superstar was technologically advanced for its time, its design, like those of the other two sneakers in this volume—the Converse All Star and the Air Force 1 by Nike—grew out of a long history of functional footwear with vulcanized (temperature stabilized) rubber outsoles. Liverpool Rubber Company, in Great Britain, and Candee Rubber Company, in the United States, are often credited as the first adaptors of vulcanized rubber to footwear. The former used the material in "sand shoes" (designed for the beach) in the 1830s and the latter for croquet shoes in the 1840s, but it is not clear exactly how the rubber was incorporated into the design (it may have formed a complete rubber overshoe rather than an outsole). By the middle of the century, canvas shoes with rubber outsoles were definitively on the scene. Worn for tennis, their rubber soles offered much better traction than leather on grass courts. In the 1870s the Liverpool Rubber Company introduced a sturdier variation on its sand shoe. Its nickname, the Plimsoll, paid homage to the so-called Plimsoll mark painted on cargo ships' waterlines, a reference to the distinctive line created where the rubber outsole meets the upper—also a key aesthetic feature of the Superstar.[2]

In the 1980s, as the popularity of the Superstar waned among athletes (amid an onslaught of performance innovations by competing brands), it experienced a rebirth thanks to hip-hop. In versions with felt or leather stripes and plump, contrasting laces, the Superstar was embraced by New York's emerging B-boy scene, whose members gravitated toward the shoe for its aesthetic and its exotic European origins but also for the support provided by the reinforced toe during break dancing.[3] As captured in photographs by Jamel Shabazz, the Superstar was the preferred footwear among members of the hip-hop community, whose signature attitudes paralleled the bold look of the shoe. With the mainstream success of the Queens hip-hop group Run DMC and its 1986 hit "My Adidas," the Superstar became a cultural icon. The members of Run DMC were among the first artists to adopt street wear for performance clothes (most acts at the time wore over-the-top, theatrical costumes or flashy suits). The Superstar was thus part of a brand-new style as well as a conduit between the American

3

4

hip-hop movement and the rest of the world. As a wardrobe staple today, the Superstar has come full circle, offering comfort and cool in an athleisure fashion world that demands both. —SK

Left:
1— Jamel Shabazz, *Style and Finesse,* Flatbush, Brooklyn, 1982
2— Kareem Abdul-Jabbar, number 33 of the Milwaukee Bucks, shoots a hook shot against Wilt Chamberlain, number 13 of the Los Angeles Lakers, during an NBA game in Milwaukee, Wisconsin, 1970. Photograph by Robert Lewis
3— High-top sneaker by Perfection Rubber Co., early 1900s. Collection of the Bata Shoe Museum, Toronto
4— Run-DMC, Hollis, Queens, 1986. Photograph by Ebet Roberts

AIR FORCE 1   In 1982 Nike's Air Force 1 made its NBA debut, launching a footwear franchise that would be the blueprint for status sneakers for decades to come. This durable and playable high-top shoe incorporated the design innovations of earlier basketball sneakers but offered the enhanced comfort of Nike's proprietary Air Sole technology. The athletic footwear giant had been using its Air technology (based on an air-cell system developed by aerospace engineer Frank Rudy) in running sneakers since the release of the Tailwind in 1979, but the Air Force 1, designed by Bruce Kilgore, marked the first instance of this lightweight midsole cushioning in a basketball shoe. Historically, basketball shoes had featured a supportive and flexible upper attached to a simple rubber sole (see *Adidas Superstar* and *Converse All Star*). The integration of the full-length pressurized Air unit into the footbed of the Air Force 1 resulted in a thicker midsole, which gave the shoe its trademark profile and its capacity to absorb the shock of impact. Other features included a removable "proprioceptive belt" (ankle strap) for additional stability and a notched collar at the Achilles tendon for ankle support without compromising mobility. On the sole, the tread pattern of concentric circles at the ball and heel of the foot was designed with the pivoting motions of a basketball player in mind.

Adopted by NBA players like Moses Malone and stocked at select sportswear retailers with minimal marketing, the Air Force 1 intrigued amateur basketball players, who were drawn to its unique look and performance-driven features. Following industry custom, the shoe was discontinued in the early 1980s, after its initial run, but within several years a cadre of shrewd Baltimore footwear retailers (the owners of Downtown Locker Room, Cinderella Shoes, and Charley

Rudo Sports), backed by popular demand, persuaded Nike to reissue the "outdated" model in a limited range of colorways.[1] Released in staggered lots, these editions had pre-Internet sneakerheads plying the I-95 corridor to Baltimore to collect the latest hues in what became known as the Color of the Month Club.[2] At the behest of the public, Nike had effectively initiated the first "retro release"—now standard practice for footwear manufacturers.

In New York neighborhoods like Harlem and the South Bronx, where streetball tourneys and the burgeoning hip-hop scene shared close quarters in the 1980s, basketball sneakers became increasingly common off the court.[3] For sartorially smart hip-hoppers, looking "fresh to death" required an immaculate pair of sneakers. By the 1990s, pristine white-on-white Air Force 1s (or a pair in every colorway) were status objects that tacitly signaled one's purchasing power; the shoes were notably more expensive than Nike's other basketball high-tops.[4] As the Air Force 1's role as a street-style staple superseded its athletic origins, it became collectible, and sneakerheads began seeking out the rarer mid- and low-top models. In the thirty-five years since the shoe's launch, Nike has issued nearly two thousand versions of the Air Force 1, from mass-market releases emblazoned with flags or city names to ultra-exclusive celebrity collaborations that fetch four digits on the resale market. —LB

Left:
1— **Rucker Park, Harlem, c. 1985. Photograph by Dave Parham**
2— **Cinderella Shoes, Baltimore, n.d. Unknown photographer**
3— **Advertisement for the Nike Air Force 1, featuring basketball players Michael Cooper, Moses Malone, Calvin Natt, Jamaal Wilkes, Bobby Jones, and Mychal Thompson, 1982**
4— **Sneaker supercollector Bobbito Garcia in Air Force 1s, New York, 1987. Photograph by Ramón García**

A — 005

ARAN SWEATER In 1934 the fictional documentary *Man of Aran* memorialized (with some embellishment) the rural routine of the small fishing population of the three Aran Islands—Inis Mor, Inis Meain, and Inis Oirr—that perch in the Atlantic Ocean off the west coast of Ireland. The film, directed by Robert J. Flaherty, featured plenty of woolen tops in dark colors, born from the centuries-old Irish tradition of hand-knitted ganseys, or jerseys. Historically, the sweaters were knitted using sheep's wool that retained its naturally occurring lanolin oil. This made them water resistant and, combined with their inherent insulating quality, useful for wet weather and fishing, cornerstones of life on the Aran Isles. Then, as now, a light-colored sweater would have proven impractical for a hardworking fisherman, susceptible to stains from seaweed, oil, fish entrails, and more. The iconic off-white variation was enshrined in fashion history through contact with the mainland, initially through the efforts of Muriel Gahan, founder of Country Workers Ltd and the Irish Homespun Society, which promoted the native crafts of Ireland. Gahan opened The Country Shop on St Stephen's Green, Dublin, in 1930 and acted as the first broker between Aran women knitters and mainland Ireland.[1] The Aran sweaters she sold were made with undyed wool and with a coarser yarn than similar garments from the west coast of the British Isles, for speedier production. Gahan encouraged islanders to develop novel and unique patterns, supporting the growth and monetization of the craft—a boon for a community with limited resources.

The Aran sweater was further popularized by the Irish lawyer, journalist, and entrepreneur Pádraig Ó Síocháin, through his company Galway Bay Products, which marketed and exported Aran knitwear starting in the early 1950s.

He introduced the knitters to international sizing, created a sales catalogue, and distributed the product in Europe and North America. Aran sweater patterns were licensed by *Vogue* in the 1950s, and the garment appeared on Hollywood stars including Grace Kelly and Steve McQueen in the 1960s, assuring its ascendency. In subsequent decades, it has wavered between touristic take-home item and fashionable winter wear, between couture craft and mass-produced signifier of the changing seasons.

Various motifs and stitches, still in use today, are evocatively named for sources from the Bible and the natural world: Jacob's Ladder, Tree of Life, diamond stitch, moss stitch. Heinz Edgar Kiewe, a knitting historian and author, linked the genesis of the Aran sweater to the Book of Kells, an iconic medieval illustrated manuscript, citing (without evidence) a connection between its patterned geometries and the complex knitwork.[2] Further accounts suggested that individual knitting patterns were associated with specific families or communities, an idea rooted as much in repeated retelling as in reality. Stories designed to enchant tourists continue to proliferate, including, for example, the romanticized notion of knitting the distinctive cream-colored sweater for one's intended husband.

More broadly, this process of garment making using multiple loops of a single thread can be traced back over a millennium, through examples such as an extant early Roman-era Egyptian knitted cap and a pair of Egyptian knitted socks (c. 250–420 CE), though the precarious nature of cloth and fiber suggests that the practice is even older than the archaeological record allows us to determine.[3] —MMF

Right:
1, 2, 3— Aran sweater stitch patterns
4— Fishermen wearing Aran sweaters, purposely tight and short around the arms to minimize wet sleeves, c. 1900. Unknown photographer
5— Steve McQueen in the film *The Thomas Crown Affair,* 1968
6— Advertisement for an Aran knitting contest, Ireland, c. 1946

4

5

6

ARAN KNITTING CONTEST
for
AN ARAN JERSEY IN TRADITIONAL PATTERN

FIRST PRIZE: IRISH BROOCH AND £10

SECOND PRIZE: £5   THIRD PRIZE: £3

SPECIAL PRIZE FOR GIRL UNDER 16: £2

Certificates to all jerseys that pass the judges. All jerseys gaining certificates will be bought.

*

CONDITIONS

1. Any girl or woman in the Aran Islands of Inishmore, Inish Maan or Inishere, may enter for the contest.

2. More than one jersey may be sent by any knitter, but not more than one prize will be given to any household.

3. The jersey is to be knitted in white wool with a high neck, usual shape, man's size, good length of sleeve and body.

4. The jersey will be judged on its pattern, shape, knitting, and general appearance.

5. The maker's name and address on paper is to be sewn on to the jersey.

6. All jerseys to be knitted at home, and sent before St. Brigid's Day, 1st Feb., 1946 to The Country Shop, 23 St. Stephen's Green, Dublin, where the jerseys will be on exhibition.

AVIATOR SUNGLASSES   When the American feminist activist Gloria Steinem announced, "I no longer accept society's judgments that my group is second class," at a 1970s Equal Rights Amendment rally, her aviator sunglasses tempered her indignation with an air of unflappability.[1] And when the actor Tom Cruise declared, "I feel the need, the need for speed," as fighter pilot Maverick in the 1986 film *Top Gun,* the aviators that shielded his eyes seemed to validate his yearnings. Both in reality and in fiction, aviator sunglasses have long been the protective eyewear of choice for the strong-willed and independently minded.

In the 1910s, while aviation was still in its infancy, pilots began experimenting with high-altitude flights, and while fur-lined goggles protected their eyes from exposure to extreme cold (the typical biplane of the period featured an open cockpit), they also had a tendency to frost over, reducing or eliminating visibility. On February 27, 1920, Major Rudolph William "Shorty" Schroeder, a test pilot for the United States Army, flew his plane at a record height of 38,180 feet. Struggling to breathe and unable to see through frosted lenses, he was forced to remove his goggles to locate an emergency supply of oxygen, causing his eyes to freeze. Schroeder, though permanently blinded, managed to land his plane, and he was pulled from the cockpit by fellow test pilot Lieutenant John Macready. Macready made it his duty to address the deficiencies that had caused Schroeder's injury, and nearly two years later he set a new altitude record, flying to 40,800 feet—an achievement due in part to improved equipment. "Macready was clothed in the heaviest of furs with special helmet and goggles," observed the *Chicago Tribune.* "To insure clear vision a special gelatin was used on the goggles to prevent collection of ice."[2]

A few years later, Macready approached the optical company Bausch & Lomb, in Rochester, New York. Together they designed a goggle whose shape would seal the eyes from the cold while its frost-proof lenses provided protection from the bright sunlight in the upper atmosphere. Named Ray-Ban for its elimination of distracting rays of light, the goggles soon inspired sunglasses of a similar design, featuring green antiglare lenses embedded in a plastic frame. "My dad gave Bausch & Lomb the original shape, tint, and fit," Macready's daughter has said.[3] By 1937 Bausch & Lomb's Ray-Ban sunglasses were available to the general public, and a year later they were reengineered with a metal frame and rebranded the Ray-Ban Aviator. Early advertisements touted the new glasses' "soft green lenses that not only provide the wearer with maximum clarity, but give protection by cutting infra-red (heat) and ultra-violet rays."[4]

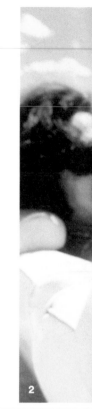

While the origins of sunglasses can be traced to British optician James Ayscough, who in 1752 advertised spectacles with tinted lenses, they only became a fashionable accessory around the turn of the twentieth century. This was due in part to a growing leisure culture and a corresponding need for resort attire, but sunglasses also became popular out of necessity, providing a more stylish alternative to the motor goggles worn in the period's windshieldless automobiles. "A pair of beautifully fitting motor goggles or sun-glasses is a Christmas gift that is sure to be used and unlikely to be duplicated," declared *Vogue* in 1925, in one of its first references to the item.[5] With a streamlined form that lent itself to outdoor sports, the Ray-Ban Aviator posed a stark contrast to the larger, brightly colored styles that were advertised for women in the 1950s and 1960s. While sunglasses were a unisex accessory, the Aviator model was primarily advertised to men, due to its association with the military, which was then mostly closed to women. When images emerged in 1944 of American general Douglas MacArthur wearing Ray-Ban Aviators while stationed in the Philippines, the style's association with rugged machismo only increased.

This all changed in the 1970s, however, when Ray-Ban introduced Aviator models with colored frames and lenses. "These are the best—this year's aviator," declared *Vogue* in 1978, "in new neutrals

[and] bold hits of color. Clean and uncluttered—glasses with the same sparseness, the same no-nonsense ease we've been seeing in clothes."[6] Given the style's evocation of a rational, sensible, cool—the opposite of frivolity—it is not surprising that Steinem, one of the period's leading feminist voices, made it a wardrobe signature. Today's aviator sunglasses differ from their forebearers only in their more complete ubiquity. For military men and women, for Hollywood celebrities, and for anyone enjoying a day at the beach, they provide protection, comfort, and an image of effortless equanimity. —SK

Left:
1— Aviation goggles manufactured by American Optical Corp., Southbridge, Massachusetts, c. 1918
2— Benicio Del Toro and Johnny Depp in the film *Fear and Loathing in Las Vegas*, 1998
3— Paul and Linda McCartney with their children, 1970. Photograph by James Garrett
4— General Douglas MacArthur (right) in the Philippines, c. 1945. Photograph by Carl Mydans

B — 007

BACKPACK From soldiers and hikers to students and urban professionals, the backpack has served a range of wearers throughout its history, evolving from an item of pure utility to one embodying style, identity, and even status. Introduced in fall 1984, the nylon backpack designed by the Italian fashion house Prada epitomizes this evolution and multidimensionality, functioning as a practical carryall that simultaneously connotes luxury. A midsize frameless sack constructed from water-proof, industrial-weight nylon of a fine twisted weave (called *vela* nylon or *tessuto vela*),[1] the backpack, conceived by company designer Miuccia Prada, was launched without any prominent branding. Having recently joined her family's name-sake leather goods company (established in 1913), Prada sought to update the firm's products to suit the needs of the modern urbanite. She soon added to the pack the triangular metal label used on the fashion house's classic luggage, thus fusing the company's heritage with the contemporary design and transforming the bag into a coveted prestige object and symbol of urban mobility, worn by both men and women for all occasions.

Humans have long sought efficient methods for transporting items on their backs, employing textiles such as the *aguayo*, used by indigenous people in the Andean regions of Bolivia, Ecuador, and Peru, and the rebozo, which does double duty throughout Latin America as an all-purpose accessory and a wrap for carrying children. The Native American cradleboard anticipated later structured backpacks for carrying heavier loads, be they children or inanimate objects. The contemporary backpack is closely connected to the development of the modern military uniform. Soldiers in U.S. and European militaries in the nineteenth and early twentieth centuries carried a small bag called a haversack. Composed of khaki canvas with a buckled flap closure, it featured a single shoulder strap; a second strap was added when the U.S. Army established the M-1910 haversack as the standard bag for infantrymen in 1910. The haversack remained in use through the beginning of World War II, with quick-release buckles added to an upgraded version in 1928.

In 1941 a larger bag, the rucksack, was introduced in the U.S. and German militaries. Offering more carrying capacity for troops stationed in colder climates, the rucksack had a drawstring closure, two padded and adjustable shoulder straps, and a heavy-gauge steel frame that posi-tioned the load just above the hips on a backrest strap.[2] The American version was eventually adopted by alpine enthusiasts, who, like soldiers, required a secure method of hands-free transport. One such enthusiast was Gerry Cunningham, an avid hiker and World War II veteran from Boulder, Colorado. In 1945 he founded the company Gerry Outdoors and began designing packs in lighter-weight materials and shapes. Nylon was first incorporated into an aluminum-frame pack in 1952 by another American hiking-enthusiast-cum-backpack-pioneer, Asher "Dick" Kelty, but Cunningham produced the first frameless nylon zippered version—the Teardrop Backpack—in 1967.

The backpack was soon adopted by another unique demographic: students. The outdoor-gear company JanSport, founded by Skip Yowell, Murray Pletz, and Jan Lewis in Seattle in 1967, located its first shop inside the bookstore at the University of Washington, where its skiing and hiking daypacks attracted book-toting students. With the introduction in 1984 of the frameless JanSport SuperBreak, a lightweight backpack designed specifi-cally for students, the school "book bag" phenomenon was firmly established.[3] Students soon began to express their individuality through bag color choice and other coded behavior. For example, while using only one shoulder strap was consid-ered cool among American students in the 1980s and 1990s, by the 2000s the rise of "geek chic" had ushered in a return of the two-strap look. Similarly, backpack mores in Seoul in the 1990s were so pronounced that they varied between districts; while students from Gangnam wore their packs as loosely as possible, extending the straps so the bags hung below their hips,

2

3

Gangbuk students strapped theirs on so tightly that the backpacks were nicknamed "tortoiseshells."[4]

This rich history, encompassing such scholastic stylings as well as military transport, outdoor athletics, and the functional luxury of the Prada bag, speaks to the adaptability of the backpack typology, demonstrating its universal function and appeal across countless social and cultural strata. —SK

Left:
1— American soldiers, Paris, 1918. Photograph by Corporal Keen Polk, Signal Corps
2— JanSport Sack 3 backpack, 1977
3— Linda Evangelista in a Prada backpack, *Vogue*, August 1989. Photograph by Hans Feurer
4— Navajo mother and child, c. 1915–25. Photograph by William Pennington and Lisle Updike

BALACLAVA The balaclava is a knitted woolen head covering with one or more holes for regions of the face; it can be worn pulled down over the chin or rolled up to form a hat. Initially designed to insulate the wearer from frigid weather, today the garment is also used to protect from UV rays or prevent facial recognition.

Balaclava is the name of a village near Sevastopol, in Crimea, that was the site of a bloody battle during the Crimean War (1853–56). The conflict is notable for the pioneering work of British nurse Florence Nightingale and for the British Army's maladministration of resources, which prompted soldiers' families to send them supplies of warm clothing and food, including lovingly hand-knitted garments. The name *balaclava*, for the hat, emerged in the 1880s; before then, the garments were known in Britain as Uhlan or Templar caps, named for similar head coverings worn by medieval knights.[1]

During World War I, publications such as the British national tabloid *Daily Sketch* and organizations such as the American Red Cross popularized knitting as a gendered patriotic pastime, encouraging women on the home front to knit for their fighting men, and distributing yarn and patterns for balaclavas, among other designs.[2] In her 1933 memoir *Testament of Youth*, a reflection on her experiences in the Great War, British nurse and pacifist Vera Brittain poignantly termed the handmade personal effects of men like her fiancé, killed in the trenches, "remnants of patriotism."[3]

Along with other protective equipment developed in wartime, firefighters, electrical workers, and racecar drivers now wear balaclavas to shield their faces from extreme conditions. Military, police, and paramilitary forces (perhaps most memorably the Irish Republican Army) use them for physical protection, for the anonymity they provide, and for their intimidating appearance—as have countless persons engaged in unlawful activity, making the balaclava a cartoonish visual shorthand for extralegal actions. These associations with violence make the recent popularization on Chinese beaches of the balaclava-like "facekini"—a thin, colorful nylon-Lycra-blend sun barrier—so humorous and disconcerting (see *Sunscreen*).

Balaclavas are not solely reserved for warmongers and crooks. Australian explorer of the Antarctic Sir Douglas Mawson (1882–1958) is a national hero in his homeland; an image of him wearing a knitted balaclava decorated the first Australian hundred-dollar bill, in 1984. Fashion houses have also embraced the balaclava, exploiting it as a provocative mask to hide what is usually flaunted.[4] Popular culture has metabolized this trend. Director Harmony Korine's cultish 2012 film *Spring Breakers* includes a memorable scene in which actor James Franco is surrounded by young women wielding weapons and clad in bikini tops, sweatpants, and pink balaclavas. The poster advertising Beyoncé and Jay-Z's 2014 On the Run tour features a closely cropped portrait of the duo, their faces almost completely obscured by balaclavas, paying homage to their 2002 hit "'03 Bonnie & Clyde" and to the accessory's felonious history. —MMF

Right:
1— Masked members of the Provisional Irish Republican Army at the funeral of hunger-striker Bobby Sands, Belfast, 1981. Unknown photographer
2— Knitted balaclava helmet with adjustable earflaps, worn during the Crimean War and reappropriated during World Wars I and II, 1941
3— Members of the punk group Pussy Riot, performing in the Cathedral of Christ the Savior, Moscow, 2012. The group was later arrested and imprisoned. Photograph by Mitya Aleshkovsky

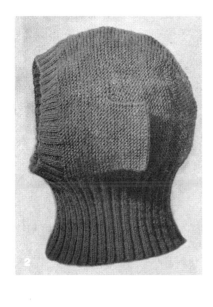

BALLET FLAT   The fashionable ballet flat derives from the flat ballet shoe, whose lineage extends to the original high-heeled, pointed, and buckled shoes worn by the female dancers of France's Académie Royale de Danse starting in 1681. The first flat ballet shoe is historically associated with French dancer Marie-Anne de Cupis de Camargo (1710–1770), who, although depicted wearing the original version of the shoe, is said to have removed the heel to improve her mobility.[1] Camargo was likely the first dancer to shorten her skirt, and as a result she was able to jump as high as her male counterparts, which allowed the role of the female dancer to begin to eclipse that of the male. By the early nineteenth century, female dancers were beginning to adopt soft, heel-less slippers to aid in their agility, a phenomenon that was also influenced by the flat lace-up shoes worn by women since the early 1800s. The flat ballet shoe was further popularized by dancer Marie Taglioni, whose revealing gauze-and-muslin layered white tutu in the 1832 premiere of the ballet *La Sylphide* elevated the shoe to an iconic status. Though credited as being the first to dance en pointe, Taglioni was not able to rise completely onto her toes: she was hindered by her leather shoes, which although heavily darned on the toe to provide some support, were no match for the later versions, which were lined with canvas and included cardboard at the toe.[2]

As the design of ballet shoes improved, one maker who helped promote them was Salvatore Capezio, an Italian immigrant to New York who, in 1887, opened a small shoe repair shop near the Metropolitan Opera House with signage that read "The Theatrical & Historical Shoemaker." Capezio became the go-to maker of toe shoes and the less structured warm-up slippers for dancers around the world, including Russian prima ballerina Anna Pavlova, who in 1910 purchased Capezio shoes for herself and her entire company. Capezio's creations eventually caught the eye of trailblazing American women's wear designer Claire McCardell, who commissioned him to create his signature slipper in fabrics that would also be used in the garments of her 1944 collection. Wartime rationing was partially the impetus for the collaboration—unlike other shoes, ballet slippers were exempt from domestic leather and rubber rationing under Limitation Order L-85. But McCardell was also responding to—and validating—the broadening lifestyles of women who, while men were away serving in the war, were expanding their participation in the labor force and in recreational activities. Promotional images from 1944 feature both leather and fabric versions of McCardell's shoe coupled with practical fashions such as "rehearsal pants" and an ensemble meant for "skating and cycling in frigid temperatures." By the end of 1944 the shoe appeared in *Vogue*, which declared, "Ballet slippers no longer confine their talents to the Stage."[3] Within months it was being promoted by stores such as Lord & Taylor and Neiman Marcus, and in 1949 a bright-yellow pair of Capezio ballet flats appeared on the cover of *Vogue*. Other designers tapped into this zeitgeist, including Valentina Schlee (known simply as Valentina), a New York–based former dancer who throughout the 1940s designed and promoted the wearing of ballet flats with both day and evening wear.

The ballet flat was soon adopted by a range of influential women. Artist and activist Diane di Prima paired hers with a black nylon leotard and jeans as a freshman at Swarthmore College in 1951 (see *Leotard*), marking her difference from those "blonde girls in cashmere sweaters with single strands of pearls [that] seem to own this place."[4] Audrey Hepburn, taking a cue from her costuming in the films *Roman Holiday* (1953), *Sabrina* (1954), and *Funny Face* (1957), became a famed devotee of the shoe, whether as an elegant foil to a dress or a modish complement to an all-black pants ensemble. Shoe designer Salvatore Ferragamo was so inspired by Hepburn's enthusiasm for the look that in 1954 he designed a round-toed flat called the Audrey. In 1956 the ballet flat received another significant endorsement when Brigitte Bardot wore a bright-red pair with red Capri pants and a Breton top in the Roger Vadim film *And God Created Woman*. Bardot herself commissioned the shoes from French designer Rose Repetto, whose namesake shop near the National Opera of Paris had been supplying pointe shoes to dancers since 1947. The Cendrillon Ballerina, as the shoe was named, ignited a new wave of popularity for the style, thanks to Bardot's combination of sex appeal and tomboyish nonchalance.

While the ballet flat fell somewhat out of favor in the mid-1960s and '70s, it came back into vogue during the 1980s, as one of the world's most beloved women, Diana, Princess of Wales, popularized the shoe as part of her preppy "Sloane Ranger" style. The ballet flat has since grown in popularity, worn by everyone from model Kate Moss to former first lady Michelle Obama. In 2006 the American designer Tory Burch introduced the Reva ballet flat, with its distinctive golden medallion logo on the toe. With more than five million pairs sold by 2013, the success of the Reva highlights the mass appeal of the ballet flat. Comfortable and practical yet romantic and elegant, the shoe entered fashion as a symbol of the modern woman, and it continues to epitomize her today.
—SK

Right:
1— **Salvatore Capezio and Claire McCardell, New York, 1944. Photograph by Frances McLaughlin-Gill**
2— **Brigitte Bardot on the set of the film *And God Created Woman*, 1956. Unknown photographer**
3— **Valentina Schlee ("Madame Valentina"), *Vogue*, November 1941. Photograph by John Rawlings**
4— **Promotional image for the Christian Louboutin Nudes collection of ballet flats, 2016. Photograph by Sofia Sanchez and Mauro Mongiello**
5— **Actress in a Claire McCardell skating or cycling ensemble in a publicity image for the film *If Winter Comes*, 1944. Unknown photographer**

BANDANNA   Practical, inexpensive, and multivalent in meaning, the bandanna is one of fashion's most versatile items. A square piece of cotton or linen fabric (or a blend thereof), the bandanna may be carried in the pocket but often is tied around a part of the body, most commonly the neck. Its distinguishing characteristic is its printed motifs, a fact underscored by its etymology. With origins in Sanskrit (*badhnāti,* meaning "to tie") and Hindi (*bāndhnū,* or "tie-dyeing"), the word *bandanna* likely came into English via Portuguese, after Portugal conquered Goa (now part of India) in the sixteenth century.

　　The bandanna's most classic design features a red ground and a centered motif of white paisleys and dots. Thought to represent a spray of flowers or a bent cedar tree, the paisley motif originated in Persia, where a less stylized iteration—the *buta* (also called the *boteh*)—appeared in textiles during the Sassanid Dynasty (224–651 CE). Reaching prolific heights during the Mughal Empire (1526–1857) in what is now India and Afghanistan, the buta was famously popularized in Europe in the eighteenth century when French emperor Napoleon Bonaparte gave his wife, Josephine, precious Kashmir shawls bearing the motif. This ignited a craze for the garment that led to its eventual mass production in Paisley, Scotland, beginning in the early nineteenth century (see *Shawl*). The paisley motif became so popular that manufacturers soon began printing it on cotton or woolen fabric, sometimes simple squares.

　　The bandanna's classic color, Turkey red—an extremely colorfast cotton dye obtained from madder root—followed a similar trajectory. This dyeing process originated in India and was imported into France in the eighteenth century, via Turkey, and was soon adapted for mass

production in Manchester, England. Turkey-red fabric was an ideal ground for roller printing, including paisley motifs, and the resulting product was a chief textile export to the American colonies.[1] It was during the American Revolution that the bandanna first took on a symbolic meaning. In 1775, to protest a British ban on textile printing in the American colonies, a bandanna was commissioned (by Martha Washington, it is believed) featuring the likeness of her husband, General George Washington, on horseback, surrounded by flags and cannons. Printed in 1776 or 1777 on a square of linen, its promotion of Washington's political image inspired the production of future U.S. political bandannas, including campaign bandannas for Presidents Andrew Jackson, printed in 1828, and Benjamin Harrison, in 1888.[2]

The bandanna gained traction among American cowboys in the second half of the nineteenth century, likely inspired by kerchiefs worn by German immigrants to the Mexican state of Nuevo León, which borders Texas. Tied around the neck or the lower part of the face, the bandanna protected the mouth and nose from dust and shielded the back of the neck from the sun; in cold weather it was worn under the hat for added insulation. The popular Western films of the 1920s and 1930s deepened the bandanna's association with the cowboy and also linked the accessory with the archetype of the outlaw, whose bandanna-covered face symbolized danger. The bandanna took on a more patriotic symbolism in the United States during World War II. As cotton was not subject to textile rationing under the government's Limitation Order L-85, the bandanna provided the perfect hair covering for the many women taking up factory jobs in the absence of male workers, and women were pictured wearing bandannas in patriotic propaganda campaigns urging them to enter the workforce. Home-sewing patterns, such as a 1943 Simplicity design called "War-Plant Hat is Made of One Bandana," offered creative variations.[3]

In the 1970s, handkerchief ("hanky") codes emerged among gay men in the United States, who used colored bandannas to communicate their sexual desires and proclivities to potential partners. Inner-city gangs, most famously the Los Angeles–based Crips and Bloods (both of which formed in the 1970s), have used bandannas to signify group identity and to demarcate turf, with Bloods wearing red bandannas and Crips sporting blue versions. In 2017 the bandanna took on a renewed political meaning as part of a global campaign called #tiedtogether. During fashion weeks, designers, models, and industry professionals wore white bandannas to demonstrate solidarity and inclusiveness amid a chaotic global political climate. A twenty-first-century moment of resistance, the campaign is just one of the many uses, both symbolic and practical, the humble bandanna has been put to throughout its long history.
—SK

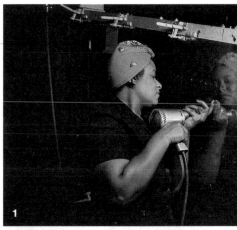

Right:
1— **Riveter at work on an A31 Vengeance dive bomber, Tennessee, 1943. Photograph by Alfred T. Palmer**
2— **Tupac Shakur, Harlem, 1994. Photograph by Michael Benabib**
3— **Portrait of General George Washington on a linen bandanna, attributed to John Hewson, Philadelphia, 1776–77**

1

BASE BALL CAPS.

NO. 21. 5 Qualities.

NO. 7.

NO. 21. Cheap Flannel.

NO. 11.

NO. 8. 4 Qualities.

NO. 13.

NO. 8. 3 Qualities.

NO. 19.

NO. 1. 1 Quality.

Cheap Muslin.

2

3

BASEBALL CAP In 1996 New Era Cap Company CEO Chris Koch received a phone call from the American film director Spike Lee, who had an unusual request. Lee, a devoted New York Yankees fan, was to attend Game 3 of the World Series in Atlanta, where his beloved Yankees would take on the Atlanta Braves. Knowing that he would be wearing his bright-red bomber jacket to the game, Lee appealed to the baseball cap producer, which had been supplying on-field caps to Major League Baseball teams since 1934: could New Era make him a red version of the classic blue Yankees cap? As New Era had maintained the exclusive license to produce baseball caps for every team in the MLB since 1993, Koch knew the request needed to be approved by Yankees owner George Steinbrenner, and since Steinbrenner both supported Lee's Yankees ardor and felt that a single hat would not affect the team's overall image, he approved. However, as the Yankees went on to win the game (and eventually the World Series), Lee was pictured on TV screens numerous times throughout the evening, and by the next day, devoted fans throughout the country were bombarding their local New Era stores with requests for the red Yankees cap. Heeding this sudden demand for caps in hues that did not reflect team colors, New Era renegotiated its license with the MLB to allow for variety, and within months the fashion-statement baseball cap was born.[1]

A quintessentially American sport, baseball had its first recorded organized game on June 19, 1846. The first official uniform, consisting of blue woolen pantaloons, a white flannel shirt, and a straw boater hat—due to the prevalence of the hat in men's summer wear at the time—was worn by teams including the New York Knickerbockers in 1849. As baseball organized semiprofessionally, early archetypes of the modern billed and curved-crown hat materialized. The "Brooklyn-style" cap worn by the Brooklyn Excelsiors in the 1860s had similarities to a jockey's hat and featured a small brim, a round, forward-leaning crown, and a button on top that joined its stitching. The "Chicago-style" pillbox cap, which emerged in the 1870s, had a flat top, a short bill, and horizontal stripes, and showed its derivation from military caps. In fact, caps were so varied during this period that an 1889 advertisement from *Spalding's Base Ball Guide* featured ten different models of varying shapes and sizes. The turn of the twentieth century saw the beginning of ball-cap standardization, with the pillbox shape disappearing in favor of a curved crown, and featuring design details such as airholes for ventilation, stitched visors for durability (with fabric sewn directly to the bill's cardboard insert), and team logos. In 1901 the Detroit Tigers became the first team to feature its logo on its caps—a running orange tiger.[2]

As more teams began to incorporate the standardized baseball cap into their uniforms in the first decades of the twentieth century, New Era Cap Company (based in Buffalo) seized on the opportunity to design its own version, and in 1934 it made its first baseball cap for the Cleveland Indians. This cap, featuring six panels for a better fit and a decorative button at its crest, along with a stitched visor, was an immediate success, and soon New Era began supplying other Major League teams, including the Brooklyn Dodgers, Cincinnati Reds, and Detroit Tigers. In 1954 New Era introduced its 59Fifty model (an identification number based on the company's internal production system), and the baseball cap as it appears today emerged. While mirroring the shape of the Brooklyn-style cap of the nineteenth century, the 59Fifty was made from lighter-weight, breathable wool and featured a host of design updates, including a layered cotton inner sweatband, ventilated airholes for each of its six panels, buckram backing to support the attached brim, and eight rows of stitching on the visor (compared to the four to six rows on earlier caps) for better support and hold.[3] The hat became the standard model for professional players—New Era was supplying caps to twenty of the twenty-four professional teams by 1974—and by the 1980s it was the go-to hat for baseball fans as well, thanks in part to

New Era's "The Cap the Pros Wear" marketing slogan.

With the introduction in 1996 of customizable colors, the result of Lee's red Yankees cap, the 59Fifty reached an even wider demographic, and New Era's annual sales doubled over the next three years. The sheer variety of the 59Fifty, which became known colloquially as the "fitted cap" (adjustable caps had been introduced in the 1940s), allowed wearers to choose a cap not simply out of allegiance to a particular team, but based on personal style. Subtle nuances—from color choices to a hat's angle on the head—became significant fashion statements. Even maintaining the New Era sizing sticker on the cap's brim was a conscious choice: it demonstrated that the cap was newly purchased and not counterfeit. Today the baseball cap is popular with wearers in all walks of life. From the catwalk to the street, its meaning has evolved as subtly as its design, facilitating its transformation from humble sports uniform to global fashion staple. —SK

Previous page:
1— **Spike Lee, New York, 1998. Photograph by Rose Hartman**
2— **Illustrations from an advertisement for baseball caps in *Spalding's Base Ball Guide*, 1889**
3— **Oil-industry welder straightens out cables, Alberta, Canada, 1982. Unknown photographer**

BERET   The beret, a round, visorless cap constructed of felt, is simple to make and dense enough to provide protection from the weather. Examples of what we now refer to as a beret have existed for millennia: archaeologists have found traces of such felt hats in tombs in Italy and Denmark that date back to the Bronze Age. In ancient Greece, both men and women, especially travelers, would wear a *petasos*, a flat, floppy hat made of straw or felt, in order to protect themselves from the rain and sun. Today this simple hat is a powerful signifier in a wide range of contexts. Its malleable shape and positioning on the head allow its meaning to shift, whether it is being worn as part of a revolutionary uniform or to convey an aura of Parisian chic.

The modern beret may be traced to the *boina*, which appeared in the fifteenth century in the Basque region of Spain and France. Originating with shepherds living on both sides of the Pyrenees, it was made in different colors— red in Guipúzcoa, white in Álava, and blue in Biscay, for example. Eventually, most Basques adopted a blue version, while the red hat became part of the provincial folk costume of the neighboring region of Navarre.[1] The red hats became associated with Spain's Carlist Wars in the nineteenth century, as part of their regulated military uniform. The cap's place as a symbol of this conflict was solidified when Tomás de Zumalacárregui, a Carlist general, was depicted wearing one in numerous portraits.

The boina is made throughout the Basque region, where it is still part of traditional dress. Boinas Elósegui, one of the oldest such factories in the region, was founded in 1858 in the town of Tolosa, where it remains. In its first years of existence, the factory produced just fifty handmade hats annually. By 1915 it had increased its yearly production to 3,500 and was exporting to South America, Cuba, the Philippines, and the United States, as well as Europe.

In France, commercial production centered in Oloron-Sainte-Marie, a small southern town, where expertise developed in the necessary knitting, felting, dyeing, brushing, and shaving processes. It is here that the last remaining historic beret manufacturer, Laulhère (founded in 1840), operates today.[2] Even though French beret manufacturing has dwindled since the 1970s, largely due to competition from producers in Asia, the hat retains strong Gallic associations that have translated into wider popular culture. Its farmer heritage appealed to bohemians living in Paris's Left Bank in the nineteenth century.[3] By the 1920s the beret was being worn by all manner of artists and intellectuals in the French capital and beyond, ranging from Pablo Picasso and Louise Bourgeois to jazz musician Dizzy Gillespie and writers Simone de Beauvoir and Ernest Hemingway. In the 1950s it became associated with the beat generation in the United States. Even though the artists traditionally associated with this literary current did not project a uniform image, by the end of that decade a stereotype had emerged that reduced beat style to a caricature of "'chicks' in black leotards and 'cats' in black turtlenecks, jeans, berets, goatees and dark glasses."[4]

Also in the 1950s, the beret became a popular choice for revolutionaries. During the Cuban Revolution (1953–59) it was part of the uniform for two of the country's most influential political leaders, Marxist guerrilla Ernesto "Che" Guevara and eventual prime minister Fidel Castro, then leader of the Communist Party. The beret was integrated into the revolutionary sartorial lexicon of the civil rights movement in the United States with the founding, in 1966, of the Black Panther Party, whose members wore a black leather jacket, black pants, a powder-blue shirt, black shoes, and their hair in a natural style, under a black beret—a nod to military uniforms worldwide. The beret was quickly adopted by other groups fighting for the rights of marginalized populations, such as the Brown Berets, a Chicano organization formed in 1967 that called for an end to discrimination and police brutality against Mexican Americans.[5]

During the 2016 Super Bowl halftime show, Beyoncé employed this provocative symbol to masterful effect with a musical performance that mixed politics with contemporary pageantry. Dressed in a militaristic style, she was accompanied by female backup dancers who wore black leather, berets, and natural hair styles—a clear reference to the Black Panthers—as the singer urged her audience to "get in formation." In this broadcast, which reached over 100 million live viewers, the beret's history was reappropriated and placed in a new context, fusing mass-televised spectacle with radical black femininity and gender politics. —AB

Previous pages:
1— **Black Panthers at a rally in DeFremery Park, Oakland, California, 1968. Photograph by Stephen Shames**
2— **A Radical Monarchs troop, Oakland, California, 2015. Unknown photographer**
3— **Beyoncé and dancers during the Super Bowl halftime show, Levi's Stadium, Santa Clara, California, 2016. Photograph by Tony Avelar**

Right:
4— **Ernesto "Che" Guevara, 1959. Photograph by Joseph Scherschel**
5— **Portrait of Tomás de Zumalacárregui, by Adolphe Jean-Baptiste Bayot, 1836**
6— **Txirrita (Jose Manuel Lujanbio Retegi) and Saiburu (Juan Jose Lujanbio Zabaleta), Basque *bertsolaris* (composers of verse), n.d. Unknown photographer**

5

4

6

BIKER JACKET   A biker jacket is a readymade exoskeleton, replete with instant meaning. Its mystique owes much to a history of provocative owners, but its appeal is equally indebted to its enigmatic design, in which streamlined sophistication is held in tension with chaotic asymmetry. The original zippered horsehide biker jacket was introduced in 1928 by Schott Brothers, a company founded in 1913 on Manhattan's Lower East Side by Irving and Jack Schott, sons of Russian Jewish immigrants. Previous motorcycle jackets, including Schott's, resembled early aviation jackets: made of brown leather with a center-front button closure and ribbed cuffs and collars, they did not provide adequate wind protection. In 1928 Irving Schott met representatives from the motorcycle parts distributor Beck Company and the zipper manufacturer Talon at a clothing conference; inspired by these encounters he designed a zippered biker jacket—the first-ever jacket to feature a zipper closure.[1] Named Perfecto (after Irving's favorite Cuban-style cigar), it featured a knitted waistband, black snaps at the wrists, two welt pockets at the waist, a single flap pocket on the chest, and a zipper at center front. Schott entered into a distribution relationship with Beck in the early 1930s, and soon introduced new design features. With the addition of a belted hem and zipper closures at the cuffs to prevent wind entry, a vented yoke to moderate the impact of wind against the back, and an off-center, diagonal zipper to maximize collar coverage at the neck, the Schott Perfecto of 1940 was a functional marvel. Epaulets, asymmetrically placed zippered pockets, and chrome snaps enhanced its usefulness while solidifying the visual impact of the design. "No matter what we tell you about this jacket you cannot half appreciate it without seeing it," declared a 1941 issue of the company trade bulletin *Beck News*. "It catches the eye and the imagination of every young fellow—to see it is to want it."[2]

Though motorcycle clubs had been growing steadily in the United States since World War I, they were not well known in the broader culture until 1947, when four thousand members of the Boozefighters biker gang rode into Hollister, California, for a three-day convention. As reported in *Life*, the event took a riotous turn: "They quickly tired of ordinary motorcycle thrills and turned to more exciting stunts. Racing their vehicles down the main street and through traffic lights, they rammed into restaurants and bars, breaking furniture and mirrors." "We like to show off," explained one participant. "It's just a lot of fun."[3] The Boozefighters and the biker jacket seemed to share the same contradictory persona: tough yet flashy, chaotic yet in control.

This tension was most famously incarnated by Marlon Brando as leader of the fictional Black Rebels Motorcycle Club in the 1953 film *The Wild One*, loosely based on the Hollister riots. The film's motorcyclists were all provided with Schott jackets; Brando wore the new Perfecto One Star, which featured a chrome star on each epaulet. At times zipped to the neck in streamlined precision and at others hanging open over the belt buckle in anarchic turmoil, the jacket signaled the character's toughness while revealing his vulnerability. After a brief lull (when many U.S. schools banned the garment as an incitement to hooliganism), sales of One Star jackets spiked, their aura of rebellion canonized in American culture.

The biker jacket was adopted in the world of rock and roll by figures ranging from the Sex Pistols' Sid Vicious to Blondie's Debbie Harry, but by the 1970s it had been worn so ubiquitously by self-styled outsiders that its cool factor had diminished in authenticity. The Ramones, a punk-rock group composed of four awkward twentysomethings from the middle-class neighborhood of Forest Hills, Queens, used it to cultivate, in the words of music critic Tom Carson, "the attractiveness of the comic loser."[4] He wrote, "Their leather jackets and strung-out, streetwise pose weren't so much an imitation of Brando in 'The Wild One' as a very self-conscious parody—they knew how phony it was for them to take on those tough-guy trappings."[5]

By the turn of the twenty-first century, the biker jacket had become a classic among fashionistas seeking to give their ensembles some edge. It received its ultimate high-style treatment in 2005, in the Ballerina Motorbike collection by the Japanese label Comme des Garçons. Featuring biker jackets paired with tutus, Ballerina Motorbike captured the irrefutable cool of the biker jacket, a garment capable of imbuing the epitome of *soft* with the essence of *hard*. —SK

Right:

1— Costume designer Jenny Beavan (left) accepts the Academy Award for best costume design for the film *Mad Max: Fury Road*, **Los Angeles, 2016. Photograph by Kevin Winter**

2— Veteran's Day parade, New York, 2010. Photograph by Michael Martin

3— Cowhide cut for Perfecto motorcycle jackets at the Schott Brothers factory, Union, New Jersey, 2015. Unknown photographer

4— Police officers at the St. Patrick's Day parade, St. Louis, 2008. Photograph by Robert Crowe

4

BIKINI   The bikini dates back to the summer of 1946 in France, where its creation is attributed to two men: Jacques Heim and Louis Réard. A respected couturier, Heim named his minimal two-piece bathing costume the Atome (the French word for *atom*), a reference to its size that may have been inspired by the nuclear tests then being conducted by the United States at Bikini Atoll, a reef near an archipelago of South Pacific islands. Though Heim's Atome was not markedly different from already extant two-piece bathing suits (the bottoms covered the navel), it emphasized the hips with a horizontal rectangle of cloth. Réard's design made its scandalous debut that same summer, on July 5, at the Molitor public pool in Paris, where Réard—an engineer by trade—organized a beauty contest to display his creation. Consisting of four triangles of fabric connected by strings, Réard's design was so revealing that models refused to wear it for the contest; Réard instead hired Micheline Bernardini, a striptease dancer at the Casino de Paris. Similarly inspired by the Bikini Atoll tests (and perhaps by Heim), Réard called his creation the Bikini, capable of igniting "the torrid heat of sexuality with nuclear force," in the words of historian Patrick Alac.[1]

The bikini exposed a new set of erogenous zones, including the navel and upper thighs, outraging some among a beachgoing populace used to seeing (and revealing) only a small section of the midriff in the two-piece bathing suits that had first appeared on European, American, and Australian beaches in the late 1920s and 1930s. Previous bathing costumes—from woolen, sleeved dresses worn over pantaloons in the 1840s to knitted "princess-style" one-piece suits worn for competitive swimming in the 1870s—had always revealed more of a woman's body than contemporaneous nonaquatic fashions, but the bikini crossed a line. It was banned almost immediately in Catholic countries such as Spain, Portugal, and Italy and was initially met with trepidation in the United States. A 1949 *Life* story titled "The Trouble with the Bikini" declared, "Abdominal scars are revealed. This has caused many women whose surgeons have left their stomachs looking like old golf balls to shun the suits."[2] In the late 1950s, the publication attributed the emerging acceptance of the bathing suit in the United States to "the vastly increasing number of home pools, where a bikini can be worn in privacy."[3]

The bikini's path to acceptance was thorny in most areas of the world, and the discourses surrounding its viability reflect the widespread politicization of women's bodies. In Australia, for example, the bikini was a source of tension between liberal youth, who embraced it early on at a number of beaches, including Queensland's Surfers Paradise, and older generations, who campaigned against it as an enabler of indecent exposure. In 1946 a Melbourne trade publication deemed the bikini "daring and NOT likely to be worn on the Victorian beaches this summer," but nevertheless predicted that eventually "the sweet young things will get their own way."[4] In 1952 the Queensland designer Paula Stafford sent the model Anne Ferguson to Surfers Paradise in one of her creations. When Ferguson was ordered to cover up by a beach inspector, the designer made five bikinis overnight and sent five more models to the same beach the next day.

Vogue Australia declared the summer of 1959 "the bikiniest summer ever,"[5] but it was not until the 1960s that the bikini gained broad acceptance internationally, thanks to celebrity endorsements, the growing power of youth culture, and innovations in textile technology—the introduction of spandex, especially. However, the bikini's move into the mainstream did not mean it was suddenly devoid of politics. In the wake of the 1964 military coup in Brazil, the bikini became a garment of protest, capturing the spirit of *tropicalismo*, a late-1960s cultural movement combining modern and traditional elements of Brazilian culture. The exposure of female bodies was an assertion of freedom and pride in Brazil's history, and the bikini-clad woman embodied a sense of cultural

fantasy in the face of rigid political hegemony.[6]

In Sicilian murals made around the year 300, women are shown doing gymnastics in scanty two-piece garments that are often cited as the precursors of the bikini; then, as now, the style allows for ease of movement and exposure to the sun. While the bikini has been an object of controversy in patriarchal cultures, where women's behavior is subject to restrictive standards of modesty, propriety, and beauty, it has nonetheless become an international fashion mainstay, a provocative yet ubiquitous beachwear staple (available at all price levels) that evokes carefree abandon and outdoor fun. Its meteoric introduction and ascent have been matched only by its enduring appeal. —SK

Left:
1— Micheline Bernardini at the Molitor swimming pool, Paris, 1946
2— Brazilian actress Leila Diniz, Rio de Janeiro, c. 1975. Photograph by Joel Maia
3— Ursula Andress in the film *Dr. No*, **1962**
4— Mosaic in Villa Romana del Casale, Piazza Armerina, Sicily, 300–400 CE
5— Model Natalie Nickerson Paine in Montego Bay, Jamaica, *Harper's Bazaar*, **May 1947. Photograph by Toni Frisell**

BIRKIN BAG According to the oft-told story, the Birkin bag—a meticulously handcrafted, yet sizeable and sturdy carryall—is the result of a chance 1981 meeting on a plane between British actress and chanteuse Jane Birkin and Jean-Louis Dumas, chief executive of Hermès. The contents of Birkin's too-small handbag spilled to the floor, prompting an offer from Dumas to design her a better one. The purse was not an immediate success when it became available to the public in 1984. But by the turn of the twenty-first century, with the explosion of a wait-list-only, limited-edition culture of luxury handbags, the Hermès Birkin had firmly solidified its position as the paragon of the It bag: luxurious yet functional, coveted yet elusive, rarified yet ubiquitous in common imagination. The term gained vernacular prominence in the mid-1990s, and first appeared in *Vogue* in 1999 as part of the phrase "die-for-it bag."[1] In 2008 *Vogue* hyperbolically described the Birkin as "that totemic accessory that announced you were owner of all that was desirable in the world."[2]

Purses date to 2600 BCE, when Egyptians created bags from sticks and animal skins. They were originally used by men to carry currency, but by 1300 CE the purse had become a unisex object, and by the 1700s its association was largely feminine. In Europe in the early nineteenth century, a handbag was a leather clutch-style envelope. Throughout the centuries, coveted iterations have appeared, from the small beaded purses of the mid-1700s to the reticules and chatelaines of the 1800s (see *Fanny Pack*).[3]

Perhaps the ultimate archetype of the It bag is Hermès's 1930s Kelly bag, rooted in the company's 1892 *haut à courroies* saddlebag. The Kelly was a simple trapezoid shape that closed with two straps and featured studs on the bottom that allowed it to remain upright on a flat surface. This fairly simple accessory became the subject of worldwide fascination when, in 1956, Princess Grace of Monaco (the American actress Grace Kelly) wielded the bag to shield her pregnant stomach, endowing it with her singular mix of Hollywood glamour and royal gravitas.

Like its predecessor—and It bags generally—the Birkin bag plays on consumers' desires and ambitions. Costing anywhere from $8,500 to nearly $300,000 (depending on materials), it is coveted for its price tag and perceived exclusivity. It takes eighteen to twenty hours to make a single Birkin bag under the guidance of one craftsperson, who begins by selecting the leather and ends by performing a series of quality-control tests. Despite its cost, the bag is often used as a utilitarian carryall. (Some owners even deface their bags with personalized scrawling or commissioned graffiti.) For shoppers on the opposite end of the financial spectrum, cheaply made knockoffs and reinterpretations abound.

In 2016 the American designer Mary Ping explored the phenomenon of the It bag by creating a series of purses that divorce craftsmanship from luxury branding. Collaborating with Italian leather studio Montanari, Ping conceived the production of the bags as a choreographed performance, an astute "commentary on how some luxury houses have chosen to use the atelier as a marketing tool."[4] —SK

Right:
1— Jane Birkin with her eponymous bag, 1996. Photograph by Mike Daines
2— Prince Rainier III of Monaco with Grace Kelly, Philadelphia, 1956. Photograph by Howard Sochurek
3— Metamorphosis, by Slow and Steady Wins the Race, the label founded by designer Mary Ping, 2016. Photograph by Josefine Forsberg

BODY MEETS DRESS—DRESS MEETS BODY

Changes of fashion throughout history can all be stripped down to one fundamental pursuit—the search for new relationships between the naked body and a textile (or multimedia) shell through a manipulation of the space between them. What we call a silhouette is a negotiated visual and material form unifying body and dress. It carves out the micro-universe in which we live and move, and it draws the body across multiple thresholds in space and time. Through the silhouette, we interact with the world and become part of it.

Body Meets Dress—Dress Meets Body, the spring 1997 ready-to-wear collection by the Japanese fashion house Comme des Garçons, foregrounds this relationship between body and clothing. The collection, designed by Rei Kawakubo, features gowns inflated into shocking silhouettes, with pads protruding beneath stretchy nylon fabrics. Ambiguous shapes swell in unlikely zones: in some looks, the overgrown bumps threaten to burst the dresses open; in others, pads are visible through sheer textiles, creating a disturbing impression of anatomy. Press reports have ridiculed the designs as "Quasimodo-style" and likened the protrusions to "cancerous cells" or a "flotation device," while scholars have celebrated the garments as transgressive, seeing in them a feminist subversion of beauty norms or a conceptual remapping of disabled or pregnant bodies.[1]

Kawakubo, who admits none of these interpretations, was not the first fashion designer to explore irregular bulges in women's dress. In her autumn/winter 1986 collection Lumps and Bumps, the English avant-garde designer Georgina Godley experimented with a similar look, slipping a rayon jersey dress over an undergarment sprouting pads across the buttocks. Godley's avowedly feminist rejection of padded feminine forms in the Western tradition was buttressed by her essentialist vision of natural fertility in "primitive cultures."[2] In this, she shared a simplification and bias with the modernist art historian Bernard Rudofsky, who, writing in the 1940s, criticized historical silhouettes that involved bodily modification (such as corsets, bustles, and various forms of adornment) as irrational and unhealthy deviations from the "natural body" as defined by classical antiquity.[3]

With Body Meets Dress, Kawakubo presented neither an essentialized femininity nor a particular vision of a natural body. The designer simply contemplated the silhouette itself through powerful visual forms, leaving its meaning an open-ended question. "I want to rethink the body, so the body and the dress become one. The idea is, no references," she said.[4] For this collection, she "started to design the body," not deforming a norm or privileging a marginalized physical state, but creating a new body, a body of the present and the future.[5] The pads, in molten, ambiguous forms—unlike any others used in fashion history to define curves or lines—express an uncertain state of becoming; the body is open and metamorphic, far from self-contained and complete. The collection presents an image of the body expanding into the surrounding space and being reconfigured by it, or what fashion scholar Caroline Evans has described as "a series of poetic speculations on the theme of embodiment in the modern age."[6] A contour of the body is a silhouette of selfhood—contingent and in flux in the digital age—that has congealed in an instant in an unpredictable form.

These silhouettes are deliberately grotesque. Grotesque like the carved monsters Saint Bernard de Clairvaux observed in medieval cloisters, with their "strange kind of shapeless shapeliness, of shapely shapelessness."[7] Grotesque, also, like the supernatural bodies abundant in East Asian spectral tales—fantastical and frightening, but also deeply vulnerable. The grotesque has long signaled danger and a threat to the established order, and in the modern era, in particular, it functions "as the leading edge of cultural change," as art historian Frances S. Connelly has pointed out.[8]

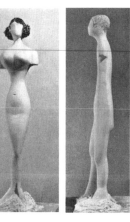

Twenty years after Body Meets Dress, Kawakubo went even further, describing her fall 2017 ready-to-wear collection as "the future of silhouette."[9] The dilated, bulbous masses that encase the body in these designs take on suffocating forms and an unsettling materiality; it would be futile to try to discern a coat or a dress, breasts or hips. The silhouette unfolds like a gigantic, entangled wasteland blooming into chaos: we are no longer certain whether it engulfs the body or is generated by it. —MMR

Left:
1— Plaster figures showing women's bodies as they would have appeared had they fit into Western clothing during four points in fashion history (1875, 1904, 1913, and the 1920s), designed by Bernard Rudofsky and sculpted by Costantino Nivola, as presented in the exhibition *Are Clothes Modern?* at The Museum of Modern Art, New York, 1944–45
2, 3, 4— Models on the runway for the Comme des Garçons spring 1997 Body Meets Dress—Dress Meets Body ready-to-wear collection. Photographs by Guy Marineau
5— Dancer Michael Foster wearing a Rei Kawakubo creation in *Scenario*, by choreographer Merce Cunningham, Düsseldorf, 2014. Photograph by Gert Weigelt

BRETON SHIRT Every culture cele-brates a few deeply entrenched sartorial stereotypes. For the French, the striped jersey pullover, or *marinière*, is an undispu-table signifier of Gallic chic. The marinière became an official part of the uniform of the French Navy in 1858 and has remained so to this day, with the number of stripes varying over time.[1] Stripes were adopted by European seamen as early as the mid-seventeenth century for their visibility at a distance, and striped tops made for civilian use are often called Breton shirts, a name derived from the Brittany region of France, the base for many sailors and fishermen.[2]

    Two historical currents contrib-uted to the spread of the marinière to civilian dress: the appropriation of the sailor style for children's clothing and the growing popularity of seaside recreation, both trends that flourished during the Belle Époque. In this period, sailor suits were widely worn by young boys and girls of the aristocratic and bourgeois classes across Europe, and the French version featured the striped shirt as the under-layer. A de facto uniform of childhood and adoles-cence, the nautical style implied a carefree, innocent world clearly separated from that of adulthood. The child is "a kind of outcast," historian Michel Pastoureau writes, "and the stripe remains, in the long run, the specific mark of that exclusion."[3] Striped bathing suits and beachwear also prevailed in the coastal towns of the French Riviera and Normandy, which had grown into fashionable seasonal resorts. There the dominant themes of nature and health called for a casual and sporty clothing style, with stripes connoting hygiene, leisure, and joyful agility.[4] In alluding to sailors' garments, stripes also imparted a sense of adventure and liberation, suggesting romanticized escapades on the sea.

Drawing on these sartorial practices, in his 1912 novella *Death in Venice* Thomas Mann clothed his character Tadzio—a beautiful adolescent boy desired by the older male protagonist—in several nautical outfits and striped bathing suits. In the text, Tadzio's clothing shimmers as an exquisite sublimation of his nudity, saturated with his observer's secret homoerotic desire and poignant spiritual struggle. In Luchino Visconti's 1971 cinematic adaptation of Mann's novella, Tadzio also wears a Breton sweater. In this garment, the director idolizes Tadzio's ephebic beauty and juvenile defiance, sensitively aestheticizing the shirt's dual association with angelic unattainability and demonic seduction. Visconti's eroticization of the nautical style points to the link in the broader cultural imagination between maritime masculinity, embodied by the sailors' uniform, and gay identity. This stereotype is explicitly explored in Rainer Werner Fassbinder's 1982 movie *Querelle*, a homosexual fantasy of sailors' life adapted from Jean Genet's 1947 novel *Querelle of Brest*.

The marinière that the sailors sport in *Querelle* directly inspired the French fashion designer Jean Paul Gaultier, who adopted the garment as a staple of his own wardrobe and uses it as a leitmotif in his designs.[5] For Gaultier, the Breton shirt is an all-purpose piece that transgresses couture genres, and he delights in manipulating the materiality of the stripes, animating them into architectonic swirls or deconstructing them into kinetic layers. In some portraits of the designer, he uses trompe l'oeil stripes to play on an appearance/disappearance and assertion/cancellation of the body, a visual game that reflects on the tenuousness of existence and is also a comment on the anonymity of the Breton shirt.[6] Above all, Gaultier celebrates the marinière as a gay camp outfit. As such, it is theatrically immortalized in a 1990 photographic portrait by Pierre et Gilles, in which Gaultier affects a bewitching smile and a coquettish gesture, framed by floating daisies reminiscent of tourist postcards. A miniature Eiffel Tower peeping from the background unabashedly asserts the Frenchness of the garment.

The French predilection for the Breton shirt as a fashion item and a statement of identity evolved over the twentieth century, as a constellation of iconic figures enriched its connotations

and allure. A photograph of the fashion designer Gabrielle "Coco" Chanel wearing the shirt in 1930 endorsed its effortless chic, and it was adopted by the iconoclastic artist Pablo Picasso and the eccentric mime Marcel Marceau, who were attracted, perhaps, by the ambiguous message of exclusion, transgression, and playfulness embedded in the stripes. New Wave film actresses such as Brigitte Bardot, Jean Seberg, and Jeanne Moreau wore the *marinière* in nonconformist roles, lending it a youthful charm and a rebellious aura.
—MMR

Previous pages:
1— **French sailors, n.d. Unknown photographer**
2— **Pascale, Véronique, and Nathalie Bonte, daughters of Bernard Bonte of the clothing manufacturer Saint James, 1976. Photograph by Bernard Bonte**
3— **Gabrielle "Coco" Chanel at her French Riviera home, c. 1928. Unknown photographer**
4— **Stephen Shore, *Andy Warhol, Gerard Malanga*, 1965–67**
5— **Pierre et Gilles, *À nous deux la mode*, a portrait of Jean Paul Gaultier, 1989**

B — 018

BRIEFS   At once the province of fusty old men, muscular models, and deliberately retrograde fashion, briefs—"pants" or "Y-fronts" in British parlance—are poised at the intersection of virility, comedy, and an ambiguous eroticism.

Perhaps the earliest direct precedents of the brief are the loincloth garments worn in ancient civilizations from Greece to the Indian subcontinent and which are still in use today in some parts of Asia.[1] Medieval men wore knee-length *braies*, or breeches, that fastened at the waist under a tunic, with an opening to allow for urination—a precursor to the long underwear that proliferated as the Industrial Revolution peaked in the West in the eighteenth and nineteenth centuries. Originally created as a less restrictive female undergarment, the U.S.-patented union suit (1868) was soon enthusiastically adopted by men. In the early twentieth century, it split in half to become long johns and undershirt (see *White T-Shirt*). In 1918 the French hosiery manufacturer Pierre Valton (who would go on to found Petit Bateau) cut the legs off long johns and added an elasticized waist; boxer shorts were developed in 1925 by Jacob Golomb, founder of the boxing-equipment company Everlast; and the French underwear company Jil created a brief with a side-opening fly in 1929.

Cooper's, a hosiery manufacturer established in 1876 in Kenosha, Wisconsin, debuted its Jockey Brief Model 1001 in the window display at Marshall Field's Chicago department store on January 19, 1935. It was made from a soft, rib-knit cotton blend with a waistband and leg openings of Lastex, an elastic yarn. Foreshadowing other underwear crazes (see *Wonderbra*), even during a heavy snowfall it sold like the proverbial hotcakes—six hundred pairs in the first three hours and twelve thousand in the next week alone. The

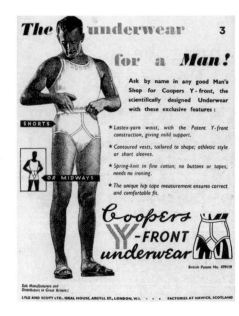

Calvin Klein Underwear

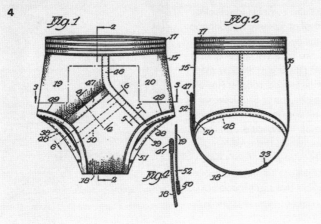

garment's name comes from the fact that it offered support similar to the jockstrap's, a familiar athletic association that Cooper's executive Arthur Kneibler felt customers would appreciate. Kneibler had been inspired to instruct his designers to create the brief when, searching for new product ideas to bolster the company during the Great Depression, he received a holiday postcard from a friend in the South of France showing a man in truncated swimming shorts. By the early 1970s, the term "jockeys" had come to so powerfully define an entire class of underwear in the United States that Cooper's changed its name to Jockey International, Inc.

Cooper's added the Y-front opening to the brief a few months after the initial product was unveiled. This design feature was intended to sync spatially with the wearer's fly opening, allowing him to urinate while almost completely clothed. It also offered support: its front pouch held the wearer's genitals in a more fixed position than boxer shorts could. This approach corresponded to wider discourses in the 1930s on improved hygiene and modern garb pioneered by, among others, the psychologist J. C. Flügel, a leader of the British Men's Dress Reform Party.

Although the material functionality of briefs has not, until very recently, been subject to the same fetishized, erotic, and sensual design imaginaries as women's underwear (in mainstream culture, at least), advertising for the garment—Jockey's included—initially drew on provocative ambiguity. Dress historian Shaun Cole has highlighted the lexicon of early-twentieth-century men's underwear ads—in particular those by the noted, prolific (and purportedly gay) illustrator J. C. Leyendecker. Leyendecker's ads traded on desire for the male body and for the fabrics that would adorn its most intimate reaches, complicating the gaze "without either alienating those who weren't [gay] or incurring censorship, by mobilizing camp irony and inbetweenism."[2] At midcentury such deliberate equivocality had been gradually replaced by imagery of virile sportsmen and conservative husbands—sports stars acting as brand ambassadors or "everyman" models cropped at the neck and thighs—next to product illustrations. These campaigns were meant to appeal to midcentury men but also accord with the heteronormative expectation that it was ultimately women who would be making the purchase. By this time, even Superman wore (bright red) briefs.

In 1982 a giant billboard advertising Calvin Klein briefs appeared in New York's Times Square. Shot by Bruce Weber on the Greek island of Santorini and produced by the In-House Agency, the iconic image of Brazilian Olympic pole vaulter Tom Hintnaus—his taut, tanned body highlighted against a whitewashed wall, and his foregrounded loins encased in magnificent white briefs—immediately made "Calvins" shorthand for sexy. Fabien Baron took over Calvin Klein's art direction in 1992, the year "Marky" Mark Wahlberg began his tenure as model and brand ambassador. As British journalist (and originator of the term *metrosexual*) Mark Simpson has pointed out, it is not "Marky's penis itself which is being sold but the confusion of it with underwear."[3] The exaggerated bulge—the intersection of biology with the perfect camera angle—fueled frenzy around "CKs" as "fetishistic objects of desire."[4] This fervor peaked in 1999, when Christie's auctioned a pair of Calvin Klein briefs originally owned by Andy Warhol for $7,000. —MMF

Previous pages:
1— **"Cellophane Wedding,"**
a publicity event for the
Jockey Brief, Chicago, 1938.
Unknown photographer
2— **Advertisement for**
Calvin Klein underwear,
featuring Tom Hintnaus, 1982.
Photograph by Bruce Weber
3— **Advertisement for**
Cooper's Y-front underwear,
1950
4— **Technical drawing**
of the Y-front Jockey Brief,
by Arthur Kneibler, 1935

BUCKET HAT   The bucket hat's connotations are as varied as its adopters, in spite of its highly specific design and function. Also known as a fisherman's hat and crusher hat, its pre-twentieth-century origins are vague, though they seem to draw from fishermen's protective headgear as well as children's outdoor wear. With its round, flat top and flexible, flared brim, often covered with concentric topstitching for added structure, the hat's design allows for versatility, a quality that is underscored by its typically soft fabric composition. Intended to protect the face and neck from the sun (or rain, depending on the material), its malleable visor can also be inverted, allowing for contact with the elements.

The utilitarian omnipresence of the garment has contributed to its symbolic significance, as in the case with the *kova tembel,* the bucket hat worn by the early settlers of Israel. Manufactured by the ATA textile company (whose acronym stands for "fabrics manufactured in our land") starting in 1934, the hat was a standard component of work wear in the emerging state, which increasingly embraced Zionist and socialist ideologies. It became a symbol of nascent nationhood in the decades preceding and following the founding of the country, in 1948, and was immortalized starting in 1956 by the Hungarian-born Israeli cartoonist Kariel Gardosh, whose character Srulik wore the hat (along with shorts and sandals) as a representation of an average-looking Israeli. It is unclear when the kova tembel, which literally translates as "fool's hat," acquired its derogatory name, but its existence highlights the significance of this item within the context of Israel's fraught political history.

The bucket hat has also had political connotations in areas of South Africa, where it is known as an *ispoti*. It is

especially popular with those performing pantsula, a quick-stepping syncopated dance that emerged in the 1950s and '60s in the townships around Johannesburg. Pantsula manifested in impromptu street performances and competitions, and as it evolved and spread throughout the country, a street culture with a signature clothing style developed. Following the end of apartheid in 1994, pantsula persisted as an expression of cultural roots for black South Africans who had lived under the oppressive regime, and today the ispoti plays a fashionable role in youth culture. Wanda Lephoto, a member of the Johannesburg design collective the Sartists, has asserted, "There are several types of fold[s] regarding ispoti: one to the front, one to the back and several to the sides. . . . These attitudes are usually based on 'gangster' mannerisms and wanting to appear as 'hardcore,' for a lack of a better word."[1]

The bucket hat has also been associated with unique forms of expression in the United States, although none have been so politically charged. The hat has been a staple among outdoor enthusiasts and sportsmen since its emergence at the turn of the twentieth century, and it was particularly popular by midcentury among fishermen, who found its soft crown an ideal location for pinning lures. Beyond its use in sports, however, the bucket hat's cultural relevance in the United States, as in Israel and Africa, has superseded its utilitarian design. Similar to the kova tembel, it has been at times associated with the archetype of the clownish fool, including, for example, Bob Denver's character Gilligan on the 1960s television sitcom *Gilligan's Island*. The bucket hat has also symbolized a certain subversive nonchalance linked with cultural rebels, such as the writer Hunter S. Thompson in the 1960s, and it has played a prominent role in hip-hop, a uniquely American cultural contribution. Sugarhill Gang's Big Bank Hank wore a bucket hat in the video for the group's 1979 song "Rapper's Delight," and the rapper LL Cool J performed on the TV show *American Bandstand* in 1986 rocking a red Kangol Bermuda Casual model. The hat has since come to symbolize the streetwise cool of contemporary artists like Tony Yayo and Rihanna, as well as, specifically for women, a tomboyish insouciance that was first personified in the 1970s by the actress Lauren Hutton; the bucket hat was

cited by *Vogue* in 2010 as one of its "ten sharp menswear pieces" for women.[2] In the hearts of many, the item will also be perennially associated with one particular British pop-cultural champion: the children's literary hero Paddington Bear. —SK

Previous pages:
1— **Moalosi Leeuw, Loyiso Nombanga, and Akido Malabela from the Rozary Productions pantsula dance crew, Dukathole, Johannesburg, 2014. Photograph by Chris Saunders**
2— **Director Akira Kurosawa on the set of the film *Seven Samurai,* 1953. Unknown photographer**
3— **Bob Denver in the TV series *Gilligan's Island,* 1966**

Right:
4— **Angora, Lycra, and nylon knitted bucket hats by designer Zhi Chen of the fashion label i-am-chen, 2017. Photograph by Chen Chen**
5— **Settlers building the first house at Kibbutz Ein Zeitim, in what is now the Galilee region of Israel, 1946. Photograph by Kluger Zoltan**

MONIKA MOGI

1

BURKINI   The burkini is an amalgamation of two very different garments: the burqa—the long, religiously prescribed garment that covers the whole face and body worn by some Muslim women—and a skimpy two-piece swimsuit (see *Bikini*). Aheda Zanetti, a Lebanese-born Australian designer, created the first such ensemble in 2003, which she tradmarked as the Burqini. Zanetti wanted to help her niece participate in school sports and national beach culture while also adhering to the Islamic sartorial tenets interpreted by some as requiring that women cover their head and neck (see *Hijab*).

The two-piece ensemble combines leggings and a tunic top with an affixed, close-fitting head covering, all made of high-performance polyester. One advertisement for the Burqini shows a group of women wearing the suits while running confidently along the beach, their smiles framed against the slogan "Freedom. Flexibility. Confidence." Zanetti has spoken of the joy she felt when she first swam in her creation: "It was my first time swimming in public. . . . It was beautiful."[1]

The garment became better known in 2007 when a young Muslim woman, Mecca Laalaa Hadid, participated in a training program in Australia designed to increase diversity among lifeguards. The project, called On the Same Wave, evolved from the riots that took place a few years before in Cronulla, a beach suburb of Sydney, sparked by tensions between Anglo-Australian and Lebanese-Australian youths. Hadid wore a Zanetti-designed burkini in the lifeguard team's colors; images of her were subsequently disseminated in the media, and Zanetti's company, Ahiida, was inundated with orders.

In August 2016 the burkini was again in the headlines. Following the violent terrorist attack in Nice that July, on Bastille Day, some cities in the South of France imitated an earlier ban on face-covering headgear in France by enacting laws against wearing the modest swimsuit on public beaches. In one widely publicized encounter, police officers approached a woman in a burkini who was peacefully enjoying the seaside, fined her, and forced her to remove the garment, causing both public censure as well as a spike in anti-Muslim rhetoric in the country. As scholar Lila Abu-Lughod has noted, public unveiling on the grounds of selective secularism is not new, from historical colonialism to the neocolonial rhetoric of "saving" women and girls from the veil as a partial justification for the so-called war on terror.[2]

Women's swimwear has long been used to police propriety and behavior in public, from the nineteenth-century British bathing hut—an enclosed wooden cart wheeled into the sea and used as a changing room, allowing complete seclusion and segregation—to the "modesty skirts" required on women athletes' competitive swimsuits well into the 1970s (see *Speedo*). Today women from many cultural and religious backgrounds have embraced the burkini, whether because they are disenchanted by other swimwear choices, concerned with modesty, or taking precautions against exposure to the sun. The burkini underscores the fact that swimwear remains politically charged—and that women's bodies are still a battleground for larger questions of personal choice, societal norms, and morality. —MMF

Previous page:
1— **Surf lifeguard, Australia, 2011. Photograph by Narelle Autio**
2— **Mecca Laalaa Hadid alongside fellow lifesavers, Cronulla beach, Sydney, 2007. Unknown photographer**

CAFTAN   The caftan (or kaftan, from the Ottoman-Turkish *qaftan*), a long-sleeved, ankle-length outer garment in cotton or silk, is characterized by its columnar body, defined sleeves, and loose, flowing profile. The exact provenance of the caftan is not perfectly known. It is sometimes traced back to the floor-length, woolen, front-fastening coats found in the Bronze Age graves of nomadic herding communities in the Taklamakan Desert (now northwestern China) and to the robes found in ancient Persian palace reliefs dating to 600 BCE.[1] The name is sometimes used —incorrectly—as a catchall for everything from the hooded djellaba to the muumuu, a Hawaiian tented dress. It is especially often confused with the more voluminous abaya.

Over the centuries, the caftan has been carried across borders via migration and invasion, among other means. It was part of Byzantine medieval court dress, and by the time of the Ottomans in the thirteenth and fourteenth centuries—when it was used as a diplomatic gift—the caftan was considered an elite garment in the Mediterranean and parts of Asia, sometimes worn with a sash or belt, or layered to invoke physical or material stature.[2] Caftans are noted in sixteenth- and seventeenth-century personal inventories in Central and Eastern Europe, and they influenced what would become a staple silhouette of conservative Jewish dress for men in these regions and beyond. Morocco, in particular, has long embraced the caftan. Makers in the cities of Fès and Tétouan are known for incorporating gold and silver embroidery in the garments, the patterns guided by detailed paper overlays, while styles from other cities assimilate traditions such as French brocade.

Caftans made their way to Western Europe in the nineteenth century, where they were often worn at home as an expression of artistic tendencies that lionized—and appropriated—the trappings of "exotic" others. Although the French designer Christian Dior created caftan-style evening coats in the 1950s, the garment became an overnight craze in evening wear in the late 1960s and early 1970s thanks to an international group of designers, including Thea Porter ("the mother of bohemian fashion"), Oscar de la Renta, Halston, and Yves Saint Laurent, who had a home in Marrakech and was often photographed wearing loose robes.[3] These designers, and others in their wake, married the prevailing bohemian chic with a deliberately nonconformist silhouette that could be worn by women (and men) of all shapes and sizes.

When Porter—who herself had French and English roots, and was born in Jerusalem, raised in Damascus, educated in London, and lived as an adult in Beirut in the 1950s and '60s—opened an interior decor shop in London in 1966, she initially imported caftans to create throw pillows. They quickly became springboards for her own robes in jewel-toned ikat, tie-dye, and boldly patterned silk and chiffon, nodding to the earlier, pioneering work of designer Paul Poiret (see *Harem Pants*). *Vogue* put a spotlight on the style—steered by editor-in-chief Diana Vreeland, who visited Morocco in the early 1960s—with editorials featuring the "gypsy" looks of Porter, Bill Gibb, Ossie Clark, and Laura Ashley, as well as the glamorous ovoid silhouettes of Saint Laurent, Jean Patou, and Halston, who employed luxurious hand-painted silk by Japanese textile artist Reiko Ehrman. These designs largely ignored contemporary struggles with postimperial identity, focusing instead on the fabrics and fantasies of northeast Africa and the Arabian Peninsula, and catering to a class of jet-set "beautiful people" (in Vreeland's parlance) for whom the world was their ever-expanding oyster.[4] Clients such as Elizabeth Taylor, Mick and Bianca Jagger, Talitha Getty, Barbra Streisand, and Princess Margaret, accustomed to shorter hemlines and more rigid silhouettes, swooned.

The style soon edged further into popular culture and everyday fashion. Caftans proved extremely versatile, finding currency as maternity wear, flight attendant uniforms, DIY sewing patterns, and

even the long robes worn by the character Endora on the television series *Bewitched*. Like certain styles of footwear (see *Clog*), the caftan was embraced by members of the hippie generation, who, turned off by consumer culture, sought loose clothing and comfortable shoes that seemed more attuned to a "back-to-the-land" lifestyle. It was also part of the sartorial arsenal of designers and consumers interested in unisex looks (see *Unisex Project*). Today designers have demonstrated fluency with both traditional forms and variants using new fabrics, surface decoration, and silhouettes. Caftans are worn by everyone from "Real Housewives" to royalty (Princess Lalla Salma of Morocco regularly dons one, to public acclaim). Vintage designs by fashion legends have also found second lives, prized by museum curators and fashion disciples alike, affirming Porter's ambition to create garments that live "beyond trend and tat, that thirty years from today will still be beautiful."[5]
—MMF

Previous pages:
1— **Elizabeth Taylor in a caftan by Emilio Pucci, 1967. Photograph by Henry Clarke**
2— **Princess Lalla Salma of Morocco leaving Westminster Abbey after the wedding of Prince William and Kate Middleton, London, 2011. Photograph by Pascal Le Segretain**
3— **Portrait of Selim II (1524–1574), sultan of the Ottoman Empire, Turkey, 1570**
4— **Collection of Elizabeth Taylor's caftans before auction at Christie's New York, 2011**

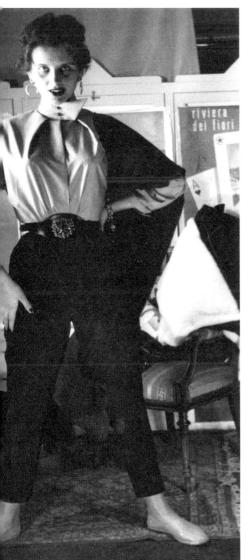

CAPRI PANTS A close-fitting trouser that extends to just above the ankle and is typically composed of sturdy fabric, such as cotton sateen or gabardine, Capri pants entered the fashion lexicon in the 1950s, though signs of their development were already evident in the 1940s. Named for the Italian resort island of Capri—due in part to self-promotion by Italian designers who had stores there—the pants were associated with leisure wear. In 1949 *Vogue* described an American-designed playsuit and cropped pair of pants that "blew in from Capri," while in its "New York Resort Openings" editorial the same year, *Women's Wear Daily* touted tapered black sailcloth "Capri slacks."[1]

The introduction of Capri pants is often attributed to the Italian designer Emilio Pucci, who sold this style of pants along with printed silk blouses from his shop La Canzone del Mare, in Capri's Marina Piccola. Though Pucci helped promote the new silhouette, he was only one among a group of Italian designers and boutiques that endorsed the style, including Simonetta Visconti of Rome, whose "narrow satin pants" were featured in a 1951 *Vogue* story on Italian leisure wear.[2] In December 1953 the magazine published a full-page image showing a model sporting a Pucci-designed ensemble of red corduroy Capris and printed silk blouse ("a costume that's at home in a beach house or a ski lodge"); additional iterations of the pants followed in subsequent pages, including examples designed by American manufacturers, such as Tribute Silks.[3]

The history of Capri pants was also shaped by a lesser-known contributor, the Bavaria-based designer Sonja de Lennart. Having fled the persecution of her native Prussia at the hands of the Soviet Union in early 1945, de Lennart ended up in Nazi Germany. She began designing clothes in order to support her family, constructing them from a hodge-podge of materials, including curtains, bedspreads, blankets, and parachute silk. The island of Capri was a symbol of freedom, peace, and happiness to the politically oppressed designer, and she borrowed its name for her first collection, which consisted of jackets, skirts, blouses, and body-hugging ankle pants with *schlitzchen* (little slits) on the outer hems. Publicity photos from 1945 show de Lennart's slim black cotton pants on the German model Karen Miller; this image predates even the earliest references to Capri pants in the fashion press. De Lennart's influence on the style highlights the limitations attached to attributing fashion innovation to a single source, and it also points to the way fashion history has privileged certain geographical locations, leading to the contributions of a variety of pioneers being overlooked.

Regardless of their origin, Capri pants have universally symbolized freedom and ease. Though they were primarily relegated to leisure wear and children's wear in the 1950s—a 1957 advertisement for Shire-Tex slacks by Davenshire, for example, shows a woman wearing the garment while riding a bicycle[4]—by the 1960s they had come to represent a more liberated woman, who chose to wear pants in opposition to proscribed social protocol. Audrey Hepburn ignited the garment's association with the rebellious single girl in her role as Jo Stockton in the 1957 film *Funny Face*, while Marilyn Monroe helped endow the pants with an aura of nonchalant sex appeal. "I found a wonderful photo of her taken during the time the film is set, cycling in the English countryside," recalled Jill Taylor, costume designer for the 2011 film *My Week with Marilyn*, set in 1956. "She is wearing capri pants, flat loafers and a chunky navy cardigan. She had a very natural, understated way of dressing. I think she was rather ahead of her time, in fact."[5] But it was Mary Tyler Moore as stay-at-home mom Laura Petrie on the *Dick Van Dyke Show* in the early 1960s who used Capri pants with the most effect to subvert a cultural norm, upsetting the period's image of a dutiful housewife. "I had Laura wear pants, because I said, 'Women don't wear full-skirted dresses to vacuum in,'" Moore explained in 2004. Although sponsors originally urged the television network to limit Moore's pants-wearing appearances to one scene per episode, she gradually increased their frequency, eventually making them her signature look.[6] Credited as the first woman to wear the garment on an American television sitcom, Moore brought the image of a woman living her everyday life in pants to millions of families throughout the United States.

Capri pants have since continued to embody a synergetic combination of abandon and practicality, and they have served as a catalyst for the acceptance of all forms of trousers within women's wear. In the twenty-first century the garment has come full circle in its ubiquitous spandex athleisure incarnation (see *Yoga Pants*), which, paired with sneakers, has come to symbolize the ultimate combination of style, practicality, and autonomy. —SK

Previous pages:
1— Model in Emilio Pucci pants, *Vogue*, December 1953. Photograph by John Rawlings
2— Model Karen Miller in winter-style Capri pants designed by Sonja de Lennart, 1945. Photograph by Hardy de Lennart
3— Mary Tyler Moore on the *Dick Van Dyke Show*, November 1962

C — 023

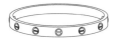

CARTIER LOVE BRACELET   In the popular imagination a diamond is forever, but once bolted onto the wearer's wrist the Cartier Love Bracelet may have a greater sense of permanence. The bracelet, predicated on the idea of the medieval chastity belt, is deliberately designed to be too small to slip on or off the wrist. It is punctuated at regular intervals on its outer surface by miniature flathead screws, two of which may be unscrewed (to open the bracelet) with the accompanying gold screwdriver, which is meant to be worn around the neck of the bestower. Affection secured through gifts of jewelry is both ancient and cross-cultural, as is the ideal of everlasting love and the paternalistic desire to secure the virtue of one's intended partner.

Designed in 1969 for the French company Société Cartier by the Italian émigré jeweler Aldo Cipullo, the Love Bracelet was intended to be unisex, a concept explored in contemporaneous avant-garde clothing by designers such as Rudi Gernreich (see *Unisex Project*). It was Cipullo's first design for Cartier, and it was a strong seller from the outset: more than two thousand of the bracelets were sold in the first few years, for approximately $300 each. His reputation quickly secured, Cipullo went on to design other iconic works, many of which are so popular that they enjoy discounted second lives as copies on the thriving counterfeit circuit.

In the twentieth century, jewelry was subject to style in the same way that garments were, and its design was every bit as important as the value of the materials used in its creation. Fashion designers such as Elsa Schiaparelli and Gabrielle "Coco" Chanel recognized jewelry, like fragrance, as profitable extensions of their brands.[1] While second-wave feminism and the availability of the contraceptive pill suggested free love and female agency,

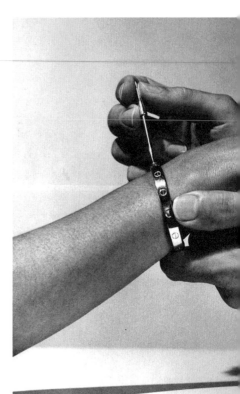

1

2

Cipullo's Cartier bangle jockeyed for space with other jewelry that presented traditional notions of romantic union in a new, sleek, modern shape (see *Diamond Enagement Ring*). Modeled exclusively by heterosexual couples (and the odd singleton) in contemporary advertisements, at its debut the Love Bracelet was indelibly associated with male/female celebrity couples of the 1970s: Robert Evans and Ali MacGraw, Dyan Cannon and Cary Grant, Oscar de la Renta and former *Vogue* editor Françoise de Langlade, and—perhaps most famously—Richard Burton and Elizabeth Taylor, who wore one in the 1972 film *X, Y, and Zee.* As Cipullo cannily recognized, Taylor was "synonymous with important jewelry" and could influence popular buying trends.[2]

Originally gold-plated, the Love Bracelet now comes in solid precious metal versions, some featuring diamonds or other gemstones in place of some of the screwheads. It is now sported by well-known (and well-photographed) male personalities, too, such as musicians Kanye West and Justin Bieber, who flaunt wrists stacked with the jewelry on social media. The bracelet is so pervasive that some emergency service and airport security workers keep a Cartier screwdriver in their kits.

Tokyo-based design duo Verbal and Yoon have created their own take on the Love Bracelet. In their 2017 design, nails and screws are driven through a solid-gold bangle. Their ends, protruding into the middle of the ring, represent different types of relationships: some long, some short, and some sharper and more painful than others. —MMF

Left:
**1— Aldo Cipullo putting a Love Bracelet on a model's wrist. Photograph by Gary Bernstein
2— Nineteenth-century copy of a medieval wrought-iron chastity belt**

CHANEL NO. 5   By the time Gabrielle "Coco" Chanel launched Chanel No. 5, her legendary fragrance, in 1921, she had made her name as a fashion designer offering women a streamlined and practical wardrobe. Like most of the stories surrounding her life, the perfume's inception remains murky. It usually begins with Chanel commissioning chemist and perfumer Ernest Beaux to create "a woman's perfume, with the odor of woman."[1] Women in the prewar years still favored scents that smelled like exotic flowers, and single-note floral aromas prevailed. By contrast, Chanel No. 5 is an abstract perfume that draws on synthetic components to give it a complex, layered profile.

Chanel was not the first couturier to create a perfume. Paul Poiret had already done so in the 1910s, but Chanel was a pioneer in revolutionizing perfume and linking it to the modern spirit. No. 5 was the first perfume to use aldehydes— molecules taken from natural compounds and synthesized in laboratories. The chemicals accentuated the base of No. 5— jasmine extract mixing with benzyl acetate —and added more layers to the fragrance. The result was clean and fresh, but with complex undertones that resonated with the modern woman, personified by Coco Chanel herself.

Equally revolutionary were the name and bottle of No. 5. Most perfumes from this time favored ornate flacons and atmospheric names, such as Poiret's Nuit de Chine and Mea Culpa. Various theories attribute the choice of "No. 5" to the formulation being the fifth sample of Beaux's test versions, or five being Chanel's lucky number, but none has a solid basis. The mysterious number gave an immediate impression of a rational industrial world and an orderly, standardized modern life. As art historian Kenneth Silver has remarked, numbers were "the perfect vehicles for the dematerialized aesthetic of the avant-garde" and "new forms of poetic expression."[2] Chanel herself designed the minimalist flacon—an angular, clear-glass bottle with a plain label, inspired by the pharmaceutical containers carried by gentlemen in their travel bags. The sleek bottle embodied modernist design principles of clarity, simplicity, and functionality. Except for slight modifications in the early years, it has remained unchanged to this day.

For nearly a hundred years, Chanel No. 5 has been an enduring fashion obsession, its mystique and allure perpetuated through images of free-spirited, complex femininity. In 1937 Chanel herself appeared in an advertisement in *Harper's Bazaar,* posing in a black evening gown of her own design in her apartment at the Hotel Ritz. In the 1950s the actress Marilyn Monroe boldly commented that she wore nothing but a few drops of the perfume to bed. Today Chanel campaigns often revisit the enigmatic paradoxes stereotypically ascribed to women: she is innocent and mature, masculine and feminine, and pure and artificial. Chanel No. 5 has become a default perfume for women around the world, as well as an aspirational scent offering an entry into a world of luxury. —MMR

Madame Gabrielle Chanel in her new apartment in the Ritz, Paris

Photo by Kollar, courtesy Ha

Madame Gabrielle Chanel is above all an artist in living. Her dresses, her perfumes, are created with a faultless instinct for drama. Her Perfume No. 5 is like the soft music that underlies the playing of a love scene. It kindles the imagination; indelibly fixes the scene in the memories of the players.

LES PARFUMS

CHANEL

GLAMOUR de CHANEL   GARDENIA de CHANEL   CUIR de RUSSIE (Russia Leather)

No.5
CHANEL

1

Right:
1— Gabrielle "Coco" Chanel in an advertisement for Chanel No. 5, *Harper's Bazaar*, 1937. Photograph by François Kollar

CHEONGSAM This quintessential Chinese women's dress is characterized by a fitted cut, standing collar, asymmetrical closure, and side slits. Although it is called *cheongsam* (meaning "long robe") in Cantonese, a name adopted in English during the dress's heyday in Hong Kong in the 1950s and '60s, it is known as *qipao* (Manchu banner gown) among Mandarin-speaking communities. While the two words are largely interchangeable, each term encapsulates cultural nuances that speak to the garment's history and evolution.

The dress was called qipao when it first emerged in Shanghai in 1921, suggesting an origin in Manchu women's gowns from the Qing dynasty. The qipao in this period featured a straight, angular shape resembling men's long robes. Both Manchu women's gowns and men's robes were cut in one piece, differing from the two-piece ensembles worn by Han Chinese women. For this reason, the qipao was regarded as radical, and its ambiguous name and style, reminiscent of a fallen dynasty and of male dress, lent itself to loaded discourses on social disorder and gender transgression. But the dress was not worn by most women as a self-conscious political statement; rather, its modern silhouette embodied the cosmopolitan Shanghai culture of the 1920s and '30s. In sync with Western fashion, the qipao in the mid-1920s echoed the loose cut and exuberant embellishment of the Jazz Age chemise dress. Around 1930, as part of an international classical revival that idealized a balanced and well-proportioned body, it shifted to a more close-fitting shape, which became the garment's defining feature. Retaining traditional two-dimensional tailoring, with a folded length of fabric along the shoulder line and no darts, the 1930s dress was narrow and flowing, with minimal surface decoration. It gently caressed a woman's curves without regulating or modifying her body, while the side slits permitted movement without disrupting the overall silhouette.

The qipao played a central role in conveying the image of modern Chinese women, from students and professionals to film stars. More demure versions found their way into the wardrobes of prominent political women, exemplified by Soong May-ling, wife of Generalissimo Chiang Kai-shek, the leader of Republican China beginning in 1928. In the early 1940s Madame Chiang wore elegant qipaos while on a speaking tour in the United States to lobby support for China in the Second Sino-Japanese War. Her qipao-clad portraits appeared on the covers of *Time* and *Life* magazines, propagandizing the images of empowered, sophisticated Chinese women and modern China. In the West the dress also became a symbol of stereotyped Chinese femininity. Chinese-American actress Anna May Wong, whose various roles in 1930s Hollywood films embodied stereotypes such as the "lotus blossom" or "dragon lady," often wore qipaos and qipao-inspired gowns, infusing the garment with an aura of sensuality and danger.

After 1949, when the Communist Party governed China, the qipao was dismissed as a bourgeois garment incongruous with proletarian spirit, and it swiftly faded from the wardrobe of women in mainland China. In Hong Kong and Taiwan, however, it continued to flourish as everyday wear throughout the 1950s and '60s, and among Chinese women overseas the garment was celebrated as a symbol of identity. The characteristic midcentury Hong Kong qipao—better known there as cheongsam—featured three-dimensional construction that tightly clung to the body and highlighted feminine contours. At that time, fashionable women wore corsets and hip pads to achieve the desired curves. From the late 1950s to the early '60s, the highly popular play and film adaptions of the 1957 novel *The World of Suzie Wong*, a story about a Hong Kong prostitute, made the wriggle-style cheongsam well known to Western audiences.[1] The character of Suzie Wong, performed by actress Nancy Kwan onscreen, exuded an explicit sexual allure, both reinforcing the cliché of eroticized Oriental women and announcing the liberating force of

such a garment. Since the 1970s, with the increasing dominance of Western-style clothing in daily life in Hong Kong and Taiwan, the cheongsam has withdrawn to the domains of school uniform, costume, and ceremonial attire even while flourishing in the West as special-occasion wear and in mass-market mutations.

Wong Kar-wai's 2000 film *In the Mood for Love* turned a nostalgic eye on the vanishing cheongsam in a poetic tale of restrained love set in 1960s Hong Kong. More than twenty cheongsams worn by actress Maggie Cheung visually and psychologically structure the film's slow-paced storyline. Her meticulously tailored, brightly patterned gowns in the midcentury style create a tangible period texture. A nostalgic longing also characterized the new craze for the qipao in mainland China in the wake of Wong's movie. Seemingly overnight, shops selling bespoke qipaos bloomed in Shanghai's Changle Road, in the heart of the former French quarter. Bringing a romanticized past into the present, these new qipaos conjure the glamour and decadence of the city in the 1930s while reasserting the contemporary relevance of such a style. —MMR

CHINOS Over the last hundred years, chinos have played wildly differing roles in fashion, signaling military uniformity, subversive individualism, buttoned-down conservatism, and irony-tinged nostalgia. Also known as khakis (the Urdu word for "dust-colored"), chinos are trousers produced from a cotton twill fabric, typically tan in hue.[1] They entered British fashion as military attire in the 1840s, when Lieutenant-General Sir Harry Burnett Lumsden, commander of a colonial reconnaissance unit, replaced his men's traditional red-coated British Army uniform with the tan cotton pajama-style dress worn locally in the Punjab region of India, where the unit—the Corps of Guides—was stationed. Colored with a dye made from the local mazari palm, the khaki material deflected sunlight and was unobtrusive, thereby facilitating the unit's intelligence-gathering missions. Khaki was officially adopted by the British military in 1885, and by 1896 it had been approved for wear in all foreign stations.

The United States had been experimenting with khaki for military uniforms prior to its participation in the Spanish-American War, in 1898, but the conflict solidified the color's association with soldiers in the public consciousness, as images of Theodore Roosevelt's "Rough Riders," the 1st U.S. Volunteer Cavalry, captured the men in full khaki garb in Cuba. The war also introduced the term *chino* into the American vernacular. Spanish slang for a Chinese person, the word was used by American soldiers stationed in the Philippines to refer to pants in general; their uniform trousers were made of lightweight cotton twill produced in China. The word became widely associated with the khaki hue when troops returned from the Philippines wearing the light-colored garments. The first chinos produced in America were issued as part of the Class C Army field uniform during World War II. They featured restrained slash pockets and tapered legs, a response to wartime cloth rationing.

By the 1950s chinos had become a signature garment of American counterculture, favored by figures ranging from the beat novelist and poet Jack Kerouac to the actress Katharine Hepburn, an early advocate of pants for women. As fashion historian Richard Martin has written, the trousers "imply order, but their relaxed cotton and non-specified contours allow nonchalance and independence, defying uniformity."[2] The style's adoption among collegiate youth in the 1960s (mainly men, though women wore them for sports) underscored this duality: chinos were neat, projecting the studious gravitas favored by the establishment, but they were also versatile and conducive to individual expression.

A few decades later, the garment's aura of adventurous insouciance was abruptly replaced by one of compliant conformity. In 1992 Levi Strauss & Co. launched a campaign to increase its share of the business-wear market, and its Dockers-branded signature chinos emerged as the de facto uniform of casual white-collar work wear. By that time, the Dockers brand (established 1986) was so closely associated with chinos that "dockers" had become a generic term for the style. Seeking to capitalize on the nascent "business-casual" culture in the company's home city of San Francisco, Levi's sent twenty-five thousand style guides titled *Casual Clothing in the Workplace: Resources* to human resources managers across the United States, featuring sample casual-dress policies and research in support of the implementation of casual business attire ("Making the Case for Casual Businesswear with Senior Management"). "Combine some of your existing business wardrobe with casual attire; for example, try wearing a button-down shirt with khakis and loafers," the company recommended.[3] By the mid-1990s chinos had replaced the suit as the standard garment of the cubicle-dwelling male office drone.

At the turn of the millennium, chinos began to reclaim their place as a garment worn by outside-the-box thinkers and laid-back dissidents, spurred in part

by the American retailer The Gap, whose 1998 series of commercials "Khakis Rock," "Khakis Groove," and "Khakis Swing" sought to reclaim the garment's legacy by associating it with youth, active lifestyles, and alternative music. Chinos have since been featured in numerous ready-to-wear collections (from Helmut Lang's "techy" take on the classic in spring/summer 2000 to Rag & Bone's more archetypal version in spring/summer 2017), and Dockers have received a makeover. Introduced in 2011, Dockers Alpha Khaki chinos, a slim-fitting, low-rise rugged pant, was pronounced "a game changer" by the brand's head of global design, Doug Conklyn, who recalled of its launch, "All of a sudden, khakis became an affirmation [of style]."[4] A few years later, the business-casual aesthetic of the 1990s—including chinos—reappeared intact as part of a backward-looking trend dubbed normcore. In its convoluted evolution, the garment is a metaphor for the system of fashion itself. As *Esquire*'s Joshua David Stein has written, "Today's chino is yesterday's chino, which is tomorrow's chino, too . . . what seems so contemporary and relevant—be it a slim fit, a flat front, our own certainty of how good we look—is just a moment in the pendular swing of time and trend."[5] —SK

Right:
1— **Knightsbridge, London, 2011. Photograph by Matthew Chattle**
2— **Rear view of crowded stands at a demonstration of live ammunition by the 9th Air Force, Eglin Field, Florida, 1948. Photograph by Frank Sherschel**
3— **Cover of *A Guide to Casual Businesswear*, a booklet produced by Levi Strauss & Co., 1995**
4— **Kabelo Kungwane, a member of the South African design collective the Sartists, 2015. Photograph by Keagan Kingsley Carlin**

CLOG   Nearly every culture has developed its own variant of the wooden-soled shoe; the enduring Western version is the clog. For at least two millennia wood has served as a pragmatic material for the making of footwear: it is readily available, durable, and inexpensive, and it can be worked to fit the wearer's foot. Owing to the biodegradability of the material, few examples of wooden shoes made in Europe before 1200 have survived, though a clog-style shoe dating from around 1250 was found in the Netherlands. One of the clog's likely antecedents is the patten, a wooden, platform-soled overshoe affixed to the feet with leather or fabric straps that dates back to the twelfth century in Europe. Pattens were devised as a practical means of elevating the wearer above the filth and dampness of the medieval street and of protecting the valuable leather or fabric shoes only the wealthy could own.[1]

The archetypal clog is the Dutch *klomp,* a wooden, whole-foot slip-on shoe embraced by farmers, laborers, and peasant workers for centuries. *Klompen* protected feet not only from injury but also from the wet climate and were prized for their hard-wearing, practical nature. The wooden footbed absorbed sweat, which prevented slipping and kept feet warm in winter and cool in summer. These shoes could be plain and utilitarian or intricately decorated for formal occasions. Elsewhere in Europe, regional variations on the clog favored a fabric or leather upper affixed to the wooden sole for greater comfort when worn as everyday footwear. Hundreds of years later, clogs have remained a traditional and practical shoe in many European countries, although they are still most closely associated with the cultures of Scandinavia and the Netherlands.

The humble clog forayed into popular fashion in the early 1970s. The

Swedish *träskor* clog, which features a flexible upper stapled or tacked to the wooden sole (usually made from birch or alder), became the most popular type. Usually backless and plain, the uppers could also be perforated or woven. With their thick wooden soles, clogs dovetailed neatly with the vogue for chunky footwear and platform shoes that helped define that decade's look (see *Platform Shoe*). In the United States, the rise of yoga and jogging culture during the 1970s brought greater awareness to the importance of correct posture and gait and to the dangers of foot, back, and leg injuries caused by improper shoes. In 1968, the American footwear-maker Dr. Scholl's had extolled the orthotic benefits of an inflexible wooden footbed in hawking the brand's wooden-soled Exercise Sandal, designed to provide arch and heel support without sacrificing fashionability or "feminine appeal." Along with the Danish-designed Earth Shoe (released in the U.S. market in 1970), wooden clogs provided a fashionable option for ergonomic footwear, since the wooden sole dampened the impact of walking on hard surfaces and provided even support for the entire foot. Brands such as Skandal, Olof Daughters, Sven, Torpatoffeln, Troentorp, and Trolls were adopted by men and women who embraced the traditional Scandinavian clog as a stylish symbol of authenticity and down-to-earthness. In 1969 coverage of the nascent trend, *Time* magazine commented that the footwear style looked like "matching gravy boats. . . . Thumbscrews would seem more comfortable to wear. Still, such is the rage for wooden shoes these days that no one cares";[2] a Sears Roebuck advertisement from 1970 describes the mass retailer's take on the Scandinavian style as "deliberately cloppy, frankly floppy, sorta shoes." By 1977 even the Swedish pop juggernaut ABBA had capitalized on the craze, releasing collector's edition clogs emblazoned with the band's logo and manufactured by Tretorn.

Like the platform shoe, the clog fell out of fashion as the decade progressed. Wooden shoes were perhaps too plebeian and bohemian for the more ostentatious, technology-obsessed 1980s. Today the clog remains both loved and loathed by the fashion world. Shoe designer Christian Louboutin once quipped, "I hate the whole concept of the clog! . . . And I hate the concept

1

3

2

of comfort!"[3] while in 2007 the Dutch fashion house Viktor & Rolf updated its homeland's traditional klomp by adding a sexy heel. Karl Lagerfeld resurrected the träskor-style clog for the Chanel spring collection in 2010.

The clog's practical appeal persists to this day, the shoe finding favor especially among occupations requiring extensive standing or for which traditional lace-up shoes pose a particular hazard. (Clogs are prevalent among nurses and chefs, for example.) Rediscovery of the slip-on ease and comfort of a clog-style shoe contributed to the explosive popularity of foam-rubber Crocs in the early 2000s. Though manufactured from a thoroughly modern, synthetic material, the Croc's klomp-like form is unmistakably indebted to the ancient wooden-soled clog. —LB

Left:
1— **Shearling clog boot by Sven, 2017**
2— **ABBA posing for an advertisement for Lois, a jeans manufacturer, Stockholm, 1975. Photograph by Bengt H. Malmqvist**
3— **Advertisement for Swedish Gypsy Virgin clogs, 1971**

CONVERSE ALL STAR   The Converse All Star, the cap-toed sneaker originally designed as an athletic shoe, is an enduring and ubiquitous icon of modern American footwear; it has not changed since 1949. Its simple canvas upper and rubber sole find their antecedents in the very first sneakers, which were produced beginning in the 1830s following the development of vulcanization, a process that improved the durability and flexibility of the latex rubber that was then being imported from the jungles of Brazil and Central America (see *Adidas Superstar*). These early sports shoes, which were designed for recreational activities such as badminton, croquet, tennis, and going to the beach, met the needs of an upper-class market that had both the time and the income to spare for such leisurely pursuits.

The Converse Rubber Shoe Company was founded in 1908 in Malden, Massachusetts, as a manufacturer of weatherproof rubber footwear. By 1915 it had expanded into the athletic market with shoes for court sports, and two years later it released the All Star, a shoe well-suited to the relatively new sport of basketball (a game that was also invented in Massachusetts, in 1891). This high-top sneaker—with its lightweight construction, flexible and non-marking rubber sole, and form-fitting canvas upper—was ideal for the leaping, running, and pivoting motions of basketball players. It could be laced tight for optimal support but was "loose-lined," with an inner layer of canvas designed to shift with the foot during movement and thus reduce the chafing and blisters that can result from repeated abrasion. The trademark rubber toe guard was devised as a form of protection against injury and a means of prolonging the life of the shoe by shielding the softer canvas from wear.[1]

The All Star quickly became the shoe of choice for basketball players looking for speed and stability on the court, competing with high-top designs by fellow American brands Spalding and Keds. In 1921 Charles Hollis "Chuck" Taylor was hired as a sales representative for Converse. A basketball fanatic and natural coach, he would become an irrepressible ambassador for the brand. Taylor spent his life traversing the country promoting the sport and the All Star shoe among players and athletic directors alike. His endorsement helped Converse sell millions of pairs of All Stars, and in 1932 Taylor's name was added to the shoe's protective ankle patch.[2] The All Star was the official shoe of the 1936 U.S. Olympic basketball team, and during World War II it was adopted by the U.S. Air Force as part of its physical-training uniform.

Through the 1960s "Chuck Taylors" remained popular basketball sneakers, dominating pickup games on schoolyard courts as well as professional matches on NBA hardwood. Wilt Chamberlain was one of the All Star's many devotees, and he was wearing the shoes when he famously became the first player to score one hundred points during a pro game, in 1962. By the 1970s the All Star's ubiquity on the court was challenged by competing models featuring the latest technical advances in materials, shock absorption, and support, including both the Adidas Superstar and the Nike Air Force 1 (see *Air Force 1*).

The world's love affair with the All Star goes beyond basketball, however. In the 1930s, as the price of rubber products fell and the efficiency of manufacturing rose, sneakers like the All Star became more affordable and thus more commonplace, especially outside the realm of sports. With the growth of consumer culture during the postwar economic and population booms, these simple sneakers (and the many designs that imitated them) became the unofficial footwear of children everywhere: they were inexpensive, rough-and-ready, and easily disposable when they inevitably wore out.

The overwhelming appeal of the shoe to a market of casual wearers prompted the release, in 1957, of a low-cut oxford style. In the 1960s and '70s, the All Star, now available in a rainbow of bright colors and patterns, also gained a following among numerous countercultural groups, including punk rockers,

skateboarders, and grunge musicians, and it found a place as well within Chicano cholo/a style. Today its widespread popularity transcends subcultural and style boundaries, and its mass appeal has made it a footwear fixture internationally. Through all of these changes, the Converse All Star has remained the archetypal high-top sneaker—a versatile staple and a universally recognized symbol of twentieth-century casual fashion. —LB

Left:
1— Basketball practice, 1925. Unknown photographer
2— Converse contingent in Boston's Pride Parade wearing shoes from the company's Pride collection, 2016. Photograph by Paul Neumann
3— Advertisement for Converse Chuck Taylor All Star sneakers, 1951
4— The Ramones, New York, 1981. Photograph by Ebet Roberts

COPPOLA Tourists travelling in Sicily often capture a familiar scene with their cameras: elderly local men relaxing outdoors in a group, all wearing a flat cap, or *coppola*. Typically made of tweed or corduroy, the coppola is a shallow cap with a soft back and a structured, curved peak that is often snapped down or sewn to a small stiff brim. The coppola is so deeply linked to Sicily in the popular imagination that in the 1972 movie *The Godfather,* director Francis Ford Coppola dressed the leading character, Michael Corleone, in one during his exile in Sicily. Corleone's Mafia roots reinforce the stereotype associated with the coppola in the twentieth century—that it signified a tie to organized crime. Although it is true that low-level members of the Mafia wore the coppola (often set at an angle to signify their sector identity), this practice simply reflected a broader sartorial convention among working-class Sicilian men. The dubious fame of the coppola led many to abandon the cap, but it has been making a comeback in recent decades among ordinary Sicilians and Italians in general. Cap manufacturers such as La Coppola Storta have striven to restore its reputation by promoting it as an icon of the Sicilian people. The name of the company, literally "crooked coppola," suggests the Mafia association while reclaiming the iconic accessory for civilian wear.

Though deeply associated with Sicily, the coppola is neither Sicilian in origin nor unique to that island. In fact it is traditional headgear in England, where it is simply called a flat cap and dates back at least to the fourteenth century. During the sixteenth century, exotic hats in tall shapes and with feather adornments exemplified the fashionable Italianate style in England and denoted high social status, whereas flat caps, primarily worn by urban tradesmen and merchants, evoked modesty and utility. Representing integrity (it did not obscure the face) and indigenous restraint as opposed to foreign extravagance, the flat cap came to symbolize the "good, old values of English urban civility."[1]

In the nineteenth century the flat cap transcended its working-class roots as it was adopted as gentlemen's country sportswear, used especially for hunting. With the golf boom in the late nineteenth century, it also became part of the gear of elite golfers: a 1936 photograph shows King Edward VIII on a golf course wearing a matching tweed flat cap and coat. An accessory meant to project a certain *soigné* casualness, the flat cap is an essential part of classic English country style.

When English and Irish immigrants came to the United States in the late nineteenth century, they brought the flat cap with them. In the ensuing decades, it grew widely popular, adopted by working-class men, schoolboys, and college students alike, as its nicknames suggest: newsboy cap, cabbie cap, and ivy cap (for students of Ivy League universities). Fashionable young men in the 1920s paired the flat cap with baggy knee-length trousers called knickerbockers. With the emerging popularity of the baseball cap in the 1940s, the flat cap was quickly replaced as a favorite accessory of schoolboys and college students, but its iconic association with the carefree youth of the Roaring Twenties is deeply anchored in cultural memory. It has gained the name "Gatsby cap" in retrospect.

Until the mid-nineteenth century, the most popular headgear among Sicilian men was a hat similar to the fez, a brimless bonnet worn in the Ottoman Empire and North Africa. Various types of English headgear were introduced in Sicily during the second half of the nineteenth century, brought by English investors and Sicilians who returned from abroad. The full-brimmed tall hat, or bowler hat (*cappello*), was exclusively worn by the wealthy and the noble, while the coppola became a symbol of the people.[2] In Sicily its popularity increased in the early twentieth century, especially among drivers, as the flat cap proved practical as a screen from sun and wind. Though it gradually became associated with the Mafia, it remained a functional accessory of working-class men.[3]

The coppola exudes a charm evocative of life on the street and in the open air. In Jean-Luc Godard's 1960 film *Breathless*, the swaggering, nihilist petty criminal Michel (played by Jean-Paul Belmondo) sports a coppola during his run from the law. His "bad guy" braggadocio is completed with a cigarette and a pair of Ray-Bans (see *Aviator Sunglasses*); he dreams of fleeing to Italy. The coppola is also a staple of contemporary high fashion. The London fashion house Burberry touts it as part of its classic English country style, and the Milan-based designer duo Domenico Dolce (born in Palermo, Sicily) and Stefano Gabbana celebrate its buoyant mischievousness, evoking the sunny streets of southern Italy. —MMR

Right:
1— **Common at the launch of his hat line Soji at La Coppola Storta, New York, 2007. Photograph by Amy Sussman**
2— **Sporting scene by Leslie Saalburg, from *Apparel Arts*, mid-twentieth century**
3— **Miners at Heol-y-Cyw, South Wales, c. 1935. Unknown photographer**
4— **Petralia, Sicily, 1977. Photograph by Ferdinando Scianna**

D — 030

DASHIKI A waist-length tunic with roots in the Yoruba culture of West Africa, the dashiki was introduced to the United States in 1967—and, a few years later, to *Webster's Dictionary*. This entry into the North American lexicon of a garment that originated over five thousand miles away was in great part due to New Breed Ltd., an Afrocentric clothing company founded at the height of the civil rights movement in the United States. New Breed was the vision of young urban professionals Jason and Mabel Benning, shoe designer Howard Davis, and a handful of their friends and acquaintances in New York.[1] Launched with the modest sum of $250, New Breed quickly grew to encompass nineteen storefronts across the country, including the company's headquarters in Harlem, at 147th Street and St. Nicholas Avenue. New Breed's mission was "to uplift the black man by working toward economic independence and developing pride in his heritage," and indeed the company's clothing was part of the sartorial backdrop for the Afros and raised fists of the black power movement in the 1960s and early 1970s.[2] Most prominent among the styles New Breed retailed to enthusiastic customers, including activists and celebrities (Sammy Davis Jr. and Aretha Franklin among them), was the dashiki.

    The brightly colored dashiki tunic was—and still is—a staple of both informal and ceremonial menswear in West African countries such as Ghana and Nigeria, where it is often teamed with a kufi cap. New Breed co-opted the style, though not the exact form, as a means of fostering black American identity through fashion at a crucial moment in the civil rights era (see *Kente Cloth*).[3] Mabel Benning sewed the first dashikis by hand in the Harlem storefront (a former brownstone parlor room decorated with African print textiles and a portrait of Malcolm X) before the company secured a factory space in Bedford-Stuyvesant, a Brooklyn neighborhood that has been predominantly black since the First Great Migration of the 1920s.[4] Adhering to the smocklike, over-the-head style of the traditional dashiki, New Breed designs deviated from the African archetype in terms of their surface detail. Eschewing the traditional garment's embroidered or printed decoration around a keyhole neckline, hem, and sleeves, the American-made dashikis were fashioned from plain, striped, or block-printed fabrics that were restrained in color and design and often featured a diamond-shaped pocket in front. Typically teamed with a turtleneck underneath, the dashiki was a powerful symbol of a black-owned and -operated business from which could be built, in the words of writer Herbert Simmons, "an industrial complex for black people[as well as] cultural identification through practical, comfortable, quality merchandise."[5]

Like its West African forebearer, New Breed's garment was roomy and loose, similar to the caftan that was co-opted by the American fashion mainstream around the same time (see *Caftan*). Both items of clothing became enmeshed in the hippie counterculture that arose concomitantly with the civil rights movement in the 1960s, and they were worn by people of any skin color looking to shake the system. A statement of racial solidarity but also a fashion that enjoyed sustained popularity among a broad spectrum of consumers, the dashiki was made from the 1970s onward by countless purveyors. It was brought home to the U.S. on the backs of returning Peace Corps volunteers and offered to DIY-ers as make-at-home patterns endorsed by designers like Willi Smith.[6]

While many enthusiastically embraced the dashiki, others responded more critically to a symbol that was easy to don without significant commitment to the cause it purported to represent—and that later became, in part, a nostalgia item that served to homogenize the black experience of the 1960s and '70s. Gil Scott-Heron's track "Brother," on his acclaimed 1970 album *Small Talk at 125th and Lenox*, chides those who "deal in too many externals": "Always Afros, handshakes, and dashikis / Never can a man build a working structure for black capitalism." Or, as the Black Panther Bobby Seale remarked in a 1970 prison interview,

5

making a stark juxtaposition between sartorial symbolism and effective action: "Power doesn't grow out of the sleeve of a dashiki . . . power grows out of the barrel of a gun."[7]

Today the dashiki is proudly worn on the African continent, in the U.S., and beyond as a symbol of identification with African heritage (with newly powerful connotations in the wake of the Black Lives Matter movement). Designer Ron Bass's dashikis printed with sports-jersey–style letters and numbers have been worn by the likes of Beyoncé, and New Jersey high school student Kyemah McEntyre "broke the Internet" when she deployed the traditional dashiki pattern—often used in African wax-print cloth—to create her own masterful prom dress (see *Dutch Wax*). The dashiki continues to be co-opted as a signifier of faddish bohemian-lite, most recently in a 2015 editorial by *Elle* Canada, which proclaimed the garment "the new caftan," prompting protests on Twitter under the hashtag "mycultureisnotcouture." —MMF

Left:
1— New Breed co-founder Howard Davis, c. 1968. Unknown photographer
2— A dashiki shop, Balogun market, Lagos, Nigeria, 2016. Photograph by Michelle Millar Fisher
3— Prince performing at the Coachella music festival, Indio, California, 2008. Photograph by Kevin Winter
4— Modeling clothing at New Breed fashion boutique, Harlem, New York, 1968. Unknown photographer
5— Designer Kyemah McEntyre adjusts her dashiki-inspired prom dresses. Photograph by Jalese Ayana

DIAMOND ENGAGEMENT RING

In *Amores,* a book of poetry written in the first century BCE, Ovid evoked the ring as a sign of devotion between lovers; Macrobius's *Saturnalia* from the fifth century mentions it as a marriage object. This latter text also states that the ring should go on the fourth finger of the left hand, because from there a vein flows directly to the heart. By the Renaissance period, the tradition of ring giving had been firmly established among European Christians. For royals and aristocrats, the rings were adorned with gems, with diamonds being the most precious.[1] A diamond ring was depicted in a commemorative Roman wedding album in 1475: Hymen, the Greek god of marriage, wears a tunic patterned with diamond rings and stands next to an altar crowned by a gigantic diamond ring joining two torches together. The accompanying text declares, "Two wills, two hearts, two passions are bonded in marriage by a diamond."

Until the late nineteenth century, diamonds were found only in certain areas of India and Brazil. Production was extremely limited, and consequently the gem was reserved for sovereigns and other elites. With little intrinsic value, diamonds were only as precious as they were scarce. The discovery in 1871 of large diamond deposits near the Orange River in South Africa threatened to dilute the gem's market price, and monopolizing the supply became the sole means of guaranteeing profits. In 1888 British businessmen operating in South Africa founded De Beers Consolidated Mines for the purpose of controlling the worldwide diamond trade.

The myth of the diamond ring as the indispensible token of engagement is a modern invention. In 1938, with Europe on the verge of war, De Beers shifted its focus to the American market. The company's advertising agency, N. W. Ayer, devised a marketing strategy designed to persuade the public that the size and quality of a diamond gift was commensurate with the size and quality of one's love. This campaign, first introduced in the 1940s, has flourished over the decades. As the diamond ring came to mark the culmination of romantic courtship, sales increased dramatically. Influencing mass psychology continued to be a successful strategy. In 1948 De Beers launched the slogan "A Diamond Is Forever," imbuing the stone with a sense of timeless sentimentality in an effort to ensure that betrothal rings would be retained as family heirlooms and thus kept out of the resale market.

In the mid-1960s De Beers furthered its international expansion. In Japan, where ring giving was not part of the betrothal tradition, the diamond engagement ring was introduced as an embodiment of modern Western values, and by 1981 Japan had become the second-largest market for diamond engagement rings, just behind the United States.[2] A similar transformation has been taking place in China. Beginning in the late 1990s, the practice of giving engagement rings—also new to that country—has swiftly spread among young urban couples, for whom the rings convey both romance and financial status. In less than a century, strategic marketing has created a widespread belief in the symbolism of the diamond, successfully transforming international customs of love and betrothal.
—MMR

Right:
1— Designers Tobias Wong and Philipp Mohr's Killer Ring, which features a diamond solitaire set upside down, 2004
2— Diamond rings pictured in an album commemorating the wedding of Costanzo Sforza of Pesaro and Camilla d'Aragona, Rome, 1475
3— Image captioned, "Preparing for her anniversary, a good wife restores the sparkle of her engagement ring," from *The Book of Diamonds: Their History and Romance from Ancient India to Modern Times* (1965), by Joan Younger Dickinson

DIAMOND STUD The diamond stud earring has become a pervasive status symbol, attainable across multiple tiers of socioeconomic aspiration. Its adaptability to a range of cuts and sizes has made it the accessory of choice for everyone from royalty to hip-hop artists. A solitaire whose setting is attached to a post that passes through a pierced ear, the diamond stud is part of a lineage of earrings stretching back to Egyptian antiquity.

Although diamonds had long been used in European earrings, by the seventeenth century they featured more regularly due to improved methods of gem cutting and the declining cost of the stones. (Vast deposits were discovered in Brazil in the early eighteenth century.) The opening of South African diamond fields in the late 1860s further facilitated the decline in prices and the rise in popularity of diamond solitaires. By the century's end, diamond studs (also called screws) had emerged.[1]

Popularized at the turn of the twentieth century by international style setters like Queen Alexandra of England, diamond studs were worn with both evening and daytime attire, even by young girls. Though diamonds had been used in numerous forms of elaborate evening jewelry during the last decades of the nineteenth century as a means of displaying wealth, their incorporation into everyday life demonstrated a new, blasé attitude toward affluence.[2]

The diamond stud's popularity in the 1990s among a new demographic—male rappers—amplified this phenomenon. "[Just as] New York's industrialists and their wives looked across the ocean to European royalty for their inspiration about how to convincingly portray their wealth," asserts diamond historian Rachelle Bergstein, "hip-hop artists did too, eager to show off their success. Between the Gilded Age railroad baron and the late-century rapper, there's an unexpected through line; the nagging insecurity that often comes with new money."[3] Indeed, the same diamond studs that were popularized as a symbol of gentility among young women by Queen Elizabeth II in the 1950s now bedazzled the lobes of Sean Combs (aka Puff Daddy) and Jay-Z. Though earrings had been a fashionable accessory for heterosexual men by the 1970s, after an almost three-hundred-year absence, hip-hop artists' (and male professional athletes') penchant for the diamond stud reaffirmed the accessory's importance in the conspicuous display of newly acquired wealth.

Inspired by a range of influences, from black musicians of the 1970s like Isaac Hayes and Barry White, who displayed their success via extravagant jewelry, to the inner-city pimps and drug dealers who wore diamonds to convey supremacy, hip-hop culture embraced the gemstone so pronouncedly that by the late 1990s the term *bling*—popularized by rapper B.G. (Baby Gangsta) in his 1999 single "Bling Bling"—quickly evolved from a playful onomatopoeic representation of the sound of light glancing off a diamond to become the very rubric for the fruits of unabashed conspicuous consumption. In the 1990s jewelers who catered to the tastes of hip-hop artists emerged, including New York's Jacob Arabo ("Jacob the Jeweler"), whose princess-cut stud became wildly popular. Though diamonds had for centuries been used as markers of wealth, their incorporation into the language of men's hip-hop fashion solidified their role as a declaration of arrival, one bling at a time. —SK

Left:
1— Footballer Diego Maradona watching the Primera Division Championship soccer match, Buenos Aires, 2013. Photograph by Marcos Brindicci
2— Queen Mary of England, c. 1911. Unknown photographer
3— Sean Combs at the *Vanity Fair* **Academy Awards party, Los Angeles, 2002. Photograph by Stewart Cook**

D — 033

DOOR-KNOCKER EARRINGS

The door-knocker earring, typically a hoop of gold or silver (sometimes square, triangular, or heart-shaped) is distinguished by its ample size and a weighty quality that recalls the piece of domestic hardware for which it is named. The most recognized door-knocker earring is the gold bamboo hoop, a style that became popular in the early 1990s, culminating with Cartier's double bamboo hoops. The bamboo-style door-knocker was promoted in the late 1980s by the hip-hop artists Salt-N-Pepa, Roxanne Shanté, and MC Lyte, and by 1990 it was such a staple that the rapper LL Cool J incorporated it into an idealization of a confident, streetwise love interest: "I want a girl with extensions in her hair / bamboo earrings, at least two pair."[1] Door-knocker earrings played an important role for Latina women in the United States in this period as well. As Ivette Feliciano, a journalist of Puerto Rican descent, describes, they were "often gifts from family members wanting to mark life's important stages—birthdays, graduations, weddings, funerals. Our families couldn't afford to pass on homes or trust funds or inheritances, but they had these bright, dynamic, and noteworthy gold or silver objects."[2]

The earrings were also key accessories in West Coast chola subculture, beginning in the 1980s and 1990s. Cholas—typically "working-class, young Mexican American female[s] from the barrios of the southwest"[3]—cultivated a look that paralleled that of their male counterparts (many of whom have been associated with California's gang culture) but also asserted an uncompromising femininity: workwear separates, such as Dickies pants, and plaid flannel shirts were juxtaposed with extravagant makeup and jewelry, including heavily lined lips and prominent door-knocker earrings. Cholas are descended culturally

2

from *pachucas*, young Mexican American women who, in the 1930s and 1940s, rejected the patriotism associated with World War II in protest of the mass deportation of Mexican Americans from the United States in that era. They wore tight sweaters and sometimes trousers (like their zoot-suited male counterparts) and often styled their hair in high, teased pompadours; like cholas, they used fashion as a form of resistance. Indeed, hoop earrings have a subversive power in many contexts, including their role as an integral component of Afrocentric dress. "In African-inspired clothing and large hoop earrings and sporting Afros and cornrow braids," scholar Tanisha C. Ford has observed, "Americans and Britons of African descent envisioned soul style as a symbolic baptism in freedom's waters through which they could be reborn, liberated from cultural and social bondage of their slave and colonial past."[4]

In the last several decades, the door-knocker earring has made its way into mainstream fashion. As a style with deep significance for women of color, it has been the centerpiece of a hotly contested debate around cultural appropriation. In March 2017 three Latina students at California's Pitzer College painted the message "White Girl, Take OFF your hoops" on the campus's free speech wall. "Within higher education, women of color are robbed of their 'aesthetic' through stigmatizing our historical Pachuca presence as 'ghetto,'" they explained. "If we don't conform, it becomes difficult to access campus resources, find job opportunities and create professional networks. . . . White upper-class elite women are able to appropriate fashion created by marginalized groups with no consequences to their well-being, social acceptance, and academic success."[5] These sentiments are magnified when appropriation leads to profit. In 2001 Patricia Field, costume designer for the American television series *Sex and the City*, outfitted the show's trendsetting character Carrie Bradshaw (a white Manhattanite) with a pair of name-plate "Carrie" door-knocker earrings and a matching necklace, igniting a fad among the show's predominantly white, affluent viewers. Transposing the door-knocker's cultural value into fashion novelty, Field cited "the kids in the neighborhood" of her New York shop as her inspiration.[6]

While Givenchy designer Riccardo Tisci came under scrutiny after presenting his fall 2015 Chola Victorian collection, which featured interpretations of door-knocker earrings, Marc Jacobs, who incorporated door-knocker hoops into his fall 2017 collection titled Respect, inspired by the early days of hip-hop, was praised in the fashion press. Jacobs explained his use of the door-knocker as "an acknowledgment and gesture of my respect for the polish and consideration applied to fashion from a generation that will forever be the foundation of youth culture street style."[7]

The line between inspiration and appropriation is a fine one; it is crossed when no acknowledgment is made of history and privilege. "When people wear things that are rooted in cultural traditions and acts of resistance by communities of color," Feliciano explains, "they should be thinking about the price that was paid to make those items 'acceptable' to a mainstream audience."[8] But as the American designer Gabriella Khorasanee emphasizes, the value of a style is not dependent on the approval of elites: "Before they were trendy, bamboos would be looked down on by high fashion as being too 'street.' But once they decided it was 'cool' then it became OK. Guess what? They were cool all along; high fashion just didn't get it."[9]
—SK

Left:
1— **Members of the M.I.S.S. crew in clothes from the Mama fall/winter 2008 Mi Vida Loca collection, San Francisco. Photograph by Amanda Lopez**
2— **Salt-N-Pepa at the Diamond Pop Awards, Antwerp, 1988. Photograph by Eugene Adebari**
3— **Sarah Jessica Parker as Carrie Bradshaw in the TV series *Sex and the City*, 2001**

DOWN JACKET   Down—the light and fluffy feathers found beneath the tough, water-repellent quills of geese, ducks, and swans—has been used for centuries as insulation, from the eiderdown-filled silk comforters made by the Vikings in the Middle Ages (from the eider duck) to the animal-skin anoraks lined with down and fur worn by the Inuit of Canada and Greenland to this day. The modern down jacket was born in 1935, when the American outdoor enthusiast and entrepreneur Eddie Bauer was prompted to design an insulating coat after a near-fatal bout of hypothermia during an ice-fishing trip in Washington state. Inspired by the tales of his uncle, a Cossack officer during the 1904–05 Russo-Japanese War who credited his winter survival to the Russian military's down-insulated coat liners, Bauer designed a goose-down jacket quilted in a diamond pattern to keep the fill in place.[1] Lightweight and water resistant, the Skyliner jacket was patented in 1936 and quickly became go-to outerwear for cold-weather sports. Though Bauer's invention was not without precedent (the Australian alpinist George Ingle Finch had created down-padded jackets for a 1922 Mount Everest expedition, for example), his application of quilting to sportswear was a breakthrough.

Meanwhile, visionary Anglo-American couturier Charles James was adapting down fill for high fashion, designing a quilted satin jacket for American socialite Mrs. Oliver Burr Jennings in 1937. Using a technique typical of an eiderdown bedspread, James reduced the filling's thickness around the neckline and armholes to allow for ease of movement, thereby producing a garment with graduated and curving forms reflective of the period's Streamline Moderne style of Art Deco architecture. It was described in *Harper's Bazaar* in 1938 as "the newest, the most deliciously feminine of evening jackets . . . that are quilted and padded like the jackets of Chinese princesses."[2] The synchronicity of Bauer's and James's designs, created for two very different purposes, underscores the unique dual aspect of quilted down-filled garments: the very features that make them useful and practical also endow them with a distinctive and unmistakable look.

As the wealthy jet set took up outdoor sporting activities in the 1950s and 1960s, luxury designers adopted the down jacket, and European fashion houses from Emilio Pucci to Christian Dior developed skiwear that demonstrated the fashionable potential of performance clothing. French sportswear company Moncler introduced its down-filled quilted jacket in 1954 and soon began supplying a series of high-profile sporting events, including the 1968 Grenoble Winter Olympics, where it outfitted the French downhill ski team. In 1980 Moncler added topstitching, lacquered fabric, and bright colors to the company's classic style, and the down jacket took on a rugged, urban aesthetic. It soon became a coveted status item among the fashion forward, mainstream shoppers, and even children.

The variety in the shape, size, and surface design of the down jacket expanded vastly during the last decades of the twentieth century, as the garment became a favored site of experimentation for designers. During a camping trip in 1975, the American designer Norma Kamali wrapped herself in her sleeping bag one evening to make a late-night run to the bathroom. She recalled, "As I was running, I was thinking, 'I need to put sleeves in this thing.'"[3] Thus the legendary Sleeping Bag Coat was born. Photographed in the 1980s and early '90s on cocktail-dress–clad models traipsing chilly streets in stiletto heels, Kamali's reimagined camping gear became a favored avant-garde accessory.

This interplay between form and function came full circle in 2016, when Shayne Oliver of the American fashion house Hood By Air sent a coat down the runway that could open up completely into a two-dimensional structure resembling a sleeping bag. Constructed from individual down-filled panels of a lacquered fabric similar to that used by Moncler, and sectioned off by horizontal zippers, Oliver's coat may be read as a mediation on the luxury commodification of the utilitarian garment.

Seen on the runway, in shows by Junya Watanabe (who based his fall 2009

collection on the garment) and the design houses Balenciaga and Alexander McQueen (fall 2016), and on the backs of hip-hop artists like Drake and Rihanna, the quilted down jacket—or "puffer," as it is now known—represents a unique nexus of style and function. Whether it is worn as specialized sporting gear, for daily practicality, as a fashion statement, or to signal one's elevated purchasing power and luxury lifestyle—or for all these reasons combined—the down jacket is an indispensable cold-weather wardrobe item worldwide. —SK

Left:
1— **Model in satin evening jacket designed by Charles James,** *Harper's Bazaar*, **October 1938. Photograph by George Hoyningen-Huene**
2— **Skier in a Moncler jacket, New Zealand, 2013. Photograph by Max Dayan**
3— **Model on the runway with a Hood By Air coat, 2016. Photograph by Marcus Tondo**
4— **Model in a Norma Kamali Sleeping Bag Coat,** *Elle*, **September 1990. Photograph by Gilles Bensimon**

D — 035

DR. MARTENS Known colloquially as "Doc Martens," "Docs," or "DMs," the Dr. Martens 1460 boot has been associated almost from its inception with youth subcultures, from punk to ska to goth. Easily identifiable as the signature footwear of countless musicians, including Joe Strummer, Eddie Vedder, and Gwen Stefani, the Dr. Martens boot had, by the twenty-first century, gone mainstream.

The inaugural pair of 1460 boots cleared the production line in Northamptonshire, U.K., on April 1, 1960, the product of some thirteen years of prototyping. The boot's innovative design was originally conceived in the mid-1940s by German doctor Klaus Märtens, who envisioned a sole composed of an air-filled material rather than conventional leather.[1] In 1947 Märtens and Dr. Herbert Funck began to hand produce orthopedic shoes whose honeycomb sole provided excellent shock absorption. As Märtens recalled in 1985, "Our timing was perfect, the whole of Europe had just spent five years in [notoriously uncomfortable] Army boots. . . . The shoe was the right answer at the right time."[2] In 1959 the Northamptonshire-based bootmaker R. Griggs Company acquired an exclusive license to produce the air-cushioned sole. The company applied it to a sturdy black work boot that featured a leather upper with a unique bulbous shape, distinctive yellow welt stitching, eight lace rivets, and a two-toned, grooved sole edge. The boot was given a new brand name, AirWair (which appeared on a yellow heel loop), and called the Dr. Martens 1460, after its original creator and date of birth. Costing only two pounds, the 1460 was worn primarily by blue-collar workers, who found its combination of comfort and durability invaluable.[3]

The first and most significant youth subculture to assimilate Dr. Martens into its dress were the skinheads.

Denizens of London's war-ravaged East End and the grim proletarian neighborhoods of industrial cities like Glasgow and Birmingham, the skinheads were descendants of the hard mods of the early 1960s, who emphasized working-class pride by adopting the steel-toed boots and jeans worn by manual laborers. Though the term *skinhead* (derived from the extremely short haircut these youths favored) was not used until the end of the 1960s, the group formed in the early part of the decade, combining the hardscrabble class heritage of the hard mods with the musical influence of soul and Jamaican ska favored by the "rude boy" subculture of Jamaican immigrants.[4] While miners' boots with steel-toe caps had been preferred by these groups, they were soon classified as weapons (used in fights at soccer matches), and the Dr. Martens 1460 proved the ideal replacement. The boot not only offered extreme comfort, but its air-cushioned sole also provided height. "Dr. Martens were the boots to have for any aspiring young skinhead," recalls Jonathan Freedman, owner of the skinhead-preferred shirt brand Brutus. "They . . . made you feel that little bit taller and that little bit tougher—and that's what the movement was all about."[5] The 1460 became so popular among skinheads that Griggs's production skyrocketed from one thousand pairs a week to six thousand by the mid-1960s. Its centrality to the subculture's style even landed its rendering on the seven-inch sleeve of the ska and reggae band Symarip's 1970 single "Skinhead Moonstomp."

While the Dr. Martens 1460 has perennially connoted utility and antifashion, its meaning evolved as it moved through different subcultures. Though punk fashion was a non-uniform, individualized expression that varied among members, the 1460 emerged as a recurrent component due to its accessibility: it was inexpensive and available in far-flung areas of England. Even women began adopting the boot. "I started wearing boys' DMs with dresses in 1975/76," recalled Viv Albertine of the female punk band The Slits. "How I wore them was particularly different because I put them with ballet tutus, my brownie uniform and short flowery vintage dresses."[6]

Punk was responsible for the 1460's gradual infiltration into the United States and its eventual adoption by grunge rockers in the 1990s. Frequently

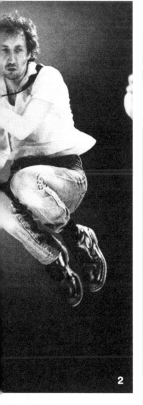

worn with colored laces left untied, tongue flapping loosely around the ankle, and emblazoned with personalized drawings and band names, the 1460 reached its pinnacle of individualized expression toward the end of the twentieth century. Utilitarian in design yet individualized in meaning, the Dr. Martens 1460 has garnered an enduring popularity perhaps best explained by one of the boot's first prominent champions, The Who guitarist Pete Townshend. In a publication celebrating the brand's history, he wrote, "That night on stage was a revelation. . . . The Dr. Martens boots were the real bonus. I had always given my feet a hard time on stage. I kind of stamped around in those days, . . . but my trademark jumping, scissor-kicks, . . . and knee leaps, all featured for the first time as a medley that evening. With my new 'Air Soles' I literally started to fly."[7] —SK

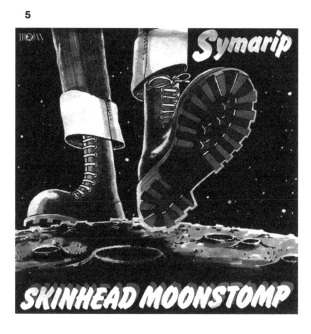

DUTCH WAX Widely associated with West Africa and its diaspora, Dutch wax textiles are used by celebrated designers and at-home seamstresses to create a multitude of casual and ceremonial garments and accessories. The boldly colored and patterned cloth is made through a multistep resin-resist dyeing and block-printing technique that decorates bleached cotton with rich jewel-toned motifs on both sides. Worn by millions, the textiles are also gifted and stored as heirlooms in their unstitched state or used for interior decoration.

Based on the batik technique, which was perfected in Indonesia before the thirteenth century, wax-print textiles were imported from South Asia to Europe beginning in the seventeenth century along trading routes monopolized by the Dutch East India Company.[1] Batik was labor-intensive and thus expensive, and dealers, hoping to sell to lucrative Indonesian and European markets, industrialized the process in factory mills in Britain and on the Continent. Received lukewarmly in their intended markets, from the late nineteenth century the machined textiles were exported with more success to countries in West and Central Africa—including Nigeria and Ghana. There local consumers, retailers, designers, and manufacturers so profoundly shaped its motifs, uses, and history that some insist on calling the textile African wax print rather than Dutch wax.

The Dutch textile company Vlisco has sent wax-print textiles to West Africa since 1876. While the company is comparatively unknown in the Netherlands, its textiles are expensive status symbols in the African market, which it cultivates assiduously.[2] It and other European

manufacturers have tailored production to regional tastes, responding to demands not only for "certain colors, but for some quite specific designs: blackboards, the alphabet, numbers, emblems of chiefly authority and designs based on the visualization of local proverbs."[3] Market traders and storefront retailers give motifs names based on current events, local knowledge, or whimsy, further embedding them in local culture. One recent Vlisco textile decorated with a handbag motif became known as "Le Sac de Michelle Obama," a reference to the Louis Vuitton purse that the former U.S. first lady carried during her 2009 visit to Ghana. An early motif called "A, B, C, D" includes children's lettered building blocks, a design later appropriated to spell the names of political parties or other messages. The "Staff of Kingship" design (in production as early as 1904) features an image of "a wrought-iron sword captured from the Asante and acquired by the British Museum in 1896," scholar John Picton has written, acknowledging the fraught colonial legacy of the wax-print textile. Wearing this design, popular throughout the century since its debut, "gave Gold Coast people an opportunity to register their opposition to the colonial pretense to authority. They could quietly flaunt their regard for local authority."[4]

African textile factories emerged in the mid-twentieth century, producing their own wax-print designs that sampled Indonesian, Dutch, and British examples. Like kente cloth, wax print—ironically, given its colonial origins—became "a symbol of nationalist revival in the wake of political independence in Africa, a sign of the new continent, of pride and difference" in the 1960s, worn by African political figures and adopted by the Black Power movement in the United States and Britain (see *Kente Cloth*).[5] In London the internationally acclaimed artist Yinka Shonibare uses wax-print textiles in his art practice, employing them, he has said, as an "apt metaphor for the entangled relationship between Africa and Europe and how the two continents have invented each other."[6] Fashion designers such as Dries van Noten, Jean Paul Gaultier, and Junya Watanabe have included Dutch wax textiles in their collections.[7]

Today a multitude of companies produce wax-print textiles, including Chinese versions that ape the quality of Vlisco (prompting the Dutch company to introduce security measures, such as an encrypted bar code) and tertiary fakes that offer the consumer ever more choice while further complicating the concept of authenticity in relation to this complex fabric.[8] At the sixth annual Lagos Fashion and Design Week, in fall 2016, Vlisco collaborated with young West African designers—including Elie Kuame and Loza Maléombho, from the Ivory Coast, and the Nigerian Lanre Da Silva Ajayi—who produced capsule collections using the company's textiles. The established Nigerian designer Lisa Folawiyo closed the four-day event with her collection of asymmetrical and appliquéd ensembles, all of which employed Ankara wax-print textiles (made in West Africa through the Dutch wax process) as their base. There is no single "African fashion" on the fifty-four-country continent, and the seesaw of tradition and modernity is an exhausted metaphor in this context. Yet, the passion with which the Dutch wax textile—whether foreign or homegrown—has been taken up by consumers and designers in West and Central Africa makes it a potent symbol of the continent in its own eyes and in those of the world. —MMF

Left:
1— **Model in a dress from the Dries van Noten spring/summer 2010 ready-to-wear collection. Photograph by Nathalie Lagneau**
2— **Wax-print textiles for sale, West Africa, 2009. Photograph by Alexander Sarlay**
3— **Vlisco factory, Helmond, Netherlands, c. 1950. Unknown photographer**
4— **Model in an outfit from the Vlisco Hommage à l'Art campaign, 2013. Photograph by Koen Hauser**

ESPADRILLE How did a grass shoe make it to the modern era? Sandals made from this material have been found in ancient Egyptian, Roman, and Native American archaeological sites, and they are also traditional in several African cultures and in Japan and Korea. The Spanish version of the grass shoe is the espadrille (also known as an *alpargata* or *esparteña*). The defining element of the espadrille is its sole, which is made of jute (originally esparto grass) that has been braided, coiled, and sewn to a linen or canvas upper, resuling in a resilient, breathable, and comfortable shoe. An early example from Granada dates to the sixth century BCE, and others have been documented in the Pyrenees over the centuries. The shoe migrated to the Americas along with Spanish colonizers and missionaries, finding an especially strong footing among late-nineteenth-century Argentine cowboys, or gauchos. In the nineteenth and early twentieth centuries, espadrilles were common in Spain—worn by farmworkers, fishermen, laborers, and priests—but it wasn't until the 1930s that they began to appear as practical leisure wear throughout Europe. During this period, manufacturers began painting the shoe's jute sole with rubber, increasing its resilience.

The adaptation of the espadrille as stylish street wear is credited to the Italian shoe designer Salvatore Ferragamo, who made creative use of hemp, raffia, cork, and textiles in his designs, when trade embargoes against Italy in the 1930s and 1940s led to a scarcity of materials, especially high-quality leather. A Ferragamo sandal from 1937, for example, resembles an espadrille in materials and silhouette, featuring a woven raffia upper and wedge heel wrapped in braided rope.[1] Movies spread espadrilles further into the territory of fashion: Lauren Bacall wore them in 1948's *Key Largo* and Grace Kelly sported a pair in *To Catch a Thief* in 1955.

In the 1970s the espadrille was reinvented again by Yves Saint Laurent, who found a traditional shoemaker willing to wrap braided jute around a wedge sole, elevating the heel. With the addition of color and high ankle ties, wedge espadrilles stepped onto the runway in 1976, igniting a trend. Since then, designers such as John Galliano, Stella McCartney, and Stuart Weitzman have regularly introduced luxury footwear that evokes the traditional, utilitarian espadrille.

In 2006 the American entrepreneur and philanthropist Blake Mycoskie introduced a new espadrille-inspired shoe, marketed under the brand name Toms (short for "tomorrow's shoes"). Mycoskie encountered the alpargata during travel in Argentina: "I saw this incredibly versatile shoe everywhere: in the cities, on the farms, and in the nightclubs," he has said.[2] Working with traditional shoemakers, he modified the conventional rubber outsole and added a leather insole, and released the shoe in a broad range of colors and patterns. The success of these revivals and reinventions, along with this simply constructed, ecofriendly shoe's continuous use as beachwear, help to explain how this ancient form of footwear has endured into the twenty-first century. —JT

Right:
1— **Emmanuelle Alt, editor-in-chief of** *Vogue* **Paris, 2014. Photograph by Silvia Olsen**
2— **Salvador Dalí, Portlligat, Spain, n.d. Photograph by Melitó Casals**
3— **Spanish troops at the outbreak of the Spanish Civil War, 1936. Unknown photographer**
4— **Working jute by hand to create a Las Pacas espadrille, La Rioja, Spain, 2017. Photograph by Ana Sanz**

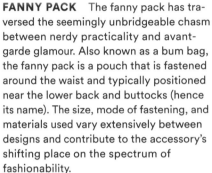

FANNY PACK The fanny pack has traversed the seemingly unbridgeable chasm between nerdy practicality and avant-garde glamour. Also known as a bum bag, the fanny pack is a pouch that is fastened around the waist and typically positioned near the lower back and buttocks (hence its name). The size, mode of fastening, and materials used vary extensively between designs and contribute to the accessory's shifting place on the spectrum of fashionability.

The concept of the fanny pack is ancient, as both women and men have been tying belongings around their waists for centuries. The chatelaine, for example, in use in Europe as early as the sixteenth century, consisted of a group of chains that hung from a hook on a woman's belt or waistband. While in the sixteenth and seventeenth centuries the chains were ankle-length and used for hanging Bibles, keys, and fans, in the eighteenth century the chatelaine's chains hung at the hip and typically bore sewing tools, smelling boxes, and watches. By the nineteenth century, the chatelaine came its closest to resembling the modern-day fanny pack, as it began to feature pouches known as chatelaine bags.[1]

Early iterations of pockets also relied on the waist. The tie pockets worn during the seventeenth, eighteenth, and nineteenth centuries were bound around the midsection over a woman's upper petticoat and underneath her dress. Accessed via a slit in the main garment's side seam, the tie pocket was, like the chatelaine, used to carry sewing materials, keys, and handkerchiefs. Its sturdy cotton or linen fabric was often embellished by fine needlework.

The fanny pack can also be traced to the waist-suspended pouches worn by soldiers, hunters, and sportsmen to hold arms, ammunition, and other small objects.

From the Native American buffalo pouch, made of animal hide and decorated with beadwork, to the Scottish sporran, made of leather or fur and worn as part of traditional Highland dress, the ancestors of the fanny pack came in culturally specific variations. The sabretache, a flat pouch suspended from the belt of cavalry officers, is one of the oldest archetypes; early examples hark back to tenth-century Magyar warriors. Decorated with metal plating and eventually featuring intricate embroidery of regimental crests, these functional pouches anticipated the twentieth-century deployment of fanny packs as logo-bearing promotional tools.

Used as sports equipment during much of the twentieth century (especially by skiers, cyclists, and mountaineers), the fanny pack became a popular fashion item in the 1980s, boosted by the influence the 1970s fitness craze exerted on fashion (see *Leotard* and *Tracksuit*) and by an overall relaxation of standards of formality. Available en masse in inexpensive multicolored nylon versions but also offered in handcrafted leather adaptations, the fanny pack was adopted by tourists, busy suburban parents, businessmen, and chic travelers. When influential designers like Rifat Özbek and Karl Lagerfeld (for Chanel) weighed in with their interpretations in the early 1990s, the fanny pack became an idiosyncratic accessory for the fashion conscious. (Özbek's fanny pack featured prominently in a 1990 *Vogue* editorial.)

The launch of MTV in 1981 spurred rampant cross-pollination between music and fashion, and the fanny pack became an essential accoutrement for the emerging "MTV generation." When the cable TV music channel released its own line of clothing and accessories, its products included baseball caps, T-shirts, and, of course, fanny packs. Available in brightly colored nylon and festooned with the MTV logo in an equally bright contrasting color, the MTV version came to symbolize the item's mass-market appeal.[2]

In the 1990s and 2000s even high-fashion houses like Chanel and Gucci grafted their logos and brand signatures onto the accessory. However, it was designer Vivienne Westwood who produced the quintessential couture interpretation of the fanny pack with her 1996 bum bag for Louis Vuitton. Constructed of leather in a rigid, bulbous shape, so as to reference the Victorian bustle, Westwood's bag accentuated the peculiarity of the fanny pack's

form while calling into question its place in twentieth-century fashion. Her incorporation of the famed Louis Vuitton monogram (in celebration of the motif's hundred-year anniversary) served as the ultimate commentary on the fanny pack's use as a site of promotion.

Although the fanny pack's popularity has waned in the twenty-first century, a comeback can never be ruled out for this quirky and functional item. From octogenarians living in Florida to the runways of Alexander Wang (2016) and Gucci (2017), the fanny pack's reach is wide and its devotees loyal. —SK

Right:
1— Absaroka man with a beaded pouch, c. 1908. Photograph by Edward S. Curtis
2— Model with a Vivienne Westwood Faux Cul bag, 1996. Photograph by Inez Van Lamsweerde and Vinoodh Matadin
3— Portrait of a young girl with a gold chatelaine hanging from a ropework belt, early seventeenth century
4— Hiskey and Kiger families on vacation, Coco Cay, Bahamas, 1990. Unknown photographer

2

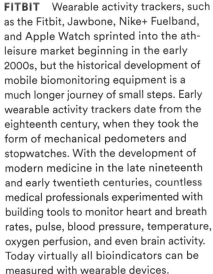

FITBIT Wearable activity trackers, such as the Fitbit, Jawbone, Nike+ Fuelband, and Apple Watch sprinted into the athleisure market beginning in the early 2000s, but the historical development of mobile biomonitoring equipment is a much longer journey of small steps. Early wearable activity trackers date from the eighteenth century, when they took the form of mechanical pedometers and stopwatches. With the development of modern medicine in the late nineteenth and early twentieth centuries, countless medical professionals experimented with building tools to monitor heart and breath rates, pulse, blood pressure, temperature, oxygen perfusion, and even brain activity. Today virtually all bioindicators can be measured with wearable devices.

In the twentieth century, interest in pushing the boundaries of where human bodies can go and in increasing physical fitness—or at least the appearance of it—drove demand for consumer-oriented biomonitoring devices. In the 1940s the development of scuba diving spurred the design of wearable equipment to monitor depth, elapsed time, water pressure, and oxygen consumption. Similarly, space suits have long incorporated biotelemetry, such as the devices famously disconnected by the Apollo 13 astronauts during their ill-fated 1970 mission.[1] Diving watches became dry-land status symbols in the 1960s, early digital watches began to incorporate timers in the 1970s, and wearable heart-rate monitors started to peek out from under running gear in the 1980s.

At the turn of the millennium, widespread interest in fitness ran headlong into digital, networked life. The iPod, launched in 2001, added a soundtrack to spatial odysseys, and the debut of the iPhone in 2007 heralded the era of total connectivity, selfies, and social media. Fitbit founders James Park and Eric

4

Friedman saw an opportunity, launching a dedicated activity-tracking device in 2009. Built around an accelerometer and digital display, the clip-on Fitbit Tracker quantified walking, stair climbing, and sleep, along with the option to upload the results to a website—making physical activity a collective endeavor. Newer versions added features such as an altimeter, stopwatch, and reminders to move. With the introduction of the wrist-worn, wireless Fitbit Flex in 2013, activity tracking became even more visible as a public pursuit.

It's not clear where these steps are leading. Evidence is mixed on activity trackers' effects upon physical or mental health. Anecdotally, some claim that wearing the devices increases activity, one of the few in-depth studies finds no positive effect upon fitness, activity, or weight loss.[2] Moreover, targets such as steps per day have proved largely arbitrary, resulting in effects that are more mental than physical. As one psychologist notes, "The negative effects of measurement are really where you were just doing something for fun. Measurement makes it not fun."[3] —JT

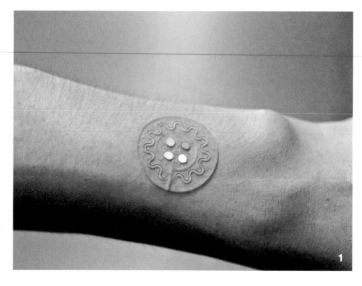

FLEECE In 1979, experimenting with polyester textiles, Malden Mills CEO Aaron Feuerstein managed to produce a novel material: It's light but insulates well. It resists water and stays warm if it gets wet. It's non-allergenic, and it breathes. It's durable, machine washable and dryer safe, and needs no ironing. It has a pleasing elasticity yet keeps its shape, and doesn't fray. It melts instead of burns, and it can be made out of plastic bottles. It's unpatented—and ubiquitous. This material is known today as fleece (or Polartec, as trademarked in 1981). To make it, fine polyethylene terephthalate (PET) strands are crimped and chopped to take on the elasticity of wool, then spun into thread and woven into cloth. The cloth is brushed to raise a plush layer of loops on both sides, and this nap is then sheared for an even finish.

Key to fleece's popularization was its development for use in outerwear, pioneered in collaboration with Yvon Chouinard, CEO of the outfitter Great Pacific Iron Works (later Patagonia), which introduced a precursor Soft Fleece sweater and jacket in 1978. The material was an alternative to "pile," a synthetic similar to fleece but less pliable. It was too thick and stiff for an internal pocket, so the distinctive patch pocket associated with today's fleece outerwear was originally a work-around. In 1985, after further development, Patagonia (using Synchilla as the fabric name) introduced a pullover called the Snap-T. Its functionality and bright color palette took fleece out of the woods and onto the street. In the years since, fleece has been adapted into different weights and finishes, enabling applications from lightweight sheets to industrial carpeting. Fleece textiles interwoven with fiber optics, biosensors, and even USB ports were developed for the military in the early 2000s.

Fleece's environmental impact is much debated. It has a substantial carbon footprint, and its microfibers are entering the food chain. According to the Higg Index, which assesses the impact of producing industrial materials, polyester fabric production is half as impactful as cotton and wool and three times less than silk, but this doesn't account for post-production effects.[1] In particular, PET doesn't biodegrade, and much of it ends up in landfills. Some producers have focused on socially responsible production—including a recycled fleece made from recovered fleece or other PET products, such as soda bottles, that debuted in 2006—but the long-term impact of the material remains a concern.

Despite its environmental disadvantages, fleece remains highly popular. Several generations have now grown up in fleece—starting with indestructible onesies, moving on to team jackets, and graduating to outdoor gear. As a *Vogue* journalist reflected in 2014, "Everybody had one and everybody wore one. They were 'it.' And the thing is, they kind of still *are*."[2] This ubiquity puts fleece at the fuzzy center of normcore, a consciously bourgeois, mainstream style of dress. Fashion designers, too, are riffing on this pervasiveness, often by rendering a standard fleece garment in a luxurious material such as shearling or mohair, exemplified by the Patagonia-style jackets of Joseph Altuzarra, Patrik Ervell, Kim Jones, and Phillip Lim. Other desigers have gone in the opposite direction, as with the tailored suit by Comme des Garçons made up in humble fleece. —JT

Left:
1— Yvon Chouinard free-climbing, Yosemite National Park, California, 1964. Photograph by Tom Frost
2— Cameron Ridgeway, daughter of Rick Ridgeway, Patagonia's vice president of environmental affairs, exploring tide pools, Cannon Beach, Oregon, c. 1987. Photograph by Rick Ridgeway

FLIP-FLOP Like its woodsier cousin (see *Clog*), the flip-flop (also known as a thong, *jandal*, *paduka*, and *hawai chappal*) is virtually universal. Documented globally among ancient and traditional cultures, with surviving examples dating back ten thousand years, the flip-flop is essentially a flat sole held on the foot by a strap or peg gripped between two toes. Functionally, flip-flops protect the bottom of the foot while leaving the top open to the air. They are compact, simple to take on and off, and easily made using age-old techniques and sustainable materials.

Twentieth-century flip-flops are believed to derive from traditional Japanese *zori* (thonged sandals made of fiber or other natural materials) and *geta* (wooden, often elevated, slip-on shoes). Cast-rubber versions were a substantial export between 1905 and 1938, while traditional zori with added rubber and cork soles were popular domestically. It is believed that the first Japanese flip-flops were made in Osaka, using neoprene insulation recycled from airplanes and emergency equipment, inspiring copies produced elsewhere by 1949. Synthetic rubber became a viable substitute for natural rubber during World War II, and neoprene, invented by DuPont in 1931, soon became the spongy standard. By the mid-1950s, these flip-flops were an established export product.[1] When Japanese swimmers wore them at the 1956 Summer Olympics in Melbourne, sports-gear manufacturers began to develop commercial athletic versions.

By the 1960s, cheap synthetic flip-flops were widely available in the West, and in 1962, Robert Fraser, a Scotsman with family ties to the textile business, was inspired by Japanese sandals he observed in Hawaii and his adoptive Brazil to prototype a rubber version. These Havaianas (the trademark is Portuguese for "Hawaiian") soon became ubiquitous in Brazil and began to spread abroad through tourism. In the 1990s, as domestic sales slowed, the Brazilian manufacturer Alpargatas organized a successful campaign to market Havaianas internationally, now as a fashion accessory.[2]

Socially, flip-flops variously represent beach or beat culture, low or high social status, and even ethnic exoticism. When worn by public figures such as the Dalai Lama or Mahatma Gandhi, the symbolic humility of the gesture paradoxically amplifies the wearer's social power (a pair of the Dalai Lama's flip-flops are now enshrined in the collection of Toronto's Bata Shoe Museum; sales of flip-flops bearing Gandhi's image recently provoked heated controversy in India). In American culture, "flip-flopping" signifies ambiguity or equivocation.

Like many ubiquitous clothing forms, the flip-flop is periodically reinvented by fashion designers, including *zori* reinterpretations by Yohji Yamamoto in 2003 and 2004 and traditional shoemaker Gion Naito's Jojo line, spotted on an Issey Miyake runway in 2017. The flip-flop may even evolve into a activity tracker (see *Fitbit*). The Texas-based footwear maker Hari Mari's Nokona flip-flop is embedded with an information-gathering, app-connected chip that supposedly benefits the wearer as well as the marketer. Thus flip-flops, one of the few footwear types named for their sound, continue to be heard around the world. —JT

Right:
1— Meeting between the Dalai Lama and U.S. president George W. Bush at the White House, Washington, D.C., 2001. Photograph by Mai
2— Brass *paduka* sandals, n.d.
3— *Zori,* made in Japan, 1980–87. Collection of the Bata Shoe Museum, Toronto

3

FUR COAT Few garments are as controversial as the fur coat, an object imprinted with messages of power, fortune, sexuality, vanity, and cruelty. Its rise and fall—from the height of prestige and glamour to a symbol of brutality—is embedded with tensions between desire and hatred, pleasure and guilt, as well as polarized notions of femininity and ecology. In early modern Europe fur belonged exclusively to monarchs, nobles, and the Church. Ermine, in particular, denoted royalty, appearing in majestic coronation robes. In the prosperous Qing dynasty in China, the emperor and court officials adopted fur-lined silk robes as winter wear. In Europe, China, and beyond, fur symbolized not only extravagance, but also the exclusive power to mobilize and control global resources. The fur trade was a major impetus for the European colonization of the vast land that is now Canada. Likewise, fur in China in the eighteenth and nineteenth centuries came from Russia, and the fur trade monopolized by the Qing court profoundly impacted the Russian economy and environment. The trade in fur over the centuries demonstrates the interconnectedness of global history and the dynamic processes of cultural exchange and exploitation.

Although fur had long been used for linings, trimmings, and accessories, the full fur coat did not become a fashion item in the West until the late nineteenth century. In the 1920s and '30s the fur coat epitomized the extravagant style of Hollywood actresses. The mink coat became an object of desire for aspiring middle-class women in the 1950s, giving rise to a long-lasting stereotype of the trapped bourgeois housewife.[1] But the fur coat at midcentury also embodied more complex and diverse femininities. For example, Marguerite Duras, the feminist and Marxist writer, wore raccoon and leopard fur coats like a personal uniform in her interviews and at political protests. African American jazz singers such as Billie Holiday and Dinah Washington sported mink coats as flamboyant signs that announced, "I've made it." As recently as 2015, singer Aretha Franklin performed at the Kennedy Center in Washington, D.C., wearing a mink coat, dropping it to the stage floor in a dramatic climax. As David Remnick wrote in the *New Yorker,* "Dropping the fur—it's an old gospel move, a gesture of emotional abandon, of letting loose."[2]

By the late 1960s, when the cult of youth culture and futurism in fashion had rendered the fur coat somewhat outmoded, the label Blackglama, founded by the Great Lakes Mink Association, launched the advertising campaign "What Becomes a Legend Most," promoting black mink as timelessly elegant through glamorous images of actresses, divas, and fashion icons. With the rise of animal-rights movements in the 1970s, however, efforts were made to dramatically shift the meaning of the fur coat from glamour and luxury to cruelty and bad taste. During the 1980s and '90s organizations such as Lynx and PETA (People for the Ethical Treatment of Animals) successfully raised public consciousness of the harsh realities of fur production. From the mid-1980s the campaigns increasingly condemned female fur wearers, demonizing them as brutal, ugly, and immoral.[3] The misogynistic undertone in Lynx's posters was strong enough to provoke feminist protests in Britain.[4] In the most aggressive cases, anti-fur campaigns involved paint spraying and physical assault. While these movements have achieved advancements in ethical standards for animal treatment, they have also been criticized for their negative impact on the economies and cultures of indigenous people whose livelihoods depend on the fur trade. Inuit designers in Canada have continued to feature fur fashion as part of their tradition,[5] and others have argued that fur is a sustainable resource and more environmentally friendly than synthetic fibers created through a petrochemical process.[6]

In the literary and artistic imagination, since the late nineteenth century the fur coat has been firmly associated with sexual fetishism, a stereotype established by psychoanalytical theories. Sigmund Freud famously associated fur with female pubic hair,[7] and Leopold von Sacher-Masoch's 1870 novel *Venus in Furs* immortalizes the image of the fur-clad woman as a dominatrix. In his 1974 photograph *Laura, Avenue George V*, Helmut Newton blatantly visualizes this link between fur and female sexuality: a model strides along the Parisian street baring her lower body beneath a wide-open fox cape. PETA's influential campaign "I'd Rather Go Naked Than Wear Fur," launched in 1989, reinforced the stereotype of sexually charged female nudes and fur, as if women had no choices other than fur or nakedness. —MMR

Children in Winter— with all the fur in Winter

$15,000 Tune: Clad in mink coats valued at a total of $15,000, singers Dinah Washington and Laverne Baker team to belt out a tune in a Chicago bistro. Miss Washington's coat was Christmas present from "admirer," Miss Baker's was gift from comic Slappy White.

"I'd rather go naked than wear fur."
—Christy Turlington

Right:
1— **Canadian postcard showing Inuit children with furs, n.d.**
2— **Portrait of Sigismund Baldinger, by George Pencz, 1545**
3— **Singers Dinah Washington and LaVern Baker in Chicago,** *Jet,* **January 1959. Photograph by James Nave**
4— **Supermodel Christy Turlington in a PETA anti-fur campaign poster, 1993**

OMAR VICTOR DIOP

J
♣

♣
ſ

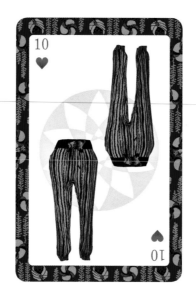

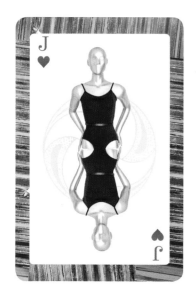

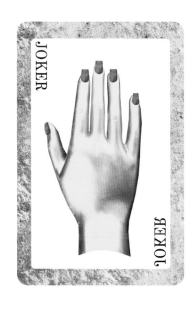

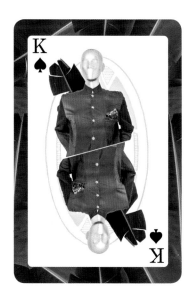

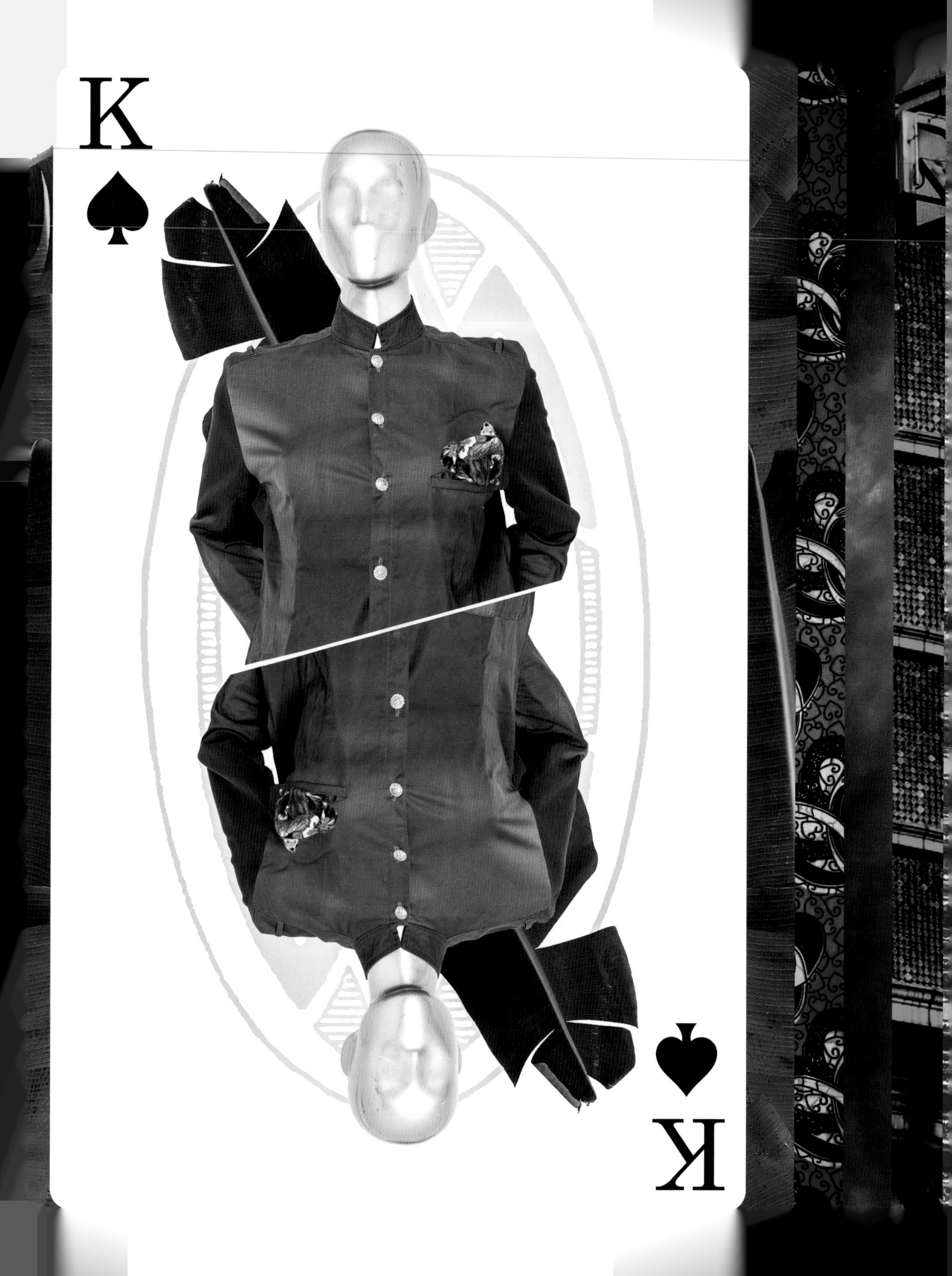
K
K

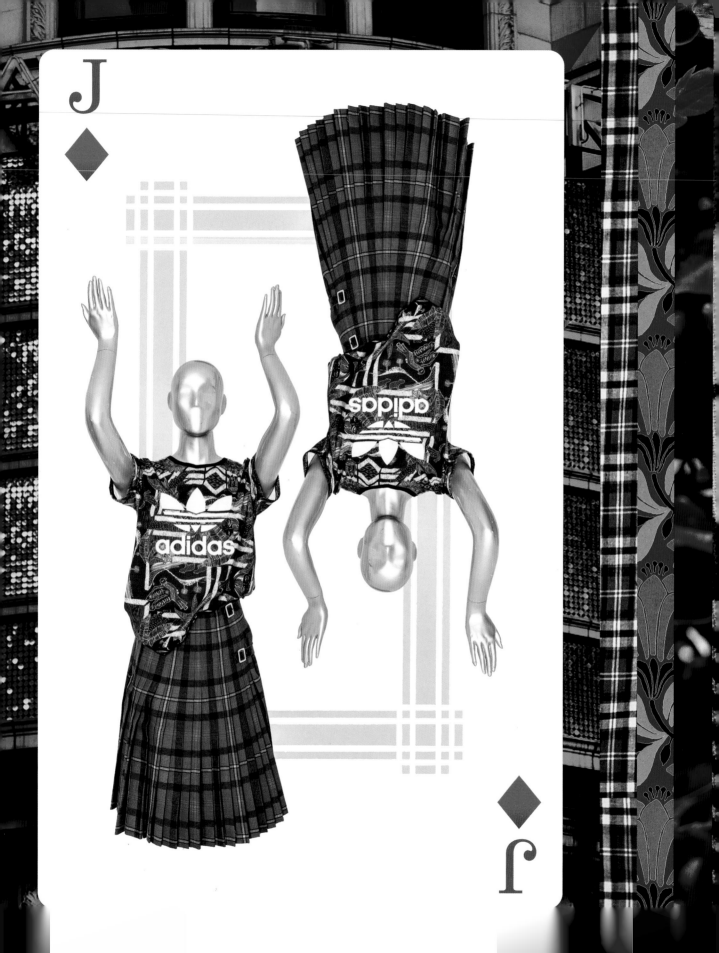

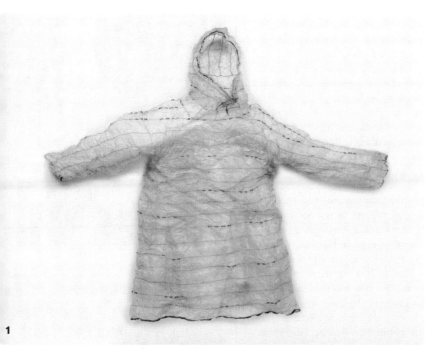

1

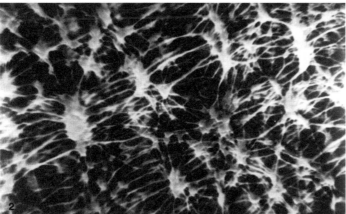

2

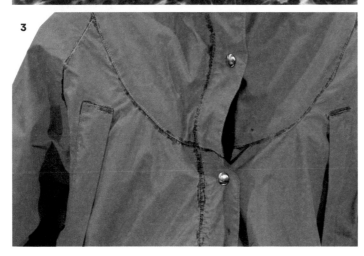

3

GORE-TEX Gore-Tex is not a garment, it is a material. Yet since its 1976 introduction by manufacturing behemoth W. L. Gore & Associates, Gore-Tex fabric has become shorthand for the high-performance outdoor wear favored by those braving the best and the worst that Mother Nature has to offer. All-weather top garments can be traced back to the innovative use of seal and whale intestines by the Inuit in Canada, Greenland, and Alaska, as well as to the grass capes of early Neolithic peoples in South America. Fabrics specially treated to repel moisture appeared in Scotland (waxed cotton) and China (oiled silk), but waterproof outerwear did not become a wardrobe staple until the nineteenth century, with the British development of the rubberized mackintosh raincoat and waterproofed gabardine fabric (by Thomas Burberry). The latter gained wide use for military trench coats during World War I.

It was the development of a lightweight and highly flexible waterproof, windproof, and breathable fabric in the mid-twentieth century, however, that changed the nature of high-performance outdoor gear. On January 1, 1958, Wilbert L. (Bill) Gore, in partnership with his wife, Vieve, founded W. L. Gore & Associates in the basement of their home, with Bill leaving his full-time job as a chemical engineer at the American conglomerate DuPont shortly thereafter.[1] The Gores were convinced of the potential of a polymer developed at DuPont in 1938 called polytetrafluoroethylene (PTFE)—a linear polymer consisting of fluorine and carbon molecules—and first used it to insulate wire and cables, astutely predicting the burgeoning computing field. In 1969 their son Bob Gore, who had joined the company in 1963, found that heating and pulling the material at accelerated speeds produced expanded polytetrafluoroethylene (ePTFE), a microporous polymer that features a high strength-to-weight ratio, is noncombustible, and offers a high thermal resistance, among many other useful characteristics.[2] At 70 percent air to 30 percent polymer, ePTFE presented opportunities for novel applications in the wide variety of fields that can benefit from lightweight, flexible textiles. In 1970 the company applied for the first of what became many patents for Gore-Tex.

Although Gore manufactures a small volume of branded garments using ePTFE, consumers generally encounter Gore-Tex through the two arenas in which the textile is licensed: specialized, technically oriented protective uniforms for the military and for first responders like police officers and firefighters, and commercial gear for outdoor activities such as camping, hiking, skiing, and mountain climbing. Gore-Tex, which looks and feels like silk, is used as a laminate in two- or three-layer composite textiles in garments and as one of up to five layers in shoes, acting as a barrier to extremes of temperature and moisture. As the layer is not visible on the exterior of the final product, color, design, and other aesthetic considerations can be foregrounded. Outfitters like Early Winters and Marmot were among the first to adopt Gore-Tex for tents and, ultimately, the jackets and associated garments that help their customers brave the elements. Early advertisements featured the companies' young founders putting their Gore-Tex products through R & D testing personally, inspiring a cult following and rapid, loyal uptake by a growing base of customers.

Gore tried out a number of marketing slogans—including "Keeps you warm and dry regardless of what falls out of the sky," part of a memorable print ad featuring an illustration of a Magritte-like man in a bowler hat, unperturbed by a sky populated by falling cats and dogs— before settling on the emphatic and enduring promise "Guaranteed to keep you dry" in 1989. Equipped with a "rain room" at its Wilmington, Delaware, headquarters that offers controlled precipitation for garment testing, as well as environmental chambers that can mimic intense heat, cold, wind, and solar exposure, Gore associates work with each manufacturer to ensure

that products incorporating Gore-Tex meet the company's guarantee.[3] In the early years, this led to the creation of Seam Seal to plug the tiny holes made by stitches in assembly. The resulting seams, noticeably pasted over, became an aesthetic embraced as a badge of pride by hardy outdoors enthusiasts. Gore designers continue to work on developing—and improving—a range of strategies to achieve the material's highest performance, including lips over seams and pockets that deflect rain, and seam stitching that bars the elements.

Gore-Tex is but one product of a company that applies over two thousand patented applications for the polymer to the fields of medicine, electronics, cable, filtration, and fiber technologies, to name just a few; if you floss, chances are that you have used a Gore-patented technology to do so. The polymer is also biocompatible and chemically inert, making it possible to employ it as a scaffold for human tissue generation—as part of hernia surgery, for example. Gore-Tex garments and fibers have found their way to the summit of Mount Everest as well as the surface of the moon, and they continue to exemplify everyday design obsessively refined and recalibrated to protect the ordinary consumer during less far-flung excursions, whether it be a blustery office commute, an outdoor patrol, or a weekend hike. —MMF

Previous page:
1— Parka made of the intestines of sea animals, Aleutian Islands, Alaska, 1869 or earlier
2— Electron micrograph showing the membrane structure of Gore-Tex, c. 1976
3— Detail of a Gore-Tex parka, c. 1978, showing the technique for sealing the seams

GRAPHIC T-SHIRT If the white T-shirt is the ultimate sartorial blank canvas, a quintessential product of twentieth-century modernity (see *White T-Shirt*), the graphic T-shirt is its all-knowing, expressive, postmodern sibling. While its mass ascendancy would not come until the 1960s and '70s, early archetypes emerged around the same time as the white tee's fashionable rise. In 1942, for example, *Life* featured a soldier on its cover wearing an "Air Corps Gunnery School" T-shirt, bearing its logo of an anthropomorphized animal firing a gun.[1] And when New York governor Thomas Dewey ran for president in 1948, he is said to have distributed T-shirts with the slogan "Dew-it-with Dewey." By the mid-1950s graphic T-shirts had begun to appear as promotional items for tourist destinations, including Disneyland.[2]

Technological advancements in screenprinting and the development of colorfast inks in the 1960s made the production of graphic T-shirts efficient and inexpensive.[3] This, coupled with a growing current of individualized expression within fashion, led to the graphic T-shirt flourishing in a variety of manifestations: promotional tool, mouthpiece for advocacy, and display of allegiance.

Both timeless and ubiquitous, the original "I Love NY" T-shirt is the ultimate promotional graphic tee. Created by the graphic designer Milton Glaser, and introduced in 1977, the logo (with a red heart standing in for *Love* and the characters grouped in quadrants) was commissioned by the New York State Department of Commerce at a time when New York City—experiencing a billion-dollar budget deficit, rampant crime, surging unemployment, and union strikes—was in dire need of image rehabilitation. With the success of the T-shirt and related marketing, New York tourism boomed, and the graphic became a symbol of hope worldwide.[4]

Designer Katharine Hamnett's bold tees with protest phrases such as "Preserve the Rainforests" and "Worldwide Nuclear Ban Now" exemplify the graphic T-shirt's ability to advocate for a cause. Invited to meet British prime minister Margaret Thatcher after being named Designer of the Year by the British Fashion Council in 1984, Hamnett wore her "58% Don't Want Pershing" shirt to the reception as a sartorial declaration of dissent on behalf of the British public, a response to Thatcher's aim to bring cruise and Pershing missile stations to the United Kingdom. "It was empowering to think you could get away with it," Hamnett said. "[The T-shirt] was all about democracy, and it's still about that."[5]

A third type of graphic tee—the rock T-shirt—is about freedom of choice and the ability to display that choice via allegiance. "You were expressing support for fellow members of a loose-knit community of wandering gypsy minstrels," noted seminal no-wave musician Lydia Lunch.[6] Though iconic graphic rock tees abound, from Nirvana's distorted yellow smiley face to Black Flag's quartet of thick vertical lines, few other band graphics have proven more evocative or enduring than the Rolling Stones' "Tongue and Lips" logo, otherwise known as "Hot Lips." Though asked to design a likeness of Kali, the Hindu goddess of everlasting energy (who boasts an agape mouth with a hanging tongue), the logo's designer, John Pasche, was so taken by Jagger's own luscious lips that his inspiration ultimately derived from the rock star himself.[7] Debuting on the band's 1971 Sticky Fingers LP, Hot Lips has been the Rolling Stones' band logo for almost fifty years, emblazoning countless tees and distilling the band's essence into a single image worn by legions of fans.

As an informal piece of duplicable clothing, the graphic tee has come to signify deep-seated memory, identity, experience, and connection for its wearers, as typified by the T-shirt–collecting ethos surrounding street-wear brands like Supreme (New York) and Palace (U.K.). "When we opened we made three T-shirts," recalled Supreme founder James Jebbia, "one with an image of [Robert] De Niro from Taxi Driver, one with an image from the 1970s of a skater with a cool afro, and one with our box logo. . . . The first day we opened I was really surprised because those three T-shirts were pretty much the only things that sold that day. . . . Tons of people coming in and sensing that it was something new and fresh."[8] Supreme is now famous for the seemingly haphazard selection of imagery and graphics on its wildly popular T-shirts, which have moved beyond expressing mere personal allegiance to manifesting a larger philosophy and lifestyle. "Supreme spreads style," noted renowned journalist Glenn O'Brien, "but it also spreads thought and information. Culture is its business."[9] The same can be said about the typology of the graphic T-shirt itself: personal yet public facing, explicit yet open to ambiguity, it is sagacious even as it traffics in pastiche. Though postmodern in its fluid ephemerality, its timelessness and enduring significance make it one of fashion's modern players. —SK

Previous pages:
1— Folk singer and songwriter Alix Dobkin in a T-shirt made for Labyris Books, New York, 1975. Photograph by Liza Cowan
2— Protestor at a peace march organized by the New York Congress of Racial Equality (CORE), New York, 1961. Photograph by Diana Davies
3— Student Megan Stoyles at an anti–Vietnam War protest in Canberra, Australia, 1966. Photograph by George Silk
4— Participant in the Million Mask March, London, 2014. Photograph by Jordan Mansfield

Right:
5— Patti Smith in a T-shirt featuring Keith Richards, New York, 1974. Photograph by Frank Stefanko
6— British prime minister Margaret Thatcher greets designer Katharine Hamnett at 10 Downing Street, London, 1984. Unknown photographer
7— Tourist in an "I Love New York" T-shirt, New York, 2010. Unknown photographer

6

5

7

G — 045

GUAYABERA The guayabera—
a loose-fitting, lightweight shirt with
pockets, vertical pleats, and embroidery—
has long been worn throughout Latin
America. It is widely associated with Cuba
in particular, and although its origins are
uncertain, it is commonly believed that
the guayabera first appeared in the Cuban
city of Sancti Spíritus in the early eighteenth century, when a wealthy *hacendado*
(landowner) asked his wife to make him
a shirt with multiple pockets out of a
lightweight cotton fabric called *batista*
(batiste).[1] His workers took a liking to the
garment because it seemed practical and
well suited to withstanding the heat, and
they decided to copy the style, calling it
yayabera after the nearby Yayabo River.[2]
By other accounts, the garment was named
for its large pockets, in which workers
could carry multiple *guayabas* (guavas),
a fruit that grows in the region.

By 1948 the guayabera was so
prominent in the streets of the Cuban
capital that a group of women who
belonged to the Lyceum Lawn Tennis
Club of Havana, a prominent upper-class
country club, organized a panel of intellectuals to discuss the shirt's growing
popularity and its pitfalls.[3] Rafael Suárez
Solís, a renowned writer, expressed his
dismay at the "wholesale adoption of the
shirt at all hours of the day and evening
by rich and poor alike."[4] He advocated for
a "dividing line" of 6 p.m., before which it
was appropriate to appear in a guayabera,
but after which it was uncivilized and
in bad taste.[5] The speakers were mostly
concerned about "guayaberismo," which
the writer Francisco Ichaso defined as "the
attitudes, habits, states of conscience,
even the ideas which this systematic use
or abuse of the garment produces."[6] They
were afraid that by wearing the guayabera,
locals were perpetuating the stereotype
of Latin Americans as lazy and dishonest.

Suárez Solís, for example, used the Spanish
word *fresca,* which means "fresh" but also
connotes impoliteness and shamelessness,
to describe the shirt and to argue for its
inappropriateness.[7] Ichaso, in turn, claimed
that the vogue for the guayabera in Cuba
was due to Miami's influence on the island.[8]
In his view, the growing presence of
shorts-wearing tourists from Florida was
causing Cubans to adopt a more casual
attitude toward dress. "Miami is a city at
the service of the beach," he said. "Havana
is a city at the service of civilization."[9]

Today the guayabera is most
visible on the streets of Miami. Cuban
immigrants in the United States don the
style as a way to maintain a connection
with the country many of them felt forced
to leave, and it has become a symbol for
Cuba's recent history of migration. The
story of Ramón Puig exemplifies the
guayabera's journey. Having made a name
for himself in Havana as a guayabera tailor,
Puig relocated to Miami's Little Havana
neighborhood in 1971 and brought his
business with him. In the years that followed, his shop became one of the most
prominent in town, providing handmade
shirts to politicians like Ronald Reagan.
After Puig's death in 2011, his son, Ramón
Puig Jr. took over the business and
rebranded it to appeal to a younger audience. "The guayabera is the coolest
thing in the world," he told the *Wall Street
Journal.* "It's not just your dad's shirt any-
more. It's Cuban cool."[10] Cuban Americans
wear the shirt at all hours of the day, with
jeans and other casual clothing, but in
Cuba the shirt is considered formal attire.
In 2010 the Cuban government even
declared the guayabera the official garment for diplomatic and state events,
making it a required uniform for diplomats
and politicians.[11] This decree was the
culmination of a shift that began decades
earlier, after the Cuban Revolution
(1953–59), when the Communist Party
embraced the garment's humble origins
and its members began wearing it to
formal functions.

Despite its strong links to Cuba,
in the last century the guayabera has also
become a sign of a broader Latin American
identity, frequently worn by politicians
from across the region during international
political summits to signify unity. In 1994
Cuban leader Fidel Castro caused a stir
when he appeared in a guayabera, instead
of his usual military uniform, at the
Ibero-American Summit in Cartagena,

Colombia. "My guayabera and my uniform are the Latin America of which [Simón] Bolívar and [José] Martí dreamt," he explained; by referring to two nineteenth-century figures who played prominent roles in struggles for independence in Latin America, Castro aligned the guayabera with a broad populist political vision.[12] Aside from its popularity with politicians, the guayabera is a formal and an informal wardrobe staple for most men in warm regions across Latin America. The shirt is also worn in Southeast Asia and other parts of the world with humid climates. Today most guayaberas are mass-produced in China and Mexico. They are sold internationally and called by various names: a Yucatán shirt in Mexico, a *chacabana* in the Dominican Republic, and a bush jacket in Jamaica.
—AB

Right:
1— **Members of the Indian Communist Party protest U.S. intervention in Cuba during the Bay of Pigs invasion, India, 1961. Unknown photographer**
2— **Fidel Castro at the Fourth Ibero-American Summit of Heads of State and Government, Cartagena de Indias, Colombia, 1994. Unknown photographer**
3— **Cuban émigré in Calle Ocho, Miami, 2009. Photograph by Robert Harding**
4— **Ernest Hemingway and Gary Cooper in Havana, 1956. Unknown photographer**

H — 046

HAREM PANTS   In 1911 the Parisian fashion designer Paul Poiret introduced a new collection loosely inspired by Middle Eastern costumes and accessories. It was presented that year at his fancy-dress ball, "The 1002nd Night," and in a catalogue illustrated by the French artist Georges Lepape. The *jupe-culotte,* also known as harem pants, was a central piece in the collection, and it came to exemplify Poiret's signature style. These high-waisted, ballooning trousers tied at the ankle were worn with a lampshade-style tunic or a simple, revealing top.

Then more generally known as "Turkish trousers," the style had long been part of the European visual vocabulary. From the heyday of *turquerie* in paintings and decorative arts in the eighteenth century to the French Orientalist paintings of the nineteenth century, the garment embodied a romanticized vision of the East, closely associated with the opulence and decadence of the harem. In the early twentieth century, with a new French translation of *The Thousand and One Nights* by Jean-Charles Mardrus and the wild success of Sergei Diaghilev's Ballets Russes across Europe, Orientalism seized France with a new frenzy. In 1910 the company staged the ballet *Schéhérazade,* featuring various eroticized "harem dresses" designed by the Russian artist Léon Bakst, including wide trousers in exuberant fabrics, which may have inspired Poiret's jupe-culotte a year later (although Poiret fiercely denied this).[1]

The jupe-culotte appeared at a time of heightened zeal around dress reform, a movement that rejected corsets and bustles and advocated a natural body and comfortable garments for women. Poiret, together with his contemporaries

Callot Soeurs and Mariano Fortuny, was a pioneer in drawing on the Eastern and European pasts and mixing these elements to fashion new silhouettes and aesthetics. Abandoning the taut, disjointed forms of contemporary fashion, Poiret's simple, billowing shapes created a more unified and intelligible image of the body and highlighted its vivacity and sensuality. His harem pants were mainly reserved for private soirées and interior settings, but they were adapted into day wear by other designers, in outfits that manifested a new sense of physical mobility, often tied to outdoor activity.

Poiret's jupe-culotte immediately stirred up controversy. As fashion scholar Nancy Troy has outlined, criticism centered on the design's racially marked exoticism, which was foreign to French couture taste, and on its perceived threat to traditional gender roles.[2] Before the twentieth century, trousers were not part of mainstream women's wardrobes in the West, and in the nineteenth century women's rights activists (such as Amelia Bloomer) had adopted Turkish trousers as a statement of independence and health.[3] In published defenses of the style, Poiret denied any political implication, especially in relation to women's suffrage and gender transgression. But the gender flexibility implied by very name of the garment— poised between skirt (*jupe*) and trouser (*culotte*)—was one of its most provoking characteristics in the popular imagination, and the flexibility worked in both directions. Vaslav Nijinsky, the star of the Ballets Russes, wore shimmering gold Turkish trousers and a brief bejeweled top in his performance as the Golden Slave in *Schéhérazade.* In Lepape's painting of Nijinsky in this costume, the dancer ascends from a bed piled with colorful pillows, his face and gestures feminized like an Oriental odalisque. The English writer Virginia Woolf used the androgyny of Turkish trousers in her 1928 novel *Orlando: A Biography*, a fantastic tale in which the hero lives for more than three hundred years, changing from a man to a woman partway through. Orlando's transformation occurs mysteriously, during sleep, while the character is in Turkey, and her trousers, a style worn there by men and women alike, disguise the metamorphosis and distract her from contemplating her new sex.

Liberty, simplicity, movement, and androgyny—in many ways the jupe-culotte redefined the female body, leaving the Belle Époque behind and anticipating modernist fashion. But it was not modernist in spirit. Far from the machine-driven logic of speed, functionality, and rationality—the characteristics that reshaped fashion in the 1920s and 1930s—Poiret's trousers indulged in a realm of timeless fantasy, historicism, and decadence. Poiret may have changed the way women dressed and felt about their bodies, but he did not revolutionize the way they lived—unlike, for example, the contemporaneous designer Gabrielle "Coco" Chanel (see *Little Black Dress*).

Poiret's harem pants fell out of favor around 1935, when streamlined, straight-legged masculine trousers found their way into women's wardrobes, but the style had a curious reemergence in the 1980s, when hip-hop recording artist MC Hammer popularized a version as an essential component of his choreography and stage performance. Loose and flowing above a tight ankle, like the jupe-culotte but with a more prominently draped crotch, "hammer pants" sustained the dynamic spirit of Poiret's design and also imbued it with the distinctive cultural cachet of the nascent hip-hop genre. —MMR

Right:
1— **MC Hammer on** ***The Oprah Winfrey Show,*** **1990. Photograph by Eugene Adebari**
2— **Barbara Eden in the pilot for the TV series** ***I Dream of Jeannie,*** **1964**
3— ***The Bloomer Costume,*** **lithograph by Currier and Ives, 1851**
4— **A dancing-girl costume design by Léon Bakst for the ballet** ***Schéhérazade,*** **1910**
5— **Paul Poiret and his wife, Denise, at his party "The 1002nd Night," 1911. Photograph by Henri Manuel**

2

3

5

HEAD WRAP Encircling part or all of the head with a length of textile is a long-standing custom in many parts of the world. It is rarely only a fashion choice, especially for women, but instead is often a mark of identity and status, whether religious or secular. Though they are associated with Africa and the African disapora, head wraps (or head ties) are worn in many other cultures and contexts; the Sikh turban or *dastaar,* prestitched wraps made of stretchy synthetics, and repurposed silk scarves worn by Orthodox Jewish women are three examples. It has functioned variously as a metaphorical augmentation of stature; a signal of modesty or religious observance (a woman's uncovered hair is interpreted by some cultures as erotic); practical protection from sun or sleep damage; indicators, often overlapping, of embellishment, ceremony, identity, and belonging; or just a way to conceal a bad hair day. It has also been an enforced mode of dress, in particular for African American slaves in the United States and during periods of colonial rule in Africa.

European women covered their heads for modesty and display of rank at about the same time that elaborate turbans appeared on the head of the king symbolizing the continent of Africa in medieval and Renaissance depictions of the biblical Three Wise Men.[1] This latter wrap, the *toca de camino,* was worn by Muslim Moors in North Africa and was transmitted in the fifteenth century to Christians in Spain (and travelers to New Spain), and eventually became *un tocado nacional*, or national headdress. A Flemish courtier on a trip to Spain observed the head wraps worn "wound several times around the head, all made of cloth," and in Spain's colonies in South America, they "[distinguished] a colonialist Spanish elite from the mass of indigenous peoples."[2]

The scholar Helen Bradley Griebel has argued that the African American head wrap began in West Africa, where it was used as ceremonial dress as well as everyday wear denoting social or marital status and changed according to local aesthetic standards.[3] It may have first come to North America with the slaves taken to the West Indies, as a powerful reminder of their origins. It was a vexed garment, at times worn by choice and at others by coercion. From the eighteenth century until the abolishment of slavery, parts of the American South, including the Spanish colony of Louisiana, had laws that mandated the wearing of a head wrap by enslaved women, in order to visibly demarcate their bondage and to maintain class and race distinctions. Yet contrarily, the *tignons* they wore became a source of racial and geographic pride as well as a subversive canvas for imaginative folding and bejeweling, thus, according to the historian Steeve O. Buckridge, "resist[ing] the system of slavery that sought to rob them of their pride, their dignity, and . . . African identity."[4]

The head wrap is not solely the preserve of one community or culture. The historian Willard B. Gatewood recorded the exotic turbans worn during the Harlem Renaissance, in the early twentieth century, by the socialite A'Lelia Walker, a form that has also appeared in contexts as varied as the Hasidic enclaves of Brooklyn, New York, and the Royal Ascot races in 1989, when Diana, Princess of Wales, wore a striking blue turban hat designed by Philip Somerville.[5] In the past several decades, some women and men have actively reclaimed forms of the head wrap to signal opposition to conservative and exclusionary attitudes or to celebrate their pan-African identity.[6] Its adoption by actors and musicians and their fans has brought other forms and meanings to light. Think of Bob Marley, with his Rastafarian dreadlock wrap, or of Erykah Badu, for whom wearing head wraps was a symbol of racial pride. When a South African television station cut a segment by the reporter Nontobeko Sibisi because she wore a *doek,* which the station considered informal and unprofessional, a social media campaign rose up to defend her.[7] And the head wrap has become part of a complex conversation about cultural appropriation. In but one example, the *iduku,* the head wrap sometimes worn by women employed as domestic workers in southern African cities, has been taken up as a fashion accessory by affluent young women and celebrities;

activists and others have decried the divorcing of such a charged garment from context and history.[8]

The head wrap today is proudly and widely worn, by people as diverse as the American singer, songwriter, and actress Janelle Monáe and the South African television personality Bonang Matheba. At a film premiere in 2016, the actress Lupita Nyong'o wore a *gele* (a Nigerian head wrap made of tight overlapping folds) in tandem with a Carolina Herrera dress—a powerful mix of coutures and cultures in a single ensemble. —MMF

Left:
1— **Jacques Guillaume Lucien Amans, *Creole in a Red Headdress*, c. 1840**
2— **Nigerian model Mayowa Nicholas in a *gele*, Lagos Fashion and Design Week, 2016**
3— **Erykah Badu on the Smokin' Grooves tour, 1997. Photograph by Estevan Oriol**
4— **Sikh men, United States, 2013. Unknown photographer**
5— **Women praying at the Western Wall (or *Kotel*), Jerusalem, 2013. Photograph by Laura Arsie**

HEADPHONES Headphones date to the nineteenth century, but only in the late twentieth would they become public accoutrements that redefined social conventions. If the late-nineteenth-century predecessors served to amplify opera performances, aid hearing, and block noise, the headphone as we know it arrived in 1910 when one Nathaniel Baldwin proposed an over-ear set to the U.S. Navy; it remained the miltary standard through two world wars. Headphones (and earphones) entered consumer headspace in the 1950s with the popularization of portable transistor radios and stereo LPs. The audio manufacturer Koss introduced the first stereo headphones in 1957, pairing them with its Model 390 stereo phonograph, which came in its own suitcase, presaging the idea of a mobile private sound system.

Stereo sound became truly mobile with the introduction of the Sony Walkman Portable Audio Cassette Player (TPS-L2) and Stereo Headphones (MDR-3L2) in 1979. Though a master narrative of the Walkman's development is elusive, the device established the idea of personal isolation within public space, a phenomenon that was intensified by the advent of the iPod in 2001 and the subsequent ascendancy of the smartphone.[1]

That the *New York Times* first reported on the Walkman as a fashion phenomenon rather than a technological advance would prove prescient in 2008 when the sleek, upscale Beats by Dre headphones—born of a fraught collaboration between audio innovator Monster and the music industry team of Jimmy Iovine and Dr. Dre (Andre Young)—transformed a piece of audio equipment into stylish headwear and made celebrity endorsement a design criterion. As one tech critic put it, Iovine and Dre "took decent headphones that could swamp

your ears with low-end [sound], isolate you from street noise, and keep your skull relatively comfortable during a long walk, and made all of these qualities irrelevant under a sheen of rapper-lure."[2]

Socially, the Walkman with headphones and MP3 player or smartphone with Beats engendered a radically new experience of space, which curator Paola Antonelli has termed *Existenzmaximum* (a critical reaction to *Existenzminimum*, early-twentieth-century functionalist architects' conception of the minimal spatial requirements for human comfort). She locates its origins in the 1960s and '70s, when new social attitudes, materials, and media were mobilized by architects and designers into "the revolutionary concept of expanding, growing, breathing, walking, and digesting structures and cities." At human scale, she has observed, such design "enables us to inhabit a comfortable space whose boundaries are protective rather than oppressive, such as the cocoon one forges on mass transit."[3]

These visionaries also anticipated the realm of quasi-public networked information known today as cyberspace. In fact, author William Gibson's 1982 coinage emerged from his experience with the Walkman and early personal computers: "If there is an imaginary point of convergence where the information this machine handles could be accessed with the under-the-skin intimacy of the Walkman," he wondered, "what would that be like?"[4] As headphones transmute into multisensory, smartphone-driven virtual-reality headsets, we may soon find out. —JT

Right:
1— **Subway riders, New York, 1981. Photograph by Dick Lewis**
2— **Commuters in the women-only carriage on the metro, New Delhi, 2015. Photograph by Anna Zieminski**
3— **Drake and Lil Wayne wearing diamond-studded Beats by Dre headphones at the 2012 NBA All-Star Game, Orlando, Florida. Photograph by Ronald Martinez**

HIJAB   Contrary to predictions that have been made for more than half a century that the hijab would wane in use and fade from women's wardrobes, the veil remains a mainstay of contemporary dress for millions of Muslims across the globe.[1] Worn to cover the head (and often the neck), hijabs are shaped by a multitude of overlapping concerns, including doctrinal distinctions, local and global fashion trends, personal choice, and transnational trade. Related modes of veiling include the longer, enveloping chador and the niqab and burka, which cover the face.

Modesty for men and women alike is a key tenet of Muslim culture. Referring to the pre-Islamic veil worn on the Arabian Peninsula at the time the prophet Muhammad founded Islam in the seventh century, the Koran enjoins women to "draw their *khimar* over their breasts and not display their beauty." Modesty is, of course, wholly subjective, a constructed set of social norms—whether pertaining to short skirts, tight jeans, or religious garb. Like any other major world religion, Islam is heterogeneous, and opinions on the hijab—from style to substance—are diverse and hotly debated both within and outside the faith. While some countries mandate its wearing by law (e.g., Iran and Saudi Arabia) other countries (for example, France, with its explicit separation of church and state) have strict proscriptions against its wearing in public and governmental spaces, where the garment intersects with issues around security, immigration, assimilation, and Islam's position in the West. In some Muslim-majority countries (Morocco, for instance), the hijab is often officially discouraged, seen as a sign of support for a political Islam that stands in conflict with secular governance. Under the current authoritarian government of Turkish president Recep Tayyip Erdoğan, to the contrary, the hijab—once banned in government offices and schools—has been instrumentalized as "a symbol of religious freedom from the strictures of secularism."[2]

The fall and rise of the hijab in the twentieth century can be traced from the implementation of democratic socialism and the concomitant unveiling in countries such as Egypt and Turkey in the 1920s through the 1960s to the subsequent disillusionment with failed policies of Westernization, the rise of Saudi Arabia as a regional power and promoter of Wahhabism, and a renewed commitment to an activist Islam throughout the Middle East and beyond.[3] After the attacks on September 11, 2001, the hijab was increasingly stereotyped in the West as an oppressive, gender-normative prescription and a sign of religious separatism. But this is nothing new.[4] Indeed, the long intersection of colonial rule and interventionist unveiling is precisely what made the hijab a rallying cry of opposition to the West during independence and nationalist movements. Still, many Muslims have argued that veiling should not be compulsory, given that the practice predated Islam on the Arabian Peninsula and was tied as firmly to class as it was to religion: working women, especially of low status, were often unable to veil or seclude themselves and in ancient cultures were sometimes even legally prohibited from doing so.

Hijabs today, like those historically, come in a range of shapes, styles, and textiles, from plain black fabric lengths (the proper donning of which requires both skill and pins) to preformed cowls and turbans. The common al-amira ("princess") style comprises a tube that covers the crown from forehead to nape and a second piece that drapes around the head and neck. In Turkey, silk scarves are typically tied at the chin, while black Muslims from different parts of the globe sometimes use traditional forms of African or African American headdress to satisfy Islamic standards of modesty.[5] From New York to London to Dubai, where women of diverse professions choose dark, monochrome business-wear ensembles, a black hijab— all too frequently imbued with sinister connotations in Western media—blends in and becomes part of the mundane workday uniform.

Contemporary retailers and designers have capitalized on a fast-growing market for modest fashion. Sports led the way. In 2001 the Dutch designer Cindy van den Bremen founded the company

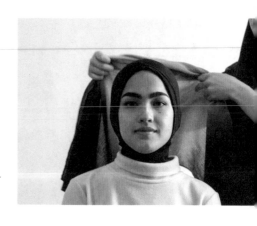

Capsters with the goal of empowering hijabi women in sport. (Nike launched its own version of the sports hijab in 2017.) Two years before medaling at the 2016 Summer Olympics in Rio de Janeiro, Ibtihaj Muhammad—the first American to compete in a hijab—founded the modest-fashion line Louella. Major houses such as Dolce & Gabbana, DKNY, and Tommy Hilfiger now design Ramadan capsule collections, astutely aware of the buying power of Muslim consumers. In 2015 the young British designer Hana Tajima began collaborating with the international Japanese brand Uniqlo to create a modest-fashion line complete with floor-length hemlines and chic, hoodlike hijabs. In the last five years, an efflorescence of blogging, social media content, and YouTube hijab tutorials from modest fashionistas such as the British Egyptian Dina Torkia (who has more than a million followers) has emphasized personal style over the fastidiousness of religion. Despite such changes in contemporary attitudes, which increasingly foreground secular themes of aesthetics and personal identity, the hijab remains a potent symbol of faith and institutional religion around the world. —MMF

Right:
1— **Hana Tajima and model demonstrating how to wear a hijab, in a still from Tajima's video "Hana Tajima Shawl Tutorial," 2015**
2— **American fencer Ibtihaj Muhammad during the Women's Sabre Team Semifinal 1 at the 2016 Summer Olympics, Rio de Janeiro. Photograph by Tom Pennington**
3— **Market shop, Damascus, n.d. Unknown photographer**
4— **Palestinian students, early 1990s. Photograph by Peter Turnley**
5— **Model on the runaway for the Anniesa Hasibuan spring/summer 2017 collection. Photograph by Frazer Harrison**

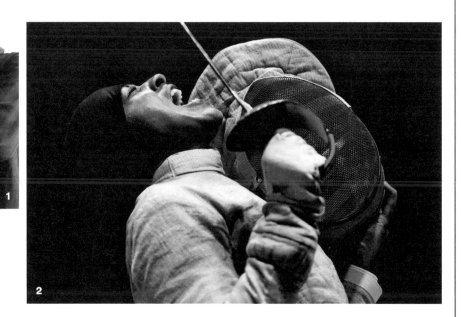

HOODIE   A mainstay of American casual wear, the hooded sweatshirt is a loosely cut zip-front or pullover sweatshirt, typically made of thick cotton jersey or polyester and distinguished by the attached head covering, which can be tightened with a drawstring. A practical garment, the hoodie (as it is now widely known) appeals to people in many different walks of life, including athletes, suburban parents, college students, hip-hop artists, rebellious youth, weekend adventurers, and tech billionaires, shifting in meaning from congenial to defiant, humble to arrogant, and intimate to political, depending on who wears it, and how.

Hooded garments have long been part of the Western sartorial heritage, valued primarily as shields from the elements. In Europe, medieval and Renaissance monks wore hooded cloaks, and noble ladies in the mid-eighteenth century favored a short traveling jacket called a Brunswick, which featured a hood. The modern hooded sweatshirt was invented in the 1930s by the Rochester-based sportswear manufacturer now known as Champion, intended to fit over competition gear and to keep athletes warm before and after training. It was subsequently adopted by workers in coldstorage units and on construction sites. Both of these early associations with the garment—sports and labor—are key thematic elements in the 1976 film *Rocky,* in which the eponymous working-class hero struggles toward success as a professional boxer in a worn-out gray hoodie.

In the 1950s and '60s the hooded sweatshirt became popular among university students, in part promoted by young women who appropriated their boyfriends' football and track-and-field gear. Emblazoned with the logos of college sports teams, the garment became further associated with athleticism but also with the status implied by an elite education. Today the hoodie plays a paramount role in the quintessential look of the young American student, often as a statement of belonging to—or an aspiration to soon become a part of—a venerated institution or admired clique, or even of affiliation with a fashion brand (hence the pricey runway versions). In other cases it is driven by an anti-elite, democratic, or intellectually oriented "anti-fashion" attitude, or perhaps simply by a desire to conceal lingering adolescent awkwardness in homogeneity and invisibility. As Troy Patterson has written in the *New York Times Magazine,* "The hood frames a dirty look, obscures acne and anxiety, masks headphones in study hall, makes a cone of solitude that will suffice for an autonomous realm."[1] When college kids transform overnight into newly rich tech-industry leaders, the hoodie becomes their power dress. The hoodie is the signature garment of Mark Zuckerberg, founder of Facebook, who wears it in public appearances and at high-profile business meetings. Openly disrespectful of established business dress codes, his sweatshirt celebrates the power to reset the rules and redefine success.

In the mid-1970s and '80s the hoodie took on a new meaning as a street style, as hip-hop culture burgeoned in New York City. Graffiti writers pulled up the hood while they worked, and break dancers warmed up in the sweatshirts before hitting the ground. On the West Coast, the closure of many skate parks drove young people to the streets, where they skated illicitly with their hoods up. In the 1990s hard-edged rappers such as Wu-Tang Clan further developed the hooded sweatshirt as a sign of anonymity and resistance. The cover of the group's 1993 debut album *Enter the Wu-Tang (36 Chambers)* represents the members wrapped in black hoodies, all faceless.

As fashion historian Joanne Turney has noted, numerous fictional and real figures associated with evil and crime have worn hoods, ranging from the Grim Reaper of Victorian tales to members of the ultra-racist Ku Klux Klan in the American South.[2] In contemporary cities, the hoodie directly confronts the modern surveillance system (designed for crime prevention and detection), acknowledging the presence of ubiquitous CCTV cameras by shielding the wearer from them. In recent history,

1

3

the American Ted Kaczynski, known as the Unabomber, conducted a deadly mail-bombing campaign between 1978 and 1995; he first came to public attention in a forensic sketch in which he was disguised in a hooded sweatshirt and sunglasses.

Today these negative associations with hooded figures have merged with racist stereotypes to make targets of young African American and Latino males. On February 26, 2012, seventeen-year-old Trayvon Martin was shot dead on a residential street in Sanford, Florida, by George Zimmerman, a neighborhood watch volunteer, who had identified the teen as behaving suspiciously. Zimmerman noted to a police dispatcher before the shooting that the African American teenager was wearing a "dark hoodie."[3] Ironically, Martin may have pulled up the hood of his sweatshirt because he was scared of Zimmerman, who had been following him down the street. In the aftermath of the killing, Martin's supporters organized Million Hoodie Marches across the country, rallying around the garment as a material embodiment both of the vulnerable black body it failed to protect and of deeply entrenched racial prejudice. In identifying themselves with the victim through clothing, the protesters turned the stigma of the hoodie into a political statement against race-based violence and social injustice. —MMR

4

Left:
1— New York City Council members at a press conference organized to call for justice in the killing of Trayvon Martin, New York, 2012. Photograph by Allison Joyce
2— Model on the runway for the Vetements fall 2016 ready-to-wear collection, 2016. Photograph by Daniele Oberrauch
3— Sylvester Stallone in the film *Rocky Balboa*, 2006
4— Illustration from a Champion catalogue, c. 1966

JUMPSUIT A jumpsuit is a garment with pants and top combined. The name derives from the one-piece uniforms worn by World War I parachute jumpers, but the garment's origins can be traced to the one-piece knitted long underwear known as the union suit—a version of which, the "emancipation union under flannel," was patented in the United States in 1868 as a more comfortable, and liberating, alternative to the standard constricting undergarments worn by women. While it served as a key component of women's dress reform, it soon found purpose for men as well, particularly as an extra layer of warmth for soldiers.

When all-in-one garments began to appear as general wardrobe items in addition to underclothes, utility and practicality continued to be emphasized. The Lee Union-All, designed in 1913 by the H. D. Lee Mercantile Company in Kansas (later Lee Jeans), was a loose but durable workwear coverall worn originally by mechanics and eventually adopted by farmers and factory workers after World War I. About this time, the one-piece jumpsuit also found application in more rarefied settings: in 1911 the French couturier Paul Poiret introduced his pantaloon gown (*jupe-sultane*), a one-piece bifurcated dress made of lightweight silk that enabled free movement for outdoor activities.[1]

The jumpsuit was also looked to as an ideal garment to eradicate social divisions. In 1914 Futurist artists put forth a manifesto on men's fashion that called for the abolition of frivolous styles composed of heavy fabrics and useless adornment. In 1919 the Futurist artist and illustrator Thayaht (Ernesto Michahelles) proposed the TuTa—a T-shaped jumpsuit fastened with a belt—to serve as a universal item of menswear and a do-it-yourself, antibourgeois statement. These sentiments were echoed in 1923 by the Russian Constructivist artists Varvara Stepanova and Aleksandr Rodchenko, who viewed the jumpsuit as a vehicle for providing mass-produced, egalitarian clothing to the working-class majority after the Russian revolution. While Stepanova designed one-piece unisex "sports overalls" governed by the principles of comfort and expediency, Rodchenko created everyday wool coveralls trimmed with leather and called them "production clothing."[2]

The jumpsuit would also serve as the basis for the siren suit that emerged during World War II, a durable garment made for civilians to easily put on for a sudden journey to a bunker in the event of a nighttime air raid. Designs varied: a 1941 example was described in *Women's Wear Daily* as "a one-piece costume of navy blue waterproofed gabardine, with a concealed slide fastener and huge pockets in each trouser leg" that could be "slipped on quickly in seven motions."[3]

In the 1960s the jumpsuit evolved from utilitarian garb to iterations that were pure expressions of fashion. Fueled by a desire to explore new expressions of modernity, designers showcased the garment as a symbol of youth, faith in technology, and optimism about the future. French designer Pierre Cardin referenced space travel with jumpsuits as part of his Cosmocorps lines (see *Space Age*), while Austrian-American designer Rudi Gernreich used the jumpsuit as a way to eradicate gender divisions (see *Unisex Project*).

It was during the 1970s, however, that the jumpsuit conquered another significant fashion frontier: women's evening wear. Although the French designer Yves Saint Laurent's tuxedo for women had already been introduced, in 1966 (see *Le Smoking*), evening-wear jumpsuits provided women with the option of wearing pants for formal occasions on their own terms, without referencing menswear or implying androgyny. Adaptations by Saint Laurent and American designers like Halston and Norma Kamali were inspired by the disco scene and its New York mecca, Studio 54. The new nightlife staple beamed luxury and glamour, its silhouette accentuating movements on the dance floor. The American designer Stephen Burrows's c. 1974 version in slinky, shimmering gold lamé, with its revealing backless halter top and loosely gathered legs, epitomized the

celebration of the new ideal of a fit body. The jumpsuit further evolved through the end of the century, assuming the hard glamour of the 1980s by gaining shoulder pads, as championed by the French designer Thierry Mugler, and the extreme body consciousness of the 1990s, as typified by Gianni Versace's bondage-inspired iterations.

In the twenty-first century, jumpsuit aficionados have reprised the future-forward, post-gender idealism seen in the earliest loose-fitting, utilitarian forms, as in the case of the American artist collective Rational Dress Society's (RDS) Jumpsuit introduced in 2016, envisioned as an "ungendered mono-garment to replace all clothes in perpetuity."[4] A response to the fast-fashion phenomenon, which conditions shoppers to continually buy inexpensive garments that do not last, Jumpsuit has a planned production of over two hundred custom sizes designed to suit multiple body types using a system based on NASA body-size data—underscoring the notion of the jumpsuit as the garment of the future. —SK

Right:
1— **The Beastie Boys on Canal Street preparing to film a video for their album *To the 5 Boroughs*, New York, 2004. Photograph by Richard Corkery**
2— **Design for a men's suit by Aleksandr Rodchenko, c. 1922**
3— **Advertisement for the "Two-Way Siren Suit" on a pattern-packet frontispiece, 1940s**
4— **David Bowie in a jumpsuit designed by Kansai Yamamoto, 1973. Photograph by Masayoshi Sukita**

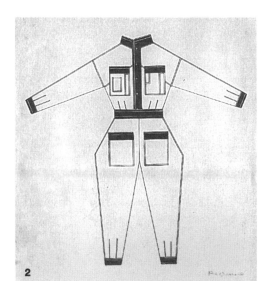

2

4

KEFFIYEH The keffiyeh, a draped head covering derived from traditional Bedouin Arab dress, emerged in the early twentieth century to both assert and blur Palestinian identity, spreading around the globe as a general symbol for political struggle decades later. Also known as a *hattah*, *shamagh*, or *ghutra*, the modern keffiyeh is a square cotton (or cotton and wool blend) cloth, usually white with a one-color motif known as "knotted net" or "dog tooth" woven in. Design scholar Hala Malak has located the origin of the keffiyeh in pre-Islamic Sumeria, positing a practical garment that evolved to connote social status through material variation and decorative imagery. She further attributes the characteristic net motif to an ancient priestly ritual that, as an abstract pattern, adapted well to Islamic culture.[1]

The keffiyeh first became a potent symbol of identity in the 1930s, during a period of Palestinian revolt against Jewish immigration. When Palestinian organizers required sympathizers of all classes to wear it as a way to camouflage keffiyeh-wearing fighters, a unifying symbol was born. In the 1960s the black-patterned keffiyeh was revived as an expression of organized resistance by the Palestine Liberation Organization leader and secular Fatah party founder Yasser Arafat, and by the Popular Front for the Liberation of Palestine member Leila Khaled. Around the same time, a red-patterned keffiyeh emerged from traditional Jordanian culture to represent its military, and in 1987 the red version became associated with the nascent Islamicist Hamas party and First Intifada fighters. The red-black distinction gained renewed significance in the early 2000s, as tensions between the two parties intensified. In the 1970s, following widespread news coverage of the continuing Israeli-Palestinian conflict, the "PLO shawl" was adopted by leftist students in Europe, spreading over several decades and continents to become a ubiquitous accessory with very loose connections to activism.

Western fashion claimed the keffiyeh as early as 1965, inspiring appropriation ever since. The year 2007 was an especially prolific one for the cloth, when it was referenced by luxury design houses from Balenciaga to Louis Vuitton.[2] Other notable references include a 2010 collection by Givenchy, a 2015 line by Chanel, and an ongoing series by the Denmark-based fashion line Cecilie Copenhagen. In popular culture, through color and pattern tweaks the keffiyeh has been appropriated for any number of purposes, with blue-and-white Israeli versions the most overtly political. At the same time, Malak has observed, the keffiyeh continues to be worn traditionally in the Persian Gulf region, untouched by fashion.

In today's global context the keffiyeh seems to become less controversial the farther it disperses—unlike other garments associated with Islamic cultures. As the fashion and style writer David Colman put it in the *New York Times*, "To some people, it suggests a vague sympathy with Palestinian movements like Fatah and Hamas. To others, less interested in politics, it just looks bohemian and, you know, nomadic."[3] —JT

Right:
1— **Leila Khaled, Jordan, 1969. Unknown photographer**
2— **Bedouin men, 1910–20. Unknown photographer**
3— **Model Brigitte Bauer in a patterned silk dress by Branell and head wrap by Halston,** *Vogue,* **February 1965. Photograph by Irving Penn**
4— **Architect Salim Al Kadi's Kevlar keffiyeh, 2016. Photograph by Marcel Rached**
5— **Yasser Arafat at an Arab Summit conference, Rabat, Morocco, 1974. Unknown photographer**

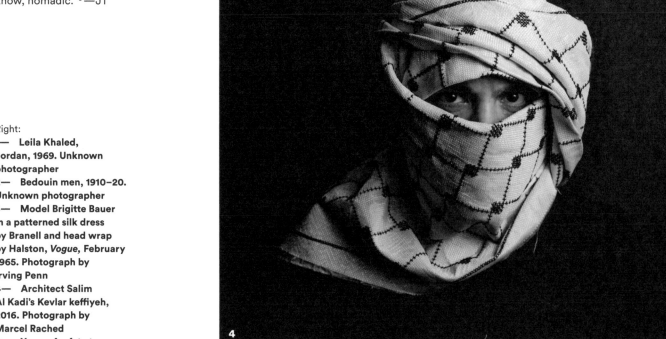

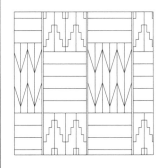

KENTE CLOTH   A traditional strip-woven fabric originating in Ghana and Togo, kente cloth has been translated widely into popular fashion across the globe, particularly since Ghanaian independence, achieved in 1957, and the ensuing birth of the modern Pan-African movement. From the tailored kente ensembles of the 1960s to the American hip-hop trio Salt-N-Pepa sporting kente-embellished kufi hats two decades later to the American designer Jeremy Scott's brightly colored kente sneaker collaboration with Adidas Originals in 2009, the cloth signals identification with (and, at times, appropriation of) African heritage.

Historically, it is the Asante (the largest ethnic group within the Akan population of Ghana and the Ivory Coast) and the Ewe (of Ghana and neighboring Togo) peoples who weave kente cloth. These two groups maintain discrete yet overlapping visual and material cultures and have at key moments shared and influenced each other's kente production. Kente cloth is made of three- to four-inch-wide textile strips (often patterned) that are woven on a horizontal treadle loom and then sewn together to create fabrics of varying sizes. Ewe kente, in particular, is frequently decorated with *adinkra* motifs, pictorial and graphic symbols meant to convey traditional wisdom. While the cloth was initially hand-loomed (a skill set almost exclusively male), machine-produced cloth has proliferated since the mid-twentieth century, as have shortcuts such as roller-printed kente fabric.[1] Often hung on walls in (Western) museums, kente is meant to be worn wrapped on the body by both men and women, a garment described by the preeminent African textile scholar Doran H. Ross as "a kinetic sculpture, part kaleidoscope and part kite."[2]

The Gold Coast of West Africa was a site of European settlers and slavers since the late fifteenth century, and it was declared a British crown colony in 1874. Led by its first president, Kwame Nkrumah, Ghana decisively broke its colonial chains, gaining independence in 1957—the first such sub-Saharan nation to do so. Nkrumah was an early architect of the modern Pan-African movement (which sought cooperative action among all people of African descent), and kente played an important role in shaping a nascent public identity for Ghana and for Africa on the international stage. Nkrumah used the Asante kente exclusively, wearing it during public ceremonial events, and an inaugural display of Asante kente (and no Ewe examples) at the National Museum of Ghana that remained on view for nearly forty years gave the Asante weave prominence. This, combined with the more dynamic and established patronage systems of the Asante elite for court regalia, explains the later prevalence of this particular brightly colored, geometric kente type in foreign markets such as the United States.[3]

Kente cloth moved from a prestige garment restricted to use by chiefs to become enmeshed in the mainstream of both globalized and highly localized fashion tendencies in the twentieth century. Juliana Norteye was the first Ghanaian-born, Parisian-trained fashion designer in the capital city of Accra in the 1960s, and her clothing made innovative bridges between the traditional and contemporary under her label Chez Julie. Norteye's Kaba ensemble pairs a length of kente wrapped into a tubular midcalf skirt with a short-sleeved formfitting blouse of the same fabric, an early and provocative example of precious kente cloth being cut and tailored into Western styles.

Over the following three decades, kente found its way into many everyday items, from backpacks to Band-Aids to Kwanzaa gifts (as well as a mid-1990s JCPenney specialty catalogue that included everything from kente-decorated crockery to kente caftans). Graduating students in many countries, not least the United States, often incorporate a kente stole into their robes to signify pride in African heritage, and figures who loom large in the public consciousness such as W.E.B. Du Bois, Muhammad Ali, and Nelson Mandela were known to wear the textile, wrapped, in tailored form, or as an embellishment.

Haute couture has continued to assimilate and appropriate kente cloth. The American designer Patrick Kelly memorably employed the patterned textile in garments—including spandex leggings—in his spring/summer 1988 runway show; more recently the Italian designers Stella Jean and Gabriele Colangelo have each extemporized on kente patterns, the latter creating a deconstructed sheared-silk kente for his spring 2016 collection.

While kente has assumed global prominence, the cloth remains a durable part of everyday and ceremonial Ghanaian dress. President Nana Akufo-Addo, a former human rights lawyer elected in 2016, proudly sports fine kente decorated with a plethora of adinkra symbols, a combination of painstakingly handwoven cloth juxtaposed with machine-made mass-produced fabrics and decorations sourced from Asia; kente masters in the Asante weaving center of Bonwire often create his ensembles. The town has become an international tourist center, producing kente that is purchased as vacation keepsakes and in bulk for distribution far and wide. —MMF

Left:
1— **Chiefs of the Agotime Traditional Area at the Agotime Kente Festival, Kpetoe, Volta Region, Ghana, September 2014. Photograph by Philippe J. Kradolfer**
2— **Graduating students at Ithaca College during commencement, Ithaca, New York, 2015. Photograph by Gary Hodges**
3— **Nana Akufo-Addo, president of Ghana, inspects a military parade after his swearing-in ceremony at Independence Square, Accra, Ghana, 2017. Photograph by Luc Gnago**
4— **Christian bride and groom, Gold Coast (now Ghana), c. 1900. Unknown photographer**

K — 054

KILT The kilt is a cipher for romanticized Scottish nationalism and rugged masculinity that has often been worn most memorably (although not always with historical fidelity) by non-Scots—including the nineteenth-century British monarch King George IV, who wore his with pink hose, and the actors Mel Gibson and Liam Neeson in the 1995 Hollywood blockbuster films *Braveheart* and *Rob Roy*, respectively.

    The kilt as we know it today evolved from a layered garment known in the sixteenth century as the *breacan an féileadh* (belted tartan, or "great kilt"), a long piece of woven cloth worn by Gaelic-speaking Scottish Highland men in the north of the country (distinct from southern Scots Lowlanders). Made of strong, durable, harsh twill in muted colors, and around six yards long and two yards wide, the fabric was wrapped around the lower body, belted, and then passed over one shoulder. Unlike the brighter hues that proliferated in the nineteenth century, early tartans (known as plaids in North America) were basic weaves achieved by juxtaposing two or more colors at right angles in a balanced check.[1]

    The garment was more formally codified in the late seventeenth and early eighteenth centuries as the *féileadh beag* ("small kilt"): pleats were sewn permanently into the back of the skirt, loops were added for ease of belting, and the top length of fabric was detached from the rest of the wrap to form an autonomous garment. Highland clans distinguished themselves with the use of different tartans, and the kilt came to symbolize familial, military, and geographic loyalties. This practice was stamped out in the wake of the House of Stuart's attempts to regain the British throne, a series of incursions known as the Jacobite Uprisings (1689–1746). The northern Scots were ultimately defeated at the Battle of Culloden in 1746.

The Dress Act of that same year restricted use of the kilt in the Highlands to the Black Watch, a Scottish infantry regiment that was part of the British Army. By the time the law was repealed by King George III, in 1782, the kilt had ceased to be a quotidian part of Highland clothing.

The kilt subsequently morphed into a sartorial expression of the Romantic era, becoming the province of Highland Societies and worn by elite landowners who fetishized Scottish antiquarianism and stylized pageantry, often inventing new traditions around its use. The kilt was paired with accoutrements still used today, including the sporran, a small carrying pouch usually made of leather and sometimes trimmed with cow or horse hide—a descendent of the medieval tie-on pocket (see *Fanny Pack*). A special kilt pin fastens the layers where they meet at the front, though the pin is sometimes ornamental, not functional. The ensemble is worn with long, woolen knee socks, out of which protrudes—on the side of the wearer's dominant hand—the hilt of the *sgian-dubh,* a small Gaelic knife originally used for practical and defensive purposes. Queen Victoria and her spouse, Prince Albert, took the cult of the Highlands to its apogee, purchasing the Aberdeenshire estate Balmoral in 1852. They decorated its interiors with tartan, wore it for everyday and ceremonial attire, and popularized the Highland Games; the kilt has since flourished as a touristic motif on shortbread tins, whiskey casks, and postcards.

Kilts were used by the British military until the mid-twentieth century.[2] In the postwar period the garment took on a particularly nostalgic symbolism for nationals in diaspora, and as a common element of girls' private-school uniforms it retains certain elite connotations. Punk subcultures, however, sought to deliberately subvert such claims; British designer Vivienne Westwood became particularly associated with the use of tartan, though not always in kilt form, sourcing from historic lowland mills in the Scottish Borders.

In the 1990s the kilt was firmly absorbed into the high-fashion mainstream and concomitantly became a mainstay of popular culture in Scotland and beyond. Photographer Arthur Elgort and stylist Grace Coddington created a memorable story on location at a Scottish castle for the September 1991 issue of *Vogue* titled "A Shot of Scotch," with Linda Evangelista modeling Oscar de la Renta and Jean Paul Gaultier tartan fashions while prancing alongside a kilted bagpiper and a Scotsman artfully preparing to toss a monumentally heavy tree trunk, or caber. A 1993 *New York Times* article noted the prevalence of the kilt at the city's gay pride parade that year, making the connection between its uber-masculine symbolism and "the gym-perfected bodies of today's generation."[3] Westwood's seminal fall/winter 1993/94 Anglomania collection was swooned over as Kate Moss and Naomi Campbell walked various kilted garments down the runway—Campbell famously falling in the precipitous blue Super Elevated Gillie platforms (see *Platform Shoe*)—while Alexander McQueen took up the baton with his infamous 1995 Highland Rape collection exploring the atrocities of the Clearances. The fashion for subversion ultimately reached its apex in a look that combined the traditional dress with wholly nontraditional hoodies and graphic T-shirts.

Today, however, kilts are still most commonly seen on guests at a Scottish wedding, uniformed schoolgirls, or bagpipers busking on the street. For most people, including the residents of Scotland, there remains a strong association with ceremonial events and national identity, performances that have been in vogue in one form or another since nineteenth-century royalty tamed the kilt and made it fashionable. —MMF

Left:
1— **Portrait of King George IV in Highland dress, by Sir David Wilkie, 1829**
2— **Ben Westwood,** *Carry On Kilts,* **promotional image for Worlds End Boutique, London, 2016**
3— **Men of the Black Watch in a French village, 1918. Unknown photographer**
4— **Naomi Campbell after falling on the runway during a Vivienne Westwood show, Paris, fall 1993. Photograph by Niall McInerney**

KIPPAH   The kippah (Hebrew, plural *kippot*) or yarmulke (Yiddish) is a small cap worn to signal Jewish faith and identity and—through variations in surface decoration, color, and method or place of manufacture—secular selfhood and individual style. A public declaration of piety under the omnipotent eye of God, it was traditionally worn only by men. However, since the 1970s, when women were included in the rabbinical class, female rabbis and laywomen have also reached for the kippah to indicate their equality within Judaism and to express their personal connection to their faith—a move not without substantial controversy.

Although in ancient texts Jewish religious leaders are described as wearing head coverings, it is not *halakhic* (explicitly required by Jewish law) for ordinary folk to cover their heads for religious or secular activities. Head coverings for men have been what scholar Esther Juhasz terms an "obligatory norm" in most Jewish communities from the nineteenth century onward, though they were voluntarily adopted haphazardly throughout the medieval Jewish world, spurred by an edict by the fifteenth-century Czech Rabbi Israel Bruna that denounced male bareheadedness.[1] As Juhasz highlights, because Jews have had to identify themselves by wearing differentiated clothing throughout their long history of persecution, covering one's head has at times been a compulsory practice, as was the case in Europe as early as the medieval period. In turn, covering one's head also became an act of resistance against such laws, one enforced by rabbis as a way of "transforming their experience of vestimentary apartheid into a condition of Jewish law."[2] The Talmud—the commentary on the Torah, the central text of Judaism—does suggest that covering the head is an appropriate sign of awe or *yirat shamayim* (fear of heaven) before the Divine Presence, though there is no mention of what material or exact form the covering might take (except that it may not be made of wool and linen blend, which Jewish law prohibits).

Precursors to the kippah varied vastly, taking on different forms based on regional differences and surrounding cultures, including various styles of skullcap, the French beret for Yemenite and North African Jews, and the karakul in Uzbekistan and Afghanistan. The close-fitting skullcap is today the most universally recognizable Jewish headgear, its many variants functioning as public symbols of allegiance to a particular sect within Judaism. Hasidic and other very observant Jewish men wear a large black velvet kippah at all times, removing it only to bathe and to sleep, when they leave it on the nightstand to be donned again immediately upon waking. Zionist Jews prefer a knitted or crocheted head covering (the *kippah serugah*), its handmade construction underlining the critique of consumer culture embedded in the kibbutz culture that played a role in founding the modern state of Israel. Disposable kippot are sometimes used to commemorate special occasions; they might bear the event's date and the names of couples getting married or of bat mitzvah celebrants and are often picked up at the entrance to the ceremony.

In the 1970s kippot options flourished: distinctive surface decoration, motifs ranging from cartoon characters to baseball team logos, and multicolored and jazzy textiles embellished the heads of wearers. With this trend the religious head covering definitively entered the realm of fashion, creating new patterns of consumption, display, and identity formation. Almost as important as the kippah itself is securing it to the head, accomplished in a number of ways—with a color-coordinated clip, a bobby pin, a comb, or Velcro. Given the rigors of combat, a secure kippah is especially important for Jewish U.S. military personnel who, along with their Sikh colleagues, won the right to wear "neat and conservative" religious headgear when President Ronald Reagan passed into law the Religious Apparel Amendment in 1988.

Strongly observant married Jewish women have always traditionally covered their heads, be it with wrapped textiles, turbans, or wigs. In the past half-century, which saw the development

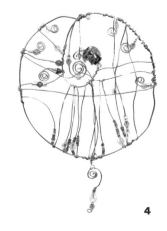

1

4

6

8

of second- and third-wave feminism, some women in liberal Reform congregations have chosen to use kippot instead, selecting traditional versions or ones in distinctive and sometimes overtly gendered colors such as pink or decorated with beads or lace. The New York–based Jewish feminist magazine *Lilith* stoked the debate on this trend in the 1980s and '90s, running articles about whether women should move in this direction.

Contemporary developments include embellishing kippot with everything from LED lighting to emoji patterns and making them using eco-conscious and ethical materials and labor practices. Whether mass-produced or handmade (fashioning and decorating a kippah for an intended romantic target used to be a popular pastime at Jewish summer camps), the kippah is a sartorial statement that bridges the everyday and the sacred and traverses geographic, religious, and secular terrains. —MMF

2

3

5

7

9

Left:
1— Jewish man, Kishinev, in the Russian Empire (now Chişinău, Republic of Moldova), c. 1889. Unknown photographer
2— Crocheted and hand-decorated kippah, designed and made by women artisans of Santiago Atitlán, Guatemala, n.d.
3— Crocheted kippah with Star of David, purchased in 2017
4— Women's kippah handcrafted of copper wire and glass beads, 2017
5— Custom needlepoint kippah for an American bar mitzvah, 2015
6— Suede kippah, purchased in 2017
7— Emoji kippah made in the United States, n.d.
8— A 3-D-printed kippah by computer science professor Craig Kaplan of the University of Waterloo, Ontario, Canada, 2014
9— Crocheted kippah, made in Guatemala, 2017

L — 056

LAPEL PIN The lapel pin exercises considerable agency for the small amount of real estate it occupies; it is a tiny but mighty signifier of achievement and allegiance, whether political, social, cultural, or aesthetic. Usually affixed to a collar using a post-and-clasp system (and sometimes with a horizontal or hinged pin), lapel pins also migrate to bags, coats, and the brims of hats, and they share commonalities of form, function, and meaning with badges, patches, and brooches.

Precious ancient medieval fibulae anticipated the positioning (near the collarbone), rationale (declarations of status, diplomacy, and belonging), and decoration (then, metal or richly colored cloisonné; now, often enamel) of the modern lapel pin. Men's outerwear first incorporated lapels in the nineteenth century, and fashionable fresh or silk boutonnieres were partial inspiration for some later enamel pins.[1] In the late 1890s the National American Woman Suffrage Association produced lapel pins inscribed with the year 1848 (the year of the Seneca Falls Convention, in New York) within a sunflower, which were worn until U.S. women won the right to vote in 1920. Since World War I the red poppy has symbolized commemoration, and in the United Kingdom public officials, royalty, and citizens wear paper poppies around Remembrance Day, on November 11—a tradition so strong that those who do not participate face censure.

The iconic peace sign started its life on the lapels of activists in the Campaign for Nuclear Disarmament. In 1958 Gerald Holtom, a graduate of London's Royal College of Art, created the motif from the positions of semaphore flags spelling out "ND" and painted it on ceramic pins. The red AIDS ribbon, a similarly powerful emblem, first appeared on a public figure when the actor Jeremy Irons wore it to the

Tony Awards in New York in 1991. Conceived by the Visual AIDS Artists' Caucus, it quickly became a staple accoutrement of the red carpet and was rapidly adopted by citizens desperate to raise consciousness of the worldwide pandemic; subsequent global campaigns have used the twisted-ribbon form in a range of colors. The American flag pin has been a fixture of patriotic display since at least the Nixon era, when those in support of the Vietnam War proudly wore it (and protesters sewed the flag onto the seat of their pants).[2]

Lapel pins may also signal membership in certain groups, such as the Girl Guides (with its globally recognized trefoil) or obsessive *Star Trek* fandom (denoted by Starfleet insignia). Most lapel pins are produced in China, although boutique companies have emerged in the last several years; the inventory of the Brooklyn-based company Pintrill includes homages to rap lyrics, emojis, and limited editions created in collaboration with artists, designers, and retailers. In 2016 a controversy erupted over the alleged theft, by the fashion retailer Zara, of pin (and patch) motifs that were copied and sold without license or credit to the original artists.[3] Cheap to produce, lapel pins have become part of the fast-fashion landscape for some, while remaining unchanging fixtures for others. —MMF

Right:
1— **Queen Elizabeth II at the annual Remembrance Sunday ceremony, London, November 11, 2011. Photograph by Eddie Keogh**
2— **President Barack Obama and Republican presidential candidate Mitt Romney, Denver, Colorado, 2012. Photograph by Win McNamee**
3— **Paul Newman and Elizabeth Taylor at the Academy Awards ceremony, Los Angeles, 1992. Photograph by Jim Smeal**
4— **Portrait of Charles Cordier, by Jean-Auguste-Dominique Ingres, 1811**
5— **Young man at a march for nuclear disarmament, U.K., 1966. Unknown photographer**

LE SMOKING Yves Saint Laurent's Le Smoking was revolutionary in its approach to gender. Presented in July 1966 as part of the designer's fall/winter couture collection, it was an adaptation of a classic men's tuxedo for women's evening wear (*le smoking* being how the tuxedo is referred to in French). Gloria Emerson, a *New York Times* reviewer, described the ensemble as comprising a "ruffly white shirt, a big black bow at the neck, a wide cummerbund of satin, and satin stripes down the rather wide pants." Emerson speculated that it had been inspired by the French artist Niki de Saint Phalle, a friend of Saint Laurent's, who had taken to wearing "black tie trouser suits" (and who had contributed sculptures to Saint Laurent's Rive Gauche boutique).[1]

Le Smoking was initially met with a lukewarm reception by the house's established clients—staunch couture wearers accustomed to spending sizeable sums on custom-made gowns—who simply could not fathom the notion of wearing a pantsuit for evening. Saint Laurent had been known for pushing the boundaries of couture's formality since his first collection, in 1962, so this reaction was not surprising. It was the designer's astute understanding of how the fashion climate was being increasingly influenced by a younger generation that allowed for Le Smoking's eventual success. He incorporated the ensemble into his new ready-to-wear label, Saint Laurent Rive Gauche, which launched in September 1966, and it became a hit with a new clientele, one that would not necessarily have bought couture but could afford Rive Gauche's more realistic prices. The new label, which embodied Saint Laurent's vision

of modern fashion, premiered with the opening of a boutique at 21 rue de Tournon in Paris, and marked new territory in luxury ready-to-wear. Its ideal customer, in the words of Saint Laurent's business partner, Pierre Bergé, was a woman "who drove her own car to her office, her desk at the newspaper, or her business."[2] In adapting a menswear garment for women, Saint Laurent reflected the zeitgeist of the 1960s, which saw more women assuming agency rather than deferring to men. Although he softened the suit's tailoring to conform to a woman's body, he retained the angularity of the tuxedo cut and maintained the formal elements so closely affiliated with the rationality and intellect ascribed to menswear. The result was something beyond the old associations: "How do you wear this tuxedo?" asked a writer for *Vogue* Paris in December 1966. "It's such a new uniform that there aren't any rules on the art of wearing one."[3]

Le Smoking was not the first instance of trousers being worn by women for evening (Paul Poiret's *jupe-sultane* and *jupe-culotte* were introduced in 1911, for example),[4] but it was the first to be directly derived from a menswear design. Modern evening clothes for men emerged in the last quarter of the nineteenth century and were named for Tuxedo Park, an enclave of mansions in upstate New York. The suit was conceived by Pierre Lorillard, a resident of the village, whose friend James Brown Potter had been introduced to the dinner jacket—a new style of evening jacket worn by the Prince of Wales (later Edward VII) —by the prince himself. A black, tailless garment reminiscent of a shawl-collared smoking jacket, the dinner jacket gradually replaced the tailcoat for men's semiformal evening wear in England. The tuxedo version caught on and quickly became de rigueur in New York society.

Considered the outward manifestation of man's intelligence and sobriety, men's suits, in the words of the historian Anne Hollander, embodied "the image of unadorned masculine perfection . . . an abstract statue of the naked hero carved according to tailors' rules."[5] Saint Laurent's co-opting of this powerful signifier for women, within a trajectory of fashion long dominated by extravagant gowns with artificial silhouettes and elaborate detail, was groundbreaking. Indeed, when put together with stiletto heels and dramatic makeup, Le Smoking constructed an uncompromising image of femininity, one devoid of any association with delicacy or frivolity. Helmut Newton captured this idea in the 1970s in a series of photographs in which shadowy film noir–style backdrops, angular postures, and hints of androgyny further destabilize the links between femininity and fragility.

The significance of Le Smoking has since shifted in ways Saint Laurent could not have predicted, confirming outdated notions of gendered dress rather than shattering old stereotypes. Hari Nef, the transgender model and writer, has observed of a famous Newton photograph, "The discourse around this image is that a woman . . . gains this power, this sort of dominance, this sexiness from donning a man's suit. But if she is sourcing this new sense of power and sexiness . . . from a signifier of a masculinity, then how sustainable is that as a power source?"[6] Such questioning of the suit's patriarchal power, in the sectors of contemporary culture that have begun to challenge the binary construction of gender, gives the iconic ensemble a new position in the discourse of fashion. Nevertheless, Le Smoking remains one of the most fascinating, controversial, and influential designs in modern fashion history. —SK

Right:
1— Catherine Deneuve with Yves Saint Laurent at the opening of the first Saint Laurent Rive Gauche boutique, Paris, 1966. Photograph by Alain Nogues
2— Bianca Jagger arriving at Heathrow Airport, London, 1972
3— Helmut Newton, *Retro Verseau, French Vogue, 1979*, 1979

1

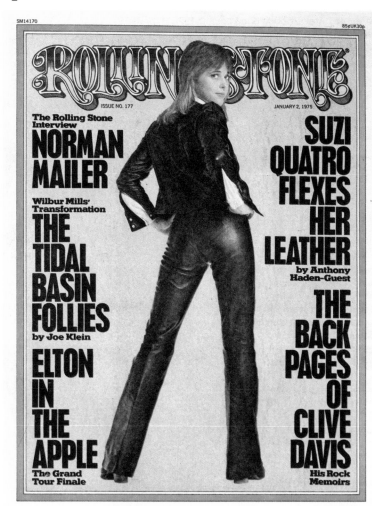

2

LEATHER PANTS In the American West, herders on horseback have typically worn pants made of rawhide or tanned leather.[1] These are known as chaps and derive from Native American buckskins as well as the riding wear of Mesoamerican vaqueros, which in turn was influenced by Spanish dress—in particular that of Spanish landowners in the region of Salamanca, who wore low-crowned hats, bolero jackets, sashes, tight-fitting trousers, and spurred boots.[2] Chaps are made to be worn over trousers and have no seat and no crotch piece; the two legs are joined at the waist by a belt. (Originally, the leather was simply wrapped around the legs and attached to the saddle.) The leather provides a barrier against the elements as well as the sharp brush and cactus plants native to the American West. The chaps (and jackets) worn by charros—gentleman ranchers of Mexico—typically featured a fringe of leather strips that served to dispel water; they started influencing North American Western wear in the 1830s. The arrival to the West of American frontiersmen such as Daniel Boone and Davy Crockett, who adopted aspects of local dress, helped establish the cowboy as a classic trope of masculinity.

In the early twentieth century, the image of the solitary, rugged American cowboy was romanticized in Hollywood westerns, and his getup ultimately made the leap from function—and costume— to fashion in a mash-up of Western wear and motorcycle gear (see *Biker Jacket*). Many subcultures saw the attire worn by outlier personas such as the cowboy and the biker as adaptable symbols of transgression. During the 1960s, for example, The Doors front man Jim Morrison consistently wore a pair of custom-made, skintight brown leather pants cut to look like the Levi's jeans favored by cowboys (see *501s*). They were inspired by the snakeskin jacket Marlon Brando wore in the 1960 film *The Fugitive Kind*—a look described by his fellow band member Ray Manzarek as "like a black mamba."[3] Morrison's leather pants signified both a raw eroticism and nostalgic visions of the American West, thus helping to build another archetype of male masculinity: the sexually charged male rock star.

In the following years, female musicians from Suzi Quatro to Debbie Harry to Joan Jett and Chrissie Hynde appropriated leather pants to challenge stereotypes of gender in music. In a 1977 interview with *Rolling Stone,* Quatro explained the impact of skintight leather on her fans (described by the magazine as "those adoring girls in their rough-tough leather stuff") by stating, "I think they see me as representative of a changing world. I mean, when I started doing what I'm doing . . . a girl couldn't play bass. But now it's not so strange."[4] Leather pants became a rock and roll staple suitable for disparate genres—from hard rock to glam rock to punk to heavy metal to hip-hop. In 1978 they were also brought firmly into the mainstream with the wildly successful musical film *Grease,* in which costume designer Albert Wolsky used skintight leather pants to signal the climactic sea change from demure ingénue to smoking-hot sexpot for Olivia Newton-John's character Sandy Olsson (opposite John Travolta's Danny Zuko).

Concurrent to their rise in the music scene, leather pants also assumed a major role in the sartorial practices of gay subcultures, beginning in the 1950s, "when disenchanted ex-servicemen with a penchant for rough sex and motorcycles had begun putting together a 'heavy' look."[5] When the first gay biker club in the United States, the Satyrs, was formed in Los Angeles in 1954, there were no purveyors of ready-made leather sex clothes, so biker pants were acquired from Harley-Davidson and chaps came from Western-wear shops. Within twenty years, as underground gay clubs began to proliferate, the leather look codified a culture that celebrated hypermasculinity via bondage, dominance, sadomasochism, and role play. In this arena, chaps are frequently worn not over denim but with nothing but a jockstrap (often leather) underneath, for maximum exposure. Artists like Tom of

Finland and Robert Mapplethorpe, whose stylized drawings and explicit photographs, respectively, of leather clubs and BDSM practitioners helped take the fetish look to the mainstream but also sparked questions of censorship that brought the scene to the American national consciousness.

Sexy, pliable, and fitting like a second skin, leather pants naturally found their way into the collections of many fashion designers. Gianni Versace's controversial 1992 leather collection of S/M–inspired leather pants (and dresses) was simultaneously criticized for objectifying women and praised for empowering their sexuality.[6] In 1996 Alexander McQueen introduced his infamous low-slung leather "bumster" trousers, cut so low in the back as to expose the crevice of the buttocks. Within this high-fashion realm, leather pants have come to symbolize both subversive notions of sexuality and mainstream ideas of cool in one simple garment, the latter embodied in *Vogue* in 1996 by model Stella Tennant in a slick, slim pair by Jean-Claude Jitrois, epitomizing 1990s downtown chic. —AB

Previous page:
1— Bill Murray (New York), Guy Baldwin (Los Angeles), and Mitch Davis (Boston) accepting their awards at the International Mr. Leather contest, Chicago, 1989. Unknown photographer
2— Suzi Quatro on the cover of *Rolling Stone,* January 1975. Unknown photographer

Right:
3— Jim Morrison during a Doors concert, Frankfurt, 1968. Photograph by Michael Ochs
4— Stella Tennant in leather pants, *Vogue,* December 1996/January 1997. Photograph by Jean-Baptiste Mondino

LEOTARD Worn by dancers, gymnasts, roller disco aficionados, and stylish professionals alike, the leotard is a fashion crossover whose success lies in its adaptability to everyday life. When designer Bonnie August joined Danskin in 1975, the New York–based company had primarily been associated with dancewear and knitted activewear, having supplied tights, tutus, and leotards to dancers since its founding in 1882. Creating imaginative variations on the company's classic leotard, including styles with surplice detailing, plunging necklines, and spaghetti straps, August not only helped broaden Danskin's appeal, but also contributed to the cultivation of the body-conscious look of the late 1970s. Though August's other designs for Danskin (stirrup tights, crop tops, and leggings) helped nurture the body-wear aesthetic of the period, it was her leotard that triumphed, arming women with a versatile garment that could be worn as easily under a pair of jeans as over a pair of workout leggings. With the introduction of a wrap skirt to further ease the transition from the dance studio, August earned a prestigious Coty American Fashion Critics' Award in 1978 (fashion's highest honor at the time), prompting Danskin to rebrand its image with the clever tagline "Danskins Are Not Just for Dancing."

The leotard owes its name to the nineteenth-century French acrobat and international sensation Jules Léotard, who redesigned his costume into a one-piece knitted suit that was gusseted between the legs and cut low on the neck, allowing for ease of movement while minimizing the danger of becoming entangled in the trapeze ropes. Originally referred to as a maillot, the garment resembled a skimpier version of men's knitted bathing costumes of the time. By emphasizing Léotard's physique, it contributed to his fame, which culminated in the popular 1867 music-hall

song "The Daring Young Man on the Flying Trapeze."

In the first half of the twentieth century, the leotard was promoted by modern-dance pioneer Martha Graham. The term *leotard* was applied liberally at the time, encompassing also a legged version now known as a unitard. The flexibility the garment afforded soon led to its being embraced by another demographic: college-age women. For a September 1943 cover story on leotards, *Life* magazine featured two models sporting versions by contemporary designers, including Claire McCardell, proclaiming that the popularity of "acrobats' tights" lay in the fact that "college girls, although allegedly faddists, like to be comfortable . . . with nothing but a brassiere or panties underneath, a skirt or a jumper over, a girl can be snug and warm indoors or out."[1]

The leotard continued to serve on-the-go women throughout the twentieth century, from countercultural beatniks in the 1950s (both authentically and as typecast by the media) to off-duty dancers à la Broadway's 1975 production *A Chorus Line.* The leotard's emergence in the 1980s as a multipurpose power garment, as perfected by Donna Karan (see *Seven Easy Pieces*), proved the ultimate testament to its practicality, bringing the garment full circle as an expression of prowess and adaptability. —SK

Previous page:
1— Jules Léotard in a hand-colored carte de visite, mid-nineteenth century
2— American gymnast Simone Biles during the Artistic Gymnastics competition at the 2016 Summer Olympics, Rio de Janeiro. Photograph by Tim Clayton

Right:
3— Promotional poster for Danskin, c. 1980
4— Picture from a feature promoting short leotards, a new college fashion trend, *Life,* 1943. Photograph by Philippe Halsman

LITTLE BLACK DRESS "Ten out of ten women have one," proclaimed *Vogue* in 1944, "but ten out of ten want another because the little black dress leads the best-rounded life. [It] is a complete chameleon about moods and times and places. [It] has the highest potential chic (only if well-handled). [It] has the longest open season."[1] Indeed, the little black dress is a fashion phenomenon whose centrality in the vernacular of fashion has been rivaled only by the attention it has received from scholars.

The concept of the little black dress was born in 1926, when *Vogue* featured a sketch of Gabrielle "Coco" Chanel's black crepe de chine long-sleeved sheath alongside the caption "The Chanel 'Ford' —the frock that all the world will wear."[2] Considered trailblazing in its use of a color that had generally been associated with mourning, and innovative in its versatile silhouette suggestive of the day's tennis and bathing costumes, the dress's comparison with a Ford car implied the efficiency of the Model T's assembly-line production but also emphasized the practicality of its color: in 1923 Henry Ford famously said, "Any customer can have a car painted any color that he wants so long as it is black."[3] This early exposure in *Vogue,* augmented by Chanel's own self-promotion, led to the little black dress becoming synonymous with the designer for decades to come.

Yet fashion historians have debunked the mythology surrounding the little black dress: it was neither an invention of Chanel's nor the first instance of black being worn as a fashionable color rather than a symbol of mourning. Expensive to produce with natural dyes, black textiles had long conveyed the wealth and refinement of the upper classes, as in the case of fifteenth-century Spanish aristocracy. The introduction of aniline dyes in the nineteenth century made the hue more accessible, and black attire began to be associated with the lower classes (due, likely, to its obscuring of stains). When the color was adopted by fashionable women of the era, it was considered a statement—as famously captured in John Singer Sargent's 1884 painting *Portrait of Madame X*, in which socialite Virginie Gautreau is dressed in a form-fitting, décolletage-revealing black evening gown.

Chanel herself declared, "Scheherazade is easy; a little black dress is difficult." Historically, the garment has served as a way to explore symbolic associations: sophistication, elegance, sex, power, rebellion, and charisma. It is neither overstated nor understated; it conveys precisely what is needed in any context. "The little black dress is not a style per se," the fashion historian Valerie Steele has opined, "but it's a conceptual fashion that's entirely versatile. There are many ways to design it. It's modern, it changes, but it's always the same. And it's always a kind of chic armor."[4] The long black Givenchy dress Audrey Hepburn wears as Holly Golightly in the opening scene of the 1961 film *Breakfast at Tiffany's,* as she peers into the windows of the legendary New York jeweler while nibbling a pastry and sipping coffee, perfectly encapsulates this notion. A sleeveless gown with a fitted bodice, slightly gathered skirt, and elegant cut-outs revealing the shoulder blades, it has an air of effortlessness mirrored by the nonchalance with which the character enjoys her early morning breakfast while decked out in full evening attire.

The sartorial mystique of the little black dress is highlighted by its emphasis on silhouette. This has manifested in a variety of forms, from demure, full-skirted designs of the 1950s reflective of Christian Dior's waist-accentuating New Look to Azzedine Alaïa's signature 1980s micro-knit "fit and flares." A more recent example is Rick Owens's 2014 take—a two-piece composed of short sheaths of futuristic materials and embellishments and modeled by members of American step teams, conveying strength and rebellion.

In constancy, the little black dress's color is second only to its mutability, which offers a metaphor for fashion itself. "Fashion is . . . like a vampire," Steele has asserted. "It's undead. . . . The promise of fashion is always that you're going to be reborn with a new look."[5] This notion is exemplified by Thierry Mugler's 1981 version, which pushed the silhouette to the extreme. Featuring a corseted bodice, cinched waist, and short skirt overlaid with a nineteenth-century-inspired peplum, Mugler's vampirish dress (complete with a fanglike neckline) represented his ideal of a sexy, modern powerful woman. Taking up the mantle in the twenty-first century is the American design duo Nervous System, whose 2014 Kinematics Dress, composed of thousands of interlocking nylon pieces, is produced using a 3-D printer; it is as elegant as any of its conventionally crafted predecessors. Timeless but ever evolving, the little black dress has allowed its wearers to summon fashion's past while simultaneously pushing the limits of possibility into its future.
—SK

Previous page:
1— "The Chanel 'Ford'— the frock that all the world will wear," in an illustration by Mainbocher, *Vogue*, October 1926
2— American step team performing on the runway for Rick Owens's spring/summer 2014 collection show, Paris, 2014
3— Nervous System's Kinematics Dress, with 2,279 unique triangular panels and 3,316 hinges, 3-D-printed as a single piece, 2014. Photograph by Steve Marsel Studio
4— Dress by Thierry Mugler, 1981
5— Givenchy evening dress in black satin, black cording, sequins, and jet beads, 1968

LOAFER The loafer is a laceless, un-lined leather shoe with a low or flat heel.[1] The penny loafer, a variant that features a moccasin-style seamed upper that includes an instep strap incised with a small decorative slit, was a sartorial staple for numerous twentieth-century subcultures, from British teddy boys and mods to Jamaican rude boys and American preps, and has become a mainstay of Western footwear.

While the loafer has a broad and ancient precedent in the Native American moccasin, the penny loafer has its roots in a leather slip-on shoe that Norwegian peasants wore starting in the early 1900s.[2] Before long, sportsmen from the Continent who traveled to Norway to fish adopted the style, and through them it found its way to the rest of Europe. From there the look spread to North America, and in 1936 its stylishness was confirmed in the pages of *Esquire* magazine, in illustrations documenting the Norwegian-style footwear being worn at the fashionable resorts of Palm Beach, Florida.[3] The American manufacturer Bass jumped on the trend, and the loafer it released the same year—called the Weejun in reference to its Norwegian origins—would soon become the standard.[4] Available in shiny black and brown leather, Weejuns could be dressed up and were often paired with a single-breasted suit jacket and cuffed chino trousers as part of the preppy "Ivy League" look popular with young American men in the 1940s and '50s.[5] Conversely, the loafer's simplicity and comfort made it ideal for the increasingly informal dress of the postwar era (a Bass advertisement from 1962 described it as "a symbol of elegant leisure"). At some point, young Americans of both genders, whether for playful or practical reasons, began slipping shiny pennies into the decorative slit on the shoe's instep—hence the term "penny loafer."

This Americanized version of the loafer is what the Italian fashion house Gucci encountered when it opened its first stateside boutique in the early 1950s. Not to be left out of the trend, Gucci produced a luxury take on it, using calfskin leather in a range of colors. The snaffle horse bit that Gucci later placed across the vamp was a trademark detail that made its loafer a signifier of wealth and taste for the remainder of the century.

Celebrities of all kinds have worn classic penny loafers over the decades, but it was Michael Jackson, the "King of Pop," who literally put the shoes center stage in the 1980s, incorporating them into the elaborate costumes he donned for his performances. Jackson's influence, combined with a cultural nostalgia for the preppy look of the 1950s, ensured that the penny loafer's popularity soared again in this decade. The casual minimalist style of the 1990s saw penny loafers paired with light-washed form-fitting denim and simple, comfortable knitwear, and the recent surge of interest in heritage brands has kept these old-school shoes current, affirming their enduring relevance and adaptability. —LB

Previous pages:
1— **Michael Jackson performing "Billie Jean" on the TV special** *Motown 25: Yesterday, Today, Forever*, **1983. Photograph by Paul Drinkwater**
2— **Advertisement for Toflers loafers, 1936**
3— **Moccasins made by Sioux women of the Pine Ridge Reservation, South Dakota, 1970. Photograph by Dave Buresh**
4— **Student Anna McCann, Wellesley College, Wellesley, Massachusetts,** *Holiday*, **1954. Unknown photographer**
5— **Rude boys Chuka and Dubem Okonkwo, the "Islington twins," London, 1981. Photograph by Janette Beckman**

MANICURE The word *manicure* broadly means "care of the hands" (Latin: *cura* and *manus),* which usually includes nail trimming and buffing, cuticle maintenance, skin moisturizing, and hand massage in addition to nail polishing. Maintaining pampered nails and soft hands has always been a signifier of economic status, given their centrality to manual labor. Recorded across cultures and millennia, dyed nails were historically common in parts of North Africa, the Arabian Peninsula, South Asia (using henna), and China (beeswax lacquer).

In the Western world, nails were generally colored with tinted powders that were buffed on until the development of a colored liquid nail enamel by the American company Cutex in 1917.[1] The suntan, made fashionable by Gabrielle "Coco" Chanel (among others) in the 1920s, was the perfect foil to the deep red nail lauded as the epitome of chic.

Cosmetics giant Revlon, formed in 1932, initially specialized in nail polish, a recession-proof affordable luxury. The naming of nail colors played an important role in helping the consumer try on new identities. Revlon's 1952 bright-red Fire and Ice, for example—advertised with a personality questionnaire—was positioned as a nail polish for bold, adventurous, and emancipated women (see *Red Lipstick*). It crystalized the tension around cosmetics in general (and painted nails in particular) in the twentieth century: increasingly part of an independent modern woman's public identity and yet still associated with the artificiality of "those icons of deception, actresses and whores" (see *YSL Touche Éclat*).[2]

The 1970s birthed the tawny, white-tipped French manicure, and chipped polish and muddy dark tones emerged as a style for both sexes—worn by gender-bending rock musicians Freddie Mercury and Lou Reed as a means to subvert what fashion designer André Courrèges declared to

be "obviously outdated sexual references —the red lips, red nails, black eyebrows."[3] Technical innovations like self-adhesive press-on nails and acrylic nail extensions provided the durability needed for longer nail lengths that helped bring artistic expression (with the use of pens, stencils, and appliqués) to new heights—as epitomized by Olympian Florence Griffith Joyner's elaborately decorated six-inch nails.[4]

The manicure is now an $8.5 billion annual industry. Nail salons operated by Vietnamese and Korean immigrants began to proliferate in the United States in the late twentieth century, transforming the marketplace by offering fast and inexpensive walk-in manicures.[5] At the same time, the aesthetics of the manicure were profoundly shaped by a small subset of celebrated and sought-after nail artists such as New York–based Bernadette Thompson, who created the "money manicure" for rapper Lil' Kim in the early 1990s using strips of U.S. paper currency, as well as Japanese innovator Sachiko Nakasone, who pioneered 3-D nail art.

Today nail polish is used as a vehicle for brand extension by designers, companies, and celebrities. Perhaps the most famous has been Chanel's 1994 Vamp, developed under the tenure of Karl Lagerfeld, a color that sold out almost immediately, instigated waiting lists, and was memorably described by *Washington Post* critic Robin Givhan as possessing "the gloomy blackberry tones of dried blood."[6] —MMF

Left:

1— Model Ina Balke with nude nails, *Glamour*, **1964. Photograph by Gene Laurents**
2— Raimund von Stillfried, *Fille de Lanxchow* **(Daughter of Lanxchow), 1870s**
3— Manicurist at work creating complex acrylic nail art, Japan, n.d. Unknown photographer
4— American track-and-field athlete Florence Griffith Joyner holding her medals at the Summer Olympics in Seoul, 1989. Photograph by Tony Duffy

M — 063

MAO JACKET In 1974, after returning from a trip to China, the French semiotician Roland Barthes recorded his impressions of the Chinese people: "As for the body, the obvious disappearance of all coquetry (neither fashion nor make-up), the uniformity of clothes, the prose of gestures, all these absences, multiplied along a dense crowd, invite this incredible feeling . . . : that the body is no longer to be understood, that there, it insists not to signify, not to be caught in an erotic or dramatic reading."[1] The Chinese sartorial landscape that puzzled and frustrated Barthes was a sea of so-called Mao suits—all-purpose, loose-fitting ensembles worn by both men and women in the subdued colors of black, dark blue, gray, or khaki green.

A modified military uniform, the Mao suit consisted of a jacket with a high, turned-down collar and matching trousers. The men's jacket featured four symmetrically placed front pockets, whereas the women's usually had just two pockets, either on the chest or below the waist. This outfit was first popularized in the early 1920s by Sun Yat-sen, the founding father of the Republic of China, and it is better known among the Chinese as a *Zhongshan zhuang* (Sun Yat-sen suit). Incorporating elements drawn from German military uniforms, the neatly tailored Zhongshan suit represented a newly disciplined, modernized China and embodied Sun's revolutionary spirit and democratic agenda. In 1929 the Nationalist Party officially adopted the Zhongshan suit as formal attire; Mao Tse-tung and other male leaders of the Communist Party began to wear it in the late 1920s. "Progressive" Communist women, such as Mao's wife Jiang Qing, sported modified versions of the Zhongshan suit, in a symbolic rejection of bourgeois femininity and a celebration of empowered proletarian womanhood. Firmly associated with the ultra-Communist ideology of progression,

liberation, and egalitarianism in Mao's China (1949–76), the Zhongshan suit gained the new name *renmin zhuang* (people's suit) or simply *zhifu* (uniform), and it was the state-sanctioned clothing style for daily life from the mid-1950s to the mid-'70s. Driven by a heightened sentiment opposed to feudalism and capitalism, the elegantly structured form of the Zhongshan suit gradually gave way to a baggy style for both genders, an outfit that obscured sexual difference and subsumed the body into an ideological vision of class solidarity and gender equality. During the Cultural Revolution of 1966–76, Mao mobilized the Red Guards—a student paramilitary movement—against Communist Party members and city dwellers suspected of bourgeois habits. The uniform of the Red Guards was a "people's suit" in khaki green, with the addition of a belt and a red armband with Mao's slogan. The strident military style expressed a revolutionary zeal, an anarchist passion disguised as a totalitarian pursuit of order.

 In the West the so-called Mao jacket is anchored more in a romanticized vision of Maoist China and the Cultural Revolution than in any clearly defined original or authentic Chinese style. It first appeared in Paris in 1967, the year that a craze for Maoism seized French intellectuals and university students. The advent of the Cultural Revolution a year earlier had excited French Maoists, who saw in it a promising model for overturning French bourgeois society. A new style of structured jacket featuring a standing collar, initiated by French designer Gilbert Feruch in 1965, swept Parisian streets. This style is now often called a Nehru jacket, after the Indian prime minister, but in 1967 it was unmistakably tied to Mao, which led American *Vogue* to report that "in Paris, the great leap forward is into the 'Mao' suit. . . . The rigidly constructed, austere costumes . . . are not worn by the Chinese but by a goodly part of *le tout Paris*."[2] The Mao suit was one iteration of the utopian youth fashion of the late 1960s: an "intellectual chic" merged with a future-oriented "techno-chic."

 Despite his indifference to the Chinese revolution and his somewhat veiled criticism of China and Chinese clothing in the 1970s,[3] Barthes chose to pose in an authentic Mao jacket—probably obtained in China—in a series of portraits taken in the mid-to-late 1970s. The overloaded surface symbolism of the Mao jacket,

combined with its semiotic opacity, is a close parallel to Barthes's perception of the fundamental inauthenticity of photographic portraits.[4] Deliberate inauthenticity also defines the artist Tseng Kwong Chi's self-portrait series made between 1979 and 1989, in which the central character is a Mao suit. A Hong Kong–born Chinese/Canadian/American, Tseng never lived in Communist China. Posing in the outfit at iconic Western sites such as the Statue of Liberty and the Eiffel Tower and blatantly titling his photographs *East Meets West*, Tseng employed the Mao suit to perform a parody of both monumentality and identity. —MMR

Left:
1— **Mao Tse-tung with his wife Jiang Qing, c. 1945. Unknown photographer**
2— **Red Guards during the Cultural Revolution, China, 1966. Unknown photographer**
3— **Tseng Kwong Chi, *East Meets West: New York, New York*, 1979**
4— **Roland Barthes, Paris, 1978. Photograph by Sophie Bassouls**

MINISKIRT   A symbol of women's liberation, youth culture, and modern design, the miniskirt has been a subject of fascination from the moment it emerged in the 1960s—mythologized, analyzed, and even used as a barometer for economic prosperity.[1] Attempts to definitively attribute the miniskirt to a single "inventor"—typically either Mary Quant or Parisian couturier André Courrèges—have been mostly unsuccessful. Quant herself dismissed the notion that she, or any one person, created the style. "Fashion, as I see it, is inevitable," she has said. "It wasn't me or Courrèges who invented the miniskirt anyway—it was the girls in the street who did it."[2] There is no disputing, however, that Quant played a fundamental role in popularizing it. In 1955, in collaboration with her friend Archie McNair and her future husband, Alexander Plunket Greene, she opened a shop called Bazaar in London's Chelsea neighborhood, which was the site of a growing youth counterculture. Quant, who was in her twenties at the time, felt that clothing for her age group simply did not exist, so she decided to offer designs of her own that reflected the energy of "swinging London." She was inspired by a range of looks, from the minimal, monochromatic uniforms of Chelsea's beatniks to the short skirt, tights, and patent-leather shoes worn by a girl in a tap dancing class she remembered from her childhood. By 1958 Quant had introduced above-the-knee skirts, often paired with brightly colored tights, which would soon become her signature and would eventually inch their way even further up the thigh.[3] Around the same time, Courrèges was also experimenting with youth-oriented styles but through the lens of the future-facing space age (see *Space Age*). Although Courrèges proposed above-the-knee skirts starting in the early 1960s, it was his spring/summer 1964 collection

that solidified his association with the style. Favoring a stark and futuristic aesthetic, Courrèges paired the miniskirt with calf-high white-leather boots and showed it alongside sculpted tunics and high-fashion pants, another revolutionary look for women. He would eventually claim, "I was the man who invented the mini. Mary Quant only commercialized the idea."[4]

The miniskirt changed the direction of fashion with regard to women's bodies. By flaunting their legs rather than hiding them, women signaled their rejection of traditional notions of ladylike propriety and the sartorial rules that reinforced them. First adopted by young women (in the face of resistance from parents and teachers), the miniskirt was soon embraced by customers of all ages and taken up by many designers. Emerging in an era that saw the invention of the birth control pill and other advances for women, the style came to symbolize their sexual freedom, although it was also the target of disdain and, in some parts of the world, prohibition.[5]

Requiring very little material and simple in construction, the miniskirt was relatively affordable, and even more so when it became part of the trend for disposable clothing. In 1967 the British paper company Dispo (Meyersohn & Silverstein Ltd) made a cheap version from a bonded cellulose fiber, called Bondina, that could withstand washing and be worn at least six times.[6] With a bold design inspired by ancient Egyptian writing, the simple skirt called attention to its wearer. As the fashion historian James Laver put it, "Long, hampering skirts were fetters to keep a woman at home. The very short ones scream: 'I am stepping out.'"[7] The miniskirt reached its apogee in 1969 with what became known as the "micro-mini," and, although it lived on, by the following year the midi and the maxi lengths were equally popular, prompting *Vogue* to announce, "This is the year to do your own thing with your hemline."[8]

The miniskirt was the culmination of the hemline's long history as a site for debates about women's bodies and attempts to regulate them. When the tuberculosis bacterium was discovered in 1882, for example, doctors blamed long, trailing skirts for sweeping up germs on the streets and infecting their wearers. Hemline fluctuations were limited to a few inches near the ankle and foot until the 1920s, when young women started

revealing a lot more leg with styles that hit just below the knee, including an asymmetrical design called the "handkerchief hem." The "controversy over the lengthened hem-line, the uneven hem-line and the shortened hem-line," as *Vogue* described it in 1921, involved questions about what was "decent," which came up again with the emergence of the miniskirt.[9] In 1966 Dr. William E. Mosher, commissioner of the Erie County Health Department in upstate New York, warned of the perils of wearing miniskirts in frigid weather: "Hemlines 3 to 4 inches above the knee expose more of the lower extremities." However, in a testament to the agency encapsulated by the miniskirt, Mosher was also compelled to acknowledge that "the decision to wear or not wear a miniskirt still depends on the individual female."[10] —SK

Left:
1— Gloria Steinem being interviewed for a *Time* magazine profile, 1968. Photograph by Carey Winfrey
2— Brittany Murphy, Alicia Silverstone, and Stacey Dash in the film *Clueless*, 1995
3— High school girls pose for a formal portrait, c. 1925. Unknown photographer
4— Mary Quant adjusting a miniskirt on a model, 1967. Unknown photographer

MONOGRAM Monograms are identity markers formed from the initials of a name. Assimilated into human dress etiquette and social customs, early European monograms took the form of royal seals and artisanal marks, often derived from heraldry and family crests. From the Middle Ages to the present day, the monogram has functioned as a distinctive symbol of authorship, ownership, and social status.

In the industrial era, monograms took on new cultural—and legal—significance. As mass production distanced maker from buyer, and as products (and images) became easily reproducible, copyright, patent, and trademark law became major design considerations. At the same time, the professionalization of advertising engendered the notion of brand identification, and the monogram was deployed as both company sign (think of the interlocking initials of Yves Saint Laurent and Gucci, for example) and as surface decoration that exponentially enhanced the marketability and pricing of the garments and accessories it graced.

As a merchant class emerged, so too did desire for identity symbols comparable to those of titled families, and so monograms proliferated in the Victorian era, finding their way not only to silverware and letterhead but also to clothing, which provided retailers and consumers alike a rich and diverse platform for the display of such signifiers. Monogramming in this period was also practical, establishing ownership of items put into public circulation, as with a garment sent for laundering. This practice continues today with initials inscribed on clothing en route to camp or boarding school or machine-embroidered on towels, backpacks, or the ubiquitous L.L.Bean tote bag.

Fashion monograms originate in products for the elite, such as couture. There the monogram is rooted in the early garment labeling of nineteenth-century Paris, when licensing, franchising, and copying became standard practices. Luxury goods for travel are another origin point, with luggage maker Louis Vuitton a prominent early example. In the late nineteenth century, the company integrated sturdy canvas into an innovative design for stackable, light, and water-resistant suitcases. To discourage copying, canvas printed with Vuitton's initials was introduced in 1896.

The 1960s and '70s saw an explosion of monogram deployment by designers, including Karl Lagerfeld, who introduced the double-F insignia for Fendi in 1965, and James Galanos, who referenced his roots in a summer 1970 dress decorated with his name in Greek lettering. But while fashion houses in the postwar era have used monograms to affirm the status quo, others use them to subvert existing norms and rules. In the 1980s and early '90s, self-taught designer Dapper Dan (born Daniel Day) sold custom clothing for African American celebrities from his Harlem storefront, emphasizing the exuberant appropriation of monograms. In the late 1990s the Dapper Dan aesthetic was then resampled by the luxury lines themselves, with Fendi, Vuitton, Gucci, and others adopting bold, repeat patterns in homage. In today's environment, in which appropriation is a form of authenticity, authorship is fluid, and individuals consider themselves to be social-media brands, the practice of monogramming reflects the ever closer intertwining of self and symbol. —JT

Right:
1— Work by the Brooklyn-based artist GucciGhost (Trevor Andrew), 2016. Photograph by Kevin Tachman
2— Olympic sprinter Diane Dixon in a custom-made Dapper Dan jacket, Dapper Dan's Boutique, New York, 1989. Unknown photographer
3— Model in a Gucci skirt with motifs inspired by GucciGhost, *Harper's Bazaar* Spain, 2016. Photograph by Michael Schwartz

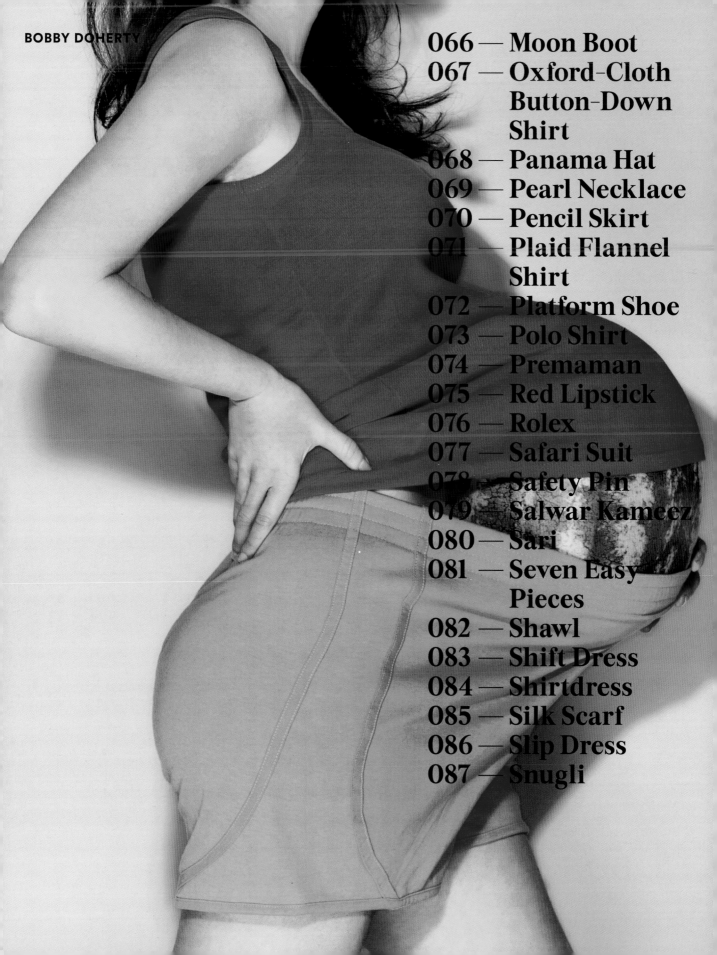

BOBBY DOHERTY

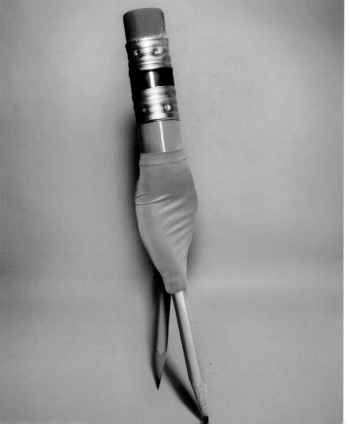

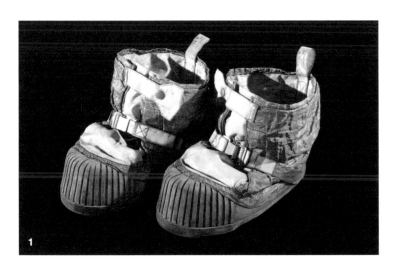

MOON BOOT   The Moon Boot is a trademarked type of outdoor footwear designed for cold, snowy, and wet weather. Introduced in 1970 by the Italian winter-sports company Tecnica, it was the brain-child of company cofounder Giancarlo Zanatta, a second-generation bootmaker who, after witnessing the glory of the first moon landing the previous year, was moved to create a boot based on the shape and technology of the Apollo 11 astronauts' lunar footwear. The name has since been applied to countless examples of similar design and concept.

The boots in which Neil Armstrong and Buzz Aldrin took the famous "giant leap for mankind" in 1969 were designed to protect against extreme lunar surface temperatures as well as abrasion from unpredictably sharp dust-covered rocks. An inner boot, composed of non-flammable, honeycomb elastomer, served as a pressure chamber, providing comfort, and was equipped with a flexible sole for wear within the spacecraft. The outer boot was strapped over the inner boot, like a galosh, for walking on the moon. Twelve layers of chemically stable and insulating materials, including Mylar and Dacron, as well as a silicone sole with quarter-inch tread and a covering con-structed from a stainless-steel textile, provided protection from wear and tear.[1] Zanatta's Moon Boot, though not as technologically advanced, offers similar features for the outdoors enthusiast, particularly for winter wear. Composed of polyurethane foam for insulation and covered in waterproof nylon, the boot's thin rubber outsole and foam-rubber midsole provide traction in snow while simultaneously suggesting the effect of a low-gravity moon bounce. Just like the outer boots worn by astronauts, Moon Boots lack differentiation between the right and left foot. Initially manufactured in a variety of bright colors and prominently featuring the brand name across the shaft—rendered in the bubbly Amelia typeface (designed by Stan Davis in 1964) that was used for the title of the Beatles' 1969 album *Yellow Submarine*—Moon Boots were quickly adopted as a practical and fashionable après-ski accessory at European alpine resorts.

The Moon Boot's early popularity reflected the general fascination with space travel that pervaded fashion in the 1960s and early '70s. Collections by leading Parisian designers Pierre Cardin and André Courrèges were directly inspired by outer space; the former launched his geometric Cosmos line in 1964 (see *Space Age*) and the latter incorporated vinyl and plastic into simple A-line dresses, even introducing helmetlike hats. The Moon Boot, though by no means a budget purchase (costing about 7,500 lire in 1972, the rough equivalent of $75 today), nonetheless made this high-design trend accessible to a wider audience.[2]

Curiously, after a lull in the 1990s, in 2004 Moon Boots experienced a sharp increase in popularity among fashion-conscious American women, who took to wearing them with dresses and jeans even on mild days. Described in the *New York Times* as "a true rarity, a fashion fad that seems to have surfaced spontaneously," the Moon Boot revival was soon taken up by designers worldwide, from Marc Jacobs to Christian Dior. Though the *New York Times* attempted to pinpoint the origin of the sudden trend to the footwear's appearance in Anna Sui's fall/winter 2003 runway show, it seems unlikely that a single source generated the fad.[3] Perhaps the Moon Boot's twenty-first-century resurgence was in part a reaction to the ubiquity of the Ugg sheepskin boot in the early 2000s or, simply, to the timelessness of its functionality. A predecessor of both Uggs and Moon Boots can be found in various prehistoric boot forms, including the kamiks of the Dorset—and eventually Inuit—culture of the North America Arctic, which feature inner and outer layers made of the fur and skin of seals and caribou.

In 2017 the London-based concept-footwear designer Liz Ciokajlo reimagined the Moon Boot for the twenty-first century, developing the Mars Boot, grown from a combination of water and mycelium. While Tecnica's original Moon Boot was a reflection of a material culture based on synthetics, exemplified by the space age, Ciokajlo's Mars Boot evolves the typology toward a future of human life on Mars, where materials are scarce and the ecosystem tenuous. The quantity of matter needed to produce the boot is minimal; Ciokajlo envisions the loading of mycelium spores onto a spacecraft and the use of a space traveler's filtered sweat to feed their growth while en route to Mars. Encouraging wearers to visualize a life in which their own bodies may be a material source for fashion, the Mars Boot is the ultimate foil to the highly inorganic Moon Boot. While the Moon Boot embodied a utopian vision of the future, the Mars Boot references a dystopian view of our neighboring planet's scarcity, reflective of the 1897 H. G. Wells novel *The War of the Worlds*. Though still a concept, the Mars Boot highlights the appeal of space exploration for designers. With 23.5 million pairs sold as of 2016,[4] the terrestrial Moon Boot, and the world's enduring fascination with it, is a testament to the hope, optimism, and wonder embodied by its lunar forerunner. —SK

Previous page:
1— Extravehicular overshoes worn by American astronaut Eugene Cernan, commander of Apollo 17, when he walked on the moon in 1972
2—   Paul McCartney playing the sitar, Abbey Road Studios, London, 1972. Photograph by Linda McCartney
3—   Swiss Alps, summer 2008. Photograph by Tobias Lundkvist

OXFORD-CLOTH BUTTON-DOWN SHIRT

The Oxford-cloth button-down shirt, as its name explains, is a shirt made of Oxford cloth and with collars turned down and secured by a button. Its subtle details embody diverse personas: the sporty, the business casual, the preppy, the jazzy, and the mod.

Men's fashion in early modern Europe was characterized by splendid fabrics and ornate jabots, cravats, and cuffs. From the late eighteenth century onward, with the rise of neoclassicism and Romanticism, men's dress became increasingly simplified and somber, and flamboyant accessories gave way to restrained collars and cuffs. The Romantic poet Byron was often credited with inventing the modern shirt collar by laying the points flat against the collarbone rather than wearing them upright around the neck.[1] In the 1920s the Duke of Windsor and his brothers popularized the turndown and attached collar, which represented a more comfortable and clean look (previously, collar and shirt had usually been separate pieces).[2]

The American menswear company Brooks Brothers introduced the button-down shirt around 1900. John Brooks, the retired president, took inspiration from English polo players' shirts, the collar points of which were buttoned to the shirt body to prevent them from flapping during riding.[3] The button-down shirt has since become the signature style of Brooks Brothers and is firmly associated with the brand. The most classic type is made of Oxford cloth—a cotton fabric of plain basket weave with a slightly coarse appearance. Other than white, Oxford cloth often features unsaturated shades created by interweaving color warps and white weft threads. Pink and blue are the most popular colors of Brooks Brothers Oxford-cloth shirts.

In modern men's shirting, the subtle variations of buttons and collar shapes are coded with nuanced meanings, denoting profession, cultural background, social status, occasion, and personality. The button-down represents a sporty spirit transformed into business attire. Its charm derives from an ambiguity between casualness and formality. As fashion journalist and historian G. Bruce Boyer has written, "The button-down collar is at the casual end of the business shirt spectrum and is the jauntiest collar that one can wear in the office or boardroom. Its purposefully nonchalant roll acts as a counterpoint to an otherwise sedate outfit and tends to give the impression of dressed-down and approachable respectability; figuratively as well as literally, it softens the stiff edges of the appearance."[4]

The Oxford-cloth button-down shirt has long been a staple of Ivy League style, or the preppy look, which originated in top-echelon universities in the American Northeast. Ivy style is a studied, elite look that strives to appear carefree and effortless. An understated and versatile garment, the Oxford-cloth button-down shirt easily complements unpadded sack suits, tweed jackets, khaki trousers, Shetland sweaters, madras sports blazers, and Bermuda shorts —items that constitute the Ivy wardrobe— helping to achieve the desired air of carelessness. From midcentury onward, the shirt has also played a part in the female counterpart of the Ivy look, the Seven Sisters style, so called after the seven most prestigious women's colleges on the East Coast. In 1949 Brooks Brothers introduced the women's button-down, and a pink version—a color up until then associated with men's shirts in the Brooks Brothers lexicon—with long collar points was advertised in the August college issue of *Vogue* that year, announcing the beginning of "a new tradition."[5] Also novel was the mixture of Dacron polyester and cotton that Brooks Brothers introduced in 1953, creating an early wash-and-wear shirt (a feat repeated in 1998, when the company brought out a successful 100-percent cotton non-iron shirt).[6]

Midcentury American jazz musicians and the English mod generation infused new character into the button-down. In the 1950s, when jazz swept American campuses and transformed from dance music to listening music, jazz stars shed the oversize zoot suit and adopted the clothing of their collegiate audiences. Exemplifying the "Jivey Ivy" style, Miles Davis, Dave Brubeck, and John Coltrane, among others, injected the nerdy, elite preppy look with a hipster, bohemian spirit. On the other side of the Atlantic, in the 1960s, mod youth in Britain turned to the button-down as a rebellious sartorial statement. Members of rock bands like the Kinks and the Yardbirds sported button-downs with skinny ties, and Roger Daltrey, lead singer of The Who, was known to pair outrageously large-collared shirts with bright-colored jackets, while smartly dressed young men in button-downs and formal suits affected the gesture of laying brown paper bags down on bus seats to protect their outfits from dirt. More recently, designers (such as Ann Demeulemeester) have looked to the Oxford shirt as a cipher for cool-headed minimalism, and the item has also been reinvented to accommodate differently abled bodies, as in MagnaReady shirts, which close with small magnets to allow those with a limited range of digital motion (due to arthritis or other issues) to more easily "button" their button-downs. —MMR

Previous pages:
1— **Students at a football game, from the Wofford College yearbook, Spartanburg, South Carolina, 1988. Unknown photographer**
2— **Model Hélène Fillières on the runway for an Ann Demeulemeester show, summer 1997. Photograph by Marleen Daniels**
3— **Model in a Brooks Brothers shirt, *Vogue*, August 1949. Photograph by John Rawlings**
4— **F. Scott Fitzgerald, 1900. Unknown photographer**

PANAMA HAT The Panama hat, more accurately named a toquilla straw hat or Montecristi hat, is a brimmed headpiece crafted out of toquilla, a palmlike plant native to Ecuador. The hat is finely woven by artisans in Ecuador's coastal Manabí province, in the weaving town of Montecristi, where it may take up to six months to fabricate one hat.[1] To begin, toquilla stalks are harvested and cut into strips, their interior fibers extracted and then boiled. The fine fiber strings, called *cogollos*, are bundled while still steaming, beaten against poles, dried for several days, and then bleached using sulfur. The resulting color and the fineness of the fiber determines the quality of the hat.[2] Both men and women artisans in the region are taught this practice by their elders in their adolescence, and it takes several years to learn the intricate process. The weaving starts with the rosette, or center of the crown, which is made from a number of toquilla strands woven in a tight lattice pattern. Scholar Beverly Chico has written, "The fineness and value of the hat depends largely on the number of circular rows inside the crown: Five to seven knot-rows make an ordinary hat; nine to thirteen, a better one; more than fifteen, a hat of very high quality and price."[3] It is common for other artisans to be involved toward the end of the process, creating the shape of the hat, tightening it, and cutting off the edges. Finally, the hats are dried in the sun for further bleaching. In 2012 the Ecuadorian toquilla straw hat, a prime example of the meeting point between craftsmanship and design, was added to UNESCO's Intangible Cultural Heritage of Humanity list.

Straw hats were made and worn by descendants of the Incas and were commonly worn in the region that is now Ecuador when the Spanish conquistadors arrived in South America in the sixteenth century.[4] By 1630 native weavers in the Manabí region were making and selling straw hats, which they called *jipijapas*, for the local mestizo population. In the 1840s large quantities of toquilla hats were sent to Panama, where they were bought by travelers en route to the gold mines of California.[5] Because of where they were purchased, the hats were known as Panama hats in the United States. The construction of the Panama Canal, from 1904 to 1914, helped cement the link between that country and the hat, as thousands of laborers wore inexpensive straw hats as protection from the sun. By the time U.S. president Theodore Roosevelt visited the Canal in 1906, wearing a "Panama" of extremely fine weave, the hats were already widely regarded as hailing from that region.[6] Panamas became an international hit, worn by movie stars such as Gary Cooper and Humphrey Bogart in the 1940s. Hat connoisseurs then and now, however, know that a true *fino* (fine hat) is made in Ecuador, by a skilled artisan from Montecristi or Manabí. —AB

Previous pages:
**1— Workers lining up for dinner at the Commission Hotel, Nueva Gorgona, Panama, early twentieth century. Unknown photographer
2— Men attending Pitti Uomo, Florence, 2014. Photograph by Marta Rovatti
3— Holger Domingo Carranza weaving a Panama hat in Pile, a small village near Montecristi, Ecuador, 2017. Photograph by Hugo Gonzenbach
4— Theodore Roosevelt, c. 1911. Unknown photographer**

2

4

PEARL NECKLACE The pearl, a lustrous, gemlike substance formed within the shells of certain mollusks, has long been treasured as a wonder of nature. For thousands of years, pearl fishing was centered in the Arabian Gulf, the Red Sea, South India, and Sri Lanka, and trade in pearls crossed the vast continents, from Asia to Europe. A natural pearl is formed serendipitously when the mantle tissue of a shellfish creates a crust around intruding parasites. Artificial pearl culturing involves implanting an irritant that triggers the mollusk to release the nacreous coating, keeping the shape of the generated pearl under control. This method was practiced in China beginning in the eighth century, but a technique to produce spherical pearls was perfected in Japan in the first decade of the twentieth century, particularly by Kōkichi Mikimoto, who revolutionized the pearl farming industry.[1] Today, natural pearls harvested through traditional fishing are extremely rare.

Whether natural or artificial, the quality of a pearl is determined by size, luster, and uniformity of shape. Pearl necklaces are typically knotted between each bead—for better hanging and to prevent a whole strand of pearls coming loose if the string were to break—and they are sold in a series of conventional lengths that have evolved over time: collar, choker, princess, matinee, opera, and rope, which is at least forty-five inches long and is often worn looped into a knot.

The mysterious formation and miraculous beauty of the pearl lends itself to multiple symbolic meanings. In medieval Europe, pearls represented the power and authority of churches and sovereigns; as a Christian emblem, they indicated the chastity of the Virgin Mary. Pearls were also believed to possess magical and medicinal values, enabling the changing of one's fortune or the strengthening of

the heart.[2] Although pearls had long adorned religious and royal regalia, strands of pearls were not common until the Renaissance. During this period, as in ancient Rome, pearls were associated in the poetic and artistic imagination with the goddess Venus, an incarnation of both sacred and profane love, whose seductive beauty is idealized in Botticelli's painting *The Birth of Venus* (c. 1486). In Italian portraiture, young brides wore choker-length pearl necklaces with a pendant—a symbol of purity and innocence. The dual representations of the pearl, chastity and power, converged in 1588 in a propagandist portrait of Elizabeth I, the Virgin Queen of England, in which the austere monarch, dressed in forbidding splendor (including abundantly long strands of pearls), celebrated her victory over the Spanish Armada. Flash forward four centuries, and another ruler—this time the Indian Maharaja of Baroda State, Sir Sayajirao Gaekwad III—sits resplendent in pearl necklaces for his official portrait.

Apart from virtue and virginity, pearl necklaces as feminine jewelry also denoted both maternity and death. In the genre of pregnancy portraits popular in the late sixteenth and early seventeenth centuries, strings of pearls on noble ladies signified fertility.[3] They also marked another stage of life: widowhood. In the Renaissance and Baroque eras, pearl necklaces were the only appropriate adornment for the mourning period. The association of pearls with death and grief goes back to the classical myth that they are the teardrops of the gods.[4]

The various connotations of the pearl necklace have become all the more pronounced in modern times. In the Jazz Age it took on a new dynamism as an image of seduction, with dramatic cascades dangling around the liberated bodies of flapper girls. Silent film actresses Louise Brooks, Clara Bow, and Pola Negri tantalized audiences with long, sweeping strands. Also in the 1920s, Gabrielle "Coco" Chanel popularized the wearing of multiple artificial pearl necklaces—both draped down the front and flipped over the back—in open defiance of conventional definitions of wealth and class. Worn this way, the pearl necklace was a modern expression of freedom, caprice, and independence, which were embodied in its accessibility and captivating kinetic sway.

In the mid-twentieth century the choker length took precedence. Pearls strung close to the jugular subtly called attention to the erogenous qualities of the neck and collarbone yet tended to symbolize pure femininity. In England, for example, a pearl necklace was presented as a gift to brides and to young women celebrating a twenty-first birthday, marking their entry into womanhood. In the 1950s and '60s, images of the ideal American housewife featured a woman in an elegant dress and sensible pearls, serenely overseeing her cheerfully spotless, efficient domain: the necklace—like those worn by Grace Kelly or the triple strand favored by Jackie Kennedy—announced her propriety and her comfortable life. While some styles of this moment were strung with uniform pearls, others used graduated sizes, with the largest pearls at the center of the strand for a more affordable look. On the other end of the sartorial spectrum, political women—exemplified by British prime minister Margaret Thatcher in the 1980s and more recently by the American presidential nominee Hillary Clinton in 2016—continue to endorse the pearl necklace as a symbol of power and domination. —MMR

Previous pages:
1— Margaret Thatcher and cabinet minister Norman Tebbit at a press conference, London, 1983. Unknown photographer
2— Louise Brooks in the film *The Canary Murder Case*, 1929. Photograph by Eugene Robert Richee
3— Portrait of Queen Elizabeth I by an unknown English artist, c. 1588
4— Bride, c. 1950. Unknown photographer

PENCIL SKIRT At once revealing (of the body's form) and restrictive (of the body's movement), the pencil skirt straddles the line between liberation and oppression. It has had a varied life—worn by everyone from the film-noir femmes fatales of the 1940s to the power-suited working women of the 1980s, but has consistently remained both straight and narrow.

Although the pencil skirt entered mainstream fashion in the 1930s, traces of its form were evident earlier. The full-length hobble skirt of the early twentieth century is a forerunner. Often attributed to French designer Paul Poiret, this garment tapered toward the hem and at times was even banded below the knee, impeding movement; its name referred to a device put on horses and other animals to immobilize them. Although it is shorter, the pencil skirt likewise restricts its wearer's stride. In 1919 *Women's Wear Daily* featured a piece titled "Women Doctors Differ over the Tight Skirt," in which the "lead pencil skirt" was described as "mak[ing] a normal step impossible" and—when combined with high heels—affecting "indirectly the chest, the pelvis and the whole nervous system."[1]

In spite of these concerns, the pencil skirt gained prominence in the 1930s, promoted by designers including Edward Molyneux, who paired it with long double-breasted jackets, and Elsa Schiaparelli, who offered options for both day and evening that were dubbed "narrow as pencils" in *Vogue* in 1940 (the magazine's first overt reference to the style).[2] During World War II, as the fashion industries of the warring nations were impacted by materials rationing (as prescribed by the Utility Scheme in Great Britain and Limitation Order L-85 in the United States), the pencil skirt came to signify practicality; simple and easily cut

THE NEW SKIRT AND THE POETRY OF MOTION.

Edith (breaking into a hop). "HURRY UP, MABEL; YOU'LL NEVER CATCH THE TRAIN IF YOU KEEP ON TRYING TO RUN."

on the straight grain, it did not require an abundance of material. In the work of American designers such as Adele Simpson, the pencil skirt became an integral component of the wartime silhouette, which emphasized a defined shoulder in an otherwise simple jacket and a narrow waist and hipline.

Although the pencil skirt did not fall out of favor, it was overshadowed in the late 1940s by the fuller and longer silhouette that emerged as an exuberant reaction to the end of austerity measures, encapsulated by Christian Dior's 1947 New Look, a collection featuring markedly full skirts that necessitated multiple yards of fabric. Despite his association with this opulent turn, in the following decade it was Dior who helped promote the more restrained pencil skirt, with his H-line collection, whose silhouette was described in the *New York Times* as "almost a straight line from shoulders to hem."[3] Named for the way in which its garments resembled the capital letter *H* (with straight vertical lines and a horizontal "crossbar" of hemline or embellishment at the hipline), the collection featured curve-hugging pencil skirts that emphasized the hip and narrowed at the knee. Other designers, including Pierre Balmain and Cristóbal Balenciaga, showed pencil skirts at this time, but Dior's H-line crystalized the form.

The pinnacle of smart refinement and feminine elegance, the pencil skirt went on to become an integral wardrobe item for women of varied walks of life, from pregnant homemakers (for whom *Harper's Bazaar* suggested a "bouffant camisole circling a pared-to-a-pencil skirt" in 1954) to the women who were entering the workplace in ever greater numbers.[4] When the designer Janie Bryant was costuming the character Joan Holloway for the 2007–15 television drama *Mad Men*— set in a 1960s advertising agency—she chose the formfitting pencil skirt. "There is a level of empowerment in wearing that garment and a woman feeling feminine and strong," Bryant explained.[5] The pencil skirt became Joan's signature, its simultaneously constricting and freeing shape a metaphor for her state as a woman who makes professional gains but remains trapped in a misogynistic work environment.

The pencil skirt had particular resonance in the 1980s, when it was shortened to well above the knee. The American designer Calvin Klein treated it as a separate, which *Vogue* deemed "smart and stylish,"[6] while the French designer Thierry Mugler featured it as a component of broad-shouldered, aggressive power suits. The shortened pencil skirt of the last decades of the twentieth century allowed for more mobility than its longer predecessor, signaling both a literal and a figurative unshackling as women climbed the professional ranks.

In the twenty-first century the pencil skirt has become a versatile basic for women, worn casually, even with a T-shirt and sneakers. It can still communicate power and agency, however: in 2016 the actress Emma Watson delivered a speech on university sexual assault policies to the United Nations General Assembly dressed in a camel-colored pencil skirt that she had created in collaboration with the New York–based ethical fashion brand Zady. —SK

Previous pages:
1— Model Cordula Reyer in a Chanel suit, *Vogue*, May 1989. Photograph by Wayne Maser
2— Richard Sandler, *Mad Ave.*, 1982
3— Christina Hendricks as Joan Holloway (right) in the television series *Mad Men*, 2007
4— Cartoon by Lewis Baumer, c. 1910

PLAID FLANNEL SHIRT   In December 1992, a little more than a year after Nirvana's debut album *Nevermind* propelled the meteoric rise of the American musical genre known as grunge, *Vogue* published "Grunge and Glory," an editorial spread aimed at encapsulating the fashion style that had emerged with the burgeoning alternative-rock subculture in and around Seattle. Styled by then–fashion editor Grace Coddington and featuring three of the period's most iconic models, Naomi Campbell, Nadja Auermann, and Kristen McMenamy, the spread included seven plaid shirts worn in a variety of ways (tied around the waist, open, tucked in); an image caption read, "The plaid shirt proves its staying power. Long part of a work uniform in the Northwest timber towns, the shirt has been picked up by TV (*Twin Peaks* and *Northern Exposure*) and grunge bands."[1] Though *Vogue*'s characterization of the garment was accurate, Coddington's sourcing of the examples belied the very ethos behind the item's popularity, as some of the shirts depicted had been procured from the trendy street-wear boutique Na Na; others, such as a DKNY version priced at $155, came from high-end department stores like Saks Fifth Avenue and Neiman Marcus. Of course, neither lumberjacks nor alt-rockers bought their plaid shirts from any such outlets, and *Vogue*'s editorial was disparaged for feeding the mass-media machine that sought to commodify all things grunge, including the humble, utilitarian plaid flannel shirt.

Although plaid cloth has roots in the seventeenth century—in both yarn-dyed cotton madras fabric from India and the twilled woolen tartan cloth integral to Scotland's Highland dress—its use in American work wear can be traced to Pennsylvania's Woolrich Woolen Mill's Buffalo Check shirt. First produced in 1850

and made of a soft yet durable wool flannel (a plain or twill woven fabric of slightly twisted yarns with a napped finish), the Buffalo Check shirt proved extremely successful among workers and outdoorsmen who needed to brave the elements while maintaining freedom of movement. (The name of the pattern was, apparently, an homage to the Woolrich designer's buffalo herd, but a similar plaid called Rob Roy MacGregor had appeared as early as 1704 in the Scottish Register of Tartans.) As Americans' participation in outdoor leisure activities increased during the final decades of the nineteenth century, the demand for outdoor sportswear grew, and Woolrich diversified its Buffalo Check shirt into multiple plaid patterns and colorways.[2] Soon other textile mills entered the market, including the Oregon-based Pendleton Woolen Mills, which in 1924 introduced brightly colored plaid flannel shirts made from the wool of the Umatilla area's sheep. With the baby boom of the 1950s, leisure wear became de rigueur for American dads, and the plaid flannel shirt was among its staples. Catalogues for both Woolrich and Pendleton during the period presented the plaid shirt as an important component of American culture, breaking down sartorial barriers between the white-collar worker and the outdoor laborer.

The plaid flannel shirt was associated with the extreme casualness of the 1970s—and also, as a marker of masculinity, with that decade's "gay male clone" style (especially in San Francisco's Castro district). However, it fell out of favor as a fashionable choice for casual wear among the class-conscious salarymen of the Wall Street–obsessed 1980s and flooded thrift shops and Goodwill stores. Particularly prevalent in the Pacific Northwest, where logging is a major industry, flannel shirts soon found their way into the wardrobes of financially strapped fledgling musicians based in the area. Among them was Nirvana's lead singer, Kurt Cobain, who often performed in a plaid flannel shirt worn open over layers of clothing—a look that would ultimately make him the poster child of grunge. (In fact, Cobain's layering of flannel shirts and T-shirts was a response to insecurities about his extremely thin frame, which was the consequence of a chronic stomach illness.) As Nirvana, Pearl Jam, and other bands of their ilk leapt to the forefront of mainstream music in early 1992, the media quickly attempted to dissect the scene's clothing, lifestyle, and lingo.

Unlike prior musical subcultures, such as punk, whose participants explicitly strove to make an antifashion statement and were, according to sociologist Dick Hebdige, "concerned first and foremost with consumption," the grunge scene adopted its look—of which the plaid flannel shirt was emblematic—as a matter of utility and an abstention from fashion.[3] By the time the New York Times published "Grunge: A Success Story" in November 1992, plaid shirts were available from mainstream retailers such as The Gap as well as high-end fashion houses such as Perry Ellis, whose designer at the time, Marc Jacobs, famously sent to Italy a two-dollar plaid flannel shirt purchased on St. Mark's Place, in Manhattan's East Village, to be copied in a $330-a-yard plaid silk. Acknowledging the oddity of the humble garment's newly acquired high-fashion status and noting that the ultimate fate of every trendy item is to quickly end up as a cheap knockoff, the New York Times underscored the irony that grunge wear "was already for sale at Kmart, not to mention the Salvation Army."[4] Although its popularity and fashion status have waxed and waned over the decades, the plaid flannel shirt seems to have been with us forever. Worn globally by men, women, and children, it traverses barriers and speaks volumes.
—SK

Left:
1— Kurt Cobain of Nirvana performing at the nightclub Raji's, Los Angeles, 1990. Photograph by Charles Peterson
2— Models Kristen McMenamy and Nadja Auermann, Ward Pound Ridge Reservation, New York, 1992. Photograph by Steven Meisel
3— Promotional illustration for Pendleton Woolen Mills, n.d.

PLATFORM SHOE   This twentieth-century fashion typology has roots in footwear developed throughout history with a pragmatic purpose: to give the wearer an additional one to twenty inches in height.

Some of the earliest recorded usages of height-enhancing footwear date from around 600 BCE, when platform sandals appeared on statues of fashionable Greek women of status.[1] Bathing traditions of the Levant inspired stiltlike wooden *qabâqib*, which protected bathers' feet from the hot and slippery tiles of the bathhouse floor.[2] Throughout the Middle Ages in Western Europe, wooden-soled, strap-on overshoes called pattens added extra height to keep the wearer's valuable leather or textile shoes clean, above the dampness and detritus of the street. By the 1400s, the chopine, a solid-soled platform shoe for women, had become prevalent in Spain, Italy, and particularly in the Republic of Venice, where, at the zenith of its popularity in the sixteenth century, such tall footwear could add as much as twenty inches of height.[3] Though they were concealed underneath the wearers' clothing, Venetian chopines functioned to signal wealth by increasing the length of ladies' skirts and thereby the amount of sumptuous fabric they were able to wear.

Platform footwear is not only a Western phenomenon, however. In Edo-period Japan (1603–1868), black lacquered *koma geta* (wooden platform sandals) were worn by high-class courtesans while soliciting potential customers outside their brothels.[4] Their conspicuous height, extravagant fashion, and stilted walk were intended to attract male attention. Though the practice of binding women's feet was eschewed in China's Manchu region in the nineteenth century, fashion dictated the wearing of a platform shoe known as the *qixie* (also flower-pot

or horse-hoof shoe). The shoes featured a single central heel made of wood wrapped in white fabric and a simple satin upper, often decorated with embroidery, that encouraged a dainty, measured gait.[5]

In the West in the 1930s platform footwear took off. Inspired by the Venetian chopine, French shoe designer Roger Vivier sketched out his vision for a platform sandal in 1937, a design that was later used in a collection by Elsa Schiaparelli. Manufacturers like the American company Delman transformed chunky-soled sandals and shoes from beachwear to glamorous footwear for Hollywood starlets and well-to-do women.[6] Salvatore Ferragamo produced elaborately decorative wedge heels and platform soles throughout the late 1930s, further popularizing the style—perhaps most famously with his 1938 rainbow platform wedge with a sculptural sole of lightweight cork covered with ripples of brightly colored suede. The stable platform shoe retained its favor during World War II, when civilians walked more and many women assumed factory jobs left vacant by the men who had left to fight. Leather and rubber were reserved for the war effort, but off-ration materials like cork, woven straw, and wood were used in abundance by designers to build platform soles of ever-greater heights (see *Espadrille*).

Platform shoes fell out of style with the postwar rise of the hyper-feminine stiletto heel in the 1950s (see *Stiletto*) and the more ergonomically friendly footwear favored by hippie fashion in the 1960s (see *Clog*). But by the early 1970s platform-soled shoes and boots were everywhere, on the feet of the self-celebrating women, and many men, of the "Me" generation, available through trendsetting lifestyle boutiques like London's Biba. Platforms effectively became the first tall-heeled shoe worn by men since the late eighteenth century.[7] Because they added inches and required a confident stride, the shoes were a suitably ostentatious element of flamboyant 1970s menswear, and particularly lavish pairs intensified the glamorous look of male rock stars from the period, including Gene Simmons of Kiss and David Bowie, as well as the peacocking devotees of the disco scene and sartorially outrageous R&B stars such as George Clinton of Parliament-Funkadelic.

Platform footwear continued to be prevalent among music-related subcultures. Groups affiliated with the punk movement (including ska and rockabilly) revived the crepe-soled platform creeper shoe originally produced in Britain in the 1950s, made available through Malcolm McLaren and Vivienne Westwood's formative London boutique Sex.[8] Goths and fans of industrial music, which flourished in the late 1970s and '80s, also favored heavy-looking black platform boots with gratuitous metal buckles and eyelets.[9] By the 1990s, club kids and ravers were sporting multicolored platform shoes by Swear and Buffalo to dance parties. Pop sensation the Spice Girls, specifically Ginger, Baby, and Scary Spice, were rarely photographed without their trademark platform sneakers or boots, often emblazoned with their names or a bold Union Jack. And in 1993 Naomi Campbell made headlines when she took a coltish tumble on the runway in Westwood's blue mock-croc nine-inch Super Elevated Gillie platforms (see *Kilt*). More recently, the pop star Lady Gaga has incorporated towering shoes into her provocative looks, notably Noritaka Tatehana's precariously heelless Lady Bloom platforms from 2013. A contemporary fascination with the 1990s and its fashion movements, from grunge- and skateboarding-inspired looks to the continued exploration of club-kid style, has seen a resurgence of the platform shoe in popular fashion. —LB

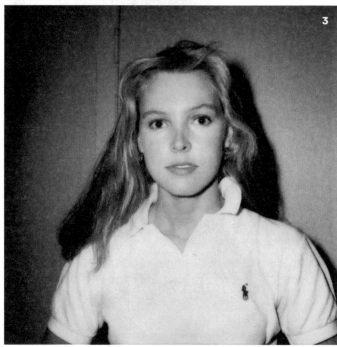

Previous pages:
1— **Blind musicians, Niigata Prefecture, Japan, 1956. Photograph by Hiroshi Hamaya**
2— **Club kid at Limelight, New York, 1994. Photograph by Steve Eichner**
3— **Subway rider, Brooklyn, New York, 1978. Photograph by Meryl Meisler**
4— **Illustration of Spanish women wearing pattens, by an unknown artist, c. 1540**
5— **Fashion muse Daphne Guinness on the Upper East Side, New York, 2015. Photograph by Josiah Kamau**

POLO SHIRT The polo shirt is a twentieth-century phenomenon of branding, associated more with its embroidered logo than its actual form. Its name is itself a product of marketing, applied to a variety of garments during the early twentieth century, ranging from jersey turtlenecks (particularly in Great Britain) to the Brooks Brothers' Oxford-cloth button-down shirt, whose label declares it "the original polo shirt" (see *Oxford-Cloth Button-Down Shirt*). It was not until the 1920s that the polo shirt consistently appeared in the form it does today: a knitted, short-sleeved pullover with a turndown collar and a center-front placket, often fastened with buttons. Named for its use by polo players and purchased by both men and women for sports and casual resort wear, the polo shirt in the twentieth century has been closely associated with tennis, especially with the French tennis champion René Lacoste.

Lacoste was ranked the world's top player in 1926 and 1927. His early competition clothing included a starched white collared shirt with long sleeves and center-front buttons. Inspired by George Horatio Charles Cholmondeley, a well-known polo and tennis player who had taken to wearing short-sleeved shirts during matches, in 1926 Lacoste commissioned a tailor to construct pullover shirts in both wool and breathable cotton with a soft but stiff unstarched collar. That same year, Lacoste's friend Robert George designed the now-iconic logo, which honored the fiercely competitive tennis player's nickname, "the Crocodile," and made its debut embroidered on Lacoste's blazer.

In 1933 Lacoste partnered with André Gillier, president of the largest French knitwear company at the time, to produce multiple versions of *la chemise Lacoste* for the masses. The Lacoste polo

shirt became a staple of the well-dressed sportsman in Europe, and by 1951 the company was offering multiple colors beyond the classic "tennis white." A year later the American manufacturer David Crystal Company made an agreement with Lacoste to license his shirts in the United States under the name Izod (named for an acclaimed London tailor). Designed with a slightly longer back hem called a "tennis tail," the Izod Lacoste polo was advertised as a status symbol of the elite sportsman and was sold in high-end shops like Brooks Brothers.

Peaking at $400 million in sales in the U.S. in 1982, the Lacoste polo shirt was adopted as a staple by American preppies. When Lisa Birnbach published the satirical *Official Preppy Handbook* in 1980, the shirt made multiple appearances. "The sport shirt of choice is the Lacoste," she advised men. "Only the all-cotton model will do, the one with cap sleeves with the ribbed edging, narrow collar and two-button placket (never buttoned)." For women, she warned, "Big boned, flat chested women can get away with the men's version, but the crocodile does tend to sit neatly on the left nipple. . . . Pink, after 6:00 p.m., is construed as dressy."[1]

Lacoste catalyzed a style since developed by other key figures. In 1952 the British tennis star Fred Perry, whose working-class background contrasted sharply with the privileged pedigree typical of players affiliated with the All England Club (i.e., Wimbledon), introduced his own take on the polo shirt, which bore a signature laurel wreath embroidered on its front. The original symbol of the All England Club, the wreath signified belonging and, for Perry, upward mobility.

The shirt was soon adopted by mods and skinheads, two British youth subcultures of the underclass. Mods wore it buttoned to the top with slim-cut, single-breasted suits, a fastidious look belying the boys' straitened circumstances. Skinheads preferred Perry's twin tipped M12 polo. Bordered on both collar and sleeves with contrasting colored stripes, it allowed one to display team allegiance, and when worn with cuffed jeans, suspenders, and combat boots (see *Dr. Martens*) it symbolized working-class pride.

The polo shirt is perhaps best known in association with Ralph Lauren, a designer who has aligned himself unambiguously with the garment's elite sporting heritage. Introduced in 1972 under his Polo Ralph Lauren label, Lauren's iteration featured the embroidered silhouette of a polo player on horseback as its logo, and it was immediately positioned as a symbol of an American leisure lifestyle.

Lauren's polo appealed to the 1980s yuppie, of course, but marketed as an aspirational status item, the shirt acquired an unintended fan base: inner-city street gangs. Formed in 1988 in Brooklyn, the Lo Lifes were a prominent Ralph Lauren–loving crew that amassed large quantities of merchandise. Acquired through a combination of thievery and black-market entrepreneurship, the polo-player–studded polo shirt allowed gang members to project an image of affluence. "It made us feel exclusive," recalled Lo Life founder Thirstin Howl III. "The colors stood out and people were able to identify us. Polo became a uniform."[2] "In a time when Polo was being made for and marketed to the aspirational white middle class," wrote *New York Times* music critic Jon Caramanica, "some of the most rigorously sourced collections were sitting in closets in Brooklyn."[3] By the 1990s the Ralph Lauren polo shirt had become an integral component of hip-hop street wear. Once again, the shirt's meaning was determined not by marketers, but by a diverse range of consumers who contextualized the garment within their lives and made it their own. —SK

P — 074

PREMAMAN Italians use the word *premaman* to describe maternity clothing and other accessories or items designed for pregnancy. While flexible maternity wear, such as the Indian sari, is ancient and global, at the turn of the twentieth century in the West, clothes for pregnant women were circumscribed. Pregnancy was considered something to be hidden from public view: a burgeoning stomach was a literal sign of sex, an unflattering silhouette, and something more safely rested at home. The clothes available to women were limited to lightly boned dresses and empire waists (at best) and repurposed garments (more often), and maternity corsets were advertised well into the 1930s. Fashion editorials addressing expectant readers in mainstream publications emerged slowly from 1900 onward; these featured darted, pleated, and laced dresses adaptable to a pregnant woman's changing shape, as well as roomier couture items that *Vogue* termed "miracles of concealment."[1] The models used, whether photographed or illustrated, invariably showed little sign of being with child.

Lena Himmelstein Bryant Malsin, a young widow, mother, and New York dressmaker, was at the forefront of the gradual shift toward supplying pregnant women—and society at large—with palatable options for masking their natural state. In 1904 she established Lane Bryant, so called thanks to a clerk's misspelling of her name, and the company's No. 5 maternity gown was an early commercial ready-to-wear dress designed for pregnancy. By 1910 the company was turning more than $50,000 in annual sales and was advertised in newspapers and magazines, including *Vogue*.[2] Malsin cannily recognized that the shape and size of women's bodies fluctuate, pregnant or not, and accordingly marketed garments with adjustable

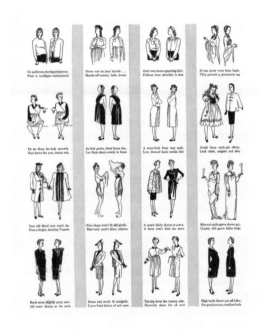

waistbands, thus connecting the history of maternity wear with that of non-sample-size fashion.

Ready-to-wear fashion was broadly established by the early twentieth century, and maternity wear rode this wave. By the 1930s stores such as Neiman Marcus and Saks Fifth Avenue stocked maternity fashions, and Bonwit Teller contained an Anticipation Shop. The noted maternity line Page Boy's Dallas store, located next to several obstetricians' offices, sold the quintessential midcentury pregnancy skirt, featuring a half circle cut from the waistband to accommodate a blossoming belly, secured with an adjustable tie.[3]

At higher echelons, the feted Hollywood designer Gilbert Adrian created maternity ensembles for his wife, and the couturier Charles James designed a maternity garment for Lane Bryant's fiftieth-anniversary catwalk show, at the Plaza Hotel in New York in 1954. Actress Lauren Bacall designed her own pregnancy wardrobe, which featured expressive, calligraphic peplum details and wrapped silhouettes. It was Lucille Ball, however, who brought maternity wear into the public eye. Her real-life pregnancy and its fashions—demure, boxy two-piece ensembles and tented muumuus—were written into her popular television series, *I Love Lucy*, in 1952. The preference of style over practicality took hold thanks to the singular allure of Jacqueline Kennedy, who in 1960 campaigned with her husband, then Senator John F. Kennedy, wearing couture while pregnant. High-profile royal pregnancies—such as those of Diana, Princess of Wales, who favored the couturier Catherine Walker, and Kate Middleton, who relied on high-street brands as much as haute couture—have influenced maternity style, and as mass and social media fuel interest in the pregnant bodies of celebrities such as the performers M.I.A. and Beyoncé, maternity fashions follow suit.

In the later twentieth century, with the advent of second-wave feminism and policies protecting the civil rights of pregnant women, there was a dramatic rise in the number of women working after childbirth.[4] Mass-market retailers (such as The Gap, an early pioneer) produced an efflorescence of clothing appropriate to various professions for the periods during and immediately after pregnancy. Women have long been adept at adapting or augmenting existing clothing, a practice now commercialized in items such as elastic belly belts used at the top of pants and an extender that fastens to a coat's lining. Contemporary international chains such as H&M and online retailers such as Asos now include maternity wear, and the rise of fast fashion means that women can buy larger sizes cheaply and discard as needed—a privileged convenience, predicated on low-paid labor (usually of other women). More recently, various businesses have tried—and often failed—to rent trendy maternity wear to be returned later.

In the United States there are roughly six million pregnant women at any given time, but museum collections, exhibitions, and scholarship have yet to fully embrace maternity fashions.[5] This is due in part to the confinement of expectant women to the domestic sphere, which continued well beyond the early 1900s, as well as the fact that pregnancy clothing often deteriorated, especially after several babies. It is due as well as to the industry's preference for lithe young models and mannequins—progeny-free, unless a child is a useful prop. The most famous celebrations of pregnancy and popular culture, in fact, have focused on the unclothed body—most notably the actress Demi Moore's *Vanity Fair* cover in August 1991, which featured her naked and seven months pregnant. The current historical and cultural moment at once fetishizes and skips over the rich contribution to the history of dress by those—mostly women—who have designed clothes for pregnancy as it has moved from the realm of the shameful and private into significant public, political, and economic realms.
—MMF

Previous pages:
1— President John F. Kennedy and a pregnant Jacqueline Kennedy with their daughter Caroline, 1960. Unknown photographer
2— Fashion advice for pregnant women, *Glamour*, 1944
3— Woman in a sari, Bengaluru, Karnataka, India, 2006. Photograph by Philippe McLean

RED LIPSTICK A pair of impeccably painted lips in intense rouge at once signals seduction and refusal, invitation and intimidation. This paradox is at the heart of the success of Fire and Ice, Revlon's legendary lipstick and nail color launched in 1952 (see *Manicure*). An advertisement shows the model Dorian Leigh in a silver-sequined sheath dress and a red coat ballooning off one bare shoulder, her lips parted and moist, and her gaze cold and direct. Announcing that its product was for "you who love to flirt with fire . . . who dare to skate on thin ice," the campaign eschewed typical tropes (romantic encounters, mirrors, lipstick prints), instead linking the lipstick to a fifteen-point questionnaire meant to uncover a woman's inner essence: "Have you ever danced with your shoes off?" and "Would you take a trip to Mars?" Here the radiance of a woman's red lips indicates her self-sufficiency, fearlessness, and power.

Lipstick was not always considered an object that emboldens and empowers. One of the simplest acts to adorn the face, lip painting has been practiced in many cultures and dates back to antiquity, but its allure has been better documented since the early modern period. In the eighteenth century the French court spread the fashion for heavy makeup among European aristocratic circles. Both ladies and gentlemen painted their faces white and reddened their cheekbones and lips with minium or cinnabar materials; facial cosmetics primarily denoted social class rather than gender. Despite the poisoning effects of such products (which contained lead and mercury), the desired red was as saturated as possible, and the French word *rouge* became synonymous with makeup.[1] The fad declined after the 1770s, along with the rise of neoclassicism and the

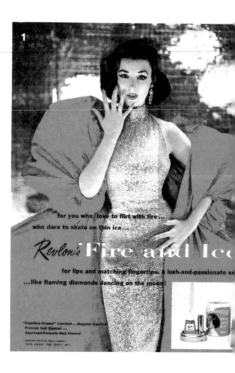

198

Rousseauean ideal of pastoral femininity that advocated natural beauty and health.

In the nineteenth century, when masculinity was redefined by rationality and sobriety, rouge became solely the province of women. But polite society preferred the restrained application of makeup in shades that more subtly played up a sense of fragile, innocent beauty. Crimson lips never ceased to be a sign of prettiness, but the color was to appear intrinsic. Popular advice offered tips on how to achieve such a look, ranging from soaking the lips in warm water, to sucking on hot cinnamon drops, to biting the lips to give an instant bloom. A heavily made-up face with sanguine lips was identified with prostitutes, whose images near the turn of the twentieth century were vividly captured in the paintings of Henri de Toulouse-Lautrec, Amedeo Modigliani, and Kees van Dongen, among other artists. Therefore, when American feminists wore red lip rouge to women's suffrage rallies, it was seen as a symbol of their emancipation, independence, unity, and defiance.[2]

The first two decades of the twentieth century saw a booming cosmetics industry, which contributed to the increasing acceptability of lip coloring. In 1915 the American manufacturer Scovill introduced modern lipsticks packaged in portable metal cases for the mass market, and by the 1920s lipstick had become an indispensable accessory in a woman's purse.[3] Scientific development gave rise to a vast array of shades and indelible, waterproof products by major companies such as Max Factor and Maybelline. Until this time, lipsticks had been colored with carmine, a red pigment extracted from cochineal insects, but the color wiped off easily and the mixture quickly turned rancid. In 1927 the French chemist Paul Baudecroux invented the first commercially successful "kiss-proof" lipstick, an eosin-based bright red, which gave the name Rouge Baiser (red kiss) to the brand.[4] American companies followed suit. The mark of the kiss bestowed the lipstick with a romantic charm while offering women the excitement of sexual empowerment.

During World War II red lips symbolized other kinds of feminine power—courage and old-time glamour. In the United States, lipstick helped women to "put on a brave face, 'conceal heartbreak or sorrow,' and gain 'self-confidence when it's badly needed.'"[5] In France, advertisements for lip rouge evoked the aristocratic life of the eighteenth century with all its extravagance and romantic intrigue—an idealization that resisted the wartime reality. After the war, putting on red lipstick continued to be celebrated as a dignified, courageous gesture that defied the banality and despair of daily life, as assessed in *Harper's Bazaar* in 1946: "Proud fingers wield their weapon. The act reinforces the spirit. The streak of red steadies trembling lips. For one poignant moment, the little stick takes on the significance of a sword."[6]

By the mid-twentieth century red lipstick had been firmly established as a classic symbol of sexiness and boldness. In the following decades, the rich, deep red never fell out of mode, withstanding the shifting of fashion caprices among hues (from purple to maroon, fuchsia, coral, pink, orange, brown, nude, and even white, black, blue, and green) and luminosity (frosted, glossy, sheer, and otherwise). But the feminine categorization of red lipstick has been ruptured. From rock icon David Bowie to the designer Thom Browne's runway shows, men in flaming lips have come to share and enrich its enigma and power. At the same time, iconoclast designers shatter the ideal of symmetrically lined, perfectly painted red lips, swelling them (Alexander McQueen), smudging them (Browne), or painting them off-center (Rei Kawakubo) to express different, deliberately subversive aesthetics. —MMR

Left:
1— Advertisement for Revlon's Fire and Ice, with Dorian Leigh, 1952. Photograph by Richard Avedon
2— Advertisement for MAC Cosmetics' Viva Glam, with RuPaul, 1994. Photographs by Albert Sanchez

ROLEX Instruments of timekeeping reflect technological advancement and social progression; they help shape interpersonal relationships and orient an individual within the natural world. Unlike clocks, which occupy shared space (a mantel, an entry hall, a classroom wall, a town square) and serve to instill group accountability—or even state control—personal timepieces synchronize private time with public time, mediating between the microcosm of oneself and the wider universe.

Mechanical watches made by the Swiss company Rolex (established in London in 1905 and moved to Geneva in 1919) embodied the new temporal consciousness developed during the twentieth century. Chronometric precision—the trademark quality of Rolex watches—ensured disciplined punctuality and efficiency, two essential demands of modern life. In the early twentieth century Rolex advanced and popularized the wristwatch, a practical accessory-tool that had begun to replace the chained pocket watches traditionally carried by men.

In 1931 the company invented the world's first self-winding mechanism, a literal and symbolic realization of a perpetual quest for speed. The "Datejust" feature, an automatically adjusting date in the window of the dial, was debuted in 1945, with a women's version following in 1957, a year after the release of the Rolex Perpetual Day-Date, which included the day of the week in addition to the date. In the 1950s, coinciding with the nascence of transcontinental commercial flights, Rolex designed a watch that could indicate the time across different time zones.

Rolex's major technological inventions were closely associated with significant advancements made by humans in natural exploration. For example, the Rolex Oyster, the first waterproof and dustproof wristwatch, created in 1926 and worn by Mercedes Gleitze during her ten-hour attempt to swim across the English Channel in 1927, famously maintained its working order; pilots making the first flight over Mount Everest in 1933 wore Rolex watches; and Rolex's Deep Sea Special was present on the first journey to the bottom of the Mariana Trench, the deepest known depression on Earth, in 1960. Throughout the century Rolex continued to develop professional watches for use by deep-sea divers, mountain climbers, and scientific explorers, launching several series, including the Explorer, the Submariner, and the Sea-Dweller. The watches' high-profile performance celebrated the human conquest of nature.

The majority of Rolex watch faces are set on metal bracelets (gold, platinum, and, since 1985, 904L steel), which offer superior longevity to leather as well as water resistance. Rolex's three bracelet designs—the Oyster (late 1930s), the Jubilee (1945), and the President (1956)—feature a distinct three-link chain design, making the watch instantly recognizable to connoisseurs and familiar to neophytes (although fakes abound).

Today Rolex remains the largest luxury watch brand, synonymous with reliability, technical innovation, and a discerning clientele as much as high living, thereby establishing itself as a symbol of wealth, status, and power. As a 1966 print advertisement for the Rolex Explorer claimed, "When a man has the world in his hands, you expect to find a Rolex (or two) on his wrist."[1] Even with the rise of smartphones and handheld digital devices, a thriving secondary market for Rolex timepieces has proliferated (through private dealers, auction houses, and a vast online exchange), prompting an inevitable and highly profitable influx of counterfeits.[2]
—MMR

Right:
1— Woman demonstrating the water-resistant qualities of a Rolex watch, n.d. Unknown photographer
2— Three generations of 1950s Rolex Oyster watches with three styles of bracelet, 2017. Photograph by Jack Forster

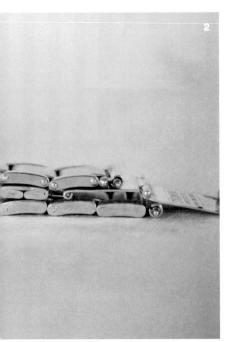

SAFARI SUIT The safari suit, a classic embodiment of colonial machismo with roots in big-game hunting, has come to represent a standard of unisex fashion. The archetype generally includes a jacket with four patch pockets (two at the breast line and two at the waist), a shirtlike closure down the front, a spread collar, buttoned epaulettes, and a straight hem; it is often accentuated by a belt of the same fabric.

While the term *safari* entered the English language from Swahili in the latter half of the nineteenth century, the concept of the safari suit can be traced to the colonial activity of the British East India Company, when men of the trading concern took to hunting wild animals such as tigers, elephants, and boars.[1] In his influential book *Seonee* (published in 1877), the naturalist Sir Robert Armitage Sterndale described the quintessential big-game hunter of the subcontinent, "clad in a close-fitting suit of stout drill, dyed with the barks of the mango and babool trees to the true shikar colour," with the shoulders "protected by pieces of leather to bear the friction of the rifle; leather-lined pockets in front [to hold] a small powder flask," and a "double-edged dagger . . . attached to a broad belt of sambhur leather."[2] Thus the image of the big-game hunter, with his unmistakable uniform, was crystallized. Sterndale's representation also anticipated the garment's signature color, khaki, a term derived from the Urdu word for "dust-colored" (see *Chinos*).

With the introduction of game laws in India in the 1880s, Africa soon became the destination of choice for thrill-seeking hunters, made especially feasible by the establishment of the Imperial British East Africa Company in 1888. The unreservedly colonialist image of the virile Western hunter dressed in a safari jacket and posing with his kill first emerged in Africa at the turn of the twentieth century. Famous American proponents of big-game expeditions such as Theodore Roosevelt and Ernest Hemingway were photographed in their safari attire, cementing its association with the heroics of man conquering beast (Roosevelt wrote that hunting "cultivates that vigorous manliness").[3] Moreover, it was adopted as a symbol of masculine hegemony by Africans, including independent Zambia's first president, Kenneth Kaunda.[4] While British hunters purchased bespoke versions in London, the ultimate safari jacket in the United States was made by sporting-gear purveyor Abercrombie & Fitch, which produced the densely woven cotton model 486 jacket in collaboration with expedition outfitter Willis & Geiger. (The model 476, featuring a sleeve pocket for spectacles, was later developed for Hemingway.)

After World War II the safari became the ultimate leisure activity of English aristocrats, Indian princes, and Hollywood movie stars, and the safari jacket began to be associated with glamour and exoticism. Yves Saint Laurent tapped into this spirit, designing women's blazers and coats with the safari jacket's signature four patch pockets for his spring/summer 1968 couture collection as well as a more stylized iteration called the Saharienne— a tunic with a revealing lace-up front placket, modeled by Veruschka in the July 1968 issue of *Vogue* Paris. Saint Laurent's recent purchase of a home in Marrakech likely contributed to his interest in Africa and exotic themes. By 1969 he had introduced full safari suits in his couture and Rive Gauche lines for both men and women, presenting the garment as the ultimate sartorial bridge between genders. Though he was by no means the first designer to adapt safari attire to fashion (Marc Bohan had featured safari-inspired skirt suits in his spring/summer 1967 collection for Christian Dior, for example), he was undoubtedly at the forefront of its promotion for both sexes. He himself was his own best model; a 1969 photograph shows him wearing a safari suit alongside one of his muses, Betty Catroux, who is posing in the Saharienne.

As the safari suit became a de facto form of casual attire for men, sanctioned by *Vogue* in 1970 as appropriate for office wear on Fridays and dubbed "a classic" by the publication a year later, it also was a key example of a unisex— or "his and hers"—style, the women's suit simply a more tailored version of the men's.[5] This unisex look, promoted by designers such as Ted Lapidus and Paul Stuart, ultimately reinforced the masculine connotations that had defined its emergence, unlike the gender-neutralizing garments of Rudi Gernreich (see *Unisex Project*).[6]

In 1978 the husband-and-wife team Mel and Patricia Ziegler founded Banana Republic Travel and Safari Clothing Company, a catalogue business aimed at selling repurposed military and safari attire. With the establishment of free-standing stores by 1983, Banana Republic contextualized the safari jacket within its earlier symbolism of exotic leisure and highlighted its simultaneously gendered and unisex appeal. As a staple of casual resort attire today, the safari jacket remains a unifying and knotty item that both bridges and reinforces a gender binary.
—SK

Right:
1— **American naturalists and explorers Osa and Martin Johnson (far left and far right) with two unidentified cameramen, Africa, 1921. Unknown photographer**
2— **Advertisement for Plaid Stallions clothing, c. 1970s**
3— **Portrait of Kenneth Kaunda, first president of Zambia, by Oenone Acheson, 1990**
4— **Model in a suit from the House of Boateng spring/summer 2012 collection. Photograph by Jamie Morgan**
5— **Yves Saint Laurent at the opening of his shop Rive Gauche in Bond Street, London, with Loulou de la Falaise and Betty Catroux (right), London, 1969. Photograph by John Minihan**

Safari for him and her.

SAFETY PIN The safety pin is a humble masterpiece of design with a history of subversive fashion applications. It is credited to Walter Hunt, who received a U.S. patent in 1849 for a bent wire "dress pin" that featured a coiled spring on one end and a clasp and point at the other.[1] Though previous iterations had been patented (and called safety pins), Hunt's innovation lay in fashioning the pin from a single piece of wire, which both forced the point into the clasp through a spring mechanism and facilitated the mass production and dissemination of the useful design.

Dating to prehistoric Europe, pin fasteners derive most notably from the fibula, first introduced in the Bronze Age. Its main components included a pin holder —often cast with decorative elements— and a wire sharpened into a pin on one end and coiled into a spring on the other, an advancement over straight-shafted pins that prevented the point from coming loose and injuring its wearer. Often present on the shoulders of garments such as the Greek chiton and peplos and the Roman toga, the fibula became a status symbol that conveyed wealth and social hierarchy.[2]

With the onset of systematized mass production in the nineteenth century, the safety pin became a utilitarian working-class item, and it is for this reason that it was eventually adopted in the 1970s as a key stylistic marker of punk subculture. While New York punks espoused a nonchalant mix of gritty, low-budget street wear and art-school sophistication, London punks took a more calculated approach, combining S/M styles like bondage straps with overtly political references. Punk fashion was an extension of an overall mindset of disillusionment with a political and cultural landscape that offered no opportunity for social mobility. The safety pin, with its connection to postwar deprivation, was an antifashion symbol that reflected a disdain for materialism and simultaneously celebrated the working-class connotations of its mass production.[3] It was used to hold together ripped clothes (systematically applied in rows) and worn as jewelry, strung together as necklaces or inserted through the ear, nose, cheek, or lip.

The look is generally attributed to Richard Hell of the New York band Television as well as the British fashion designer Vivienne Westwood and the punk impresario Malcolm McLaren, who jointly ran the legendary London boutique Sex. Their 1977 "God Save the Queen" Sex Pistols T-shirt featuring artist Jamie Reid's image of Queen Elizabeth with a safety pin superimposed through her lips was the ultimate punk symbol. The safety pin lives on as a sign of rebellion through, for example, the British designer Zandra Rhodes's use of beaded safety pins in her 1977–78 Conceptual Chic collection, Gianni Versace's defiantly sexual black dress of 1994 with strategic cut-outs fastened with oversize gold safety pins, and the object's brief resurrection as an accessory worn by concerned citizens of Great Britain and the United States in 2016 and 2017 to express solidarity with immigrants and minorities in the face of Brexit and the election of President Donald Trump. —SK

1

3

4

Right:

1— **Nick Knight, *Leigh Bowery with Skull*, 1992**
2— **Model in a coat fastened with safety pins, 1947. Photograph by Lisa Larsen**
3— **Malcolm McLaren and Vivienne Westwood, London, 1977. Unknown photographer**
4— **Elizabeth Hurley and Hugh Grant arriving at the premiere party for Grant's film *Four Weddings and a Funeral*, London, 1994. Photograph by Dave Benett**
5— **Models in garments from the Zandra Rhodes 1977–78 Conceptual Chic collection. Photograph by Clive Arrowsmith**

5

SALWAR KAMEEZ The salwar kameez (or shalwar kameez, qameez, or kamiz) is an ensemble comprising a tunic (kameez) and loose one-size-fits-all pants (salwar), which originated in Punjab long before the partition of Pakistan from India split the region in two. It is also found in communities formerly under Ottoman rule, in particular in Greece and Turkey, where the cut of the garments is similar to styles predating the Christian era.

The outfit is and has historically been unisex; women often add a long scarf (dupatta) styled in various ways. Salwar kameez are commissioned from tailors and also available in ready-to-wear options, which proliferated in the later twentieth century. The ensemble comes in a multitude of fabrics and cuts, and the kameez varies in length, collar design, and embroidered decoration depending on personal taste and prevailing regional or, today, transnational styles.

Some Muslim women have embraced the salwar kameez as part of what the scholar Reina Lewis has called a "South Asian preoccupation with dressing modestly."[1] Incursions against such modesty—by Western ideas about femininity, in particular—are played out through the salwar kameez in India's Bollywood films. The ensemble, still viewed in some contexts as "symbolic of a subdued sexuality compared with revealing Western outfits," was in others transformed, beginning in the 1960s, from an unassuming "Punjabi suit" to a more revealing, sometimes sleeveless, quite deliberately sexy outfit, as worn by movie stars such as Sadhana Shivdasani.[2]

Salwar kameez traveled on the bodies of postcolonial subjects to places such as London, Manchester, Bradford, and Glasgow during the wave of emigration from India (and other former colonies) to the United Kingdom in the 1950s and '60s, and became "frames which fixed and defined [identity] . . . visible proof of permanent difference, provoking not only curiosity but also ridicule, racism, and suspicion."[3] In subsequent generations, people have employed it variously—some, like older family members, for everyday wear; others only for ceremonial attire; still others to fulfill the modesty requirements of their faith.[4] Many schoolgirls on the Indian subcontinent wear it as their uniform, and in certain uniform-only British schools, pupils are allowed to wear one as a symbol of cultural or religious identity.[5]

The appropriation of the salwar kameez by outsiders has been considered respectful, opportunistic, or both. Chelsea and Hillary Clinton wore them, with dupattas covering their hair, on a state visit to Pakistan in 1994, and Oprah Winfrey was resplendent in a gold embroidered version at the Jaipur Literature Festival in 2012. It has also been co-opted, and its origins erased, by Western fashion: a 1998 *Vogue* article noted that the banking heiress Jemima Goldsmith "left her hip London wardrobe behind forever [when she married Pakistani cricketer and politician Imran Khan] . . . [and] revolutionized the Pakistani look by having her flowing pants made with two yards of fabric per leg instead of the usual four."[6] The scholar Meenakshi Gigi Durham has highlighted this displacement of South Asian heritage by youthful, fashionable white Western bodies, often with little regard for culture or context, focusing on pop stars such as Gwen Stefani and Madonna, who have worn nose rings, bindi, saris, and salwar kameez while performing.[7] In this new context these clothes and accessories are read as alluringly exotic rather than foreign and subject to censure; they are cut adrift from the discrimination and oppression encountered by the groups they are taken from. With the rise of terrorist threats from fundamentalist Muslim groups and the so-called war on terror, the salwar kameez has been subject to some of the same vilification and typecasting as the hijab (see *Hijab*).[8]

The salwar kameez occupies a liminal space in the areas where it has been worn for centuries. Benazir Bhutto, who, in 1988, became Pakistan's first female prime minister—and whose predecessor advocated exceedingly conservative

clothing for women, including the burqa—chose it as a middle ground between her former Westernized wardrobe of jeans and couture and the expectations of her new position. The extent of its modesty is still subject to debate: while the Kerala High Court ordered, in December 2016, that women should not be allowed to wear the salwar kameez inside Padmanabha-swamy Temple, ruling it was not pious enough, only a few months earlier a legislator in Andhra Pradesh urged schools to instate it as a uniform for girls in order to ward off sexual harassment.[9] Younger generations now wear it as an alternative to the sari; it is "thought better suited to commuting and work" in both urban and rural areas, and its associations with educated girls and women have made it a symbol of progressive social mores.[10] After the United Kingdom's hotly debated decision to leave the European Union, in 2016, the Delhi-born designer Ashish Gupta, of the British label Ashish, created a spring ready-to-wear collection that celebrated unity and diversity. His designs presented Indian culture as "an integral part of British culture," through which the salwar kameez cycled in various guises—asymmetrical tunic, billowing tea dress, spaghetti-strapped slip dress, and complement to striped tracksuit bottoms.[11]
—MMF

Right:
1— **Women on a scooter, Tamil Nadu, India. Photograph by Yogesh Chawda**
2— **Model on the runway for the Ashish spring/summer 2017 collection, London, 2016. Photograph by Catwalking**
3— **Man relaxing in Lahore, Pakistan, 1992. Photograph by Imran Ahmed**
4— **Hindu students in Kaparda village, Rajasthan, India, 2011. Photograph by Tim Graham**

SARI A major cultural symbol and a living garment in India, the sari is an unstitched, draped textile worn by women. The tradition of wearing unsewn cloth dates back at least a thousand years in India, but the origins of the sari remain murky.[1] The garment comprises a rectangular piece of cloth generally measuring thirteen to twenty-seven feet long and four feet wide. It consists of three areas: the longitudinal borders, the inner and outer end-pieces, and the central field. Although it is a two-dimensional fabric, the sari is conceived on the loom with a three-dimensional body in mind. Usually densely woven and decorated, the borders and end-pieces carry more weight than the central field. They help balance the textile around the body, while the motifs give clues to the positioning of finished drapes.

The ingenuity of the sari lies in its origami-like transformability—something that also makes it one of the most useful maternity-wear garments globally (see *Premaman*). The flat cloth can be artfully pleated, wound, tied, pinned, and draped to form shorts, trousers, skirts, or gowns, easily changeable to suit various functions and occasions, all without a single stich. With its intrinsic fluidity, the sari presents an alternative to the more common relationship between the body and sewn structures. Each sari is native to an individual woman, adapted to her shifting body and sentiments over time. The poetics of the sari reside in the fact that it is not simply put on, but is constructed and activated each time it is worn, in a delicate communication between the body and the world. In the words of writer Hélène Cixous, a sari "doesn't separate the inside from the outside, it translates,

sheltering."[2] For many Indian women, their saris encapsulate their passages of life, from young adulthood to marriage to old age, carrying in their folds an intimate journey suffused with personal cosmology.

There is no one single type of sari but a plethora of textiles, patterns, and modes of draping. The rich variations speak to the diversified regional traditions and identities in India. Sari textiles range from the handwoven Tangail fabrics of Bengal, the *bandhani* tie-dye cloth of Gujarat, and the hand-printed *kalamkaris* of Andhra Pradesh, to the gold brocades of Varanasi (the city also called Banaras). Mill-made saris, often in rayon or polyester, are worn by most working-class women today. They offer an ease of care and a more accessible price than handwoven saris. Iconic women have imbued certain types of sari with specific cultural significance. For example, Indira Gandhi, prime minister of India from 1966 to 1977 and from 1980 to 1984, wore handloomed saris from different regions as a political gesture to affirm her homegrown power. She was most famously identified with the *khadi*, the handspun and handwoven cotton cloth advocated by Mahatma Gandhi that is a symbol— along with the *charkha* upon which it is spun—of India's economic self-sufficiency and political freedom. In post-independence India, the *khadi* continued to emblematize the strengths of indigenous crafts and domestic industry.[3]

There are more than a hundred ways of draping the sari, the products of local heritages enriched by global encounters and negotiated aesthetics. For instance, in northern India, greatly influenced by its rule under the Mughal Empire, women cover their heads with the outer end-piece (*pallav*) of the sari.[4] The popular *nivi* drape adopted by most urban women today emerged only in the 1870s. It was invented by poet Rabindranath Tagore's sister-in-law Gyanodanandini when she accompanied her husband on his Indian civil service post in Mumbai. To achieve a more dignified look in the European circle where she was active, Gyanodanandini incorporated elements drawn from Western fashion—a fitted blouse and a petticoat—as an under-layer.[5] The *nivi* style is columnar and furrowed; the sari is wrapped around the lower body by pleating and tucking about a yard of cloth into the waist of the petticoat, then the remainder is passed across the front body to fall over the left shoulder.

The sari has not lost its appeal among contemporary designers even as it appears to be losing its place in urban Indian women's wardrobes, where it is being replaced by items perceived as less unwieldy (see *Salwar Kameez*) and by Western-style clothing. As Malika V. Kashyap, documentarian of the sari and its myriad drapes, has suggested, "a floor-length sari with a blouse, petticoat, and 15 safety pins may seem cumbersome to everyday living. The irony remains that most of the drapes do not have a petticoat, are often worn without a blouse, and always without safety pins."[6] As India's population continues to grow in the twenty-first century, the sari's future as a daily garment is precarious and much debated.[7] However, its existence appears all the more cutting-edge and forward-looking in today's world, with urban middle-class women experimenting by pairing theirs with collared peplum blouses and even T-shirts.[8] —MMR

Right:
1— Police officer, Darjeeling, India, 2006. Photograph by Uri Baitner
2— Prime Minister Indira Gandhi (center) in the Palace of Government, New Delhi, 1960. Photograph by Giancarlo Botti
3— Market, Ahmedabad, India, October 2016. Photograph by Paola Antonelli
4, 5— Uma Chaudhari–designed sari in a Surguja North drape, a style from Chhattisgarh, and Taanbaan-designed sari in a Mohiniyattam drape with peplum pleats, a style from Kerala, part of *The Sari Series: An Anthology of Drape*, a multimedia project by Malika Verma Kashyap, 2017. Photographs by Bon Duke
6— Bollywood actress Bhanurekha Ganesan at a wedding reception, Mumbai, 2012. Unknown photographer

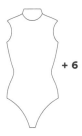

+ 6

6

SEVEN EASY PIECES   When the American designer Donna Karan showed the first collection of her namesake label in the spring of 1985, she declared, "These are not clothes we are looking at. This is not fashion we are talking about; this is a concept."[1] That concept, which became known as Seven Easy Pieces, would serve as the foundation of her future output: clothes made for the modern professional woman by a modern professional woman. It consisted of a knitted bodysuit, trousers, a blazer, a casual skirt, an evening skirt, an overcoat, an oversize shawl, and a variety of accessories, from belts to wrist cuffs, that could be mixed and matched. The bodysuit, presented in a variety of iterations, from turtlenecks to surplice blouses, was the unchanging anchor of the ensemble, a garment over which all the others could be efficiently layered in different combinations depending on time of day and season. "These interchangeable pieces form an entire wardrobe," Karan said. "They pack. They travel. They dress up. They dress down. The whole point is to simplify your life so you can get on to what really matters."[2]

Declared "close to perfection" in *Women's Wear Daily*,[3] Karan's concept resonated with fashion cognoscenti and a trend-following public that had spent the past several years contending with severe menswear-inspired power suits created for women by a host of male designers, including Thierry Mugler and Giorgio Armani (see *Suit*). As the period of second-wave feminism was drawing to a close, women were entering the workplace and climbing the ranks in record numbers, and their clothing was a key signifier and tool in the professional setting. Menswear-inspired suiting, at times heavily bolstered with shoulder pads, had become the standard for female office workers; to achieve power, it was felt, one

had to dress the part, and in a time when most high-level positions were still held by men (despite gains in gender equality), dressing like a man seemed to many women like the best option. "When I was working at Anne Klein in the '70s," Karan has recalled, "women were wearing jackets and bow ties and shirts—more or less dressing like men. Where was the sensuality of women? I don't think anyone really understood how crazy our lives were. Those suits were holding us back. We wanted to move. We wanted to be comfortable."[4] In her review of Karan's debut collection, *New York Times* critic Bernadine Morris agreed: "What makes her collection a standout is that the designer doesn't talk down to the working woman. She doesn't make her look too tailored or dowdy or like a clone of a male executive. The clothes have drama and style. In clothes for the business and professional woman, this is a major breakthrough."[5]

Through her designs, Karan encapsulated the notion of soft power that would be articulated a few years later by the American political scientist Joseph Nye in his 1990 book *Bound to Lead: The Changing Nature of American Power*. Unlike hard power, which, according to Nye, relies on coercion in order to achieve desired outcomes, soft power is subtler and is exerted through influence and by demonstrating admirable values. Karan's Seven Easy Pieces reflected this idea by encouraging women to demonstrate their abilities without reaching for a masculine language of dress to legitimatize their role; more literally, it was a softer take on rigidly tailored men's suiting. Karan's concept was also attuned to the multidimensionality of working women's lives in the 1980s, offering flexibility. "I wanted to simplify—simplify our way of life, simplify how to dress, be able to travel, do things, be in the world," Karan has recalled.[6]

Seven Easy Pieces emerged out of a history of versatile, practical clothing designed for women by women, particularly in the United States. In 1935, for example, Vera Maxwell introduced a "weekend wardrobe" that consisted of two jackets, two skirts, a pair of trousers, a jersey blouse, a riding jacket, and a cotton coverall. Intended to be mixed and matched based on the occasion, the weekend wardrobe accommodated women's busy schedules. During World War II, Claire McCardell created the chic yet practical "Pop-over" dress (see *Wrap*

Dress). With its spacious pocket, surplice neckline, and coordinating oven mitt, the Pop-over was meant to be worn while doing everything from cooking to running errands and could even be "popped over" a pair of pants. In the 1980s Sandra Garratt brought adaptability to casual knitwear with her Multiples line, which consisted of prepackaged pants, tunics, dresses, skirts, and tube tops. Made with a pliable cotton-polyester interlock knit, available in a range of colors, and generically sized at "one size fits most," the garments could be combined in a variety of ways according to the wearer's taste and needs; the packaging even offered diagrams of some possibilities.

"If people say to me that I'm designing for myself," Karan opined in 1985, "they're probably very accurate. I use myself as a barometer. That's something a man can't do."[7] By concentrating on her own needs, Karan paved the way for other women, designers included, to do the same. —SK

Right:
1, 2— Model Suzanne Lanza in a Donna Karan four-pattern package wardrobe, *Vogue Patterns*, **autumn 1987. Photographs by Benoit Malphettes**
3— Advertisement for Sandra Garratt Modular Looks Multiples, *Vogue*, **spring 1989. Photograph by Les Hall**
4— Models after the Donna Karan spring 1986 runway show, New York, 1985. Photograph by Pierre Sherman

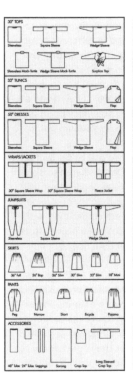

SHAWL The English "shawl" derives from the Persian word *shāl*, which itself originated in a Sanskrit term meaning finely woven wool cloth. The finest such cloth is Kashmir (or cashmere), which is made of soft hair combed from the belly and throat of Himalayan mountain goats. Over the centuries, goat hair was collected and transported to the Kashmir region in India, where it was spun and woven into shawls. Elaborate cashmere shawls featured decorative patterns formed by tapestry weave, a time-consuming craft; it could take eighteen months to three years to complete one garment.

Indian cashmere shawls had long been circulated and treasured in Asia and North Africa, reaching the vast regions spreading from China to Iran and from Russia to Egypt.[1] British colonizers in India brought home cashmere shawls as precious souvenirs, and these textiles became imbricated in European women's fashion from the late eighteenth century. They also came to symbolize masculinity for the English gentleman, as depicted in portraiture proudly glorifying them in Indian costumes, their splendid shawls embodying the British empire's political domination and material wealth made through global trade.

The rise of cashmere shawls as women's fashion in the late 1780s was directly triggered by neoclassicism in Europe, which embraced the purportedly natural and balanced beauty of ancient Greek and Roman art and inspired simplified silhouettes and unadorned fabrics such as white muslin. Shawls complemented the new style by adding a vibrant layer to the restrained color scheme. European production of shawls after the Indian prototype began at this time. These products were distinguished by their materials (a combination of silk and wool as a substitute for hard-to-obtain cashmere) and the faster weaving techniques permitted by the mechanical Jacquard loom beginning in the mid-nineteenth century.

In the 1860s shawls of low price and low quality began to be produced in large quantity in Europe, appealing to women of all walks of life, from the aristocratic to the bourgeois and the working class. Shawls subtly distinguished the wearer's social status through their origins (Indian imports vs. European mass-market imitations), materials (fine cashmeres vs. blended fibers), and drape (gaping and trailing vs. decorous and proper). French period literature such as Balzac's *Cousin Bette* (1846) and Flaubert's *Sentimental Education* (1869) structured characters and plots around this object of desire and through it sensitively captured the era's anxieties over social authenticity and mobility.[2] The economic depression that followed the Franco-Prussian War put an end to the fashion, a displacement reinforced by the new silhouettes favored in the following decades.

Shawls have remained a wardrobe staple for many, exploding as a fad from time to time. A short-lived trend for cashmere shawls (marketed as *pashmina*, another Persian word denoting wool) at the turn of the twenty-first century in Europe and the United States saw inexpensive low-quality versions flourish at tourist-city street stands.[3] It was an extreme example of trickle-down fashion: the blatant appropriation (and ultimate disposability) of luxury products manufactured for the impulse-buying everyday consumer. —MMR

Previous page:
1— A hand-embroidered shawl commissioned by Kashmir Loom, New Delhi, 2017. Photograph by Asaf Ali
2— Scarves, hats, and shawls for sale, New York, 2016. Photograph by Michelle Millar Fisher
3— Portrait of Sayyid Rajû Qattâl, Sufi saint and spiritual master of the Sultan of Golconde, c. 1690
4— John Singer Sargent, *The Cashmere Shawl*, 1911. Photograph © 2017 Museum of Fine Arts, Boston

SHIFT DRESS With its straight lines and unassuming shape, the shift dress seems a basic garment, a comfortable dress that is fitted at the bust but otherwise unstructured. "Nobody knows exactly when or where it was born," mused *Vogue* in 1938 in "Success Story of the Shift Dress," which marked the item's first mention in the magazine.[1] Its silhouette has varied with the times: in the 1930s it was ankle- or knee-length and ample in material; during World War II its shape was reduced to accommodate wartime fabric rations. *Vogue*, in 1943, printed a pattern for "an afternoon shift dress" that sat flush to the body and featured minimal construction details, assuring its readers, "If you make your clothes under *Vogue*'s guidance, you can also be sure today that they are in accordance with wartime regulations that your Government has issued."[2] The 1960s version—sleeveless, above the knee, straight and minimal, often boasting diagonal darts running from the side seam to the bustline—remains current today, appearing in iterations both professional-looking and retro-inspired. As a blank canvas for patterns and embellishment, and as a vehicle for experiments with different materials, the shift dress's seeming simplicity is its biggest asset.

In the 1960s in the United States, a screenprinted cotton version was known among its many wearers as "the Lilly." Lilly Pulitzer, a juice-stand owner in Palm Beach, Florida, began hand printing the practical shape in brightly colored patterns to camouflage juice stains. Her clothes caught the eye of Palm Beach's wealthy resort set, and she eventually opened a shop. Pulitzer's shift became a chic staple among vacationers and locals—it could be worn straight from beach to cocktail party—and among prominent figures such as First Lady Jacqueline Kennedy, who was photographed wearing it at the

Kennedys' Hyannis Port, Massachusetts, compound. The silhouette's popularity prompted *Women's Wear Daily* to declare, in 1963, "The switch to shifts is on. . . . They are selling in all price ranges . . . from Lilly Pulitzer's $45 (top retail price line) to $25 (big volume seller), down to $1.87 and even 99-cent numbers."[3]

Among the variations that subsequently became available was Marimekko's boldly colored Laine dress, a Scandinavian counterpoint to the Lilly. The designer Anne Klein demonstrated the shift's adaptability in the 1960s with her Junior Sophisticates line, which was made for petite women and was offered in materials such as crepe and linen. Earlier in her career Klein had cautioned that "extremes and misplacements" were "pitfalls for designs of the special size group," and her "long torso shift dress" made the silhouette available to women of different body types.[4]

Disposable paper versions appeared in 1966, thanks in part to a promotional stunt by Scott Paper Co. Eliminating the need for laundering and tailoring (*Time* magazine noted, "A quick snip of the scissors and the hem is shortened"), the paper dress gave women access to a variety of designs at affordable prices (some cost less than a dollar).[5] In the late 1960s the designer Harry Gordon's Poster Dresses were inspired by popular culture and politics, with packaging that suggested, "should you tire [of it] (which is doubtful), just cut open all the seams and hang it on your wall as a poster, or cover pillows."

In dresses that were similarly experimental, though not as affordable, the Spanish designer Paco Rabanne used industrial materials such as plastic and steel, which he thought necessary to "[open] up the eyes of the sleepy people who are too comfortable in the cotton-wool of their traditions."[6] A sculptural micromini dress, constructed from aluminum squares and rectangles hinged together with metal rings, was introduced in 1966 as part of Rabanne's Twelve Unwearable Dresses collection, which questioned the commonplace relationship between a garment's materials, its construction, and the body that wears it. Although somewhat graduated at the waistline, the dress nevertheless reflected the era's popular shift shape.

Helmut Lang, in the 1980s and '90s, approached materials with a keen understanding of the generation he was designing for.[7] A dress from 1994, made with his student Susanne Bisovsky, and featuring a rubber under-layer fused with Chantilly lace, was dubbed "the little rubber dress" by *Vogue*, which observed, "Lang understands that the shine on fabric worn by this generation should look more like a crinkled candy wrapper or a nylon bomber jacket than a disco dress."[8] The designer Hussein Chalayan took a more conceptual tack in Geotropics, his spring/summer 1999 collection, which featured a sheer white organza dress amplified in the front with layers of deconstructed dress components. A study in how geography forms nations and customs, the shift was a visual metaphor for the Silk Road and the cultures along its path, with its layers derived from an animated film depicting a garment's journey along the route. Chalayan felt that the dress's wearer would give it a "new sense of life . . . shaped by the ever-changing body environment"—perhaps the perfect metaphor for the shift dress itself.[9] —SK

Previous pages:
1— American socialite Wendy Vanderbilt (right) and friend in Lilly Pulitzer sundresses, Palm Beach, Florida, 1964. Photograph by Slim Aarons
2— Model on the runway for the Chalayan spring/summer 1999 Geotropics collection. Photograph by Chris Moore
3— Model Tatjana Patitz on the runway for the Helmut Lang fall/winter 1994/95 ready-to-wear collection. Photograph by Guy Marineau
4— Model in a Harry Gordon paper dress featuring Bob Dylan, Milan, 1967. Photograph by Alfa Castaldi

A YARD OF PRISC

THE MODERN

2

SHIRTDRESS The shirtdress or shirtwaist dress has been a staple of women's wardrobes since the 1930s and is a key example of American sportswear. With its front-buttoned bodice and collar, which together resemble an elongated shirt, the shirtdress was derived from the shirtwaist blouse of the late nineteenth and early twentieth centuries, itself rooted in the Garibaldi shirt of the 1860s, modeled after the red shirt worn by the Italian nationalist and freedom fighter. The shirtwaist blouse (or shirtwaist) signaled a move toward women's separates, particularly in the United States; it was proclaimed in 1862 by *Godey's Lady's Book and Magazine* to be "destined to produce change amounting to a revolution in Ladies' costume."[1] The silhouette ranged from tailored men's shirts to loose lightweight blouses trimmed with lace, and they were worn with skirts for housework, as part of a sportswear ensemble, or with bloomers for cycling. The shirtwaist represented an early turn to practicality in women's wear, a notion that would prove integral to the shirtdress as well.

The shirtdress first appeared in the 1920s in the United States. It was often referred to as a "sports dress" when worn for golf and tennis, while companies such as Best and Co. advertised it as a "shirtmaker frock."[2] It was not until the 1930s, however, that the shirtdress became a widely recognized option for women's sports clothing. Mass-market versions, such as the moderately priced dresses in cotton broadcloth, chambray, and wool flannel produced by the McMullen Company in Glens Falls, New York, were readily available by 1935.[3] The shirtdress was first mentioned in American *Vogue* in 1937, when it reported that the French

NUE, BOSTON, MASS.

1

3

socialite Madame de Léglise was "seen at the Chiberta golf club" wearing a "red-and-white silk shirt dress, and high-heeled sandals with red kid straps knotted over the ankles."[4] Its popularity as sports clothing was codified in 1938 in *Life* magazine's "Summer Sports Clothes," which featured the "classic shirtwaist dress" in its selection of ensembles.[5]

As pants became acceptable for women's sporting activities, the shirtdress moved into their daily wardrobes. For much of the 1940s a simplified version, due to shortages caused by the rationing of fabric, formed part of wartime style, but by the end of the decade its silhouette was full-skirted, cinched at the waist, and made in a variety of textiles. It was a dress that could be worn day or night; *Vogue*, in 1954, promoted "After-Five Plans for the Shirt Dress," declaring, "The shirt idea: newest when it's luxurious. Here, three shirt dresses to make for late-day parties, dinners; all a matter of simple lines in rich fabrics."[6] The same magazine declared the shirtdress one of the items to include "if you are going to compress into a time capsule the very essence of January 1, 1950," even more relevant, according to the magazine's list, than a television set.[7] Demure and respectable, appropriate for both housework and a dinner date, the dress was an expression of the ideal qualities and limited spheres for women at the time.

In the 1960s and '70s, as second-wave feminism gained a foothold in the West, women's professional and personal choices expanded. Clothing reflected this zeitgeist, and there is perhaps no better example of this than Roy Halston's take on the shirtdress. Introduced in the fall of 1972 as "model number 704," Halston's shirtdress was constructed from Ultrasuede, a trademarked nonwoven material made from needle-punched polyester microfibers that gave it a suedelike appearance. Resistant to stains and discoloration, but also washable, the Ultrasuede shirtdress was both practical and feminine. While Halston's garment—with its set-in collar, center back yoke, and two-button cuffed sleeves—certainly resembled a man's shirt, he subtly tweaked the details, making the collar oversize, shaping the sleeves to a more fitted silhouette, and cutting the dress in a slightly A-line shape. He also positioned the buttons so that they began at the breastbone rather than the

neckline, providing women with a décolletage-revealing garment for day. All of these changes rendered his shirtdress uniquely feminine while maintaining its smart versatility, so that it could be worn in a variety of contexts. In 1972 both *Women's Wear Daily* and *Vogue* reported that the shirtdress was Halston's best seller, a standout among his pared-down offerings, which included glamorous party gowns and jumpsuits, and in 1973, *Women's Wear Daily* dubbed it "the suede uniform," the "'everywhere' dress of the season" that "ladies turn out in en masse for luncheons, meetings about town."[8]

Today the shirtdress is as ubiquitous as it is varied. From the oversize version with minimal construction details that appeared in Celine's spring/summer 2017 collection to the more romantic designs incorporating sheer panels shown by Carolina Herrera in her spring/summer 2016 presentation, the shirtdress continues to offer the "power to take you everywhere," as British *Vogue* put it.[9] But it now does so in a cultural climate where femininity can mean many things: "There's a shirtdress for every woman, from androgynous types to feminine souls—just dial up (or down) the flourish."[10] —SK

Left:
**1— Sixteen designs for shirtwaists in an advertisement for the needlework magazine *The Modern Priscilla*, c. 1906
2— Model in a shirtdress, *Vogue*, February 1948. Photograph by Irving Penn
3— Model in a Halston Ultrasuede shirtdress, *Vogue*, August 1972. Photograph by Bob Stone**

SILK SCARF Women gradually discarded accessories as the twentieth century progressed—shawls, fans, parasols, dress hats, and gloves have all faded from fashion. Despite, or perhaps because of, this simplification of the wardrobe, the silk scarf has flourished. In its many modes of folding and tying, it transforms a look, pronounces a mood, or provides a quick fix for everything from a bad hair day to unexpected drizzle.

In the precursor of the modern silk scarf is the fichu, a large rectangular or square-shaped kerchief popular in Europe during the eighteenth and nineteenth centuries. Typically made of plain linen and muslin but also found in fine lace and embroidered silk, a fichu folded around the neck and shoulders, crossing in the front to tuck into the bodice to modestly cover the décolleté.[1]

In the 1920s liberated flappers wrapped long silk scarves around their bobbed hair, knotted at the side or at the nape of the neck with the tail end flowing flamboyantly down their backs. When looped around the neck, voluminous swirls of billowing silk lent an ensemble a seductive air of exoticism and drama—as worn, unforgettably, by modern dancer Isadora Duncan, who died a tragic death on the French Riviera in 1927 when her "immense iridescent silk scarf" was caught in the wheel of the convertible in which she was riding.[2] The 1960s saw multiple women's headwear fashions involving square textile swatches (see *Head Wrap*), including a crisp, long silk scarf, neatly folded into a narrow bandeau handband with ends draping down.

By contrast, the square, printed silk *carré* primarily evokes elegance and a benevolent propriety. Most closely identified with French luxury goods manufacturer Hermès but also made by other fashion houses, such as Ferragamo and Gucci, the carré was born in the late 1930s. Measuring nearly three square feet, these scarves can be worn in diverse manners, including around the handles of a handbag—a signifier of luxury even when the head or hair needs no protection. French writer Colette wore it as a huge bowtie. Queen Elizabeth II folds it in half over her head and knots it under her chin. Actress Grace Kelly popularized the "Princess style," wrapping an extra-large version around her head and tying it in the back (and, on occasion and to stylish effect, using it as a sling for her arm or as a strapless kerchief blouse while riding a horse). In the 1960s rebellious young women turned their mothers' Hermès carrés into miniskirts. In the 2000s the British singer Amy Winehouse paired retro chic with rockabilly by wrapping one around her enormous beehive hairstyle.

The most luxurious silk scarves are silkscreened and hemmed by hand. Specific designs are immediately recognizable, like Hermès's classic equestrian-themed Brides de Gala (1957). When worn, folded and knotted, the image is distorted into abstract patterns and blocks of color, rendering the design an intimate secret, each silk carré a private pleasure for its wearer. —MMR

Right:
1— NASA Hubble silk scarf by Slow Factory, from the Floating in Space collection, 2013. Photograph by Julia Robbs
2— Hainan Airlines flight attendants, Beijing, 2013. Photograph by Feng Gang
3— Workers printing silk for Hermès scarves, Bourgoin-Jallieu, France, 2009. Photograph by Kasia Wandycz
4— Princess Grace of Monaco with a Hermès silk scarf sling, followed by Aristotle Onassis and Prince Rainier, Monte Carlo, 1959. Unknown photographer/ Avalon

SLIP DRESS On November 5, 1993, Calvin Klein sent eighty-nine looks down the runway for his spring 1994 ready-to-wear presentation, a collection of dresses that the *New York Times* fashion critic Bernadine Morris described as being "in fabrics like satin and muslin, and they sometimes nestle under a cashmere cardigan. The thin fabrics offer no camouflage, so occasionally the dresses are worn over a short tank-top dress, which serves as a slip. Similar tank-top styles serve as dresses and are piled one on top of the other to cut the transparency." Klein, she observed, "who has always been a minimalist, pushes his position to its limit."[1]

Although Morris did not use the term at the time, this silhouette—a shapeless, body-grazing sleeveless dress, typically made of silk—would become the ubiquitous slip dress of the 1990s. The designation had been used for years but the '90s version would crystallize in part thanks to Klein's show, which captured the zeitgeist: its less-is-more aesthetic as well as the trend of wearing underwear as outerwear made the dress, according to the fashion writer Colin McDowell, "an oblique answer to earlier more blatantly sexual looks, [which] didn't carry with it overtones of wealth."[2] Klein's slip dresses proved integral to the season's fashion story, with examples featured in editorials in both *Harper's Bazaar* and *Vogue* in February 1994 (the latter included two of Klein's slip dresses in the same article). The association of Klein with the slip dress—the dress that "no woman could live without," according to *Vogue* in August 1994—was confirmed in 1996, when an ingénue named Gwyneth Paltrow wore a deceptively simple beaded white Calvin Klein slip dress to the Academy Awards ceremony.[3]

The word *slip* has been used since the seventeenth century to describe different undergarments for women. Slips employed as corset covers in the eighteenth century sometimes included sleeves and closures; slips since the latter half of the twentieth century have taken the form of unstructured petticoats, to be worn under dresses and skirts, either sleeveless and full-length or hanging from the waist. The term *slip dress* has also been applied to different silhouettes, from simple wool sheaths in the 1950s to slinky silk spaghetti-strap gowns in the 1970s. It first appeared in *Vogue* in 1934, describing a multipiece dress with a foundation layer; the article went on to say, "It starts out with a slip of crepe or satin. . . . Then, there may be a train that ties on, or shoulder veilings or a sheer overdress. And over this, again, there may be a tunic."[4]

The slip dress's relationship to its namesake undergarment has changed over time in accordance with standards of modesty. In 1949 the American weekly magazine *Quick* published a photo-essay that followed Henry Callahan, the display chief at Lord & Taylor department store, one evening as he escorted a model wearing a slip as if it were a dress, to "demonstrate oversimplification of [the day's] '20s-inspired evening fashions."[5] Women have worn underwear-inspired clothing at different points in history, such as Marie Antoinette and her *chemise à la reine*, of the 1780s—a lightweight dress consisting of layers of thin muslin, loosely draped and belted at the waist, considered quite scandalous in its heyday—and the bias-cut, body-skimming charmeuse gowns of the 1930s. But the codification of the slip dress in the 1990s was due not only to the period's minimalist aesthetic, but also to the element of performance brought to the garment by those who wore it—often with heavy boots and leather jackets, as if contradicting the dress's drape and fabrication; for those wearers, the slip dress seemed to be less about accentuating stereotypes of femininity than subverting them. When the model Kate Moss wore a transparent Liza Bruce slip dress to a party given by Elite modeling agency in 1993, accessorized with cotton underwear and a pair of flip-flops (along with a cigarette and a bottle of beer), the shock of the ensemble came not from its sexual overtones but from the utter nonchalance with which it was worn, "a display of pure casual rebellion," as interpreted by the *Guardian* writer Imogen Fox.[6] Courtney Love, the lead singer for the

band Hole, was famous for her brash onstage style and confrontational approach to gender issues; she often wore slip dresses for her concerts, with nothing added but a guitar and red (often smeared) lipstick. Barefoot and wailing into the microphone, Love, like Moss, destabilized the slip dress's genteel associations, using her sardonic punk style to turn it into a symbol of defiance and independence.

In all their forms—whether spaghetti strapped or tank style—slip dresses continue to be disruptive garments; skimming the body without clinging, they are, as Morris wrote, "not intended to be worn under anything. They're dresses, meant to be seen. . . . Everything is reduced to essentials."[7]
—SK

Right:
1— Courtney Love performing at Lollapalooza, Chicago, 1995. Photograph by Kevin Mazur
2— Models Christiana Steidten and Denise Hopkins with unknown male model, *Vogue*, November 1973. Photograph by Chris von Wangenheim
3— Kate Moss in a Liza Bruce slip dress at an Elite modeling agency party, London, 1993. Photograph by Richard Young
4— Model Bridget Hall on the runway for the Calvin Klein spring 1994 ready-to-wear collection. Photograph by Dan Lecca
5— Henry Callahan and Annlee Danels, dressed in a slip, on a night out in New York, *Quick*, December 1949. Unknown photographer

2

4

5

SNUGLI In the 1960s Ann and Mike Moore were living and working in Togo, West Africa, part of the first generation of Peace Corps volunteers. They observed mothers there using a length of cloth to bind their children (from infants to toddlers) to their fronts or backs, a practice that seemed to engender a close bond. After she returned home, Ann asked her mother to help her fashion something similar for her own daughter, and following several iterations the Snugli was patented in 1969. The design drew on the long history of baby wearing in Africa and beyond.[1] Baby carriers, which mimic the hands-free marsupial pouch, are known by other names, including the pan-Asian *mei tai*, Korean *podaegi*, and Mexican *rebozo*. They can be worn as a sling (sometimes fastened with a ring), wrapped and tied, or sewn or buckled into soft bucket shapes worn by the child's parent, older siblings, grandparents, and other carers.[2]

The Snugli came in denim, corduroy, and, later, seersucker, with an adjustable lateral band and shoulder straps; its early marketing claimed it was a remedy for colic and showed it being used in homes and hospitals. American parents were ready for such a development; Cold War propaganda emphasized the stability and mental health of mothers and children, and one result was the humanization of hospital childbirth: newborns were no longer whisked away to a communal nursery, and rooming-in units were provided, warmly decorated with rocking chairs, bassinets, and space for new families to bond.[3] "Is Your Wife Too Civilized?," an article in *Better Homes & Gardens* in 1949, reported the research of James Maloney, an army physician stationed in Okinawa, Japan, on the extraordinary mental resilience he observed in the local population during and after World War II; he attributed this to baby wearing, which he felt offered a "secure infancy, helping children develop into mentally healthy adults."[4] This connection between early development and adult behavior was a popular thread in parenting psychology. Dr. Spock encouraged warm physical contact in the 1940s; Jean Liedloff's *Continuum Concept*, published in 1975, was influenced by the Ye'kuana people of Venezuela; and the American pediatrician Williams Sears encouraged immersive "attachment parenting" starting in the early 1980s.[5] In each case non-Western traditions were presented, often superficially, as paradigms for the raising of healthy, loved infants (and thus adults), and almost always encouraged accessories such as the baby carrier. Such co-opting has signaled a bohemian attitude toward child-rearing in postindustrial countries since the 1960s.

During the 1960s and '70s Snuglis were made by hand by girls and women in southern Ohio, until factory production was implemented and clients such as Walmart and Target signed on. The Moores sold their company in the 1980s and formed Weego, a similar enterprise (also now sold) in the 1990s, when their grandchildren were born. Baby carriers are now popular and commonplace, with many companies—including Moby, Ergobaby, and BabyBjörn—producing versions that mediate the fashions and functions of parenting. —MMF

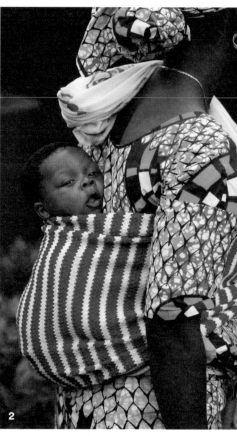

Right:
1— **Man and child using a Tula Ring Sling, San Diego, California, 2014. Photograph by Chrystal Cienfuegos**
2— **West African woman carrying her baby on her back, Togo, 2015. Unknown photographer**
3— **Snugli inventor Ann Moore carrying her daughter Mandela on the Selma to Montgomery civil rights march, Alabama, March 1965. Photograph by Morton Broffman**

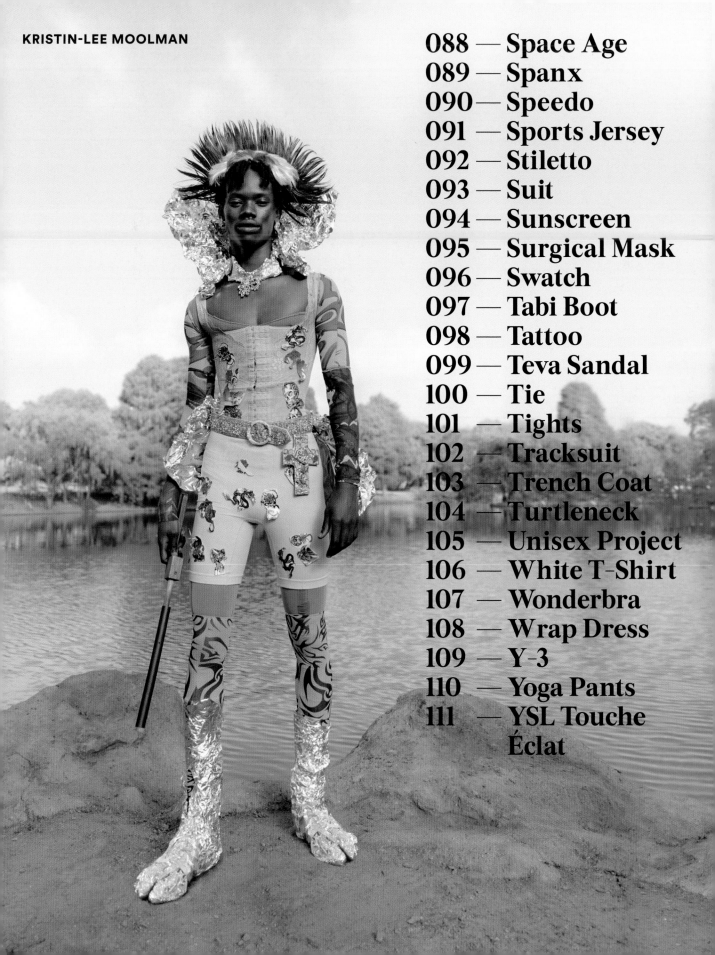

KRISTIN-LEE MOOLMAN

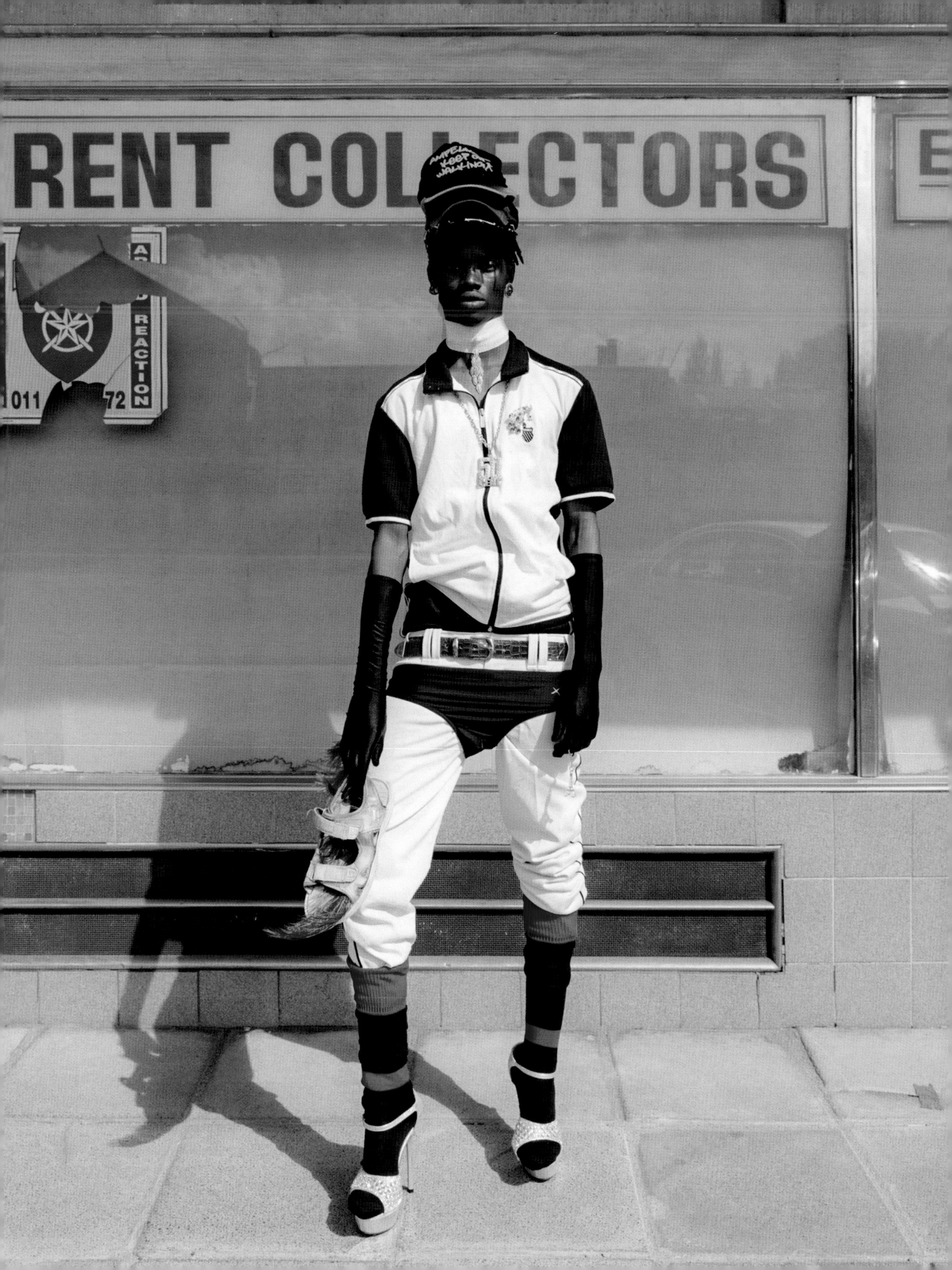
RENT COLLECTORS
REACTION

SPACE AGE   From the introduction of nylon in the 1930s to the 3-D printing of dresses and shoes in the early 2000s, fashion of the last century has constantly adopted the latest in technology. In the 1960s this future-oriented attitude was sped up by the achievements in space exploration that came to define the decade. From the Soviet Union's launch of Sputnik 1 in 1957 to the Apollo 11 moon landing in 1969, the space age wrought a new modernity characterized by the optimistic embrace of rapid technological advancement.

Fashion designers like André Courrèges and Paco Rabanne responded by exploring new frontiers in clothing design, including the use of metal, vinyl, and synthetic textiles, and employing crisp, geometric motifs and silhouettes. For Italian-born French designer Pierre Cardin, this approach led not only to material and formal innovation, but also, as exemplified by his Cosmocorps line, to a questioning of the system of fashion itself.

Introduced in 1964, the Cosmocorps line (also known as Cosmos) espoused an egalitarian method of dress and was a natural extension of Cardin's previous space-age explorations, including his 1958 felt helmet hat and his 1960 collection of brightly colored trapezoidal coats boasting oversize orblike buttons. Offering ensembles for both men and women, Cosmocorps comprised streamlined, body-skimming numbers in heavyweight woolen jersey, accented with geometric vinyl appliqué or geometric shapes cut out of the garments themselves. Circles—which "represented infinity, spinning endlessly," to Cardin, according to his long-time collaborator Jean-Pascal Hesse—featured prominently, even emerging as the central motif of the designer's signature zipper pull.[1] Men's Cosmocorps styles took the form of sleeveless tunics or jackets layered over ribbed-jersey turtlenecks and knitted pants (often over-laid with hip-hugging belts), while women's outfits were composed of sleeveless, tabard-style A-line dresses layered over jersey turtlenecks and tights. Although discernably gendered, the ensembles' coordination in silhouette, motif, and color (bold primaries, black and white) gave them an air of uniformity, while their construction entirely from knitted material espoused a modern practicality.

"What I try to do is to create a style . . . a style which is contemporary, modern," Cardin said of his work, and indeed his modernity stemmed not simply from the aesthetic of his designs, but also from the process through which they circulated.[2] Having established his couture house in 1953, Cardin caused controversy in 1959 when he presented a women's ready-to-wear collection in Paris's Printemps department store—a commercial gambit that was as yet unexplored territory for couturiers bound by Paris's governing fashion body, the Chambre Syndicale de la Haute Couture Parisienne. While haute couture was made to measure for private clients, necessitating numerous fittings and boasting hefty price tags, ready-to-wear was manufactured according to predetermined size runs and sold in shops and department stores that catered to the masses. Cardin's foray into the world of ready-to-wear resulted in his expulsion from the Chambre Syndicale, a punishment that was short-lived, as his visionary thinking soon goaded other couturiers, including Yves Saint Laurent, to do the same. "You have no idea," Cardin told *Women's Wear Daily* in 1967, "how I was criticized by my couture colleagues when I started a department at the Magasins du Printemps. But what are they all doing now? Look at Saint Laurent selling jersey dresses for $60."[3]

Indeed, in addition to capitalizing presciently on the burgeoning influence and buying power of the youth market, Cardin's vision of wider distribution also anticipated a landscape in which new fashions would be made available to the masses at a wide range of price points. Though the Cosmocorps line did not sell on a mass scale (it was dubbed "too modern for the average buyer," by Hesse),[4] Cardin's mark was nonetheless made, and his diversification into a multitude of lines (including menswear and children's wear), along with his entry into a variety of licensing agreements, set the stage for the multifarious ways designers would

propagate their artistic visions in the years to come.

Today Cardin's legacy is felt on a number of levels, from temporary "capsule" artistic collaborations between designers and brands to the proliferation of inexpensive, mass-produced fast fashion by companies such as H&M and Zara. While recent capsule projects tend to resonate with the spirit of Cardin's space-age exploration of fashion, the fast-fashion trend has only intensified the problematic if unintended consequences of his innovations in the mass merchandising of luxury brands: inextricably tied to the socioeconomics of globalization, the triumph of Cardin's model has contributed to the degradation of human labor and environmental resources worldwide. In 2017 the designer Kerby Jean-Raymond responded to this unwitting legacy by reimagining Cardin's Cosmocorps for a 2067 fashion climate, in which environmental changes that are the outcome of today's irresponsibility will necessitate functional (Haus-Rucker-esque) inflatable clothing "bubbles" to facilitate flotation in the face of rising sea levels. Coming full circle to a view of the future now turned dystopic, Jean-Raymond draws on Cardin's optimistic forms and motifs, redeploying them in response to diminishing future prospects—diminished, in fact, by the capitalist vision Cardin so earnestly celebrated. Although the space age is a vision of the future rooted in the past, its impact on fashion remains—and its implications for the future remain to be seen. —SK

Previous page:
1— **Edwina Carroll in the film *2001: A Space Odyssey*, 1968**
2— **Models in Pierre Cardin's Cosmos collection, 1967. Photograph by Yoshi Takata**
3— **Yellow Heart weekend house for two, designed by Ortner, Zamp, Pinter for Haus-Rucker-Co., Vienna, 1968**

3

SPANX Spanx is a brand whose name is synonymous with its product. The American entrepreneur Sara Blakely established the company in 2000 after coming up with a creative solution to a personal problem—the lack of suitable foundation garments that could provide a smooth look under clothing (in particular, a now infamous pair of white pants Blakely owned).[1] Shaped like a pair of leggings, Blakely's invention flattened visible bulges along the waist, hips, and thighs; Spanx was the name she gave to these "footless body-shaping pantyhose" and to the company that would sell them. Following the massive success of that first product, which is now called the Power Capri, Spanx diversified into underwear, loungewear, activewear, and even maternity shapewear; it netted $4 million in its first year and $250 million in 2012.[2]

Although shapewear is by no means a novel concept (it goes back as far as the waist-sculpting *zona* of ancient Greece), Blakely advanced it in two ways. Her first innovation was technological. She drew on the compressive qualities of control-top panty hose but eliminated the pinching at the waistline and thighs that they typically produce, therefore offering a smooth contour from rib cage to knee. Although Spanx body-shaping panty hose were fabricated in a heavy-gauge nylon-Lycra blend like their predecessors, they did not feature a stomach-cinching rubber cord in the waistband, instead boasting a tightly knitted yarn combination that extended above the lower rib cage. Blakely also applied this concept to the garment's legs, knitting the leg bands into the garment so that they did not cut into the flesh. Spanx featured a cotton gusset at the crotch (as opposed to the typical thinner cotton-nylon combination) that not only provided extra recovery when the garment stretched but also eliminated the need for underwear.

Blakely's second innovation was related to communications and marketing: she positioned Spanx as a garment designed by a woman for other women. In researching similar products, she realized that it was primarily men who had been responsible for creating them. "It made me, as a consumer who had never thought about who was making my undergarments, abundantly clear on why they had been so uncomfortable," Blakely would recall.[3] She was also shocked to learn that panty hose were tested on mannequins rather than real women: "Once I saw how little attention was being paid to how we felt in the garments, I kind of became a crusader in my desire to really show the industry that we could make things so much better for women."[4] Blakely's mission is evident even in the product's cherry-red packaging, which features playful illustrations of Spanx-clad women (including one in a superhero's cape). But while Spanx were certainly the result of a genuine effort to unshackle women, they nonetheless reinforce a prescribed beauty standard and its pursuit via physical compression and oppression.

Body manipulation has a long history, one that parallels the complex, evolving relationship between socially mandated beauty ideals and female empowerment. The Chinese practice of foot-binding is one example. It originated during the Song dynasty (960–1279) and was initially reserved for the wives and daughters of high-status men, as well as courtesans and actresses, but spread rapidly to other social groups and was practiced through the early twentieth century. Adoration of small feet ran deep in Chinese culture; the fable of Ye Xian, China's Cinderella, was published as early as the ninth century, in a collection of stories titled *Miscellaneous Morsels from Youyang*. Foot-binding, which was achieved through careful—and painful—wrapping, was never mandated (for example, women of Manchu descent eschewed the practice during the sixteenth century), but it was considered a privilege that symbolized female refinement.[5] While many women undoubtedly felt oppressed by the practice, others saw it as a way to prove their desirability, worth, and social currency. Similarly, the corset, a rigid bodice worn throughout the Western world from the sixteenth century to the early twentieth century, served to achieve an idealized body that could conform to fashionable dress. Designed to shape the female torso through constriction (typically via vertical and diagonal boning), the corset has been both criticized as a torture device and exalted as a fetishistic object of pleasure. While some wearers certainly found the corset burdensome—their complaints supported by contemporaneous medical rhetoric about the garment's health risks—many women viewed it as an item that fostered self-discipline and signified social status, respectability, beauty, and erotic allure.[6]

Both foot-binding and corsetry had vehement detractors during the periods in which they were popular, but they persisted as long as culturally decreed ideals of beauty necessitated them. While Spanx might appear to be these traditions' redemptive twenty-first-century offspring, it too raises questions about whether such garments grant women the smooth bodies they desire, or pressure them into altering their physiques in pursuit of yet another unattainable ideal. —SK

Previous pages:
1— **Stereographic image of a woman being corseted, 1897. Unknown photographer**
2— **Roussel girdle, c. 1930s. Unknown photographer**
3— **Model Ashley Graham in Spanx. Unknown photographer**

SPEEDO Can a swimsuit be faster than a birthday suit? For more than a century, designers have striven for optimal swim-wear hydrodynamics, experimenting with suits that are tight, light, nonabsorbent, and unencumbering, and at the same time meet social standards for body coverage.

In 1928 Speedo innovated a men's one-piece knitted natural-blend suit with a V-shaped back strap. This "racerback" design increased upper-body motion and reduced drag. The Australian Olympian Clara Dennis was almost denied a medal in 1932 for wearing a women's version (deemed inappropriate for exposing her shoulder blades). Men first swam topless in the 1936 Games.

Synthetic fabrics were introduced in the 1930s, and nylon knit, developed by Speedo in the 1950s for competitive swimwear, remained standard until the introduction of elasticized nylon-Lycra blends in the 1970s. These blends clung to the whole body, allowing suits to be cut smaller and tighter.

Speedos from the 1968 and 1972 Olympics were some of the first to be marketed to general consumers, a campaign aided by a highly popular poster of American swimmer Mark Spitz wearing only his Speedo and the seven gold medals he won at the Munich Games. The poster sold over a million copies and presumably a similar number of suits, ushering in a generation of men in the briefest of briefs. In 1976 the trend became the norm when Halston designed uniforms for the U.S. Olympic team, with variants sold through the retailer Montgomery Ward. Olympic licensing has since become as competitive as the Games themselves.

The women's 1968 Speedo featured a traditional scoop-style back, water-retaining center panel and lining, and vestigial skirt (a longstanding requirement for women's swimsuits eliminated by the International Swimming Federation only in the early 1970s). Patterned nylon was new at the 1968 Olympics, creating new opportunities to graphically represent national identity and market alternative colorways as fashion. The game changed in 1969 with the introduction of a radical "skinsuit" by West German doctor Konrad Döttinger, who soon marketed it as "the Belgrad". This sleek fine-cotton knitted suit was engineered for minimum water resistance, with rubber banding at the arm, leg, and neck and a mesh strip down the back. By the 1976 Olympics, Speedo and other brands were meeting the new standard with nylon-Lycra fabric, raised leg openings, and reduced linings. Women's suits, now skirtless, incorporated a high neckline and racerback straps that returned the Speedo to its roots.

In the 1990s Speedo innovated the Fastskin, designed to mimic sharkskin. Speedo then collaborated with specialized engineers and designers to develop its LZR line, introduced at the 2008 Olympic Games. Swimmers squeezed into the impermeable, full-body polyurethane suits that corseted them into streamlined form and strategically trapped air to add buoyancy. Performance effects were so strong that in 2010 new international rules limited body coverage, required permeable fabric, and prohibited fasteners. Working within that standard, designers continue to seek ever-new approaches to skin coverings more hydrodynamic than no covering at all. —JT

Left:
1— His and hers Speedos, Camber Sands, Rye, U.K., c. 2010. Unknown photographer
2— Swimmers Helene Madison of the United States and Willemijntje den Ouden of the Netherlands at the 1932 Olympics in Los Angeles. Unknown photographer
3— Kim Peyton, Shirley Babashoff, Wendy Boglioli, and Jill Sterkel of the United States celebrating their victory in the women's 4×100 meter freestyle relay at the 1976 Olympics in Montreal. Unknown photographer
4— Mark Spitz poster, 1972. Photograph by Terry O'Neill

PELÉ
10

SPORTS JERSEY When Colin Kaepernick, quarterback of the San Francisco 49ers, refused to stand for the national anthem before the first two preseason games of 2016, nobody noticed. When he repeated this behavior at the next game—this time dressed for play in a 49ers jersey bearing his surname and signature number seven—the act was national news within hours. Explaining his actions as a protest against police brutality and the oppression of people of color in the United States, Kaepernick was both praised and condemned. Within months, his jersey became the NFL's best seller.

The wearing of replicas of professional athletes' sports jerseys is so pervasive around the world that it is hard to believe that this practice is relatively new. Derived from the lightweight wool jersey-knitted pullover worn by university athletes in the 1880s, the sports jersey comes in different versions for different sports, including soccer, baseball, hockey, football, and basketball, and its evolution has been tied to technological innovations in textiles as well to the increasing public spectacle and ensuing popularity of professional sports. Before 1970, however, wearing the replica of an athlete's jersey was unheard of, and attendees of sporting events dressed formally. While players wore numbers early on, surnames didn't appear on jerseys until the middle of the twentieth century, and teams did not sell uniform replicas except in children's sizes until the mid-1960s.

Jersey replicas started appearing among sports crowds in the 1970s, at a time when fashion in general was becoming more casual, in part owing to the fitness craze and the attendant interest in athletic wear. The first image ever published in *Sports Illustrated* of a fan wearing a jersey dates to 1975; the *New York Times* ran an image in 1973 of the Montreal

Canadiens' Stanley Cup celebration in which hockey fans were dressed in replica jerseys. Produced by local sporting goods merchants and lacking official trademarks and corporate licenses during this period, professional jerseys were somewhat generic and therefore easy to replicate. In 1972, for example, Peter Capolino, owner of the Philadelphia sporting goods store Mitchell & Ness, learned that the teal jerseys worn by the undefeated Miami Dolphins football team were made by Russell Athletic, which also supplied Capolino with the jerseys he sold to local high schools and colleges. He ordered batches with players' numbers, and the jerseys immediately sold out. "I figured people were wearing them for touch-tackle games in the street," Capolino told *Sports Illustrated.* "Maybe they started wearing them to games. . . . They sure do now."[1]

A sea change occurred in 1985, when Norm Charney was granted a license to sell authentic NFL merchandise. Distributing jerseys via his NFL Pro Shop catalogue, Charney aligned himself with national distributors, and by the end of the 1980s he was selling authorized jerseys for professional baseball, hockey, and basketball. Laying the groundwork for the cooption of this business by large athletic corporations such as Nike and Champion, Charney's success underscored a bona fide yearning among sports enthusiasts to embody their favorite player. This phenomenon was hardly restricted to the United States; indeed, among the most familiar jerseys around the world is the yellow shirt emblazoned with a green number 10 and the name of Brazilian soccer superstar Pelé.

The sports jersey's crossover into street wear occurred in the 1990s when it became a hip-hop fashion staple. From Snoop Doggy Dogg, who appeared in the 1993 video for "Gin and Juice" in a Pittsburgh Penguins hockey jersey worn over a hoodie and accessorized with a gold chain, to Erik (Everlast) Schrody, who wore a Boston Celtics basketball jersey with a beaded necklace in House of Pain's 1992 video "Jump Around," the jersey emerged as a symbol of street savvy that allowed hip-hop artists to project the accomplishments of their favorite athletes—while simultaneously tailoring the garment to their personal styles. The Notorious B.I.G., for example, wore a basketball jersey that featured the name of his record label, Bad Boy, in his video

for "Juicy," while female rappers Mýa and Eve modified existing team jerseys into fitted dresses and tops. By the turn of the millennium a trend had emerged for highly prized "throwback" jerseys of retired players and defunct teams, which added to the garment's cachet as something that demonstrated specialized knowledge and was difficult to obtain.

With the increasing influence of street wear on today's luxury designers, the sports jersey's reach has grown. In 2014 Alexander Wang featured a stylized baseball jersey in his capsule collection for H&M, while Gypsy Sport showed repurposed iterations of basketball jerseys for men and women in its spring 2017 runway shows. The mounting popularity of professional women's sports has added to jerseys' popularity within women's fashion, with athletes like Lisa Leslie of the WNBA's Los Angeles Sparks generating a level of enthusiasm equivalent to that of their male counterparts. Over the past half century, the sports jersey has allowed wearers to project their ideals through a few bright colors, numbers, and names, and it is in this spirit of identification and personalization that fashion has embraced its language.
—SK

Left:
1— **Colin Kaepernick (center) kneeling before a game against the New Orleans Saints, November 6, 2016. Photograph by Brian Bahr**
2— **Pelé (top) and Jairzinho celebrating Brazil's victory over Italy at the World Cup Final, Mexico City, 1970. Unknown photographer**
3— **Model on the runway for the Jahnkoy fall/winter 2017/18 menswear collection, New York, 2016. Photograph by Oscar Landon**
4— **Abby Wambach celebrates the U.S. team's 5–2 victory over Japan in the FIFA Women's World Cup Canada 2015 final at BC Place stadium, Vancouver. Photograph by Dennis Grombkowski**

STILETTO There are few high-heeled shoe typologies as culturally complex as the stiletto heel. This twentieth-century women's shoe elevates the pump's basic form on a slender, spiky heel. Named after a medieval weapon whose needle-thin blade could easily penetrate chain-mail armor, the stiletto is characterized more by the attenuated heel's narrow shape than its height.[1] A stereotype of femininity, yet with a name and shape that are suggestive of violence, it is an object suffused with both beauty and pain, sexuality and power.[2]

French designer Roger Vivier is credited with refining the design of the stiletto heel as we know it today, although its evolution was highly collaborative and iterative.[3] Vivier established a reputation in the 1950s for architectural, often fancifully designed high heels.[4] Like the skyscraper, the stiletto's thin heel column was only possible with the integration of a steel core for structural support. It was not until after World War II, when leather and steel were no longer rationed and advancements were made in steel-extrusion technology, that these elegant designs by Vivier and others could be realized.

During the war, women's fashion and footwear were modest and pragmatic, in contrast with the eroticized stockings, garters, and high heels that figured prominently in the pinup posters so loved by American G.I.s. In 1947 Dior's flagrantly feminine New Look debuted, and its renewal of figure-hugging forms proved extremely influential on postwar fashion.[5] Vivier's perfection of the steel-cored, hyperfeminine stiletto heel for Dior in 1954 further confirmed a return to the polarized gender roles that would dominate the postwar era.

It is its physical effect on the wearer that renders the stiletto heel so controversial. Designers love them because the elevated heel elongates the leg, slims the ankle by engaging the calf muscle, and forces a posture that accentuates the buttocks and breasts. The foot is arched as though in ecstatic throes, and, in some designs, a sliver of suggestive toe cleavage is revealed. For many women, however, attaining this sexualized look comes at a dire cost to comfort. Walking or even standing in heels can be excruciating, and balancing one's body weight on a heel post as broad as a pencil makes riding an escalator, traipsing on uneven terrain, or dancing nearly impossible for many. Bunions, nerve damage, and posture problems stem from extensive time spent virtually on tiptoe.

And yet the stiletto has refused to disappear. Partly this is due to the strong affinity some subcultures have for this most extreme variant of the high heel. Drawing from its exaggerated erotic connotations, the stiletto heel has become standard female attire within BDSM and femdom fetish communities. Some foot fetishists fixate on the stiletto as a symbol of female power and an object of desire, one that with its sharp heel can become a source of physical pain, able to crush, trample, and pierce. From the late twentieth century and into the twenty-first, a few brands have gained cult status for their stiletto heels, among them Manolo Blahnik, Jimmy Choo, and Christian Louboutin. Experimental and deconstructed versions by Martin Margiela and Alexander McQueen exemplify the stiletto heel's role as an endlessly inspiring muse for the avant-garde fashion designers who continue to push its form and interrogate its broader cultural implications. —LB

Right:
1— Silk and leather high-heel pumps, designed by Roger Vivier for Delman-Christian Dior, 1954. Collection of the Bata Shoe Museum, Toronto. Photograph by David Stevenson and Eva Tkaczuk.
2— Helmut Newton, *X-Ray, Van Cleef & Arpels, French Vogue*, 1994

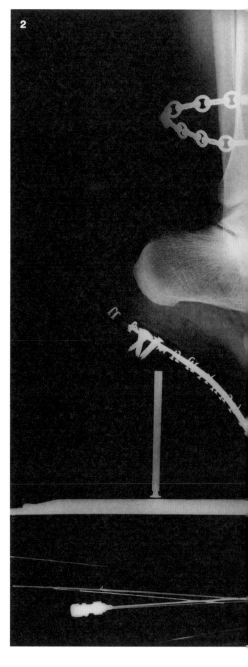

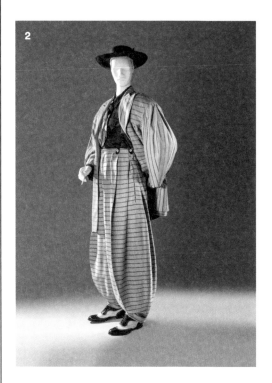

SUIT A sartorial institution, the suit—whether two-piece (trousers and a jacket) or three-piece (with the addition of a vest)—exists in constant flux between the desire to stand out through recourse to personalized tailoring and accents, and the need for homogeneity epitomized by the midcentury office drone. The genesis of the suit dates to fourteenth-century Europe, where it was a set of well-matched —but not identical—outer clothes. From the sixteenth century onward, tailors' pattern books across the continent record its increasing prevalence, but it was the introduction of the tape measure (the foundational tool in the ritual space of the bespoke fitting rooms of London's Savile Row) at the turn of the eighteenth century and the emergence of standardized patterns in the 1820s that allowed the suit as we know it today—ubiquitous and available in many styles—to flourish.[1]

The suit is often perceived as a bastion of tradition and conformity. By the mid-nineteenth century the solidly middle-class professionals who powered modern cities from Tokyo to London were uniformly clad in somber-hued suits. In his 1840 short story "The Man of the Crowd," Edgar Allan Poe memorably depicts the "tribe of clerks" who, in their suited attire, maintained "a certain dapperness of carriage, which may be termed *deskism* for want of a better word."[2] For modern architecture pioneer Adolf Loos, the suit was an archetype of progressive design in the same way a contemporary house or a car might function.[3] And as men returned from World War II to a climate that celebrated economic recovery through the consumption of such modern designs, the suit became another mass-produced object: Burton, still a staple of the British high street today, produced more than two million "demob" suits given by the government to decommissioned soldiers.[4] Yet in his catalogue for the exhibition *Are Clothes Modern?* mounted at The Museum of Modern Art, New York, in 1944, curator Bernard Rudofsky dispelled the suit's claim to modernity in his provocative data visualization of the multiple pockets, buttons, and layers a midcentury man was expected to wear when "properly" attired, crying foul on the demands of traditional dress for the current moment. Three decades later John T. Molloy nevertheless canonized the suit as the "central power garment in any business combination" in his popular 1975 book *Dress for Success*.[5]

Some men broke these constraints, not least jazz musicians and street impresarios who popularized the baggy and scandalous zoot suit in the 1930s and '40s.[6] In the contemporary era the suit is to the fashion designer what the chair is to the industrial designer—a conduit for experimentation and declaration of design identity *par excellence*. In the 1970s the British punk queen Vivienne Westwood sourced fabric from established Scottish textile manufacturers to create assertive and exciting tartan tweed bondage suits, while in the United States the suit danced onto the disco floor with John Travolta in the film *Saturday Night Fever*. During the 1980s the Italian fashion designer Giorgio Armani gestured to midcentury classics of his native cinema to create a new style, a second skin for both men and women in which he—as scholar Christopher Breward contends—"eviscerated the structure of the formal business suit, sloping the shoulders, freeing the stiffened lining, lowering the buttons and lapels, and adopting fabrics that were lighter in weight and color and texture." This was a look that suggested "a new sense of femininity . . . that was profoundly radicalizing" and, when paired with a T-shirt rather than a dress shirt, will forever be associated with the decade's hit cop television drama *Miami Vice*.[7]

Japanese designer Yohji Yamamoto deconstructed the black suit in the 1990s, inspiring new interpretations by certain *sapeurs* in the Republic of Congo.[8] In the early twenty-first century the American Thom Browne began to play with unexpected exposure with his "shrunken suits," featuring trousers that display the ankles, or even the knees. Carlo Brandelli's Unstructured suit and, later, Richard James's Naked

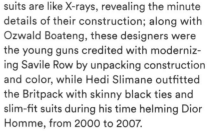

suits are like X-rays, revealing the minute details of their construction; along with Ozwald Boateng, these designers were the young guns credited with modernizing Savile Row by unpacking construction and color, while Hedi Slimane outfitted the Britpack with skinny black ties and slim-fit suits during his time helming Dior Homme, from 2000 to 2007.

Though the death knell of the suit has been repeatedly sounded, especially in the contemporary era of normcore casual and gig-economy anti-uniformity, the possibilities for standardization and insurrection posed by new directions—from tailors such as Kathryn Sargent (the first female tailor on Savile Row) and Brooklyn-based Rae Tutera, who deliberately designs against the grain of simplistic gendered identities, to robotic pattern cutters—mean the suit is an item that, like any true palimpsest, will only continue to deepen in its complexity and contradiction. —MMF

Previous page:
1— **Model in a Thom Browne classic gray suit. Photograph by Ash Reynolds**
2— **Zoot suit (1940–42) with a belly-warmer necktie (c. 1945) and spectator shoes (1935–42)**

Left:
3— **Rae Tutera fitting a client at Bindle & Keep, a custom suiting company that serves gender nonconforming clients, Brooklyn, New York, 2016. Photograph by Eric T. White**
4— **The *sapeur* Willy Covari, Brazzaville, Republic of Congo, 2008. Photograph by Daniele Tamagni**
5— **Don Johnson and Philip Michael Thomas in a publicity still for the TV series *Miami Vice*, 1984–89**
6— **Fitting for a demob suit at the British Army's Demobilization Clothing Depot, Olympia Grand, London, during World War II. Unknown photographer**
7— **John Travolta in the film *Saturday Night Fever*, 1977**

S—094

SUNSCREEN Since the debut of synthetic sunscreens in the 1930s, their use—or deliberate rejection—has reflected local and global beauty biases related to skin pigmentation. Such preferences are conditioned by entrenched sociocultural frameworks that have historically privileged porcelain-white skin and urged those born without it—or with localized pigment spots such as freckles—to consider using topical or chemical cosmetics to prevent the skin from darkening from the sun.

While various plant oils are ancient means of creating a barrier between the dermis and harmful light rays, chemical compounds such as oxybenzone and retinyl palmitate, nanoparticles of zinc oxide (ZnO), and titanium dioxide (TiO2) are more effective modern methods. First developed in the 1930s by chemists in Australia and Europe, sunscreen is either chemical, forming a thin protective layer on the skin's surface to absorb ultraviolet (UV) rays, or physical, using insoluble particles of zinc oxide or titanium dioxide to reflect UV light away from the skin. The Australian chemist H. A. Milton Blake created Hamilton sunscreen in 1932; the founder of L'Oréal, French chemist Eugène Schueller, launched his own product in 1936; and in 1938 the Swiss chemistry student Franz Greiter, assailed by reflected UV light while climbing in the Alpine snow, developed protective "glacier cream."[1] During World War II the American airman and pharmacist Benjamin Green recommended thick and greasy red veterinary petrolatum (known as "Red Vet Pet") to protect himself and his military peers. Once he returned to civilian life, Green combined the unpleasant substance with cocoa butter, coconut oil, and other ingredients to make it more palatable for a consumer market, creating the foundation for the popular Coppertone sunscreen line.

Although material barriers—including clothing, sunglasses, brimmed hats, and parasols—have all been put to work to deflect the sun's radiation, the use of synthetic topical sunscreens escalated from the 1960s onward as awareness of skin cancers and signs of premature aging such as sun spots and wrinkles increased. A triangle of opaque white zinc oxide applied to the nose (and sometimes the lips) was commonly seen on lifeguards and surfers, signifying a serious dedication to both skin safety and beach life. Developed in the 1970s, the SPF (Sun Protection Factor) chart measures how long topical barriers will protect against shortwave (UVB) rays that redden the skin, with a range of 2 to 100; since the 1980s, products have also been designed against long-wave (UVA) rays, which penetrate deeper and darken pigment.

Coinciding with the use of sunscreen was a rising fashion for the suntan. The fetishizing of deeply tanned Caucasian skin has its (apocryphal) twentieth-century genesis in Gabrielle "Coco" Chanel, who, in 1923, turned a light sunburn into a fashion statement during a vacation in Cannes. Beginning midcentury, sunscreens shared the drugstore aisle with "suntan lotions" such as Bain de Soleil Orange Gelée and Hawaiian Tropic Dark Tanning Oil, whose purpose was to coax a deep, even tan (leading to the active cultivation of prominent tan lines). American pinup illustrator Joyce Ballantyne created the memorable graphic campaign for Coppertone's suntan lotion in the late 1950s, using her three-year-old daughter as the model for the pigtailed blonde whose briefs are nipped by a playful puppy, exposing her pale buttocks and thus contrasting them with her bronzed skin below the slogan "Tan . . . don't burn!" Consumers—particularly the fair-skinned—could forego the sun altogether and achieve the look with the advent of self-tanning products such as QT (Quick Tanning) by Coppertone. The lotion, introduced in 1960, functioned similarly to many sunless or "fake" tanning products, reacting with amino acids on the skin's surface to produce a temporary bronze color. It lives on in the phenomenon of the perma-tan, the maintenance of a year-round sun-kissed glow via tanning beds or spray tans.

In the last three decades, cosmetics and clothing manufacturers have monetized concerns by consumers of all

Greetings from MIAMI BEACH

TAN ...don't burn...use COPPERTONE

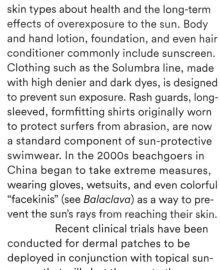

skin types about health and the long-term effects of overexposure to the sun. Body and hand lotion, foundation, and even hair conditioner commonly include sunscreen. Clothing such as the Solumbra line, made with high denier and dark dyes, is designed to prevent sun exposure. Rash guards, long-sleeved, formfitting shirts originally worn to protect surfers from abrasion, are now a standard component of sun-protective swimwear. In the 2000s beachgoers in China began to take extreme measures, wearing gloves, wetsuits, and even colorful "facekinis" (see *Balaclava*) as a way to prevent the sun's rays from reaching their skin.

Recent clinical trials have been conducted for dermal patches to be deployed in conjunction with topical sunscreen that will alert the user to the accumulated penetration of UV radiation, helping to determine when reapplication is necessary. Ease of application led to the popularity of spray-on sunscreen, a less messy alternative to lotions that is marketed especially for children (despite concerns about efficacy of coverage and the potential for inhaling the particles).[2] And in 2015 scientists studying zebrafish at Oregon State University discovered that gadusol, the compound that prevents many fish, amphibians, reptiles, and birds from burning in the sun, is not, as previously thought, produced through diet or bacteria but is instead naturally produced by metabolizing an enzyme and proteins—possibly paving the way for the creation of human-grade ingestible sunscreen. This discovery is opportune: a scientific study published in 2013 indicates that sunscreen is now a "significant source of organic and inorganic chemicals that reach the sea with potential ecological consequences on the coastal marine ecosystem."[3] —MMF

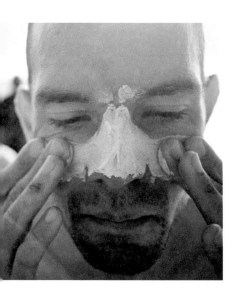

Left:
1— Beachgoers in Qingdao, China, 2013. Photograph by Hong Wu
2— Advertisement for Coppertone, 1958
3— Man applying white zinc, n.d. Unknown photographer

SURGICAL MASK Although germ theory—the understanding that microorganisms invisible to the human eye spread infectious disease—was proposed in the mid-sixteenth century, it did not become accepted in the mainstream until confirmed by the research of the French chemist and microbiologist Louis Pasteur, among others, in the late nineteenth century. The surgical mask was the accessory that made visible this change in scientific and public thought. Surgical masks were introduced at the turn of the twentieth century in a variety of medical settings—most notably the surgical theater—to prevent microorganisms from migrating from the mouths and noses of the operating staff to open wounds.[1] The flu pandemic of 1918 brought the mask to the streets, businesses, and homes, where it performed not only practically but optically for a world terrified by the threat of infection.

At their inception, surgical masks were fashioned from medical gauze tied in a strip around the mouth and, in most cases, the nose. In 1918 two doctors published findings in the *Journal of the American Medical Association* that attempted the first recorded standardization—layers of gauze to equal three hundred threads per square inch, with a surface eight inches wide and five inches high—although neither the codification nor the use of masks more generally were immediately universally adopted.[2] From the 1930s onward, designers—often doctors—experimented with thin layers of materials such as rubber, cellophane, cellulose, and polyvinyl plastic. Over the next few decades the masks incorporated ear loops for a more ergonomic fit, and the material composition of the filter became more sophisticated due to both technical innovation and a developing roster of manufacturers vying for burgeoning business. By the late 1960s masks made of fiberglass layers had introduced the practice of disposability rather than sterilization and reuse. Contemporary masks include pleats to enhance their capacity to act as a barrier.

Global health emergencies in recent years—from SARS (2002) and H1N1 flu (2009) to air pollution increasing airborne particulate matter (PM2.5) to dangerous levels in cities like New Delhi and Beijing—have engendered a resurgent adoption of the surgical mask in the public sphere. Many different masks are available for purchase in convenience stores, handed out at airports and doctors' offices as part of public health policy, and even retailed in boutique stores. Widespread use has led to the design of masks customized in different colors or with surface illustration or decoration, developing an expressive currency that mediates the uncanny disappearance of facial features demanded by its practical function. Among many such examples is the Vogmask, which was invented in California to combat airborne sand and dust at the annual Burning Man art and performance festival held in the Black Rock Desert in Nevada. The founders recently collaborated with Indian designer Manish Arora, producing limited-edition masks for the fashion conscious plagued by poor air quality on the subcontinent. Similarly, models on the runways of China Fashion Week in 2014 were equipped with heavy lower-face coverings, many of which riffed on the surgical mask, as a commentary on the severe pollution in that country. Beijing-based designer Zhijun Wang fashions masks out of sneakers— cutting into expensive collectible pairs of Nike Air VaporMax and Adidas Yeezy Boost 350 v2—becoming a darling of contemporary street-wear websites in the process. Wang's designs repurpose the ankle dips to fit snugly around the wearer's jawbone and ear. South Korean fashion brand 99%IS was founded in 2008 by Seoul native Park Jong Woo. The designer— known as Bajowoo—uses a slashed surgical mask as a signature look, describing his work in contagious metaphors: "I want what I do to be like a virus. . . . It can spread to every age, every period in history, and every culture. No matter who you are, if you catch it, you share the same experience."[3]

Surgical masks remain most prevalent in Asia, where they are used as a polite shield for those under the weather but still out in public. Japanese company

Unicharm Corporation launched the popular 3-D (*rittai*) mask in 2003, which offers close contouring for a maximum shield while tenting away from the face in order to preserve airflow and to prevent the smearing of cosmetics.

It is little surprise that the surgical mask has taken on a subcultural currency. Elision of the mouth and nose—the key to reading and communicating emotional states—is a well-worn trope of horror, science fiction, and anime that underscores alterity, danger, or damaged bodies. Paradoxically, contemporary Japanese youth have adopted the mask as a prosthetic augmentation of identity. In some cases, the mask emphasizes their eyes like a manga character; in others, it becomes a defensive shield to dissuade public interaction, or to thwart facial recognition software and surveillance, morphing from a device to manage the migration of microorganisms to a way of deflecting larger ones. All such cases fall under the term *date masuku*, meaning "just for show." —MMF

Right:
1— Policemen wearing masks provided by the American Red Cross during the influenza epidemic, Seattle, 1918. Unknown photographer
2— Woman wearing a surgical mask as part of her cosplay ensemble, Harajuku, Tokyo, Japan, 2013. Photograph by Takamitsu Kira
3— Nurse wearing a protective mask during the influenza epidemic, Brookline, Massachusetts, 1918. Unknown photographer
4— Chinese designer Zhijun Wang wearing a mask he made out of sneakers, Beijing, 2016. Photograph by Damir Sagolj

SWATCH "The genius of the Swatch," wrote journalist Nicholas Foulkes, is "its apparently oxymoronic capability of being both simultaneously high quality and disposable."[1] The now-iconic watch also signifies the reinvention of a ubiquitous product and the rejuvenation of a traditional industry. In the process, the Swiss watch has cycled from heirloom to ephemeral accessory to collectible once more.

In the early 1980s watchmakers Nicolas Hayek and Ernst Thomke, engineers Elmar Mock and Jacques Müller, and designers Marlyse Schmid and Bernard Müller converged to find a way for traditional Swiss watchmakers to compete with the inexpensive Japanese digital and quartz watches then sweeping the market. From these efforts emerged a prototype named Vulgaris (Latin for "common"), which was soon developed into a "low-cost, high-tech, artistic and emotional 'second watch.'"[2]

The project involved fusing a plastic case (traditionally metal) with a mechanism-supporting baseplate (traditionally separate), enabling fewer parts and automated assembly. The cost-saving Swatch was made of plastic—and of only 51 parts, as opposed to the 90 or even 150 parts that constitute the traditional Swiss watch. The new approach was then amplified with bold, playful styling and aggressive marketing. In 1983 the Swatch debuted with a range of designs, from the understated black-and-white GB100 to the radically transparent Jelly Fish. Swatch soon dominated watch sales, spawning a new segment of buyers and turning them into obsessed collectors.

This approach—the rapid introduction of new models responsive to pop culture trends—remains key to the brand's sustained consumer appeal. Limited-edition models, many commissioned from artists, designers, and filmmakers, are also an effective part of this strategy. An early example is the 1988 Puff, with its angora ruff wedded to a generic Swatch with a metal ring. At once resembling body hair, fan, and dandelion seed head, the fluffy halo flutters in response to motion—and coyly obscures the watch face. The designer Vivienne Westwood's 1993 Orb is packaged in a cheeky sendup of the Sovereign's Orb (part of the crown jewels of the United Kingdom), outrageously commodifying British punk sensibility.

Most conceptually rigorous, or meta, is the 2015 LooksEasy edition Swatch by the Paris-born Portuguese artist Joana Vasconcelos. In this ingenious design, filigree artisans crafted an intricate gold face that was then hand-assembled into the conventional Swatch form by traditional Swiss watchmakers. In this way Vasconcelos transformed the Swiss watch—a modernist symbol embedded with aspirations to universality, anonymity, and industrial production—into a personalized, handcrafted object. Ironically, the very ephemerality of these limited editions and celebrity designs has caused particular models to become collector's items, bringing the Swiss watch full circle to its heirloom origins.

On the one hand, the Swatch exemplifies "retrotech," a neologism defined as "everyday objects that combine the aesthetic and mechanical virtues of the past with the sophistication of contemporary technology," such as state-of-the-art "amplifiers that [do] their job without flashing" and high-tech toasters that toast "without the aid of a HAL 9000 computer."[3] On the other hand (or wrist), Swatch is developing an operating system, aligning it with smart watches and fitness trackers (see *Fitbit*).[4] That's when the design market's sweeping, invisible hand may mark a truly revolutionary movement. —JT

Right:
1— Models at a Beijing launch of Swatch watches, 1993. Photograph by Will Burgess
2— GZ010 Original Jelly Fish Swatch, 1983

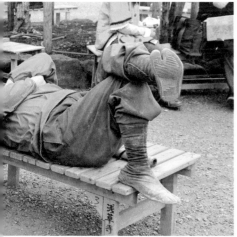

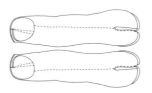

TABI BOOT Worn throughout the world by a legion of devoted fans and collectors, Maison Margiela's tabi boot, though not approachable or affordable for all, has nonetheless had a profound impact on fashion and design. Introduced in 1988 for the Martin Margiela spring/summer 1989 runway show—the first for the designer's namesake house—the tabi boot emerged as the singular shoe silhouette of the presentation, described later in the *New York Times* as "bizarre platform shoes with thonged toes."[1] A graduate of Antwerp's Royal Academy of Fine Arts who worked for Jean Paul Gaultier before establishing his own house, Margiela captivated the fashion world from the outset with his unusual approach to form, materials (at times incorporating recycled components), and technique (combining fine tailoring with raw and unfinished elements). Dubbed "*la mode* destroy" by the French press, Margiela's work seemed to challenge both the substance and the system of fashion. The tabi boot encapsulated this attitude.

"I wanted to create an 'invisible' shoe, the illusion of a bare foot walking on a high, chunky heel," Margiela explained, and he attributed its inspiration to the soft *jika-tabi* shoes worn by "the local street workers" in Tokyo. "My first show presented those tabi shoes in skin-colored suede (to evoke the nude) on high, cylindrical heels in black leather."[2] The boots were initially shown also in ivory, gray, red, and black. Even more impactful than the boots themselves was the manner in which they were presented. The designer instructed his models to walk through red paint before starting down the catwalk, and by the show's end the runway, lined with stark white cotton canvas, was transformed into a haphazard mosaic of blood-red footprints. For his autumn/winter 1989 runway collection, Margiela not only recycled the footprinted cotton into garments

(including a waistcoat taped to the body), but he also re-presented the tabi boot. In this way he used the boot to call into question both the design language of Western fashion and its organizational underpinnings of planned obsolescence, interrogating the demands of vacillating seasonal trends.

The Tokyo street-worker boots referenced by Margiela emerged in Japan at the turn of the twentieth century as a product of mass manufacturing and the development of vulcanized rubber. Meaning "socks that touch the ground," jika-tabi are named for *tabi,* the traditional Japanese socks dating to the thirteenth century that have a bifurcation between the big toe and the second toe. Designed for wearing with the *geta* sandal—a thonglike upper on a raised wooden platform sole—tabi were typically sewn from cloth rather than knit. Jika-tabi have been worn by manual laborers such as construction workers, farmers, painters, and road workers since the Meiji period (1868–1912), with their uppers typically constructed from lightweight cotton and their soles composed of a pliable yet sturdy natural rubber. While connoting different class affiliations for men during Japan's Edo period (1603–1868), depending on either color or frequency of wear, tabi maintained symbolic meaning for women, denoting female modesty at a time when footwear and sexuality were intimately connected. If respectable women were expected to wear tabi to conceal their feet from public gaze, women who worked in licensed brothels were prohibited from wearing them.

While the tabi form represented modesty and restraint in this traditional incarnation, Margiela uses it to fetishize the foot, as underscored by his decision to continue using multiple iterations of the shoe throughout his career. From ballet flats to d'Orsay-style pumps to mules, Margiela's tabi has been applied to multiple shoe shapes and constructed from materials ranging from metallic leather to suede. Though initially born out of necessity ("Because we could not afford new shoes," Margiela explained, "I put wall paint over my first collection to give it the same new feel," spawning the iconic white tabi boot), the exponentiation of tabi styles soon became a signature of the house.[3] The shoe that began as a hyperbole of the relationship between the foot and footwear soon evolved into a hyperbole of desire, as loyal devotees purchased the item in each of its iterations. "I bought them in the early days when Martin Margiela came out with those amazing collections," recounted Linda Loppa, former head of the fashion department at Margiela's alma mater in Antwerp, "because it was so different from whatever I saw in the past. I bought them immediately, but when I was wearing them people were a little shocked. You feel a little bit animalistic because of that split of the toes. People react to it skeptically, with a strange feeling that they don't know what it is. Is it beautiful? Is it scary? Is it aesthetically interesting?"[4]

In 1996 Margiela introduced a bare tabi sole, sold simply with a roll of adhesive tape for securing it to the foot. "As a lifetime observer I realize that well-chosen accessories can provoke a 'statement,'" the designer has said, but it seems that the ultimate statement about the tabi boot was his own; when asked what prompted him to have the models walk through red paint during his first runway show, Margiela replied, "Obsession. . . . I thought the audience should notice the new footwear. And what would be more evident than its footprint?"[5] —SK

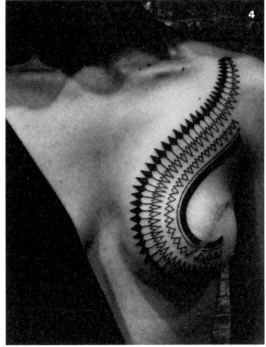

Previous pages:
1— Japanese construction worker napping, 2013. Unknown photographer
2— Tabi boots in the exhibition *Tabi Shoe Maker*, by Maison Martin Margiela and Relish, at the Relish boutique in Washington, D.C., September 2014. Photograph by Larry French
3— Maison Margiela's 1996 tabi soles. Photograph by Anders Edstrom

TATTOO Tattooing—the practice of inking permanent marks through small punctures in the skin's surface—is perhaps the most globally prevalent form of bodily adornment. With origins in a multitude of overlapping yet discrete practices, tattoos are as varied as the rationales for acquiring them. Found on Egyptian mummies as early as 3000 BCE and recorded in classical and medieval texts, permanent-ink body markings have for millennia served not only to decorate but also to identify bodies, and they have long been meted out as well to punish slaves and convicts.[1] Though the English word *tattoo* was adopted in the eighteenth century from the Polynesian root *tatau,* meaning to mark or strike, European explorers encountered irreversible body marking throughout the Americas, Asia, and Africa.

In some cultures, tattoos denote both deviance and liberation from established norms, while in others tattooed bodies *are* the norm. Tattoo designs may mark important milestones, age, status, or a community's aesthetic standards, or they may serve as expressions of selfhood. Within the last century, tattooing has experienced an efflorescence (especially in the West), becoming an established part of fashion around the world.

Japanese *irezumi* tattooing has played a formative role in global contemporary tattoo fashions. Edo period (1603–1868) woodblocks depicting heroic men decorated with (sometimes mythical) flora and fauna engendered a popularization of a similar real-life adornment, which woodblock makers happily provided. Future British king George V acquired a dragon tattoo while in Japan in 1881, highlighting the manner in which tattoos variously function as exotic adornment, signifier of cultural exchange, and souvenir. Indeed, tattoo tourism has produced quintessential tattoo stereotypes that are products of

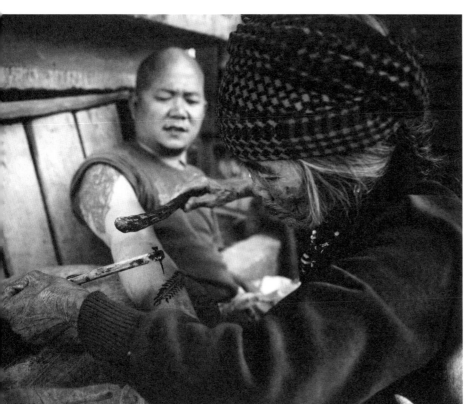

an international style. Serviceman-turned-artist Sailor Jerry—born Norman Keith Collins in 1911—was an important conduit for Japanese tattooing approaches in the United States, constructing complex tattoo designs rather than discrete icons and experimenting with shade, pigment, and tonality.

Traditional hand-done (sometimes "hand poke") tattoos are made with a thin needle, often affixed to a wooden stick or wrapped in string for grip, dipped into ink and deployed in a poke-and-stick method to achieve a line. Around 1891, Samuel O'Reilly radically changed this approach by recalibrating an engraving contraption (created by inventor Thomas Edison), transforming it into an electric tattoo machine. Tattoos became faster, cheaper, and less painful, a major flashpoint connecting tattooing with contemporary mass production, industrialization, hygiene, modernity, and a burgeoning popular culture. In the early twentieth century tattoos proliferated near U.S. military bases, and patriotic, macho wartime imagery coalesced around a relatively circumscribed repertoire, including flags, pinups, eagles, ships, and loved ones' names. Bikers introduced into the canon iconic designs such as skulls, and sayings such as "born to lose" and "live to ride."

From the 1970s onward in the West, "suddenly, tattoos [became] mainstream, middle-class and respectable . . . craft, if not art, in studios from Main Street to the malls." Lyle Tuttle, a well-known tattoo artist and the founder of the San Francisco Tattoo Museum, suggests that "the popularity stems from the late 1960s and early 1970s when women's liberation kicked in because all of a sudden half of the human race opened up" as potential clients.[2] In the era of birth control and bra burning, getting a tattoo was another way to assert control over one's body. (Of course, gender bias remains entrenched: a woman's femininity is compromised by a "tramp stamp," whereas machismo is enhanced by ink). The prevalence of electronic needles made possible a wide range of colors, and, from the 1980s on, tattoos created by those trained at fine-art schools have flourished. Sailor Jerry protégé Ed Hardy brought the field firmly into the public eye in the early 2000s, extensively sublicensing his prolific tattoo designs for clothing, footwear, and miscellanea, cementing his aesthetic in the world of fashion.[3]

Echoing French philosopher Michel Foucault's formulation of the body-as-text, scholar Michael Rees notes that "to be a member of contemporary Western cultures is to be encouraged to construct your identity through the body," and indeed the tattoo has played an increasingly public role in individual and collective identity formation—just one more way of perpetually constructing and refining body image, as common as dieting, working out, or cosmetic surgery.[4] This mindset finally catches up to cultures such as the Kalinga ethnic tribe in the northern Philippines (now a mecca for tourists seeking souvenir tattoos), where such tattoos have for centuries denoted beauty and rank.[5]

Tattooed celebrities like Angelina Jolie and Dennis Rodman, as well as behind-the-scenes television series such as *Miami Ink* and *Ink Master*, have ensured the tattoo's mainstream ascendency.[6] Paradoxically, fashion designers who mined the social unease around tattooing (Jean Paul Gaultier's spring 1994 collection; Diesel and its Tattoo fragrances) lessened the practice's edginess. As the Brooklyn-based company Tattly subverts the permanence of the genre by commissioning artists and designers to create temporary-tattoo iconography, and museum exhibitions lend institutional validation, it is clear that the West has joined cultures worldwide in understanding the inking of the skin as a fundamental part of human expression. —MMF

1

Previous pages:
1— **Hand-colored albumen print by Baron Raimund von Stillfried-Rathenitz, Japan, c. 1870s**
2— **Woman in the U-Bahn, Berlin, 2016. Photograph by ANBerlin**
3— **Rock of Ages flash design by Ed Hardy, 1988**
4— **Mastectomy scar tattoo by Roxx 2Spirit, New York, 2013. Photograph by the artist**
5— **Kalinga tattoo artist Maria Fang-od Oggay at work, Buscalan, Northern Luzon, Philippines, 2013. Photograph by Ania Blazejewska**

TEVA SANDAL Although they are now worn everywhere, from high-fashion runways to suburban cul-de-sacs, Teva sandals were conceived for a specific context: long-duration white-water rafting. In the early 1980s, Mark Thatcher, a young engineer, was laid off from his position as a geophysicist, so he turned to a job he had enjoyed during college summers: working as a guide on the Colorado River in the Grand Canyon. Thatcher quickly realized there was a need for footwear that could withstand the various activities involved in white-water rafting, including the muscular work of hauling boats and equipment, prolonged submersion in the river, and navigating terrain on dry land. In 1984 he took the basic form of the thonged flip-flop and, using a wide strap, connected it to a sturdy nylon heel and ankle strap. This tripartite "utility" design was the first Teva (pronounced, as the company is keen to point out, "teh-vah," not "tee-vah"), named after the Hebrew word for nature. He sold two hundred pairs himself (under the snappy moniker "Amphibious Utility Sandal") before securing a licensing deal the following year through Deckers, a company that also owns Ugg, among other brands.

The design was subsequently refined: the post between the first and second toes was replaced with a flat strap straddling all five, which helped minimize blisters; triangular connecting nodes were employed in the three-strap system; and Velcro was used to create an adjustable fastening at the ankle. The soles, which had two layers—the inner designed to provide anti-slip friction for wet feet, the outer to provide grip on surfaces in and out of the water—were adjusted to cushion and lessen impact. Thus, in 1988, the "Universal" Teva (patent no. 4,793,075) was born, and it is still in production today. The open design of the sandal was particularly important. It did not trap moisture around the foot and thus guarded against a condition known colloquially as foot rot (akin to trench foot), a painful ailment contracted by rafters, guides, and other outdoor enthusiasts who immerse their feet too long in water, softening the skin and then chafing it against granular matter.[1]

When they emerged, Tevas—as they are often termed colloquially—were very much in step with broader design currents, which encouraged a boom in the U.S. outdoor apparel and product industry (see *Gore-Tex*). Along with companies such as Early Winters, Marmot, and Patagonia (see *Fleece*), Teva has inspired a cult following predicated on the perceived authenticity of its brand and founder. Aspirational slogans used in its advertising campaigns include "Free your feet and your soul will follow" and "Wear less, do more." Its wearers coined the term "Teva tan" to describe the crisscross patterns on their weather-beaten bare feet, a phenomenon that recently spawned a hashtag. Like many other sports apparel and footwear companies (see *Speedo*), Teva sponsors professional athletes—in this case, white-water rafters—who test the company's products and work directly with its designers to make improvements that then become part of a wider consumer experience.

The sandal is an essential and age-old footwear type fit for outdoor performance in water and on dry land because it does not retain moisture, is lightweight yet protects the sole in most terrains, allows the foot to move, and permits air to circulate. Sandals were worn in ancient times in Africa, Asia, and the Americas. The Anasazi, who lived in parts of the southwestern United States from 200 to 1300 CE, wove them out of yucca leaves. In many cultures throughout history, sandals have been associated with spiritual or ceremonial use.[2] Israeli popular culture is imbued with a fascination with sandals, particularly the "biblical" or "Jesus" style; stereotypically associated with members of kibbutzim, it is considered a national treasure—or horror, depending on the sartorial eye of the beholder.[3] There are several Israeli competitors to Teva, including Source, which developed very similar sandals a little less than a decade later, and Teva Naot, founded on a kibbutz in the 1940s, which makes Birkenstock-style sandals and other footwear.

Although they are marketed as a "fashion sandal," Tevas have remained relatively unchanged in terms of their core design, though variations do occur in surface decoration and color, and innovations, such as the addition of an antifungal property to the footbed, are occasionally introduced. Tevas, once referred to as "the shoe most likely to be worn by a man in a fisherman sweater with leaves in his beard," have not escaped the practical sandal's reputation for being fogyish.[4] However, like many articles of performance footwear, they have periodically experienced a resurgence of attention in more stylish realms. *Vogue* identified a flash point in the ascension of the fashionably uncool sandal in the Miuccia Prada spring 1996 Banal Eccentricity collection, whose "jarring palette seemingly taken from a '70s appliance-maker, faux-naive prints, and chunky, clunky shoes" cemented her status as the "indisputable godmother" of "pretty/ugly" footwear.[5] Today Teva sandals and their ilk regularly show up on fashion runways and on the feet of Japanese youth, who sometimes pair them with knee-high socks. —MMF

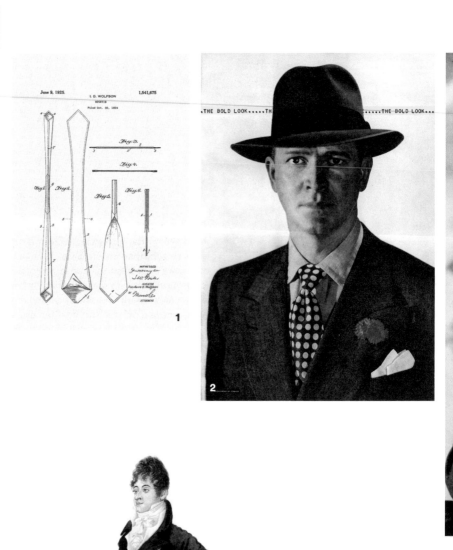

Previous pages:
1— **Teva collaboration with Danish men's fashion brand Han Kjøbenhavn, 2016**
2— **Deanna "Skydancer" Kent, Deland, Florida, 1993. Photograph by Norman Kent**
3— **Teva tans, 1989. Unknown photographer**

3

TIE Called a long tie, vertical tie, or four-in-hand tie, the modern necktie is said to have evolved from the loosely knotted neckerchiefs worn by Croatian soldiers during the Thirty Years' War (1618–48), which led to variations known as the cravat and the steinkirk (as well as to the ascot and the bow tie).[1] The concept of wearing cloth tied around the neck, however, is rooted in antiquity, as exemplified by the meticulously knotted scarves worn by the army of the first Chinese emperor, Qin Shi Huang, in the third century BCE (and captured in the thousands of terracotta soldiers buried in his tomb). From its origins, men's neckwear was designed to serve a combination of functional and symbolic purposes, protecting the skin from the elements and cumbersome armor while simultaneously conveying rank and status.

In the early nineteenth century an overall shift in men's fashion from extravagance toward understated elegance (see *Suit*) placed an emphasis on subtle details, including the pleating, folding, and knotting of the day's most prominent form of neckwear, the scarflike but stiffened cravat. Favored by British dandies like George Bryan "Beau" Brummell, the cravat required time and attention if one was to achieve the effortlessly refined appearance necessary to create an impression of aristocratic leisure (underscored by the emergence of anonymous instruction publications, such as *Neckclothitania* in 1818, aimed at demystifying the tying process).

The emergence of the four-in-hand tie during the latter half of the nineteenth century was the result of a growing white-collar workforce.[2] Early versions of the style were constructed from basic rectangular strips of silk, wool, or cotton, and as stiff collars became softer and worn with the points turned down, the four-in-hand was adopted by the leisure classes as well. Production methods soon adapted to the growing market for neckties. In 1923 the New York tie maker Jesse Langsdorf patented the three-piece Resilient Construction tie, a mass-manufacturing concept that inspired many other patents. These approaches not only standardized methods of mass-production but also improved the drape and elasticity of the tie by using strips that were cut on the bias (a forty-five-degree angle), minimizing the twisting that could result from knotting.

On the other end of the spectrum, the seven-fold tie, constructed from meticulous, origami-like hand folding and edge stitching, provided the wealthy man with a status symbol communicated through fine construction and nuanced details. Also cut on the bias, its seven precisely measured folds created a lining from the tie's own fabric, providing the perfect balance of drape and stiffness. With origins in the last decade of the nineteenth century, the seven-fold tie gained prominence concurrently with the mass-produced four-in-hand tie, with such companies as the family-owned E. Marinella of Naples promoting the design method early in the twentieth century.

The status of a tie wearer is also signaled by the tie's material, length, width, color, pattern, and knot (such as the Windsor varieties), and by the use of accessories (such as tie bars, which fasten the front of the tie to the back as well as to the shirt placket), all of which have evolved to follow fashion trends or in response to changing norms. The period after World War I saw a rise in a more flamboyant look, with silk ties hand-painted with motifs and pictorial imagery, a fashion that held until the 1950s. The development of synthetic fibers such as rayon and nylon contributed to the availability of affordable neckties in the 1930s and '40s, when silk was rationed during World War II. *Esquire*, in an attempt to reinvigorate men's fashions after the war, declared a new, assertive style in 1948 that it called the Bold Look, which led to the proliferation of brightly colored and boldly patterned ties produced by American companies such as Arrow and Van Heusen.[3] This laid the foundation for the statement styles and patterns that would emerge in the following decades, such as the skinny knitted tie with a squared bottom rather than a tapered point fashionable in the 1950s, and the exaggeratedly wide polyester ties of the late 1960s and '70s. One of the most enduring styles is the repp (or "rep") tie by Brooks Brothers (see *Oxford-Cloth Button-Down Shirt*), closely aligned with the schoolboy look of the preppy set and featuring alternating downward-sloping stripes (modeled after the British regimental tie but with the direction reversed).

By the end of the twentieth century, the move away from wearing ties in professional settings and social occasions coincided with a resurgent interest in a more discriminating, discerning approach to menswear, and the seven-fold tie saw a rise in popularity. Today both the mass-produced and bespoke tie continue to proliferate. Though not nearly as standard as it was during the first three quarters of the twentieth century, the necktie remains a menswear mainstay. —SK

Previous pages:
1— **Diagrams submitted to the U.S. Patent Office by Isadore D. Wolfson in 1924 to secure a patent on a method of making neckties**
2— **"The Bold Look,"** *Esquire*, **April 1948**
3— **Fiat president Gianni Agnelli, Turin, 1968. Photograph by David Lees**
4— **Portrait of George Bryan "Beau" Brummell, by Robert Dighton, 1805**
5— **Terracotta statues in the tomb of Chinese emperor Qin Shi Huang, Xian, China. Photograph by Danny Lehman**

TIGHTS The twentieth-century history of women's hosiery is a conversation between technological innovation and marketing, the result of which has alternately freed and hindered women through the mediated exposure of their legs. Though multiple terms have been applied to thigh-high knitted stockings attached to underwear of the same composition (including *panty hose* and *hose*), the term *tights* is the most universal and all-encompassing, and can include both sheer and opaque fabrications.[1]

Stockings became readily available with William Lee's invention of the stocking frame knitting machine in 1589, which simulated the movements of hand knitters while allowing for more rapid production. Until the nineteenth century, both women and men wore stockings that extended above the knee, although they were stylistically more integral to menswear as a display of masculinity. The shift away from the exposure of men's legs led to stockings becoming associated strictly with women, and technological innovations catered to this tightened demographic. Newly available synthetic dyes developed from coal tar in the 1850s allowed for brighter, modern colors, and women took to matching their stockings to the color of their dresses, petticoats, or shoes. Though legs were primarily concealed, with only the tops of the feet or the ankles visible, their eroticization through stockings was nevertheless present. Innovation in knitting-machine technology in 1857 inadvertently resulted in another sexually suggestive aspect of stockings: the sinuous, curve-hugging seams that ran up their back.[2]

The introduction of the more affordable rayon stocking in the 1910s

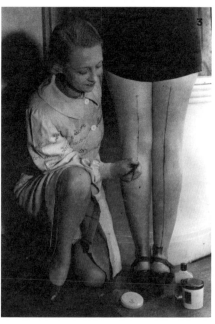

Glen Raven Panti-Legs are made in 5 sizes. We know all women aren't shaped alike.

THIS SYMBOL IS ON EVERY BOX OF GLEN RAVEN PANTI-LEGS® IF YOU DON'T SEE IT, YOU'RE NOT GETTING A GENUINE PRODUCT OF GLEN RAVEN MILLS, INC.

AT THESE STORES AND BRANCHES: LORD & TAYLOR, NEW YORK JORDAN MARSH, BOSTON & MIAMI JOSKE BROTHERS, HOUSTON BROADWAY DEPARTMENT STORES, LOS ANGELES THE CRESCENT, SPOKANE OR FOR THE STORE IN YOUR CITY, WRITE GLEN RAVEN MILLS, INC. 1430 BROADWAY NEW YORK 10018

Glen Raven also creates *ClanCrest* fabrics used in the most wanted women's and children's sportswear

1

4

allowed for greater access to fine hosiery among women (rayon was called "artificial silk" prior to 1924) and resulted in increased advertising efforts geared toward this growing market. Manufactured from cellulose, rayon was extremely lustrous and was available in skin-simulating tan colors. Coinciding with the rise of dress hemlines in the 1920s, the eroticization of women's legs reached new heights. Daring young women took to rolling their stockings below their knees, revealing their kneecaps and shinbones, and hosiery expressed an air of emancipation when coupled with the day's uncomplicated silhouette.

With the development of nylon, stockings became a symbol of smart practicality.[3] Displayed by DuPont at the World's Fair in New York in 1939, nylon boasted the same luster as rayon, but nylon recovery was stronger and thus nylon stockings did not sag. When they were introduced to the American market on May 15, 1940, over four million pairs sold within hours.[4] However, nylon stocking production was halted during World War II, when the fiber was reallocated for military purposes, which led to the repositioning of stockings from an item of modern practicality to one of patriotism. Substitute "victory textures" were advertised by such companies as Belle-Sharmeer, while leg makeup that simulated the look of stocking seams was marketed as the pinnacle of wartime sensibility.[5]

Hosiery reached a new frontier in the early 1960s with the introduction and proliferation of tights. The concept of attaching stockings to underpants was investigated in the 1950s by a few textile companies in the United States, many of whom applied for patents around the same time. Glen Raven, a North Carolina mill that had been in operation since 1880, emerged as the most influential, due not simply to the strength of its design but also its consistently dynamic marketing campaigns. Patenting the garment under the name Panti-Legs in 1959, the company soon advanced its machines to create seamless versions. While Panti-Legs sold slowly at first, the gradual shortening of hemlines (see *Miniskirt*) soon rendered them a must-have item among fashionable women, and Glen Raven seized the opportunity to position its product alongside the emancipating new skirt lengths as a liberating garment for a range of women. Market research determined the ideal leg dimensions for their models, who were often depicted in profile in print ads (a clever way to skirt pelvic nudity), but the taglines indicated a more inclusive approach to their customer: "Glen Raven Panti-Legs are made in 5 sizes. *We* know all women aren't shaped alike."[6] This sales approach captured the zeitgeist of the 1960s and set the stage for the marketing of hosiery for decades to come.

With the emergence of a variety of bright colors and textures by the mid-1960s, tights became a symbol of personal expression and individuality, and marketing efforts toward women followed suit. "They're for introspection, intellectualizing, inspirations and being incorrigibly lazy," declared a 1968 ad for Danskin tights; "it's no wonder they understand every young body."[7] Today the diversity of hosiery marketing ranges from the practical, on-the-go packaging of Hanes's L'eggs to the sexualized print-ad imagery of luxury hosiery brand Wolford. This variety is matched by the new technologies now used to fashion tights, including digitally designed versions such as the Japanese brand Somarta's Skin Series, which boasts a seamless manufacturing process for its highly conceptual full-body lace tights. —SK

Previous pages:
1— **Somarta Skin Guardian bodysuit, designed by Tamae Hirokawa, 2006. Photograph by Sinya Keita**
2— **Model in yellow tights with Mary Quant (right foreground), London, 1967. Unknown photographer**
3— **A Max Factor beautician paints lines on a woman's legs to simulate stockings during a wartime shortage, 1940. Photograph by A. R. Tanner**
4— **Advertisement for Glen Raven Panti-Legs, *Vogue*, November 1964**

TRACKSUIT   The tracksuit is a two-piece ensemble of elasticated, tie-waist pants and a (sometimes hooded, often zipped) jacket originally designed for athletes. Introduced as early as the 1930s and initially monochromatic with decorative piping or lettering, the garments were devised to be worn over lighter sporting uniforms. The tracksuit converged with fashion in the 1970s, as synthetic polyester and velour met newly acceptable modes of informal dress alongside a new fanaticism for pastimes like jogging and jazzercise.[1] Clad in red during his star turn on the television crime drama *Longstreet* (1971–72), martial arts legend Bruce Lee was an early popularizer of the ensemble. Today labels from Versace to Vetements have assimilated the item in their collections, and it has become a staple of the modern wardrobe.[2]

Adidas pioneered the tracksuit as fashion with a version for the German soccer star Franz Beckenbauer in 1967, and in the 1970s the company produced tracksuit tops that aped the style and tailoring of the leisure suit in their inclusion of lapels, buttons, and breast pockets—a clear link between athletic and contemporary casual wear. Hip-hip group Run-DMC's 1986 song "My Adidas" celebrated the company that made their stage outfits and cemented its wares as coveted items of fashionable attire (see *Adidas Superstar*). Subsequent musicians have taken up the baton, including Missy Elliott, who adopted an Adidas three-stripe tracksuit—accessorized with copious gold jewelry—as one of her signature looks. In 2003 Yohji Yamamoto pioneered the designer-sports high-fashion collaboration in conjunction with Adidas (see *Y-3*).

Beyond status attire for a range of celebrities and their followers, the tracksuit was also the chosen outfit for society's peripheral actors—on stage and screen

as well as the street. Mafiosi (as sent up in HBO's series *The Sopranos*) and graffiti kids from France's *banlieues* wore it like a uniform. The British working class (as satirized in the BBC comedy *Little Britain*) was devoted to the tracksuit, favoring sports labels like Fila, Ellesse, Le Coq Sportif, and Kappa as personal and collective insignia (see *Monogram*). In the U.K. the ensemble became a visual shorthand for lager louts, football hooligans, and street-corner kids (pejoratively called "chavs" or "neds") and was banned from certain schools and pubs. This counter-culture image of the tracksuit has become so literally fetishized that it even has found a place in pornography and sex work.[3]

If the tracksuit had from its inception been mobilized primarily as a projection of normative masculinity, this changed radically in 2001 when Juicy Couture introduced a velour version for women. Body-fitting, available in cashmere options and in multiple colors, and marketed as a glamorous ensemble that worked as well with nail and hair extensions as it did "off-duty" on excursions to the grocery store, the tracksuit caught on with celebrities.[4] Paparazzi images quickly established the Juicy Couture tracksuit as *the* aspirational outfit of the early 2000s, an unexpected cultural touchstone now ironically co-opted by Vetements, whose high-concept iterations retail for $1,800. —MMF

Previous pages:
1— **Bruce Lee in a red tracksuit in the TV series** *Longstreet*, **1971–72**
2— **Children at a housing project in Bradford, U.K., n.d. Photograph by Paula Solloway**
3— **Runner in Barrow Park, Cumbria, U.K. Photograph by Edward Herdwick**
4— **Missy Elliott performing at the MTV Europe Music Awards, Edinburgh, Scotland, 2003. Unknown photographer**
5— **Model Alex Boldea in a Brashy Studios Import/Export tracksuit, 2017. Photograph by Jacob Hägg**

TRENCH COAT Nineteenth-century leisure wear that was modified into military garb, the trench coat was deployed as fighting gear as early as the Crimean War (1853–56), and it was in wide use by soldiers during World War I (1914–18). Reappropriated for postwar civilian dress, it has been a mainstay of everyday fashion ever since.

The coat's name attests to its close association with military life and in particular the years the British Army spent fighting in muddy trenches on the Western Front during the Great War. But the archetype for waterproof outerwear dates to the early nineteenth century. Rubberized cotton patented by Charles Macintosh appeared in 1823 and was used for raincoats (the inventor's surname, often shortened to "mac," has become synonymous with this outerwear) and military uniforms for the remainder of the century.[1] In the 1850s the clothier Aquascutum also developed water-repellent fabrics for rainwear, and in 1888 Thomas Burberry, founder of the company that bears his name, patented gabardine, a twill-woven cloth in cotton or wool with individual fiber coating for water resistance. In the early twentieth century both Aquascutum and Burberry sold waterproof sportswear and military gear to the aristocracy—the class that would supply the British Army its officers during World War I. Well-tailored uniforms provided by the officers themselves were salient markers of social class and taste. The high-quality waterproof trench coat came to signify two essential elements of the English gentry's code of masculinity: outdoor leisure in the countryside, and patriotic duty in combat.

In 1916 Burberry began to advertise its weatherproof military coat as "Trench-Warm," from which the outerwear derived its name.[2] The so-called trench coat was a heavy-duty, highly utilitarian garment featuring a tailored form with double-breasted closure, belted waist, and knee-length flared skirt. Every part of the design had a specific purpose to suit wartime conditions and the trench environment: the short length prevented trailing in the mud; the truncated cape directed water away from the body; on the front, the buttoned-down shoulder flap helped protect against rifle recoil; pistols and other accessories could be hooked onto the D-rings of the belt; and gas masks could be secured under the epaulettes. Its trademark khaki color, adopted earlier for British military uniforms in India, provided indispensable camouflage (see *Chinos*). Reserved for officers, the trench coat was a hierarchical garment, indicating superior social as well as military rank. To a degree, the surging commercial competition to market a relatively inexpensive trench coat was a consequence of the high death rate among aristocratic officers during the war, which led to the makeshift recruitment of officers from the untitled classes, referred to as "temporary gentlemen." Their eagerness to dress like aristocrats gave rise to the increasing prevalence of the trench coat. Among civilians, both men and women adopted the garment in nonmilitary versions, as a patriotic gesture and symbol of solidarity with loved ones on the front.

After the war the trench coat was primarily worn on rainy days. It enjoyed increasing popularity in women's fashion during the 1930s and 1940s, in part due to the return of the waistline after a period dominated by loose-cut gowns. There was often an androgynous charge to the images of women in trench coats during this period. In the 1948 film *A Foreign Affair*, screen siren Marlene Dietrich, taking on the role of the dangerously alluring femme fatale, sported an oversize trench coat with a tightly belted waist. Frequently associated in cinema with seductresses, gangsters, spies, detectives, and hit men, the trench coat seemed to cloak dark mysteries beneath its utilitarian surface. The garment is inextricably linked in the minds of many to Humphrey Bogart, through his hard-boiled, lone-wolf screen roles in *Casablanca* (1942) and *The Big Sleep* (1946).

Over the decades, Burberry has become synonymous with classic, heritage trench coats, but many designers have presented versions. From the mid-1960s on, the trench coat has been

a fashion staple, effortlessly adapted to shifting styles such as the mod look in the 1960s and '70s and the power-woman look of the 1980s and '90s. A garment traditionally associated with outdoor sports and war, the coat has been transformed into a signifier of urban chic, especially for women. A sense of mystery and adventure still clings to the trench coat in the contemporary imagination, as illustrated in a suggestive fashion essay in the February 2000 issue of *Vogue*. Set in New York, one photo represents a couple casually dressed in classic Armani and Burberry trench coats contriving an "assignation on a moody-gray afternoon." The coat's legendary associations with furtive intrigue and cloaked-but-smoldering sexuality live on, though it is the fresh-faced charm of Romeo Beckham that now has the most currency, after his star turn, at age twelve, as the face of Burberry's autumn 2015 campaign. —MMR

Previous pages:
1— **British soldiers in battle, 1941. Unknown photographer**
2— **Humphrey Bogart and Mary Astor in the film *Across the Pacific*, 1942**
3— **Lauren Hutton, New York, 1983. Unknown photographer**
4— **Fashion editor Giovanna Battaglia during Milan Fashion Week, 2016. Photograph by Melodie Jeng**

TURTLENECK   In April 1925 *Vogue* declared the turtleneck sweater the epitome of spring smartness, advocating "a very fine cashmere jersey, preventing sunburn without giving too much warmth."[1] Almost four decades later, in 1963, the same publication underscored the garment's unisex appeal—and its fitness for fall and winter, too—by noting that "men's sweaters turn turtle this year."[2] That same year, the socialite Gloria Vanderbilt was included on *Life* magazine's best-dressed list, which admired her fondness for turtlenecks (paired with her "all-purpose" sable coat).[3] Flash forward to 2015, when the *New York Times Magazine* presented a soliloquy on the turtleneck in the twenty-first century by paying homage to the "objectively uncool" dancing of rapper Drake. In the video for his booty-call hit "Hotline Bling," the generous roll of a gray ribbed-knit turtleneck collar silhouetted the megastar as he gave "the public a performance of masculinity that it hadn't known it wanted."[4] Weather-appropriate, androgynous, and always ambiguously on the cusp of cool, the turtleneck is a high-low mediator whose multifaceted meanings are attested to in the fashion history and popular culture of the last century.

A T-shaped garment that manifests in different materials (from chunky knit to superfine silk) and varying sleeve lengths, the turtleneck is identified by a rolled collar that covers the wearer's neck. One precursor may be the arming doublet (also known as a gambeson or an aketon) worn in the late-medieval period under armor to mitigate chafing. The modern turtleneck is similarly flexible, emerging in the later nineteenth century as an all-weather sports uniform (worn by polo players, it is known as a polo shirt in the United Kingdom) and as part of naval, military, and school attire in many regions of the world.

Although the English playwright Noël Coward extolled its virtues in the 1920s, the turtleneck properly entered the fashion mainstream in the 1960s when designers including Halston provoked the establishment (and many a maître d') by pairing it with suits in place of a shirt. For women, Yves Saint Laurent controversially paired a mink-trimmed leather jacket with a turtleneck in what turned out to be his final collection for Dior, in 1960. These designers were quoting the anti-uniform that was already a stereotype of 1950s beatniks. Sweater girls wore theirs snug and paired them with bullet bras, teasing out curves even while providing demure cover, enshrining the turtleneck as a go-to garment for new generations of the preppy set.

In London the designer John Stephen led the mods as they linked the turtleneck to soul music and scooters. Second-wave feminists used the garment to train the public gaze toward their intellect and rhetoric, a strategy taken up by Black Panthers such as Kathleen Cleaver and Angela Davis (their male cohort followed suit). Musicians such as Françoise Hardy, Bob Dylan, Mick Jagger, Lou Reed, and Nico; artists like Andy Warhol and his muse Edie Sedgwick; actor Steve McQueen; novelist Kingsley Amis and other Angry Young Men; and philosopher Michel Foucault are only a handful of the public figures associated with the item between the 1950s and the '70s. Indeed, the list of those who did *not* wear a turtleneck at midcentury might be shorter. (This trope was parodied in the 1957 film *Funny Face*, in the costume of Audrey Hepburn's shy bookstore clerk.) It even colonized extraterrestrial sites, with the era's space-age utopianism finding a partial expression in the ribbed mock turtlenecks of *Star Trek* characters and the real ones worn by U.S. astronauts.[5]

Life prefigured perhaps the most famous turtleneck wearer, Apple cofounder Steve Jobs, when it noted in 1967 that the garment was for "people who don't have to deal with the chairman of the board and people who *are* chairman of the board."[6] Jobs embraced the turtleneck in the 1980s after visiting Sony headquarters in Japan, where employees were provided with work clothing designed by Issey Miyake—whom Jobs later commissioned to reproduce previously discontinued black mock turtlenecks, each with a barely discernable line bisecting the front.[7] Now firmly established as normcore (thanks to 1990s

figures like Jerry Seinfeld), the turtleneck can be mined for delicious irony, as when Dwayne "The Rock" Johnson lit up social media in 2014 by posting a flashback photo of himself, from two decades earlier, posing confidently in a turtleneck paired with a heavy gold chain and a fanny pack.

In recent decades, women interested in modest dress have used the garment as a way to draw attention away from their bodies. At the forefront of modest fashion discourse, designer Hana Tajima astutely highlights the turtleneck's chameleonic capability to "redefine—or perhaps undefine—a particular group of people," coming close to the ubiquity of jeans or the white T-shirt in the modern wardrobe.[8]
—MMF

Previous pages:
1— Jan Provoost, *Calvary* (detail), 1515
2— Cover art for the Italian comic book *Diabolik*, by Giancarlo Alessandrini, 2000
3— Steve Jobs, wearing a turtleneck by an unknown designer, Woodside, California, 1984. Photograph by Norman Seeff
4— Two Haredi girls, Israel, 2008. Photograph by Copper Kettle
5— Angela Davis, San Jose, California, 1972. Unknown photographer

1

2

UNISEX PROJECT "Today our notions of masculine and feminine are being challenged as never before," Rudi Gernreich asserted in 1968. "The basic masculine-feminine appeal is in people, not in clothes."[1]

An unrestricted approach to gender that could have been plucked from a twenty-first-century headline, these sentiments were a natural extension of the American designer's future-facing views about the body and its relationship to clothing. Known for avant-garde creations that tested the conventions of fashion's forms as well as its social frameworks, Gernreich is best remembered for his 1964 monokini, a topless bathing suit with a rib-cage-height bottom held up by shoulder straps. Viewed by its designer as a garment that emancipated women from "the implicit hypocrisy that made [the exposure of the breasts] in one culture immoral and in another perfectly acceptable," the monokini created a sensation and established Gernreich's reputation as a designer who used his work to interrogate outmoded social standards and practices.[2]

In 1969 *Life* editor Helen Blagden asked Gernreich to contribute to the magazine's January 9, 1970, double issue by envisaging what men and women would be wearing in 1980. Choosing to extend the parameter to the year 2000, Gernreich illustrated a series of matching ensembles for men and women, depicted with either shaved or wigged heads and distinguished only by the articulation of breasts for women and muscles for men. Predicting that the garments of the future would reflect a combination of honesty and utility, Gernreich declared, "Clothing will not be identified as either male or female. So women will wear pants and men will wear skirts interchangeably. . . . The aesthetics

3

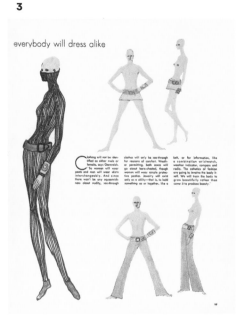

of fashion are going to involve the body itself. We will train the body to grow beautifully rather than cover it to produce beauty."[3] Linking the elision of gender markers to utility, Gernreich also projected that in cold weather, "both men and women will wear heavy ribbed leotards and waterproof boots . . . and since animals which now supply wool, fur and leather will be so rare that they must be protected, and weaving fabric such as cotton will be too much trouble, most clothes will be made entirely of cheap and synthetic knits."[4]

The Dictionary of Fashion History defines *unisex* as "a term coined to describe styles of clothing or forms of hairdressing and footwear which can be interchangeably worn by men and women."[5] Gernreich took his *Life* concept a step further. Shortly after his piece was published, Maurice Tuchman, senior curator at the Los Angeles County Museum of Art, asked Gernreich to produce a special fashion event for the U.S. Pavilion's Art and Technology Program at Expo '70, the World's Fair taking place in Osaka, Japan, later that year. Gernreich decided to produce his *Life* concept, explaining, "I felt a strong anti-statement was in order and that a drawing was vague and unreal. I believed that if I translated that drawing into clothes, it would be real. It would have an impact."[6] Though unisex clothing had been available for years, it largely involved adapting menswear items (particularly suits) for women. While seemingly offering equality, this translation ultimately reinforced the notion of a masculine standard of fashion. For Gernreich, however, unisex meant eliminating baseline constructions of gender. In bringing his pairings of pants, miniskirts, and knitted jumpsuits to life, Gernreich also eliminated stylistic markers of gender differentiation between his models, including hair. In showing both models barechested, Gernreich, as he had with his monokini, confronted the social construct of women's breasts as a sexualized part of anatomy. Photographed during a Los Angeles gallery show, the Unisex Project, as it became known, prompted the *Los Angeles Times* to declare, "Behind the shockery of completely hairless bodies and nudity, Gernreich's projection is a sincere probing of what he believes the future may be and how it will affect our appearance."[7]

Gernreich's project also looked to the past. In ancient Egypt, for example, while men of most social classes wore wrapped linen skirts (called *schenti* by some historians) and women commonly wore a wrapped linen sheath-style dress, both genders were depicted in tempera paintings from the New Kingdom (1550–1070 BCE) wearing identical pleated linen gowns, along with kohl eyeliner and polished nails. In ancient Greece, the chiton was the standard garment for both genders, particularly in its Ionic and Doric iterations from 550–300 BCE. Draped and fastened at the shoulders, the tunic-like garment was typically made of wool or linen and varied in length and fullness. Commonality in clothing during these periods was not a novel concept or practice, and Gernreich likely considered this history in conceiving his work.

The Unisex Project would not be completely realized by the year 2000, but its philosophy is reflected in a rapidly transforming understanding of gender as a fluid concept lacking a rigid masculine/feminine binary structure. From Shayne Oliver, founder of Hood By Air, who has regularly deconstructed and repurposed archetypal masculine and feminine silhouettes for a kaleidoscopic range of gender identities, to Yohji Yamamoto, whose use of non-Western techniques seems to have erased any formal conceptualizations of gender altogether, fashion designers have moved closer to a truer unisex ideal. Gernreich understood the nuances of gender and foresaw its shifting tide. —SK

Previous pages:
1— **Male and female models in identical black and white Unisex jumpsuits, part of Rudi Gernreich's Unisex Project, 1970. Photograph by Patricia Faure**
2— **The Rational Dress Society JUMPSUIT, fall/winter edition (left) and spring/summer edition (right). Photograph by Lara Kastner**
3— **Rudi Gernreich's Unisex Project illustrations, *Life*, January 9, 1970**

WHITE T-SHIRT Bruce Springsteen performs as the archetypal working-class everyman in his. James Dean embodied postwar rebellion and Sugar Ray Robinson was fight-ready in it. Harry Belafonte was smooth and *Grease*'s Danny Zuko sexy, and Elvis showed up to report for the draft—all wearing one. Madonna, Brooke Shields, and Brigitte Bardot played virgins and vixens in theirs; Kurt Cobain paired his with flannel; and Salt-N-Pepa cut theirs off at the midriff. Today skaters line up down the block to purchase theirs when streetwear labels like Supreme collaborate with brands like Hanes. From humble origins as an undergarment to mass-produced fast-fashion staple to highly collectible (and highly priced) commodity, the white T-shirt is a quintessential product of twentieth-century modernity and the ultimate sartorial and psychological blank canvas.[1] Much like denim jeans (see *501s*), over the last seventy years the white T-shirt has emerged across cultures, classes, styles, and identities as a classic, unisex wardrobe garment. Given its ubiquity, the item also serves as a conduit for conversations about some of the most pressing issues that the field of fashion and society at large confront today, including fair labor practices and the environmental toll of processing raw materials such as cotton into garments. (The fashion industry is the second most polluting industry worldwide, after oil.)[2]

As with other clothing items (see *Slip Dress*), the genesis of the white T-shirt lies in undergarments. From the early medieval period onward, simple T-shaped shirts of wool, linen, or silk were prevalent. Front and back sections were joined by seams at the shoulders and sides, with the fineness of the fabric dependent on the socioeconomic status of the wearer, and the length of hem and cuffs dependent on the prevailing style. Such

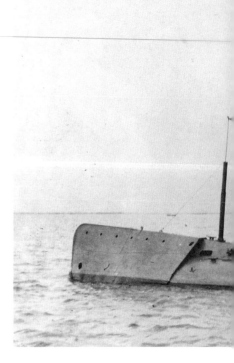

protective under-layers ensured that coarser outer garments did not irritate the skin, and that daily bodily effluents did not soil finely woven top layers. Given Christianized associations of the body and its secretions with sin, when this mediating barrier was displayed publicly, it symbolized humility.[3] With the advent of dress and sanitary reforms in the nineteenth century, undergarments were more frequently laundered, and thus the precursors of the white T-shirt helped form "the habits of organizing and meaning of laundering" that exist today.[4] The Industrial Revolution, as well as the colonial and protectionist trade in its raw materials—including slave labor—secured the dissemination of cotton products.[5]

It was at the turn of the twentieth century that companies such as Cooper Underwear (later Jockey), Hanes, and Fruit of the Loom bisected the union suit (a mid-nineteenth-century underwear invention; see *Jumpsuit*), creating long johns on the bottom and an undershirt on top. The latter was issued by the U.S. Navy during the Spanish-American war in 1898, and Hanes began to produce cotton T-shirts for the U.S. Marine Corps shortly after, in 1901.[6] Companies also marketed these undergarments for the general citizenry, using a strangely ambiguous rhetoric that played up the garment's comfort, construction, and ease of maintenance, focusing on the image of the virile, heteronormative soldier or dad on the one hand, while offering the homoerotic signifier of the taut male torso on the other.[7]

The white T-shirt was also a garment that rebellious youth could customize to suit their needs and identities—preppy, subversive, conservative, collective—whether by adding to its surface or by pairing it with other parts of an ensemble. By the time the actor Marlon Brando smoldered in a white T-shirt in the 1951 film *A Streetcar Named Desire*, his muscular arms accentuated by its taut, crisp outline, its ascendancy in the mainstream was assured. In the latter half of the twentieth century, the T-shirt's blank canvas was assimilated into fashion, also becoming a foundation for customized branding and personal expression (see *Graphic T-Shirt*). In 1991 Karl Lagerfeld paired Chanel's signature tweed cardigan jackets with white T-shirts, juxtaposing high fashion and a humble masterpiece—the simple garment serving as the perfect foil to for the iconic textured silhouette. The item has also been

imbricated in hip-hop and normcore fashion, where box-fresh tees are part of pristine ensembles. Designer Mary Ping's compelling *White T-shirt Project* (2012) investigates the many modalities and materialities of the garment, cherishing each possibility as a way of reconsidering a familiar item.

In the twenty-first century, the white T-shirt has become emblematic of the ethical and ecological implications of rapid global manufacturing and distribution in the fashion industry. Companies such as Everlane, Pact, Patagonia, and more have taken the white T-shirt as the basis for pursuing "B Corporation" status —introducing better practices to benefit all stakeholders. Thus the item is both the apogee and rejection of early-twentieth-century philosopher Walter Benjamin's ruminations on the mass-produced object. Its infinite reproducibility allows us to affordably synthesize it at will in our wardrobes, but the memories and associations woven into the favorite (white) T-shirt interrupt its disposability.[8] It exists as both marker of "auratic," authentic ritual and disassociated, plain white space. —MMF

1

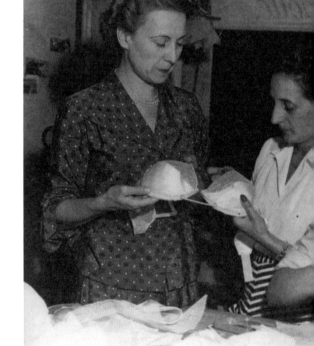

Previous pages:
1— **Officers and crew on the *USS A-2* submarine, Philippines, c. 1911–19. Unknown photographer**
2— **Cooper Underwear Company (later Jockey Intl.) union suit depicted in a painting by J. C. Leyendecker, 1915**
3— **Yarn-spinning factory, Indonesia, 2013. Photograph by David Gilkey**
4— **Harry Belafonte, 1964. Photograph by Mondadori Portfolio**

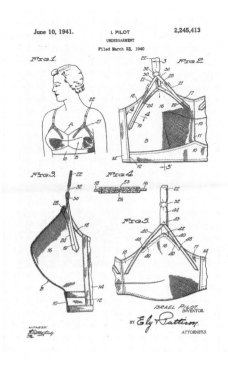

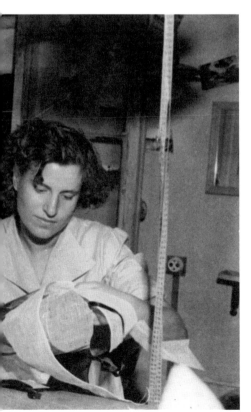

WONDERBRA The Wonderbra—for which the term *va-va-voom* might have found its perfect subject—radically redefined silhouettes and advertising strategies for women's underwear when its contemporary incarnation debuted in the early 1990s. The bra promoted unapologetically sexy cleavage and, as its name suggests, promised a magically pneumatic bosom, no matter the wearer's cup size. The Wonderbra profoundly altered tropes of femininity, sexuality, and fashion, continuing the modern tradition of bras shaping the body—literally and metaphorically.

The bra became a wardrobe staple in the early twentieth century. (The history of similar garments goes back much further; for example, athletic female figures in bra- or bikini-like attire appear in Italian mosaics dating from the fourth century CE.) Early designs included those of the French dressmaker Herminie Cadolle, who in 1889 essentially bisected the corset so that the upper half, secured with shoulder straps, bound the breasts. As restrictive corsets were slowly discarded, flapper bandeaus emerged, then gave way to supportive cups. Alphabetical sizing emerged in the early 1930s as commercial production took off. Innovations such as underwire developed in the 1950s alongside strapless dresses, as did cups that took on the streamlined (and Cold War–appropriate) form of torpedoes. Second-wave feminists urged their sisters to burn their bras in the 1960s and '70s, ushering in underwear styles that effected natural, almost-invisible lines. In a complete reversal, by the late 1990s corporate behemoth Victoria's Secret had created a carnivalesque runway spectacle to market its Miracle Bra.

Designed by Louise Poirier and commercially available in the early 1960s through Canadelle, a Canadian lingerie manufacturer, the Wonderbra was specif-

ically designed to enhance cleavage, using forty-four separate components instead of the average twenty-five, including removable cup pads and precision straps.[1] In 1968 the U.K. license for the Wonderbra was transferred from Canadelle to Courtaulds Textiles. That company's subsidiary, Gossard, sold eleven million units over the ensuing twenty-three years, notable in a country where the serviceable and sensible retailer Marks & Spencer accounted for an estimated 40 percent of bra sales and the Wonderbra retailed at an average of twice the price of other products.

It was in the early 1990s, however, that the Wonderbra really took off. Sales surged as enhanced and visible cleavage became a mainstream fashion statement, thanks to growing public acceptance of cosmetic surgery, as well as its medical refinement, and popular culture's fixation with overtly boosted breasts, exemplified by the popularity of television stars like Pamela Anderson. By the end of 1992 Gossard was producing twenty thousand Wonderbras every week for domestic and global markets. Meanwhile, Canadelle was taken over by the Sara Lee Corporation, which redistributed the Wonderbra license to Playtex. In retaliation, and to claw back its market share, Gossard developed the Ultrabra. Both companies debuted their supposedly new yet virtually unchanged and almost identical products —the Playtex Wonderbra and the Gossard Ultrabra—in early 1994, and so began the "Bra Wars."[2] Playtex hired the advertising firm TWBA to create a marketing campaign on the relatively modest budget of approximately $500,000. The resulting posters (there was no money for television spots) featured the Czech model Eva Herzigova in a black bra and panties next to various provocative slogans; one poster bore text reading "Hello boys," with Herzigova looking down and addressing her breasts. The ads literally stopped traffic with their risqué humor, and news media plastered it across their platforms. The Wonderbra's sales almost doubled that year, and its name became synonymous with the padded uplift bra.

During the mid-1990s in Britain —the Wonderbra's epicenter—the "ladette" proliferated as a cultural type.[3] Ladettes were normatively feminine in their dress but acted like lads, publicly displaying brash body confidence and matching—indeed, outdoing—their male counterparts in alcohol consumption and vulgarity; this performance was hailed by some as an expression of post-second-wave feminism. The Wonderbra and its mass-market copies became part of the ladette's sartorial symbolism, a tool for outré behavior available at an affordable price. Of course, public expectations of and judgments about gender remained predominately static, even as the pop group Spice Girls urged their own particular synthesis of ladette and lady under the banner of "girl power," singing, "We know how we got this far / strength and courage and a Wonderbra."

The desire for voluptuous cleavage is in many ways at odds with other standards of female beauty that have prevailed over the last five decades in much of the world. As the scholar Wendy Burns-Ardolino highlights, "The current feminine body ideal, the 'hot fitness body,' is so thin, so flabless, that it is necessary to rely on synthetic mechanisms to create the illusion of breasts."[4] It seems impossible that the busty, raucous ladette could coexist with the fashion industry's avant-garde heroin-chic waif epitomized by the young Kate Moss—but it did. While conceptions about the ideal breasts periodically change, savvy marketing advocating alteration of he female form is consistently profitable —and thus a constant fixture of fashion and everyday life. —MMF

Previous pages:
1— **Model Eva Herzigova in a Wonderbra advertisement, 1994. Photograph by Ellen von Unwerth**
2— **Diagrams supporting Israel Pilot's 1941 U.S. Patent for the Wonderbra, the precursor to the push-up Model 1300 developed by Louise Poirier in the 1960s**
3— **Alice Cadolle (left), descendent of Herminie Cadolle, early pioneer of the brassiere, reviewing the design and fabrication of her new collection, Paris, 1949. Unknown photographer**

1

WRAP DRESS   In 1974 the budding American fashion designer Diane von Furstenberg draped a boldly printed piece of jersey and fastened it at the waistline with a tie belt cut from the same fabric. Her wrap dress was born. Although von Furstenberg's affordable jersey sheaths and practical shirtdresses had already impressed *Vogue* editor in chief Diana Vreeland (her maxi sheath had appeared in a March 1971 *Vogue* editorial titled "Bargains in Chic"), the printed wrap dress launched her career.

Drawing on both ancient and contemporary examples of wrapping, which have long been integral to clothing across geographic and cultural lines, von Furstenberg's wrap dress both paid homage to a complex history and retooled it to reflect the contemporary moment. The *hakchangui,* for example, is a wrapped, single-layer coat worn as part of Korean traditional dress (*hanbok*), particularly by scholars and noblemen in the nineteenth century. Its relative simplicity stands in contrast to the Japanese kimono, the donning of which involves a complex and lengthy wrapping ritual.

Von Furstenberg's wrap dress was simple and intuitive, requiring minimal time and effort from its on-the-go wearer. Though not the first contemporary designer to create a wrap dress, von Furstenberg's innovative contribution came via her experimentation with different fiber blends for the printed jersey fabric. Having spent nearly a year apprenticing at the Italian textile mill Manifattura Tessile Ferretti, von Furstenberg came to appreciate the unique properties of blended fabrics. Her cotton/rayon jersey conformed to all body types, was wrinkle resistant, could be washed and drip-dried,

3

2

and allowed for a relatively affordable garment by high-fashion standards (costing between $65 and $85 in 1975—approximately $300 to $400 today). And von Furstenberg herself was the label's best promotor, embodying the lifestyle of the women for whom she designed it. "They work, they are active, yet somehow they want to be attractive," she explained. "People don't want to spend so much money on clothes, and even more than the money, they want to be comfortable."[1]

Female dress etiquette in the workplace came under great scrutiny in the 1970s as women increasingly joined the ranks of career professionals. Critics (many of whom were men) decried contemporary workplace womenswear as "aggressively feminine" and "too frilly." Von Furstenberg's assertive décolletage paired with a modest long-sleeved silhouette captured the spirit of the modern liberated woman. As she described, "It's a dress that's both proper and seductive—practical and sexy. . . . You know, you can go in a boardroom and make a presentation and feel feminine, and yet not exposed."[2]

Other twentieth-century American examples of the silhouette also helped shape the item's typology. Charles James's Taxi dress (1932)—so named because it could be removed or put on in a taxi cab—and Claire McCardell's Pop-Over dress (1942)—designed to offer busy wartime housewives an attractive dress that could go from homemaking to the outside world and meant to be "popped over" a pair of trousers or bare skin—are two examples.[3] It was von Furstenberg, however, who ultimately championed the style in its most modern incarnation. —SK

Left:
1— Claire McCardell's Pop-Over dress in a Lord & Taylor advertisement, 1940s
2— Portrait of Father Zhang Jimin and Mother Zhao, Ming or Qing dynasty (seventeenth century or later)
3— Diane von Furstenberg wearing a wrap dress in the 1970s. Unknown photographer
4— Black Taxi dress designed by Charles James, c. 1932

Y —109

Y-3 The language of Y-3 is so seamlessly embedded into the contemporary fashion vernacular that it's hard to imagine that this sports-gear-cum-luxury-ready-to-wear concept was considered an idiosyncratic novelty at its introduction only fifteen years ago. Created by celebrated Japanese avant-garde designer Yohji Yamamoto in collaboration with German sporting giant Adidas, the first Y-3 collection debuted in stores in spring 2003, with its first runway presentation taking place in October 2002. Described by *Vogue* as "something far more sophisticated than literal gym-bound design," Y-3 featured separates for women and men, many emblazoned with a variation of the Adidas three-stripe logo, and all showing some reference to classic sports clothing forms, ranging from track-style pants to elongated knitted tennis dresses.[1] While some of the garments could have been worn for sports play, the collection's driving principle was a translation of the sportswear spirit into everyday street fashion, and its ensembles—such as oversize nylon overalls with a center front-zip closure and a maxi-length hoodie dress printed with graphic flowers—certainly embodied this ethos.

　　The pairing of an avant-garde fashion designer with a global sports brand does not seem out of the ordinary in today's fashion climate of limited-run capsule collections and collaborations, but when Yamamoto telephoned Adidas to initiate a sneaker collaboration for his namesake label's fall 2001 collection, perhaps nobody was more surprised than Yamamoto himself. "When I first saw sport shoes worn by young people, I found them ugly," the designer explained. "Being well dressed means not to create an annoyance in the collective space. I stepped into this arena

to restrain the world from being visually polluted."[2] Yamamoto conducted research in the Adidas archives, and he redesigned the shoes' uppers to incorporate new materials such as mesh as well as a reimagined Adidas three-stripe logo, protruding slightly from the surface or running down the center front of the shoe. Yamamoto also incorporated his research into garments in his collection, which featured unusually proportioned iterations of the Adidas stripes on artfully draped ensembles such as hooded jackets paired with casual trousers overlaid with voluminous skirts. "Never before had a major performance-sportswear corporation crossed the path of purist fashion sensibility," declared *Vogue*.[3] Realizing that Yamamoto had tapped a new market, Adidas asked the designer to head a new clothing division, and Y-3 was born.

　　The first run of Yamamoto's sneakers for Adidas sold out completely, reaching beyond the brand's typical old-school sneaker collectors and athletic devotees to a sophisticated, design-conscious audience that spanned generations. "At the time, New York businessmen were starting to walk to work in their suits and sneakers," Yamamoto recalled in 2016. "I found this strange mix incredibly charming, a fascinating hybrid that completely inspired me."[4] Yamamoto's melding of avant-garde high-street fashion with the technical spirit of Adidas not only demonstrated that sport and fashion were complementary, but also reflected a no-rules, high-meets-low attitude that captured the essence of modern fashion at the turn of the millennium. It is not surprising, then, that the *New York Times* described Y-3's introduction as "the most innovative idea to come out of the spring 2003 collections."[5]

　　Though Y-3 represented a revolutionary blending of sports clothes with high fashion, it was by no means the first instance of this dialogue. The tailor-made suit, for example, a women's riding ensemble that emerged during the mid-nineteenth century, had evolved into fashionable day wear by the 1890s. Promoted by designers such as John Redfern of the British tailoring firm Redfern & Sons, it was inspired by men's suiting and consisted of a jewel-neck bodice over a long, trained skirt, typically constructed from woolen fabrics. It offered women a practical and comfortable alternative to more elaborately decorated day ensembles. Similarly, the informal knitwear separates of the 1920s

were directly inspired by tennis clothing. French tennis star Suzanne Lenglen helped promote the adoption of knitwear for fashionable day wear, wearing, both on and off the court, knitted ensembles designed by couturier Jean Patou. Indeed, sports clothing became so intertwined with fashion and art during the 1920s that when the Ballets Russes performed its sporting-themed *Le Train bleu* in 1924, Gabrielle "Coco" Chanel designed knitted sports costumes for the dancers that showed similarities to the knitted ensembles featured in her fashion line.

Like Y-3, these examples, along with others (see *Leotard*), do not simply represent isolated moments when sports clothing merely influenced fashion, but rather demonstrate that sports clothing permanently changed fashion's very language. It is not a coincidence that the marketing concept of "athleisure" (athletic clothing that can also be worn as leisure wear) saw a meteoric rise in the years following Y-3's introduction. Yamamoto's style language tapped into a collective mindset that increasingly viewed activity as an integral aspect of everyday life. This notion was encapsulated best by Yamamoto himself, who said, "The sports world and technology seek for necessity, practicality, or functionality while fashion is seeking the opposite. Y-3 is a strong examination of the blend of sport and style and the tension caused by mixing tradition with all that is modern."[6] —SK

3

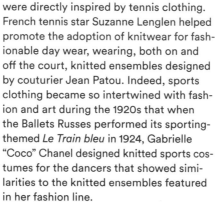

Left:
1— **Costumes by Gabrielle "Coco" Chanel for the Ballets Russes' production of *Le Train bleu*, Paris, November 1924. Photograph by Sasha**
2— **Model on the runway for the Yohji Yamamoto Y-3 spring/summer 2007 collection. Unknown photographer**
3— **Model on the runway for the Yohji Yamamoto Y-3 fall/winter 2001/2002 collection, Paris, 2001. Unknown photographer**

Y — 110

YOGA PANTS The concept of yoga pants does not refer to a distinct typology of garment, but rather reflects the diversity of yoga as a practice (both physical and spiritual) throughout its history. Yoga as a fitness activity (rather than a spiritual one) is primarily a concept of the Western world. Although some form of systematic yoga technique has existed since the fifth century BCE (the Sanskrit term may be traced to the fifteenth century BCE), before the nineteenth century yoga systems and traditions were widespread in South Asia and did not reflect a single set of beliefs or physical practices. (They were instead a diffuse amalgam of breathing, meditation, sound exercises, and *asanas*, or poses.) With the increasing popularity of hatha yoga—the earliest physical practice of yoga, which was initially developed as a vehicle to prepare the body for meditation—the notion of yoga as a fitness practice began to develop. However, even as yoga was taken up in certain European countries in the nineteenth century, a standard form of clothing was not established. According to Andrea Jain, author of *Selling Yoga: From Counterculture to Pop Culture,* "Modern yoga until the second half of the twentieth century was countercultural, elite and scandalous. . . . It was not until the late 1960s that it no longer opposed the prevailing cultural norms of Americans and Western Europeans and became readily available to the masses in urban areas across the world."[1]

In spite of its newfound accessibility during the late 1960s and early 1970s, a concretized form of yoga attire still did not exist. Some practitioners wore wrapped and draped, loincloth-like bottoms derived from the Hindu *dhoti* of the same form, while others wore all-white linen suits consisting of loose pants and tunics, reflective of the spiritually focused Kundalini school of yoga (which promoted wearing white as a method of enlightening the practitioner's consciousness). Spandex leotards, however, were ubiquitous at that time, as a widespread fitness craze took hold in the 1970s and '80s (see *Leotard*). It was not until the 1990s, when yoga gained traction as an alternative form of low-impact exercise, that items marketed specifically for its practice began to emerge on a mass scale and "yoga pants" were born.

"Yoga has the attention of popular culture right now," observed the *New York Times* in 1998. "In the current Tweeds catalogue, a woman in white drawstring pants floats along a beach, beside a caption reading, 'The pristine appeal of yoga pants in washed, corded cotton.'"[2] While the application of the term in the 1990s seemed indiscriminate (including everything from low-rise spandex culottes to sheer linen beach pants), it received its ultimate codifying boost in 1999, when yoga practitioner and studio owner Chip Wilson of Vancouver, Canada, designed the Boogie Pant for his newly established apparel line Lululemon. Made of Luon, a proprietary nylon-Lycra blend that looked and felt like cotton but offered four-way stretch and sweat wicking, the Boogie Pant was a low-rise legging with a slight flare at the ankle. Not all that distinct from other leggings composed of technical fabric, the Boogie Pant brought more innovation to the yoga apparel discourse in its marketing, as it was promoted as reflecting a larger Lululemon lifestyle devoted to healthy living and mindfulness, but also positioned as a comfortable—yet stylish—pant that could be worn for everyday use. Its versatility was underscored by its moisture-wicking capabilities and excellent stretch recovery; a yoga practitioner could in theory go straight from class into her day without looking like she came from a workout.

As the new millennium unfolded, yoga pants proliferated, prompting *Vogue* to ask, "Are Yoga Studios the Latest Runway?" and to lightheartedly assert, "Sure, a wandering ascetic in ancient India practicing the meditative exercises that would one day become what the twenty-first century calls yoga might have gotten away with wearing a loincloth while practicing his various poses. But today he would have to do a lot better than that in order to detach his mind from the external world."[3] The pant's assimilation into daily wardrobes soon led the *New York Times* to publish an article titled, "Yoga Wear, Not Yoga, Is the Mantra," in which fashion reporter Ruth La Ferla observed, "Margaret Lenon has never heard of the downward dog or praying mountain, two common yoga postures, though you might not guess that from her look. . . . Her sleek, stretchy, wardrobe, mostly ordered from a Danskin catalog, includes several pairs of yoga pants versatile enough to wear to lunch with a cashmere sweater and diamond stud earrings" (see *Diamond Stud*).[4] La Ferla's speculation presaged the rise of the athleisure trend of performance clothing designed to be fashionably current outside a sports context, a phenomenon so ubiquitous that in recent years yoga pants have even been compared to jeans in their versatility and have become a staple, especially among busy mothers. At once a symbol of a mindful lifestyle and a justification for wearing the equivalent of leggings as fashion, yoga pants, though essentially undefinable, nonetheless shed light on a variety of factors at play in the twenty-first-century fashion landscape.
—SK

Right:
1— **Yoga class in Times Square, New York, June 2016. Photograph by Justin Lane**
2— **Yoga class at a community hall, London, 1964. Unknown photographer**
3— **Hindu man practicing yoga, India, 1949. Photograph by Eliot Elisofon**

YSL TOUCHE ÉCLAT Introduced in 1992, Yves Saint Laurent's Touche Éclat ("radiant touch")—a combination concealer and face highlighter in an all-in-one tube and brush—was the brainchild of Terry de Gunzburg, then the creative director of Yves Saint Laurent Beauté. At the time of its introduction, Touche Éclat was groundbreaking for its emphasis on radiance over coverage. Inspired by de Gunzburg's technique of refreshing models' makeup on photo shoots with a homemade mixture of foundation, cream moisturizer, and liquid toner, its reflective pigments yielded a luminous look that accentuated the skin's natural tones. "Makeup artists were using powder for touch ups, which made the girls' faces look matte and crackly," de Gunzburg explained. "When I joined YSL, I suggested using this technique and making a product out of it by putting it in a click pen, easy to use and practical to carry around for touch ups."[1] The design of the makeup's applicator underscored its function as a highlighter to be swiped like a marker over the cheekbones, under the eyes, and down the nose. Considered pivotal in launching a new generation of makeup, Touche Éclat was integral in its focus on enhancing natural features rather than concealing them.

The history of cosmetics has long reflected a tension between natural beauty and artificial enhancement. Makeup is historically tied to societies with strong court cultures, in which its effect on beauty is a form of social currency. In the Imperial court system during China's Qin and Han dynasties (221 BCE–220 CE) court women and concubines applied rice powder to their faces in order to achieve the pale complexion that was associated with a leisurely, labor-free life—and therefore with power. While light face powder (often made of dangerous substances, such as arsenic and lead) was used at all levels of society in areas of Europe in the seventeenth and eighteenth centuries, lips, cheeks, and fingernails were sometimes colored red with rouge by women of the upper classes. In some societies, however, any visible trace of makeup was frowned upon and viewed as a disfiguration of one's God-given face. In 1770, for example, the English parliament passed a law annulling marriages for men who had been tricked by women who used "paints [and] cosmetic washes."[2]

By the twentieth century, negative associations with makeup had begun to wane. The proliferation of photography, the establishment of the department store industry, and the emergence of cinema all helped to create a visual culture of display and self-scrutiny.[3] In the United States during the 1910s, early pioneers such as Helena Rubinstein and Elizabeth Arden promoted makeup as a tool of empowerment (see *Red Lipstick*). The shift in terminology from "paint" to "makeup" in the 1920s underscored the idea that cosmetics were no longer a means of covering up one's looks, but rather integral to the presentation of a public persona.

With the emergence of Hollywood as a center of fashion influence, makeup innovations followed suit. Max Factor's Pan-Cake, a water-soluble foundation in cake form that was designed to smooth out screen actresses' skin tones, was introduced to the public in 1938. As access to information about beauty and makeup increased thanks to color television and an upsurge in advertising and marketing, aesthetic standards shifted. In the 1950s, for example, a more mature look consisting of arched eyebrows, matte skin, and bright lips was favored, while the 1990s saw the emergence of a subtly chiseled but natural aesthetic featuring plucked eyebrows, sculpted cheekbones, and nude lips.

The dichotomous power of makeup was laid bare on September 4, 2012, when celebrity Kim Kardashian tweeted photographs of herself mid-makeup application in a process that she described as "contouring." With various highlights and shadow lines painted on her face, Kardashian demonstrated to the world the amount of planning and calculation that went into her "natural-looking" complexion. Though cosmetics have long been used to highlight and shade various portions of the face, especially for actors of stage and cinema, Kardashian's labeling of the process substantiated it as an important tool in a bag of tricks geared at forging a specific beauty aesthetic. Soon a slew of YouTube video tutorials touting the easy-to-achieve replicability of Kardashian's look flooded the Internet. The phenomenon of contouring demonstrated not only the growing egalitarian nature of makeup, but also the demand for accessible beauty tips.

 The balancing act between the natural and the artificial remains a central concern both of cosmetics and of fashion at large. While makeup allows for self-expression—as in the case of James Charles, named CoverGirl's first-ever male spokesmodel in 2016—it can at times blur the boundary between individuality and conformity. For his spring 2016 collection, Shayne Oliver, founder and creative director of Hood By Air (now creative director of Helmut Lang), sent his models down the runway with a makeup scheme of unblended, contoured highlights and low lights, drawing attention to the tension between the natural and the artificial. Yves Saint Laurent's Touche Éclat may have advanced the trajectory of makeup toward the natural, but it also underscored the fact that no matter what the current ideal, there will always be cosmetic products that promise to help you achieve it —SK

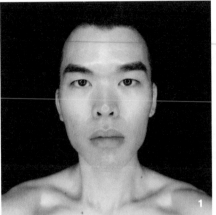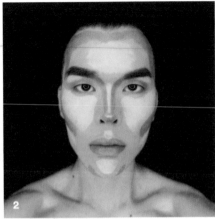

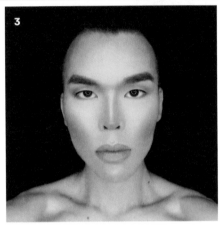

Right:
1, 2, 3— Stills from designer John Fabulin's YouTube tutorial "Highlight & Contour," 2017
4, 5— Actress Carole Lombard applying makeup to contour her face for shooting under studio lights, Hollywood, California, 1938. Photograph by Alfred Eisenstaedt

NOTES

WHO'S AFRAID OF FASHION?

1—This line appears in The Museum of Modern Art's founding charter. **2**—The garment was a gift by Mrs. Susan G. Rossbach. **3**—The other garments in the collection are a Fruit of the Loom white T-shirt acquired on the occasion of the exhibition *Humble Masterpieces* in 2004; Kosuke Tsumura's 1994 forty-four-pocket parka for Final Home, whose pockets could be filled by a homeless person with his or her belongings or with newspaper for insulation; Issey Miyake's 1997 A-POC Queen Textile, collected with the rationale that it highlights a system of manufacturing rather than fashion; four Capsters, sports headgear for Muslim women, entered in 2006; a Harry Gordon poster dress from 1967; and the 4-D-printed Kinematics dress, acquired in 2014 to complement a pioneering collection of 3-D-printed objects. Except for the T-shirt, they are all part of *Items*. The Museum of Modern Art's collection, however, does feature a distinguished selection of contemporary Japanese textiles and other textiles that may be used for interior decoration or sartorial applications. **4**—The exhibition *Deconstructivist Architecture* was on view at MoMA from June 23 to August 30, 1988, and was curated by Philip Johnson and Mark Wigley. **5**—The Victoria and Albert Museum in London has collected fashion and textiles—and art, too—since its founding in 1852, albeit from the perspective of design and the industrial arts. **6**—Suzy Menkes, "Gone Global: Fashion as Art?", *International Herald Tribune*, July 5, 2011. **7**—These issues were discussed in *The Brooklyn Rail*, March 2017. **8**—See Paola Antonelli and Michelle Millar Fisher, "Announcing Items: Is Fashion Modern?", *Inside/Out—a MoMA/MoMA PS1 Blog*, April 5, 2016. **9**—Press release for the exhibition *Are Clothes Modern?*, The Museum of Modern Art, 1944. **10**—Vanessa Friedman, "Lady Gaga Defines a New Role: Fashion Enabler," *New York Times*, March 30, 2016. **11**—*Yohji Yamamoto, Juste des vêtements*, Musée de la Mode et du Textile, Paris, April 13 to August 28, 2005. **12**—*Claire McCardell and the American Look*, The Museum at FIT, New York, October 1998 to January 9, 1999. **13**—*Utopian Bodies: Fashion Looks Forward*, Liljevalchs museum, Stockholm, September 15, 2015, to February 7, 2016. **14**—Held May 15–16, 2016, it was composed of an evening salon and a daylong "abecedarium." During this latter event, twenty-six iconic garments, accessories, and issues from the fashion universe, spanning the early twentieth century to the present, were discussed by a group of designers, curators, critics, scholars, labor activists, and entrepreneurs—one for each letter of the alphabet—in seven-minute vignettes. **15**—The term references the exhibition *Humble Masterpieces*, MoMA, April 8 to September 27, 2004, which showcased everyday marvels of design.

501s

1—James Sullivan, *Jeans: A Cultural History of an American Icon* (New York: Gotham, 2006), 32. **2**—For more on denim, see Emma McClendon, *Denim: Fashion's Frontier* (New Haven, Conn.: Yale University Press, 2016). **3**—*Vogue* introduced Lady Levi's in 1935: "Your uniform for a dude ranch or a ranch near Reno is simple-but-severe blue jeans or Levis, turned up at the bottom once, laundered before wearing (to eliminate stiffness), cut straight and tight fitting, worn low on the hips, in the manner of your favourite dude wrangler." Burt Strathers, "Boccaccio in Chaps," *Vogue*, May 1935, 73. **4**—Clare Sauro, "Jeans," in *The Berg Companion to Fashion*, ed. Valerie Steele (Oxford, U.K.: Bloomsbury Academic, 2010). **5**—Key examples include the Italian brand Fiorucci and American labels Gloria Vanderbilt and Calvin Klein. Jeans became the subject of sensational marketing campaigns, including Calvin Klein's infamous 1980 "Nothing comes between me and my Calvins" ad, featuring a fifteen-year-old Brooke Shields. **6**—This copy accompanied the sales listing for the jeans on Nordstrom's website. **7**—"Denim Jeans Industry Statistics," *Statistic Brain*, August 9, 2016. **8**—Levi Strauss & Co., "The Lifecycle of a Jean," 2015. **9**—Greenpeace, "The Dirty Secret Behind Jeans and Bras," *Greenpeace East Asia*, December 1, 2010. **10**—Paul Dillinger quoted in Elizabeth Segran, "Levi's Is Radically Redefining Sustainability," *Fast Company*, February 9, 2017. **11**—See Roberta Sassatelli, "Indigo Bodies: Fashion, Mirror Work and Sexual Identity in Milan," and Rosana Pinheiro-Machado, "The Jeans That Don't Fit: Marketing Cheap Jeans in Brazil," in *Global Denim*, ed. Daniel Miller and Sophie Woodward (Oxford, U.K.: Berg, 2011). **12**—Miller and Woodward, "Introduction," in *Global Denim*, 3–4.

A-POC QUEEN

1—Dai Fujiwara, "A-POC, A-POS, A-POM, & A-POE," in Issey Miyake and Fujiwara, *A-POC Making: Issey Miyake and Dai Fujiwara* (Berlin: Vitra Design Museum, 2001), 70. **2**—Juan de Alcega, *Tailor's Pattern Book*, 1589, trans. Jean Pain and Cecilia Bainton (Bedford, U.K.: Ruth Bean, 1979), preface. **3**—Issey Miyake, "Clothing for the Future," in Miyake and Fujiwara, *A-POC Making*, 68. **4**—Carolyne Cafaro, creative director of the McCall Pattern Company, quoted in Steven Kurutz, "Do-It-Yourself Fashion Thrives at the McCall Pattern Company," *New York Times*, August 2, 2016. **5**—Miyake, "Clothing for the Future," 68.

ADIDAS SUPERSTAR

1—For more on the design and technology of the Adidas Superstar and Supergrip, see the company's online archive. **2**—For the development of the rubber outsole and the early history of sneakers more generally, see Elizabeth Semmelhack, *Out of the Box: The Rise of Sneaker Culture* (New York: Skira Rizzoli, 2015). **3**—Bobbito Garcia provides a closer look at New York's hip-hop sneaker culture, including firsthand testimonials, in *Where'd You Get Those?: New York City's Sneaker Culture, 1960–1987* (New York: Testify, 2003).

AIR FORCE 1

1—Thibaut de Longeville tells this story in his 2010 documentary film *Air Force 1: Anatomy of an Urban Legend*. **2**—The series began life as the Shoe of the Month Club. For more about sneakerheads' pursuit of these limited-edition colorways, see Bobbito Garcia, *Where'd You Get Those?: New York City's Sneaker Culture, 1960–1987* (New York: Testify, 2003), 156. **3**—Elizabeth Semmelhack, *Out of the Box: The Rise of Sneaker Culture* (New York: Skira, 2015), 15, 108. For photographs from the emerging hip-hop scene, see Jamel Shabazz, *Back in the Days* (New York: Powerhouse, 2001). **4**—Rapper Rakim rocked Air Force 1s on the cover of his 1992 album *Don't Sweat the Technique*, with Eric B. Before rapper Nelly's eponymous 2002 ode to the Air Force 1, New York rappers Pete Nice and Jay-Z had already shouted out the shoe in 1993 and 1996, respectively, as sneaker scholar Gary Warnett noted in his 2017 article "The Forgotten History of the White on White Air Force 1, Nike's Perfect Sneaker," *Complex*, January 25, 2017.

ARAN SWEATER

1—Muriel Gahan's store was located on St. Stephen's Green until the late 1970s. For an excellent background on the birth of the Aran sweater as part of mainstream fashion in Ireland and beyond, see the didactic materials accompanying the exhibition *Romantic Stitches and Realist Sketches*, National Museum of Ireland—Country Life, Turlough Park, Castlebar, Co. Mayo, April 9–October 30, 2008. **2**—See Heinz Edgar Kiewe, *The Sacred History of Knitting* (Oxford, U.K.: Art Needlework Industries, 1971). The pamphlet was first published in the 1930s. **3**—The knitted cap (UC28150i) is in the collection of the Petrie Museum of Egyptian Archaeology, University College London, and the socks (2085&A-1900) are in the collection of the Victoria and Albert Museum, London.

AVIATOR SUNGLASSES

1—See "1970s USA Women's Liberation Rally, Gloria Steinem," YouTube video, 1:33 min., posted by "thekinolibrary," January 18, 2017. From the Kinolibrary Archive Film collections (KLR574). **2**—"Airman Climbs to 40,800 Feet. Lieutenant Macready Breaks Altitude Record," *Chicago Tribune*, September 29, 1921, 1. **3**—Sally Macready Wallace quoted in Pagan Kennedy, "Who Made Those Aviator Sunglasses?," *New York Times*, August 3, 2012. **4**—"Ray-Ban Glasses," Von Lengerke & Antoine mail-order catalogue, 1939, 33. **5**—"Features: Vogue's Suggestions for Christmas Gifts," *Vogue*, November 15, 1925,

101. **6**—"Beauty Now: Shape: Glasses—the Thinner, the Better!," *Vogue*, August 1978, 200.

BACKPACK **1**—The fabric, originally called *pocono*, was created on equipment used for making Italian military parachutes. Miuccia Prada liked it so much that she bought the entire production line of machines. It is practical, flexible, and adaptable like regular nylon, but its combination of thin and thick yarns gives it the appearance of silk. **2**—Gordon L. Rottman explores the history of the American military backpack in *World War II US Army Combat Equipments* (Oxford, U.K.: Osprey, 2016) and *US Army Combat Equipments: 1910–88* (London: Osprey, 2011). **3**—For the history of JanSport and its contribution to student life, see Skip Yowell, *The Hippie Guide to Climbing the Corporate Ladder and Other Mountains: How JanSport Makes It Happen* (Edinburgh, U.K.: Thomas Nelson, 2009). **4**—Dooyoung Choi, "Street and Youth Fashion in Seoul, South Korea," in *Berg Encyclopedia of World Dress and Fashion: East Asia*, ed. John E. Vollmer (Oxford, U.K.: Berg, 2010).

BALACLAVA **1**—See Richard Rutt, *A History of Handknitting* (Loveland, Colo.: Interweave, 2003). **2**—In the *Daily Sketch* of Thursday, March 16, 1916, a Lieut.-Commander Darke thanks the *Daily Sketch* Knitting League for "the magnificent present of comforts and socks" (9). For knitting on the American home front during World War II, see, for example, "How to Knit: Million Sweaters Wanted by Christmas," *Life*, November 24, 1941, 111. In the 1940s the British clothing company Jaeger produced "Essentials for the Forces," a pamphlet of knitting patterns with instructions for making a wartime "balaclava helmet" complete with "flaps to enable good hearing during telephone operations." **3**—Catherine Moriarty quotes Vera Brittain in "'Remnants of Patriotism': The Commemorative Representation of the Greatcoat after the First World War," *Oxford Art Journal* 27, no. 3 (2004): 293–309. **4**—Chanel's jet-black version, boldly embroidered with its logo in white, debuted in 2013; singers Frank Ocean and Sky Ferreira posed for pictures wearing balaclavas at the Metropolitan Museum of Art Costume Institute's annual gala in 2016; and Alessandro Michele's fall 2017 collection for Gucci featured models in single-color balaclavas with full-face openings. For Gucci and other examples, see Nouriah al Shatti, "Big Name Brands Are Bringing Back the Balaclava," *Vogue* Arabia, May 10, 2017.

BALLET FLAT **1**—Colleen Hill, "Ballet Shoes: Function, Fashion and Fetish," in *Dance and Fashion*, ed. Valerie Steele (New Haven, Conn.: Yale University Press, 2014), 144. **2**—For more on the evolution of the ballet flat among dancers, see ibid. **3**—"Fashion: Feet on the Ground," *Vogue*, November 15, 1944, 110. **4**—Linda Welters, "The Beat Generation: Subcultural Style," in *Twentieth-Century American Fashion*, ed. Linda Welters and Patricia A. Cunningham (Oxford, U.K.: Berg, 2008), 145–68.

BANDANNA **1**—For more information on Turkey red, see John Cannon and Margaret Cannon, *Dye Plants and Dyeing* (London: A & C Black), 2003. **2**—Hillary Weiss discusses the history of political bandannas in the United States in *The American Bandanna: Culture on Cloth from George Washington to Elvis* (San Francisco: Chronicle, 1990). **3**—Joy Spanabel Emery, "The War Years: 1940s," in Emery, *A History of the Paper Pattern Industry: The Home Dressmaking Fashion Revolution* (London: Bloomsbury Academic, 2014), 133–58.

BASEBALL CAP **1**—Jim Wannemacher, New Era Brand Historian, e-mail interview, The Museum of Modern Art, New York, January 4, 2017. **2**—For more on the evolution of the baseball cap, see Jim Lilliefores, *Ball Cap Nation: A Journey Through the World of America's National Hat* (Kentucky: Clerisy, 2009). **3**—Wannemacher interview, MoMA, 2017.

BERET **1**—Rachel Lubitz, "The History of the Beret: How a Peasant's Hat Turned into a Political Statement," style.mic, June 21, 2016. **2**—"Denis Guedon, l'artisan du béret made in Oloron," *La République des Pyrenées*, July 28, 2014. **3**—Valerie Steele, "The Black Prince of Elegance," in Steele, *Paris Fashion: A Cultural History* (Oxford, U.K.: Berg, 1998), 77–96. **4**—John Arthur Maynard, *Venice West: The Beat Generation in Southern California* (New Brunswick, N.J.: Rutgers University Press, 1991), 118. **5**—Lubitz, "History of the Beret."

BIKER JACKET **1**—The toothed closure had been available since the 1890s, but the term *zipper* was not trademarked in the United States until 1925. In 1928 the closure was primarily used for corsets, gloves, sleeping bags, pouches, and boots. By the 1930s it was just beginning to be applied to the fly front of men's pants. **2**—"Horsehide Aviation Jackets," *Beck News,* September 15, 1941. **3**—"Cyclists' Holiday: He and Friends Terrorize a Town," *Life*, July 21, 1947, 31. **4**—Tom Carson quoted in Brian Crim, "No Future: Punk Music in Postindustrial Britain and the United States," in *Sounds of Resistance: The Role of Music in Multicultural Activism,* ed. Eunice Rojas and Lindsay Michie (Westport, Conn.: Praeger, 2013), 284. **5**—Carson, "Rocket to Russia: The Ramones (Sire 6063), 1977," in *Stranded: Rock and Roll for a Desert Island*, ed. Greil Marcus (New York: Da Capo, 2007), 108.

BIKINI **1**—Patrick Alac, *The Bikini: A Cultural History* (New York: New Line, 2005), 28. **2**—"The Trouble with the Bikini," *Life*, September 1949, 66. **3**—"Splashy Suits to Swim In," *Life*, May 1959, 59. **4**—"New Season's Beachwear Styles," *The Draper of Australia*,

September 30, 1946, 68. **5**—That same year, *Women's Wear Daily* admitted in a headline, "Bikini Is Merchandise Now," after years of categorizing it as a less-than-profitable garment worn only by a daring minority. Lillian Chatov, "Bikini Is Merchandise Now," *Women's Wear Daily*, January 19, 1959, 22. **6**—For *tropicalismo* and the specific resonance of the bikini in Brazil, see Nizia Villaça, "As She Walks to the Sea: A Semiology of Rio de Janeiro," in *The Latin American Fashion Reader*, ed. Regina A. Root (Oxford, U.K.: Berg, 2005), 188–97.

BIRKIN BAG **1**—"Vogue Point of View 1999: The Rise of the Accessory," *Vogue*, January 1999, 123. **2**—Mark Holgate, "The Forever Bags: Enduring Love," *Vogue*, May 2008, 207. **3**—For more on the history of handbags, see Caroline Cox, *The Handbag: An Illustrated History* (New York: HarperDes, 2007); and Claire Wilcox, *A Century of Bags: Icons of Style in the Twentieth Century* (New York: Book Sales, 1997). **4**—Sarah Moroz, "Designer Mary Ping Is Crafting Beautiful Fake Handbags in Paris," *i-D*, October 12, 2016.

BODY MEETS DRESS—DRESS MEETS BODY **1**—For the press reports, see Kate Betts, "Women in Fashion," *Time*, February 9, 2004; David Colman, "Abandon Ship: Fashion Follies of the Year," *New York Times*, January 4, 2008; and Suzy Menkes quoted in Osman Ahmed, "Lumps and Bumps at Comme des Garçons S/S97," *AnOther*, January 5, 2016. **2**—Georgina Godley, interview by Francesca Granata in Granata, *Experimental Fashion: Performance Art, Carnival and the Grotesque Body* (London: I. B. Tauris, 2017), 30–31. **3**—Bernard Rudofsky expressed this critique in the 1944 exhibition *Are Clothes Modern?* at The Museum of Modern Art, New York, and in his book of the same title (Chicago: Paul Theobald, 1947). **4**—Rei Kawakubo quoted in "Venus Envy," *Vogue*, March 1, 1997, 434. **5**—Sanae Shimizu, *Anrimiteddo komu de gyaruson* [*Unlimited: Comme des Garçons*] (Tokyo: Heibonsha, 2005), n.p. **6**—Caroline Evans, *Fashion at the Edge: Spectacle, Modernity, and Deathliness* (New Haven, Conn.: Yale University Press, 2012), 269. **7**—The twelfth-century French abbot is quoted in E. H. Gombrich, *The Sense of Order: A Study in the Psychology of Decorative Art* (London: Phaidon, 2006), 255. **8**—Frances S. Connelly, *The Grotesque in Western Art and Culture: The Image at Play* (Cambridge, U.K.: Cambridge University Press, 2012), 18. **9**—Kawakubo quoted in Lynn Yaeger, "On the Eve of the Comme des Garçons Retrospective, the Notoriously Reclusive Rei Kawakubo Speaks Out," *Vogue*, April 13, 2017.

BRETON SHIRT **1**—Véronique Alemany-Dessaint, *Les Marins font la mode*, exh. cat. (Paris: Gallimard; Musée national de la marine, 2009), 13. **2**—For the use of the stripe by sailors and fishermen, see Michel Pastoureau, *The Devil's Cloth: A History of Stripes and Striped Fabric*, trans. Jody Gladding (New York: Columbia University Press, 2001), 69–70. As Pastoureau discusses, the iconography of the stripe has a long history, and its meaning—from diabolical or dangerous to hygienic, playful, athletic, or emblematic—has expanded and changed over time.   **3**—Pastoureau, *Devil's Cloth*, 75.   **4**—Ibid., 64–73.   **5**—See Thierry-Maxime Loriot, *Jean Paul Gaultier au Grand Palais* (Paris: RMN-Grand Palais, 2015), 62.   **6**—For example, see the 2012 portraits *Jean Paul Gaultier, Made in Mode*, by Jean-Paul Goude, and *Lost in Fashion (Jean Paul Gaultier)*, by Liu Bolin, both made in collaboration with the designer.

BRIEFS   **1**—For an excellent overview of the evolution of the brief from ancient undergarments, see Shaun Cole, *The Story of Men's Underwear* (New York: Parkstone, 2009).   **2**—Paul Jobling, "Underexposed: Spectatorship and Pleasure in Men's Underwear Advertising in the Twentieth Century," *Paragraph* 26, no. 1/2 (2003): 157. For Cole's related analysis of early advertising trends, see "Advertising Men's Underwear," in *Past and Present: Fashion Media*, ed. Djurdja Bartlett, Cole, and Agnès Rocamora (London: Bloomsbury, 2014).   **3**—Mark Simpson quoted in Jobling, "Underexposed," 147.   **4**—Jobling, "Underexposed," 147.

BUCKET HAT   **1**—Wanda Lephoto, e-mail interview with The Museum of Modern Art, New York, February 28, 2017.   **2**—"Index: Boy Wonders," *Vogue*, February 2010, 218.

BURKINI   **1**—Aheda Zanetti, "I Created the Burkini to Give Women Freedom, Not to Take It Away," *Guardian*, August 24, 2016.   **2**—See Lila Abu-Lughod, *Do Muslim Women Need Saving?* (Cambridge, Mass.: Harvard University Press, 2013).

CAFTAN   **1**—See Charlotte Jirousek, "The Kaftan and Its Origins," in *Berg Encyclopedia of World Dress and Fashion: Central and Southwest Asia*, ed. Gillian Vogelsang-Eastwood (Oxford, U.K.: Berg, 2010), 134–38.   **2**—Ibid.   **3**—For beautiful sketches and insight into Halston's vision of the caftan, see Lesley Frowick, *Halston: Inventing American Fashion* (New York: Rizzoli, 2014). Laura McLaws Helms and Venetia Porter's *Thea Porter: Bohemian Chic* (London: Victoria and Albert Museum, 2015) is also an excellent resource for the "mother" of the caftan in the 1960s and '70s.   **4**—The term "beautiful people" is often attributed to Diana Vreeland, the influential magazine editor whose fashion columns, both in *Harper's Bazaar*, until 1962, and then for *Vogue*, until 1971, detailed the style- and celebrity-obsessed culture of the 1960s and early 1970s. Marilyn Bender's book *The Beautiful People: A Candid Examination of a Cultural*

Phenomenon—The Marriage of Fashion and Society in the '60s (New York: Coward-McCann, 1967) crystallized the milieu in which Vreeland made her observations.   **5**—McLaws Helms and Porter, *Thea Porter*, 7.

CAPRI PANTS   **1**—"Fashion: Tied Pants, Wrapped Pants," *Vogue*, December 1949, 110–11; and "New York Resort Openings: Tube-Shirts: Frances Sider, Inc.," *Women's Wear Daily*, October 12, 1949, 3.   **2**—"Fashion: From the Italian Collections, Casual Clothes," *Vogue*, September 1951, 189.   **3**—"Fashion: The Fashion—Reading from South to North," *Vogue*, December 1953, 122.   **4**—Advertisement in *Vogue*, February 1957, 206.   **5**—Jill Taylor quoted in Jess Cartner-Morley, "The Magic of Marilyn Monroe," *Guardian*, November 15, 2011.   **6**—Yohana Desta, "How Mary Tyler Moore Subverted TV Sexism with a Pair of Capris," *Vanity Fair*, January 25, 2017.

CARTIER LOVE BRACELET   **1**—See Gabriele Mentges, "Jewelry," *Berg Encyclopedia of World Dress and Fashion: West Europe*, ed. Lise Skov (Oxford, U.K.: Berg, 2010), 407–12.   **2**—Aldo Cipullo quoted in Marian Christy, "Nails, Nuts, and Bolts Inspired Jewelry," *San Mateo Times*, February 23, 1972.

CHANEL NO. 5   **1**—Gabrielle "Coco" Chanel quoted in Annick Le Guérer, *Le Parfum: Des origines à nos jours* (Paris: Odile Jacob, 2010), 202.   **2**—Kenneth E. Silver, "Flacon and Fragrance: The New Math of Chanel No. 5," in Harold Koda and Andrew Bolton, eds., *Chanel* (New York: Metropolitan Museum of Art; New Haven, Conn.: Yale University Press, 2005), 31.

CHEONGSAM   **1**—The Broadway play *The World of Suzie Wong*, adapted by Paul Osborn from the novel by Richard Mason, opened in New York in 1958, and the film of the same title, directed by Richard Quine, premiered in 1960.

CHINOS   **1**—By the end of the twentieth century chinos were available in a variety of neutral colors, and they have recently appeared in brighter hues ranging from yellow to blue.   **2**—Richard Martin, *Khaki: Cut from the Original Cloth* (Santa Fe, N.M.: Tondo, 1999), 12.   **3**—"Casual Clothing in the Workplace: Resources" (San Francisco: Levi Strauss & Co., 1992).   **4**—Doug Conklyn quoted in Joshua David Stein, "The Almighty Return of the All-American Chino," *Esquire*, March 9, 2015.   **5**—Ibid.

CLOG   **1**—For further reading on the history of the clog and the patten, see Francis Grew and Margrethe de Neergaard, *Shoes and Pattens* (London: HMSO, 2001); Elizabeth Semmelhack, *Heights of Fashion: A History of the Elevated Shoe* (Toronto: Bata Shoe Museum; Pittsburgh: Gutenberg Periscope, 2008); Giorgio Riello,

"Footwear," in *The Berg Encyclopedia of World Dress and Fashion: West Europe*, ed. Lise Skov (Oxford, U.K.: Berg, 2010), 413–19; and Jonathan Walford, "Shoes," in *The Berg Companion to Fashion*, ed. Valerie Steele (Oxford, U.K.: Bloomsbury Academic, 2010).   **2**—"Cloggy Days," *Time*, August 15, 1969, 48.   **3**—Christian Louboutin quoted in Lauren Collins, "Sole Mate: Christian Louboutin and the Psychology of Shoes," *New Yorker*, March 28, 2011, 90.

CONVERSE ALL STAR   **1**—Converse All Star advertisement, 1947.   **2**—Maya Wei-Haas, "How Chuck Taylor Taught America How to Play Basketball," Smithsonian.com, August 8, 2016.

COPPOLA   **1**—Dave Postles, "'Flatcaps,' Fashioning and Civility in Early-Modern England," *Literature & History* 17, no. 2 (2008): 10.   **2**—Luigi Milanesi, "Coppola," *Dizionario etimologico della lingua siciliana* (Milan: Mnamon, 2015), n.p.   **3**—Ibid.

DASHIKI   **1**—See "The New Breed . . . Business Venture," *Afro-American Beauty and Travel*, June 1969, 24–25.   **2**—Herbert A. Simmons, "The New Breed Story," unpublished manuscript, n.d., n.p.   **3**—For more on the relationship between fashion and political struggle in this era, see Yohuru Williams, "The Art of War: The Cultural Productions of the 1950s and 1960s Black Era Freedom Struggles," in Williams, *Rethinking the Black Freedom Movement* (London: Taylor & Francis eBooks, 2015), 93.   **4**—See Ann Geracimos, "About Dashikis and the New Breed Cat," *New York Times*, April 20, 1969.   **5**—Simmons, "The New Breed Story."   **6**—For more on dashikis and home sewing, see Joy Spanabel Emery, "New Challenges: 1960s–1980s," in Emery, *A History of the Paper Pattern Industry: The Home Dressmaking Fashion Revolution* (London: Bloomsbury Academic, 2014), 178–94.   **7**—Bobby Seale quoted in Franziska Meister, *Racism and Resistance: How the Black Panthers Challenged White Supremacy* (Bielefeld, Germany: Transcript-Verlag, 2017), 186.

DIAMOND ENGAGEMENT RING
1—Andrea Bayer, ed., *Art and Love in Renaissance Italy* (New York: Metropolitan Museum of Art, 2008), 110.   **2**—This history of the diamond engagement ring in the twentieth century is drawn from Edward Jay Epstein, "Have You Ever Tried to Sell a Diamond?", *Atlantic*, February 1982.

DIAMOND STUD   **1**—For more on the history of diamonds, see Rachelle Bergstein, *Brilliance and Fire: A Biography of Diamonds* (New York: Harper, 2016); and Daniela Mascetti and Amanda Triossi, *Earrings from Antiquity to the Present* (London: Thames and Hudson, 1990).   **2**—For more on the history of earrings, see Susan Ward, "Earrings," in *The Berg Companion to Fashion*, ed. Valerie Steele (Oxford, U.K.: Bloomsbury

Academic, 2010). **3**—Bergstein, *Brilliance and Fire*, 252.

DOOR-KNOCKER EARRINGS **1**—The song is "Around the Way Girl" from the 1990 album *Mama Said Knock You Out*. **2**—Interview with Ivette Feliciano, The Museum of Modern Art, New York, June 5, 2017. **3**—Hellabreezy, an Oakland-based model and modern-day chola, in Barbara Calderón-Douglass, "The Folk Feminist Struggle Behind the Chola Fashion Trend," *Vice*, April 13, 2015. **4**—Tanisha C. Ford quoted in Erica Euse, "Who Owns Hoops Earrings? Tracing the Cultural Impact of a Classic Style," *i-D*, March 15, 2017. **5**—Jacquelyn Aguilera, Alegria Martinez, Estefanía Gallo-Gonzalez, and Gabriela Ornelas, "A Message from the Latinas Who Made the 'White Girl, Take Off Your Hoops' Mural," *Latino Rebels*, March 14, 2017. **6**—Claire Stern, "Patricia Field Explains the Origin of Carrie Necklace from Sex and the City," *InStyle*, April 22, 2015. **7**—Marc Jacobs quoted in Dena Silver, "This Season Marc Jacobs Was Inspired by the History of Hip-Hop," *Observer*, February 16, 2017. **8**—Feliciano interview, MoMA, June 5, 2017. **9**—Interview with Gabriella Khorasanee, MoMA, June 5, 2017.

DOWN JACKET **1**—For the complete story of Eddie Bauer's invention of the quilted down jacket, see Robert Spector, *The Legend of Eddie Bauer* (Old Saybrook, Conn.: Greenwich Publishing Group, 1994). **2**—"Paris Evening Fashions," *Harper's Bazaar*, October 1938, 67. **3**—Norma Kamali quoted in Ruth La Ferla, "Always in Her Element," *New York Times*, May 7, 2009.

DR. MARTENS **1**—As materials were scarce in postwar Germany, Dr. Klaus Märtens composed a crude prototype using a rubber hose for the sole and wedges of felt for the inner cavity. **2**—Märtens quoted in Martin Roach, *Dr. Martens: A History of Rebellious Self-Expression* (Wollaston, U.K.: AirWair, 2015), 11–12. **3**—For the history of the Dr. Martens 1460, the authors relied heavily on Roach's *Dr. Martens*, which was published by the manufacturer in 2015. **4**—For more on the origins and history of skinheads, see "Exodus: A Double Crossing" and "White Skins Black Masks," in Dick Hebdige, *Subculture: The Meaning of Style* (London: Routledge, 1979), 39–45 and 54–59, respectively. **5**—Jonathan Freedman quoted in Roach, *Dr. Martens*, 23–24. **6**—Viv Albertine quoted in ibid., 59. **7**—Pete Townshend quoted in ibid., 5.

DUTCH WAX **1**—For the history of the Dutch wax textile, see n. 14 in Victoria Rovine, "Colonialism's Clothing: Africa, France, and the Deployment of Fashion," *Design Issues* 25, no. 3 (Summer, 2009): 44–61. **2**—For Vlisco then and now, see Robb Young, "Africa's Fabric Is Dutch," *New York Times*, November 12, 2012. **3**—Megan Vaughn, "Africa and the Birth of the

Modern World," in *Transactions of the Royal Historical Society* 16 (2006): 150. **4**—John Picton, "Yinka Shonibare: Undressing Ethnicity," *African Arts* 34, no. 3 (Autumn 2001): 71. **5**—Olu Oguibe, "Finding a Place: Nigerian Artists in the Contemporary Art World," *Art Journal* 58, no. 2 (Summer 1999): 38–39. **6**—Yinka Shonibare quoted in Picton, "Yinka Shonibare," 60. **7**—This adoption of Dutch wax textiles by prominent international designers has not been without controversy, as when Junya Watanabe failed to include any black models on the runway for his spring/summer 2016 collection, which was heavily reliant on the fabric. **8**—Nina Sylvanus, "West Africans Are Ditching Dutch Wax Prints for Chinese 'Real-Fakes,'" *Quartz Africa*, August 30, 2016.

ESPADRILLE **1**—Stefania Ricci, *Salvatore Ferragamo: The Art of the Shoe, 1898–1960* (New York: Rizzoli, 1992), 30–31, 101. **2**—Blake Mycoskie, *Start Something That Matters* (New York: Spiegel & Grau, 2011), 4.

FANNY PACK **1**—Elisabeth Azoulay, ed., *Bagism* (Shanghai: K11 Art Space, 2016), 74–77. **2**—See Patricia A. Cunningham, Heather Mangine, and Andrew Reilly, "Television and Fashion in the 1980s," in *Twentieth-Century American Fashion*, ed. Linda Welters and Patricia A. Cunningham (Oxford, U.K.: Berg, 2008), 209–28.

FITBIT **1**—James Lovell, *Apollo 13* (New York: Pocket Books, 1994), 269. **2**—Aaron E. Carroll, "Wearable Fitness Devices Don't Seem to Make You Fitter," *New York Times*, February 20, 2017. **3**—Robinson Meyer, "The Quantified Welp," *Atlantic*, February 25, 2016.

FLEECE **1**—See a comparison of Higg Material Sustainability Index scores for various materials at http://msi.higg.org/compare/148-206-195. **2**—Alessandra Codinha, "Why One *Vogue* Editor Is Ditching Fur in Favor of a Fleece," *Vogue*, October 14, 2014.

FLIP-FLOP **1**—Martha Chaiklin, "Zori and Flip-Flop Sandal, Japan/World," in Grace Lees-Maffei, *Iconic Designs: 50 Stories about 50 Things* (London: Bloomsbury, 2014), 199–201. **2**—For more on the history of Havaianas, see "Havaianas Turns 50: The Story Behind the Most Popular Flip-Flop Brand in the World," *Huffington Post*, July 24, 2012.

FUR COAT **1**—For further discussion of the stereotype of fur-wearing bourgeois women, see Julia V. Emberley, *The Cultural Politics of Fur* (Ithaca, N.Y.: Cornell University Press, 1997), 21–35; and Andrew Bolton, *Wild: Fashion Untamed* (New York: Metropolitan Museum of Art, 2004), 57. **2**—David Remnick, "Soul Survivor," *New Yorker*, April 4, 2016. **3**—For more discussion on anti-fur movements'

targeting of "bourgeois women," see Emberley, *Cultural Politics*, 21–35. **4**—Ibid., 31. **5**—See, for example, Ashifa Kassam, "'It's Our Way of Life': Inuit Designers Are Reclaiming the Tarnished Sealskin Trade," *Guardian*, May 11, 2017. **6**—Lise Skov, "The Return of the Fur Coat: A Commodity Chain Perspective," *Current Sociology* 53, no. 1 (2005): 13. **7**—See Richard von Kraft-Ebing, *Psychopathia Sexualis: A Medico-Study* (1886); and Sigmund Freud, "Fetishism" (1927), discussed in Emberley, *Cultural Politics*, 73–82.

GORE-TEX **1**—W. L. Gore & Associates, Inc., "Our History," Gore-Tex.com. **2**—W. L. Gore & Associates, Inc., "The ePTFE Story," Gore-Tex .com. **3**—Kevin M. Brown, interview with The Museum of Modern Art, January 2017.

GRAPHIC T-SHIRT **1**—*Life,* July 13, 1942, cover. **2**—Richard Alan Schwartz, "Disneyland and Cold War Angst," in *The 1950s*, ed. Schwartz (New York: Facts on File, 2002), 251. **3**—A rotatable multicolor garment screenprinting machine was patented in the United States in 1969, for example; see Stencil Printing Machine, patent no. 3427964, February 18, 1969, United States Patent and Trademark Office. **4**—For more on the history of the "I Love NY" logo, see Paola Antonelli, *Humble Masterpieces: Everyday Marvels of Design* (New York: Harper Collins, 2005), 57. **5**—Katherine Hamnett quoted in Janet Christie, "Katherine Hamnett on Her Thrilling New Campaigns," *Scotsman,* March 22, 2015. **6**—Lydia Lunch quoted in Cesar Padilla, ed., *Ripped: T-Shirts from the Underground* (New York: Universe, 2010), 7. **7**—Robert Klara, "How Mick Jagger's Mouth Became the Rolling Stones' Legendary Logo," *Adweek,* July 20, 2015. **8**— James Jebbia, *Supreme* (New York: Rizzoli, 2010), 30. **9**—Glenn O'Brien quoted in ibid., 10.

GUAYABERA **1**—Rubén Díaz-Abreu, "Porque la guayabera es puramente cubana," *Contacto,* December 1996. **2**—Ana López, "Guayabera," in *The Encyclopedia of Latin American and Caribbean Cultures*, ed. Daniel Balderston, Mike Gonzalez, and Ana López (New York: Routledge Taylor and Francis Group, 2002), 688. **3**—Marilyn Miller, "Guayaberismo and the Essence of Cool," in *The Latin American Fashion Reader,* ed. Regina A. Root (Oxford, U.K.: Berg, 2006), 215. **4**—Rafael Suárez Solís, "El Guayaberismo," in Solís et al., *El uso y el abuso de la guayabera* (Havana: Lyceum Lawn Tennis Club, 1948), 9. Trans. in Miller, "Guayaberismo," 215. **5**—Miller, "Guayaberismo," 215. **6**—Francisco Ichaso, "El abito y el monje," in Solís et al., *El uso y el abuso,* 63. Trans. by the author. **7**—Solís, "El Guayaberismo," 9. **8**—Ichaso, "El abito y el monje," 63. Trans. by the author. **9**—Ichaso, "El abito y el monje," 63. Trans. in Miller, "Guayaberismo," 216. **10**—Ángel González, "Cuba's Favorite Shirt Tails a New Generation," *Wall Street Journal,*

December 14, 2012. **11**—"La Revolución Cubana se pasa a la guayabera," *BBC Mundo,* October 7, 2010. **12**—"Castro's Cartagena News Conference 16 June 19, 1994," Latin American Network Information Center, University of Texas at Austin.

HAREM PANTS **1**—On Paul Poiret's resistance to any suggestion that he was inspired by the Ballets Russes, see Nancy Troy, *Couture Culture: A Study in Modern Art and Fashion* (Cambridge, Mass.: MIT Press, 2002), 103. **2**—Ibid., 116. **3**—On bloomerism and dress, see Julia Petrov, "'A Strong-Minded American Lady': Bloomerism in Texts and Images, 1851," *Fashion Theory,* no. 5 (2015): 381–413.

HEAD WRAP **1**—"Africans in Medieval and Renaissance Art: The Three Kings," Victoria and Albert Museum website. **2**—"Some garments may initially have been adopted as fashionable by the upper classes, who prized the quality of Moorish textiles and often wore them for ceremonial occasions, but items such as the *toca* were eventually worn by plain folk in the Castilian countryside. Initially adopted in the mid-fifteenth century, by the early 1600s it had become widespread." Barbara Fuchs, *Exotic Nation: Maurophilia and the Construction of Early Modern Spain* (Philadelphia: University of Pennsylvania Press, 2009), 65. **3**—Helen Bradley Griebel, "The African American Woman's Headwrap: Unwinding the Symbols," in Mary Ellen Roach-Higgins, Joanne Eicher, and Kim K. P. Johnson, eds., *Dress and Identity* (New York: Fairchild, 1995), 451–65. **4**—Steeve O. Buckridge, *The Language of Dress: Resistance and Accommodation in Jamaica, 1760–1890* (Kingston, Jamaica: University of the West Indies Press, 2004), 95. **5**—The art historian Louise Siddons has contested black women's exclusive hold on the head wrap, arguing that after World War I the wrap "emerged universally as a logical extension of the increasingly close-fitting, streamlined millinery options worn by all fashionable women"—of all races. Siddons, "African Past or American Present?: The Visual Eloquence of James VanDerZee's 'Identical Twins,'" *African American Review* 46, nos. 2–3 (2013): 446. **6**—The head wrap is often worn, for example, for Kwanzaa, a cultural celebration inaugurated in 1966 by Maulana Karenga, a key figure in the Black Power movement. **7**—"UPDATE: Doek Debate Sparks Discussion," enca.com, June 2, 2016. The campaign emerged under the hashtag #RespektheDoek. **8**—Pumza Fihlani, "How South African Women Are Reclaiming the Headscarf," *BBC,* June 11, 2016.

HEADPHONES **1**—Paul du Gay, *Doing Cultural Studies: The Story of the Sony Walkman* (Thousand Oaks, Calif.: Sage, 1997), 42–43. **2**—Sam Biddle, "Beat By Dre: The Exclusive Inside Story of How Monster Lost the World," *Gizmodo,* February 7, 2013. **3**—Paola Antonelli,

Design and the Elastic Mind (New York: The Museum of Modern Art, 2008), 153–55. **4**—Daniel Engber, "Who Made That Earbud?," *New York Times,* May 16, 2014.

HIJAB **1**—Rachel Aspden, "A Quiet Revolution by Leila Ahmed—Review," *Guardian*, May 20, 2011. **2**—Tim Arango, "Turkey's Islamic Fashion Revolution," *New York Times,* September 17, 2016. **3**—See Leila Ahmed, *A Quiet Revolution: The Veil's Resurgence, from the Middle East to America* (New Haven, Conn.: Yale University Press, 2011). **4**—See, for example, Lila Abu-Lughod, *Do Muslim Women Need Saving?* (Cambridge, Mass.: Harvard University Press, 2013). **5**—See, generally, Reina Lewis, *Muslim Fashion: Contemporary Style Cultures* (Durham, N.C.: Duke University Press, 2015).

HOODIE **1**—Troy Patterson, "The Politics of the Hoodie," *New York Times Magazine,* March 2, 2016, 18. **2**—Joanne Turney, "Battle Dressed—Clothing the Criminal, or the Horror of the 'Hoodie' in Britain," in *Fashion and War in Popular Culture,* ed. Denise N. Rall (Bristol, U.K.: Intellect, 2014), 132. **3**—Mallory Simon, "911 Calls Paint Picture of Chaos after Florida Teen Is Shot," *CNN* (blog), March 20, 2012.

JUMPSUIT **1**—Such activities included playing tennis and gardening, as illustrated by Georges Lepape in a portfolio of the designs. **2**—See Daniel James Cole and Nancy Deihl, *The History of Modern Fashion* (London: Laurence King, 2015), 134. **3**—"Air-Raid Costume and Siren Suit Presented at Press Preview," *Women's Wear Daily,* October 21, 1941, 3. **4**—Rational Dress Society member Abigail Glaum-Lathbury quoted in Zach Stafford, "Tired of the Tyranny of Fashion? Wear a Jumpsuit Every Day," *Guardian,* June 2, 2016.

KEFFIYEH **1**— Hala Malak, presentation on the keffiyeh in "Items: Is Fashion Modern? An Abecedarium," The Museum of Modern Art, New York, May 16, 2016. **2**—Ibid. **3**—David Colman, "The Scarf Unwinds and Relaxes," *New York Times,* September 24, 2008.

KENTE CLOTH **1**—Doran H. Ross, ed., *Wrapped in Pride: Ghanian Kente and African American Identity* (Los Angeles: UCLA Fowler Museum, 1998), 24. **2**—Doran H. Ross quoted in Paul Richard, "Kente's Strong Threads," *Washington Post,* September 14, 1999. **3**—This robust patronage combined with greater contact (and conflict) with the colonial forces that documented Asante culture aided in its primacy, as Ross discusses in *Wrapped in Pride,* 21–23, though the author also makes the case that Ewe and Asante kente share many similarities.

KILT **1**—For a concise discussion of the kilt, see Andrew Bolton, "The Kilt" (2004), in *Heilbrunn Timeline of Art History* (New York:

Metropolitan Museum of Art, 2000–). **2**—In World War I the Black Watch were supposedly nicknamed both "Devils in Skirts" and "Ladies from Hell" by the German troops. The kilt was deemed impractical for combat and banned in the first year of World War II, although a soldier named Bill Millin famously wore a kilt (the same length of Cameron tartan worn by his father on the fields of Flanders in World War I) and played the morale-lifting bagpipes at the request of his commanding officer, Brigadier Simon Fraser—Lord Lovat, the hereditary clan chief Fraser—during the D-Day landings at Normandy in 1944. See Thomas S. Abler, "Ladies from Hell," in *Hinterland Warriors and Military Dress: European Empires and Exotic Uniforms* (Oxford: Berg, 1999), 67–98; and John F. Burns, "Bill Millin, Scottish D-Day Piper, Dies at 88," *New York Times,* August 19, 2010. **3**—"On the Street; Men in Skirts," *New York Times,* July 4, 1993. See also Shaun Cole, "Are You a Fag? 'Cos You Look Like a Fag!," in *"Don We Now Our Gay Apparel": Gay Men's Dress in the Twentieth Century* (Oxford, U.K.: Berg, 2000), 183–92.

KIPPAH **1**—See Esther Juhasz, "Men's Head Covering," in *The Jewish Wardrobe: From the Collection of the Israel Museum, Jerusalem,* ed. Juhasz (Milan: 5 Continents, 2012), 64; and Eric Silverman, *A Cultural History of Jewish Dress* (New York: Bloomsbury Academic, 2013), 161. **2**—Silverman, *A Cultural History,* 161.

LAPEL PIN **1**—In a nod to military decorations, which also grace the lapel, the French novelist Jules-Amédée Barbey d'Aurevilly declared in 1838, "I sacrifice a rose each evening to my buttonhole: Roses are the Order of the Garter of that great monarch called Nature." Sven Raphael Schneider, "The Story of How the Boutonniere Buttonhole Came to Be on the Lapel," *Gentleman's Gazette,* July 27, 2011. **2**—Gilbert Cruz, "A Brief History of the Flag Lapel Pin," *Time,* July 3, 2008. In October 2007 the presidential candidate Barack Obama was asked by a reporter why he was not wearing one—"Is that a fashion statement?"—to which Obama responded that he should be judged on his actions rather than his sartorial rhetoric (although the pin quickly became part of his campaign-trail wardrobe). Angie Drobnic Holan, "Obama Contradicts Previously Stated Pin Philosophy," *Politifact,* April 18, 2008. **3**—These artists included Tuesday Bassen and Adam J. Kurtz. Madeleine Davies, "Zara Appears to Have Stolen Over 40 Pin and Patch Designs," *Jezebel,* July 25, 2016.

LE SMOKING **1**—Gloria Emerson, "A Nude Dress That Isn't: Saint Laurent; In a New Mad Mood," *New York Times,* August 5, 1966, 53. **2**—Florence Müller and Farid Chenoune, *Yves Saint Laurent* (New York: Abrams, 2010), 26. **3**—Ibid., 66. **4**—See *Harem Pants* and *Jumpsuit.* **5**—Anne Hollander, *Sex and Suits*

(New York: Knopf, 1994), 87. **6**—Hari Nef, presentation on "Unisex" in "Items: Is Fashion Modern? An Abecedarium," The Museum of Modern Art, New York, May 16, 2016.

LEATHER PANTS **1**—The oldest known trousers—a wool pair with straight legs and a wide crotch piece found in western China and dating between the thirteenth and tenth centuries BCE—are believed to have been worn by nomadic herders. See Ulrike Beck et al., "The Invention of Trousers and Its Likely Affiliation with Horseback Riding and Mobility: A Case Study of Late Second Millennium BC Finds from Turfan in Eastern Central Asia," *Quaternary International* (October 2014): 1. **2**—Laurel Wilson, "Western Wear," in *Berg Encyclopedia of World Dress and Fashion: The United States and Canada*, ed. Phyllis G. Tortora (Oxford, U.K.: Bloomsbury Academic, 2010), 479–85. **3**—Ray Manzarek on *Kenny G's Hour of Pain*, WFMU (Jersey City, N.J.), March 25, 2009; see "Jim Morrison's Leather Pants," WFMU Live Audio Streams, http://www.wfmu.org/playlists/shows/30799. **4**—Anthony Haden-Guest, "Suzi Quatro Flexes Her Leather," *Rolling Stone*, January 2, 1975, 31. **5**—Shaun Cole, "Hell for Leather: Bikers, Fun and Fetishisation," in Cole, *'Don We Now Our Gay Apparel': Gay Men's Dress in the Twentieth Century* (Oxford, U.K.: Berg, 2000), 107–18. **6**—Daniel James Cole and Nancy Deihl, *The History of Modern Fashion* (London: Laurence King, 2015), 403.

LEOTARD **1**—"Leotards," *Life*, September 13, 1943, 47.

LITTLE BLACK DRESS **1**—"Fashion: Brief Facts re the Little Black Dress," *Vogue*, April 1944, 101. **2**—"Fashion: The Debut of the Winter Mode," *Vogue*, October 1926, 69. **3**—Henry Ford, *My Life & Work* (Garden City, N.Y.: Doubleday, Page, 1922), 55–59, 152, 154, 166, 168, 170. **4**—Valerie Steele, presentation on the little black dress in "Items: Is Fashion Modern? An Abecedarium," The Museum of Modern Art, New York, May 16, 2016. **5**—Ibid.

LOAFER **1**—"Loafer," in *The Dictionary of Fashion History,* ed. Valerie Cumming, C. W. Cunnington, and P. E. Cunnington (Oxford, U.K.: Berg, 2010), 122. **2**— According to local legend, this style was developed in the early twentieth century by Nils Tveranger, a cobbler from Aurland, Norway, who was inspired by traditional Iroquois moccasins, which he may have encountered during travels to North America. See "The Aurland Shoe," Flåm AS travel company, https://www.visitflam.com/en/aurlandskoen/historien/. **3**—"Active and Spectator Seashore Clothes," *Esquire*, August 1936, 160. **4**—Company lore has it that that Bass collaborated with editors at *Esquire* to produce a version of the shoe after it was spotted at resorts in 1935–36. A similar style,

called the Loafer, was produced by the New Hampshire–based footwear manufacturer Spalding around the same period. **5**—For more on "Ivy" style, see Patricia Mears, *Ivy Style: Radical Conformists* (New Haven, Conn.: Yale University Press, 2012); Jeffrey Banks and Doria De la Chapelle, *Preppy: Cultivating Ivy Style* (New York: Rizzoli, 2011); Teruyoshi Hayashida, Toshiyuki Kurosu, and Hajime Hasegawa, *Take Ivy* (New York: PowerHouse, 2010); and Graham Marsh and J. P. Gaul, *The Ivy Look: Classic American Clothing* (London: Francis Lincoln, 2010).

MANICURE **1**—Cutex founder Northam Warren "capitalized on the growing acceptability of makeup and introduced a rose enamel. Finally in 1932 the Cutex colour line increased to five shades ranging from 'natural' to a deep cardinal red." Kate Forde, "Celluloid Dreams: The Marketing of Cutex in America, 1916–1935," *Journal of Design History* 15, no. 3 (2002): 183. **2**—Ibid., 185. **3**—André Courrèges quoted in Suzanne Shapiro, *Nails: The Story of the Modern Manicure* (New York: Prestel, 2014), 79. **4**—George Schaeffer, founder of the dental supply business Odontorium Products Inc., switched from producing acrylic porcelains for dentures to the first acrylic nail extensions under the acronym OPI in the 1970s. **5**—A recent investigative report in the *New York Times* found that such manicurists "are routinely underpaid and exploited, and endure ethnic bias and other abuse," in addition to experiencing ill health due to repeated exposure to the chemicals in nail products. See Sarah Maslin Nir, "The Price of Nice Nails," *New York Times Magazine,* May 7, 2015. **6**—Robin Givhan, "Giving Polish a Personality," *Washington Post,* April 20, 2001.

MAO JACKET **1**—Roland Barthes traveled to China in May 1974 with a committee from *Tel Quel,* the French avant-garde literary journal founded by Philippe Sollers and published between 1960 and 1982. The committee included Sollers, Jean Wahl, Marcelin Pleynet, Julia Kristeva, and Barthes. See Barthes, "Alors, la Chine?," *Le Monde,* May 24, 1974; reprinted as a pamphlet (Paris: Christian Bourgois, 1975), 9. Trans. by the author. **2**—"Men in Vogue," *Vogue,* September 1, 1967, 231. **3**—His more forceful criticism was published posthumously. See Barthes, *Carnets du voyage en Chine* (Paris: Christian Bourgois, 2009). **4**—For Barthes's theories on photography, see *Camera Lucida: Reflections on Photography* (New York: Noonday, 1988).

MINISKIRT **1**— George Taylor's 1926 study linking the popularity of costly nylon stockings to economic prosperity (later dubbed the "Hemline Index") has by no means proved to be accurate, but it nonetheless continues to be cited during moments of major hemline change. **2**—Mary Quant quoted in Ruth Lynam, ed., *Couture: An Illustrated History of the Great Paris Designers*

(Garden City, N.Y.: Doubleday, 1972), 198. **3**—It was, in fact, the miniskirt that brought about the popularity of tights (see *Tights*). **4**— André Courrèges quoted in Lynam, *Couture*, 198. **5**—In Somalia, for example, the miniskirt was associated with prostitution, and it prompted the creation of a special police division called the "*buon costume*" (propriety) that arrested women caught wearing the garment. **6**—See *Shift Dress* for another example of paper clothing. **7**— James Laver quoted in Joel Lobenthal, "Youthquake Fashions," in *The Berg Companion to Fashion*, ed. Valerie Steele (Oxford, U.K.: Bloomsbury Academic, 2010). **8**—"Vogue's Eye View: Paris Says: This Is the Year to Do Your Own Thing with Your Hemline," *Vogue*, March 15, 1970, 41. **9**—"Fashion Hem-Lines Lengthen the Interest at Longchamp," *Vogue*, August 1921, 41. **10**—Dr. William E. Mosher quoted in "Health Aide Casts Vote for Miniskirts," *Women's Wear Daily,* December 29, 1966, 8.

MOON BOOT **1**—For more on NASA's space suit and boot technology, see ILC Dover, "Space Suit Evolution from Custom Tailored to Off-The-Rack," 1994. **2**—Information about the price of the Moon Boot was provided by Alessia Nervo, communication specialist, Tecnica Group, e-mail to staff of The Museum of Modern Art, February 24, 2017. **3**—Ruth La Ferla, "Moon Boots Back on Earth," *New York Times*, October 17, 2004. **4**—Nervo, e-mail to the Museum.

OXFORD-CLOTH BUTTON-DOWN SHIRT **1**—G. Bruce Boyer, *True Style: The History and Principles of Classic Menswear* (New York: Basic, 2015), 145. **2**—Ibid. **3**—Ibid., 147. **4**—Boyer, *Elegance: A Guide to Quality in Menswear* (New York: Norton, 1985), 49. **5**—Brooks Brothers advertisement, *Vogue*, August 15, 1949, 110. **6**—Kelly Stuart, archivist, Brooks Brothers, e-mail to staff of The Museum of Modern Art, March 17, 2017.

PANAMA HAT **1**—Holger Domingo Carranza, Manabí weaver, interview with The Museum of Modern Art, May 5, 2017. **2**—Beverly Chico, "Central American Headwear," in *Berg Encyclopedia of World Dress and Fashion: Latin America and the Caribbean*, ed. Margot Blum Schevill (Oxford, U.K.: Bloomsbury Academic, 2005), 244. **3**—Ibid. **4**—Ibid., 241. **5**—Ibid., 243. **6**—Vannie Arrocha Morán, "Historia del sombrero Panamá que popularizó Theodore Roosevelt," *El mundo*, March 25, 2015.

PEARL NECKLACE **1**—Beatriz Chadour-Sampson and Hubert Bari, *Pearls* (London: Victoria and Albert Museum, 2013), 30–31. **2**—Ibid., 46–47. **3**—Ibid., 75–76. **4**—Ibid., 74.

PENCIL SKIRT **1**—"Women Doctors Differ over the Tight Skirt," *Women's Wear Daily,* February 27, 1919, 19. **2**—"Fashion: Paris

Openings—As Usual," *Vogue*, March 1940, 51. **3**—Dorothy Vernon, "'H' Theme of Dior Clearest in Suits," *New York Times*, August 27, 1954. **4**—"Shopping Bazaar: Coiffure Portfolio Head Lines for All Ages," *Harper's Bazaar*, April 1954, 88. **5**—Janie Bryant, interview with The Museum of Modern Art, June 17, 2017. **6**—"Fashion: Smart Choices," *Vogue*, June 1987, 250.

PLAID FLANNEL SHIRT   1—Jonathan Poneman, "Grunge & Glory," *Vogue*, December 1992, 256. **2**—See, generally, Doug Truax, *Woolrich: 175 Years of Excellence* (South Boardman, Mich.: Crofton Creek Press, 2005). **3**—Dick Hebdige, *Subculture: The Meaning of Style* (London: Routledge, 1979), 94. **4**—Rick Marin, "Grunge: A Success Story," *New York Times*, November 15, 1992.

PLATFORM SHOE   1—Elizabeth Semmelhack, *On a Pedestal: From Renaissance Chopines to Baroque Heels* (Toronto: Bata Shoe Museum, 2009), 12. **2**—Rowan Bain, "Status and Power in the Hammam," in Helen Persson, ed., *Shoes: Pleasure and Pain* (London: Victoria and Albert Museum, 2015), 52. **3**—Semmelhack, *On a Pedestal*, 79. **4**—Martha Chaiklin, "Purity, Pollution and Place in Traditional Japanese Footwear," in Giorgio Riello and Peter McNeil, eds., *Shoes: A History from Sandals to Sneakers* (London and New York: Berg, 2006), 176. **5**—Lisa Small, "Rising in the East," in Small, Stefano Tonchi, and Caroline Weber, eds., *Killer Heels: The Art of the High-Heeled Shoe* (New York: Prestel, 2014), 53–54. **6**—For more on Herman Delman's innovations and influence, see Sarah Byrd and Laura Mina, *Scandal Sandals and Lady Slippers: A History of Delman Shoes* (New York: The Museum at FIT, 2010). **7**—Semmelhack, "The Allure of Power," in *Shoes: Pleasure and Pain*, 50. For a more detailed history of men and heeled footwear, see Christopher Breward, "Men in Heels," in the same volume, 128–39. **8**—Frank Cartledge, "Punk," in *The Berg Companion to Fashion*, ed. Valerie Steele (Oxford, U.K.: Bloomsbury Academic, 2010). **9**—For more on goth fashion, see Paul Hodkinson, "Goth as a Subcultural Style," in *Goth: Identity, Style and Subculture* (Oxford, U.K.: Berg, 2002), 35–64.

POLO SHIRT   1—Lisa Birnbach, *The Official Preppy Handbook* (New York: Workman, 1980), 141, 130. **2**—Thirstin Howl III quoted in Angel Diaz, "Lo End Theory: The Secret History of the Lo-Life Crew," *Complex,* September 23, 2015. **3**—Jon Caramanica, "The Gang That Brought High Fashion to Hip-Hop," *New York Times*, June 28, 2016.

PREMAMAN   1—*Vogue*, April 15, 1928, 108. The earliest such article, "A Practical Maternity Wardrobe," appeared in *Vogue*, December 15, 1913. **2**—Three years later, its revenue topped

$1 million. See Tom Mahoney, *50 Years of Lane Bryant* (New York: Lane Bryant, 1950), 7. Cited in Marianne Brown, "The Birth of Maternity Wear: Clothing for the Expectant Mother in America" (master's thesis, Fashion Institute of Technology, New York, 2009), 8. **3**—See E. Frankfurt et al., Maternity garment ensemble, U.S. Patent US2141814A, filed June 3, 1938. **4**—These policies included the Pregnancy Discrimination Act of 1979 and the Family and Medical Leave Act of 1993. **5**—There are examples of maternity fashion in the costume and fashion collections at the Museum at the Fashion Institute of Technology, New York; The Museum of the City of New York; and Drexel University, Philadelphia, for example, but it has not been a collecting focus for any institution, nor has it been the subject of many exhibitions in the last few decades.

RED LIPSTICK   1—Michel Pastoureau, *Red: The History of a Color,* trans. Jody Gladding (Princeton, N.J.: Princeton University Press, 2017), 152–55. **2**—Jessica Pallingston, *Lipstick* (New York: St. Martin's, 1999), 15. **3**—Ibid., 15. **4**—Pastoureau, *Red*, 158. **5**—Kathy Lee Peiss, *Hope in a Jar: The Making of America's Beauty Culture* (Philadelphia: University of Pennsylvania Press, 1998), 242. **6**—Quoted in Meg Cohen Ragas and Karen Kozlowski, *Read My Lips: A Cultural History of Lipstick* (San Francisco: Chronicle, 1998), 79.

ROLEX   1—See James Dowling and Jeffrey Hess, *Rolex Wristwatches: The Best of Time; An Unauthorized History* (Atglen, Penn.: Schiffer, 1996), 241. **2**—In 2009 the Geneva-based Fondation de la Haute Horlogerie estimated that the global counterfeit watch industry was worth between $250 billion and $300 billion a year, against $5 billion twenty-five years ago. Nicholas Foulkes, "Counterfeit: Reason to Resist That Dodgy Rolex," *Financial Times*, November 13, 2009.

SAFARI SUIT   1—The Swahili word *safari* in turn derives from the Arabic word *safar,* or "journey." **2**—Sir Robert Armitage Sterndale, *Seonee: Or, Camp Life on the Satpura Range; a Tale of Indian Adventure* (London, 1877), 10. **3**—Theodore Roosevelt, *The Wilderness Hunter: An Account of the Big Game of the United States and Its Chase with Horse, Hound and Rifle,* vol. 1 (New York: Scribner's, 1906), vii. **4**—See Nick Foulkes, *Mogambo: The Safari Jacket*, vol. 9, *Uman: The Essays* (Geneva: Skira, 2012), 4. **5**—"Beauty Bulletin: Mr. Charm; Today's Man," *Vogue*, November 15, 1970, 146–47; and "Men in Vogue: Be Suited to a T," *Vogue*, June 1, 1971, 67. **6**—In a 1977 Paul Stuart advertisement, for instance, the look was promoted as "the classic safari suit: cut and styled especially for women." See *Vogue,* May 1, 1977, 156.

SAFETY PIN   1—Patent no. 6281 was issued

on April 10, 1849; see Jimmy Stamp, "The Inventive Mind of Walter Hunt, Yankee Mechanical Genius," *Smithsonian Magazine*, October 2013. **2**—By the Middle Ages, fibulae gave way to more complicated brooches whose decorative significations (such as coats of arms and crests) trumped an emphasis on protective pin catches; see Bettina Arnold and Sabine Hopert Hagmann, "Fibulae and Dress in Iron Age Europe," in *Berg Encyclopedia of World Dress and Fashion: West Europe,* ed. Lise Skov (Oxford, U.K.: Berg, 2010). **3**—This was particularly the case in London, where pay caps for unionized trades in the 1970s led to widespread strikes and contempt for government.

SALWAR KAMEEZ   1—Reina Lewis, *Muslim Fashion: Contemporary Style Cultures* (Durham, N.C.: Duke University Press, 2015), 186. **2**—See Anirudh Deshpande, "Indian Cinema and the Bourgeois Nation State," *Economic and Political Weekly* 42, no. 50 (2007): 103n12. See also Rashmi Sadana, "On the Delhi Metro: An Ethnographic View," *Economic and Political Weekly* 45, no. 46 (2010): 77–83. **3**—Emma Tarlo, "Landscapes of Attraction and Rejection: South Asian Aesthetics in Islamic Fashion in London," in *Islamic Fashion and Anti-Fashion: New Perspectives from Europe and North America*, ed. Tarlo and Annelies Moors (London: Bloomsbury Academic, 2013), 73–92. **4**—Ibid. **5**—See Tahir Abbas, "The Impact of Religio-Cultural Norms and Values on the Education of Young South Asian Women," *British Journal of Sociology of Education* 24, no. 4 (2003): 411–28. **6**—Julia Reed, "Fashion: Point of View: How Sexy Is Too Sexy?," *Vogue*, April 1998, 349. **7**—Meenakshi Gigi Durham, "Ethnic Chic and the Displacement of South Asian Female Sexuality in the U.S. Media," *New York Media/Cultural Studies: Critical Approaches*, 2009, 503. **8**—See Anirudh Deshpande, "Indian Cinema and the Bourgeois Nation State," 98. **9**—Konda Surekha, quoted in "Schoolgirls Should Wear Salwar Kameez to Avoid Harassment: Woman MLA," *Hindustan Times*, March 31, 2016. **10**—Mukulika Banerjee and Daniel Miller, "Sari," in *The Berg Companion to Fashion*, ed. Valerie Steele (Oxford, U.K.: Bloomsbury Academic, 2010), 613–15. **11**—Luke Leitch, "Ashish: Spring 2017 Ready-to-Wear," *Vogue*, September 19, 2016.

SARI   1—Rta Kapur Chishti, *Saris: Tradition and Beyond* (New Delhi: Roli, 2013), 13. **2**—Hélène Cixous, "Sonia Rykiel in Translation," trans. Deborah Jenson, in *On Fashion*, ed. Shari Benstock and Suzanne Ferriss (New Brunswick, N.J.: Rutgers University Press, 1994), 98. **3**—Soha Parekh, *Saris: Splendour in Threads* (Mumbai: Red Pepper, 2012), 56. **4**—Ibid., 27. **5**—Ibid. **6**—Malika Verma Kashyap, "Why 'the Sari'?" *Border & Fall,* October 2016. **7**—Aarti Betigeri, "Can the Blouse Save the Sari?," *Border & Fall*, June 2016. **8**—I am grateful to Malika Verma Kashyap for her insight on the fate of the sari today and her kind review of this essay overall.

SEVEN EASY PIECES 1—Donna Karan quoted in Genevieve Buck, "Karan's First Collection: An Instant Hit," *Chicago Tribune,* May 8, 1985. 2—Karan quoted in Ingrid Sischy, *The Journey of a Woman: 20 Years of Donna Karan* (New York: Assouline, 2004), n.p. 3—"SA Ends with a Sophisticated Donna Karan," *Women's Wear Daily*, May 6, 1985, 14. 4—Karan quoted in Marlen Komar, "The Evolution of the Female Power Suit and What It Means," *Bustle*. 5—Bernadine Morris, "Donna Karan Stars on Her Own," *New York Times,* May 4, 1985. 6—Karan quoted in Sischy, *The Journey of a Woman,* n.p. 7—Karan quoted in Kathleen Madden, "View: Body Dressing/Sportswear Shimmer . . . ," *Vogue,* June 1985, 200.

SHAWL 1—In the Mughal court of north India, cashmere shawls were worn by royals and noblemen as part of the "robe of honor," signifying their status and privilege. 2—Susan Hiner, "Lust for 'Luxe': 'Cashmere Fever' in Nineteenth-Century France," *Journal for Early Modern Cultural Studies* 5, no. 1 (2005): 76–98. 3—William Safire, "On Language: Pashmina," *New York Times*, January 16, 2000.

SHIFT DRESS 1—"Success Story of the Shift Dress," *Vogue*, December 1938, 92. 2—"Ways to Snip Sewing-Time," *Vogue*, February 1943, 47. 3—"Shifts Move into High Gear as More Women Learn Comfort Features," *Women's Wear Daily*, March 27, 1963, 30. 4—Anne Klein quoted in "Proper Scaling Brings Style into Focus for Petites, Says Designer: Longer Skirts; Jackets," *Women's Wear Daily*, April 24, 1947, 30. For the "long torso shift dress," see "Shift, Knits, in Junior Line," *Women's Wear Daily*, October 12, 1960, 5. 5—"Paper Capers," *Time*, March 18, 1966, 71. 6—"The Now and Future Paco Rabanne," *Vogue*, March 1967, 267. 7—Amy M. Spindler, "Lang Points the Way to a New Elegance," *New York Times*, March 7, 1994, B9. 8—Katherine Betts, "Runway Report '95: Fashion's Retro-Spective," *Vogue*, January 1995, 64. 9—Hussein Chalayan, e-mail to Paola Antonelli, February 13, 2017.

SHIRTDRESS 1—*Godey's Lady's Book and Magazine* quoted in H. Kristina Haugland, "Blouse," in *The Berg Companion to Fashion*, ed. Valerie Steele (Oxford, U.K.: Bloomsbury Academic, 2010). 2—Patricia Campbell Warner, "The Americanization of Fashion: Sportswear, the Movies and the 1930s," in *Twentieth-Century American Fashion*, ed. Linda Welters and Patricia A. Cunningham (Oxford, U.K.: Berg, 2008), 79–98. 3—Ibid. 4—"Fashion: Seen at the Chiberta Golf Club," *Vogue*, November 15, 1937, 138. 5—"*Life* Looks at Summer Sports Clothes," *Life*, May 9, 1938, 25.

6—"Vogue Patterns: After-Five Plans for the Shirt Dress," *Vogue*, October 1, 1954, 153. 7—"Vogue's Eye View: Vogue's Eye View of Now . . . Right Now, of January, 1950," *Vogue*, January 1, 1950, 85. 8—"Eye: The Suede Uniform," *Women's Wear Daily*, February 7, 1973, 10. 9—Sarah Harris, "Why We All Want to Wear a Shirtdress," British *Vogue*, April 5, 2017. 10—Ibid.

SILK SCARF 1—As described in Diderot and d'Alembert's 1765 *Encyclopédie*: "With white skin, curves, firm flesh and a bosom, even the most innocent peasant woman knows how to let just enough show through the folds of her fichu." Trans. by the author. "Fichu," *Encyclopédie* (1765), vol. 6, 678. 2—"Isadora Duncan, Dragged by Scarf from Auto, Killed," *New York Times*, September 15, 1927, 1.

SLIP DRESS 1—Bernadine Morris, "Easy Dresses, Rocky Finish," *New York Times*, November 6, 1993, 30. 2—Colin McDowell, *Fashion Today* (New York: Phaidon, 2003), 410. 3—Julia Reed, "Calvin's Clean Sweep," *Vogue*, August 1, 1994, 240. 4—"Satins Go into Print," *Vogue*, January 15, 1934, 43, 45. 5—"Her Slip's Showing," *Quick*, December 19, 1949, 44. 6—Imogen Fox, "The Big Reveal: Deconstructing the Slip Dress," *Guardian*, March 7, 2016. 7—Morris, "Tank Dress: Simply Minimal," *New York Times*, November 23, 1993.

SNUGLI 1—Other practices include the cradleboards of the Plains Indian and, in China and Hong Kong, special cold-weather carrier covers embroidered with mandarin ducks, lotus flowers, and characters that spell out good omens for the child. See Valery Garrett, "Chinese Baby Carriers: A Hong Kong Tradition Now Gone," *Journal of the Hong Kong Branch of the Royal Asiatic Society* 41 (2001): 95–108; and Mary Jane Schneider, "Kiowa and Comanche Baby Carriers," *Plains Anthropologist* 28, no. 102 (1983): 305–14. 2—Elizabeth Anisfeld et al., "Does Infant Carrying Promote Attachment? An Experimental Study of the Effects of Increased Physical Contact on the Development of Attachment," *Child Development* 61, no. 5 (1990): 1, 617–27. The authors concluded that "for low income inner city mothers [the population with which the study engaged], there may be a causal relation between increased physical contact, achieved through early carrying in a soft baby carrier, and subsequent security of attachment between infant and mother." 3—Isabel Emma Eggleston Beshar, "Rooming-In: Cold War Consumer Product?," *Intersect: The Stanford Journal of Science, Technology, and Society* 7, no. 1 (March 2014). 4—See ibid., 4, for a description of the article and these words, by Beshar, describing James Maloney's research. 5—See John Bowlby, *Attachment* (New York: Basic, 1969) and William Sears, *Creative Parenting: How to Use the Attachment Parenting Concept to Raise Children Successfully from Birth Through Adolescence*, rev. ed. (New York: Dodd, Mead, 1987).

SPACE AGE 1—Pierre Cardin quoted in Jean-Pascal Hesse, *Pierre Cardin: 60 Years of Innovation* (New York: Assouline, 2010), 16. 2—Cardin quoted in Thelma Sweetinburgh, "Cardin—L'Industriel," *Women's Wear Daily*, May 12, 1967, 18. 3—Ibid. 4—Hesse, *Pierre Cardin*, 16.

SPANX 1—Spanx website, http://www.spanx.com/about-us. 2—Clare O'Connor, "How Sara Blakely of Spanx Turned $5,000 into $1 Billion," *Forbes*, March 14, 2012. 3—Blakely quoted in Caroline Bankoff, "How Selling Fax Machines Helped Make Spanx Inventor Sara Blakely a Billionaire," *New York*, October 31, 2016. 4—Ibid. 5—For more on foot-binding, see Dorothy Ko, "Footbinding," in *The Berg Companion to Fashion*, ed. Valerie Steele (Oxford, U.K.: Bloomsbury Academic, 2010). 6—For a complete history of the corset, see Valerie Steele, *The Corset: A Cultural History* (New Haven, Conn.: Yale University Press, 2003).

SPORTS JERSEY 1—Peter Carpolino quoted in Tim Leyden, "We Are What We Wear: How Sports Jerseys Became Ubiquitous in the United States," *Sports Illustrated,* February 1, 2016.

STILETTO 1—The stiletto's height can range from the modest one to two inches of rise on the so-called kitten heel to the prohibitive eight-inch heel on Christian Louboutin's practically *en pointe* Ballerina Ultima concept shoe from 2007 to Alexander McQueen's 2010 Armadillo Boot, with a heel ascending more than ten inches, pushing the form, and function, to an extreme. 2—See Camille Paglia, "The Stiletto Heel," in *Design and Violence,* ed. Paola Antonelli and James Hunt (New York: The Museum of Modern Art, 2015), 122–25. 3—Salvatore Ferragamo and André Perugia also developed stiletto heels, among other designers. 4—For more on the prodigious career of Roger Vivier, see Virginie Mouzat and Colombe Pringle, eds., *Roger Vivier* (New York: Rizzoli, 2013); Elizabeth Semmelhack, *Roger Vivier: Process to Perfection* (Toronto: Bata Shoe Museum Foundation, 2012); and Colombe Pringle, *Roger Vivier* (New York: Assouline, 2005). 5—For more on Dior's New Look, see Nigel Cawthorne, *The New Look: The Dior Revolution* (London: Hamlyn, 1996); Alexandra Palmer, *Dior: A New Look, a New Enterprise (1947–57)* (London: Victoria and Albert Museum, 2009); and Françoise Giroud, *Dior: Christian Dior, 1905–1957* (New York: Rizzoli, 1988).

SUIT 1—Kevin L. Seligman, *Cutting for All!: The Sartorial Arts, Related Crafts, and the Commercial Paper Pattern* (1996). Seligman's text, among others, outlines the many other claimants to the systematization of measuring and pattern making, including Edward Minister's *System of the Art of Cutting* (1820). **2**—Edgar Allan Poe, "The Man of the Crowd," in *The Works of the Late Edgar Allan Poe,* vol. 2: Poems and Miscellanies, ed. Rufus Wilmot Griswold (New York: J. S. Redfield, 1850), 400. **3**—Quoted in Christopher Breward, *The Suit: Form, Function, and Style* (London: Reaktion Books, 2016), 168–69. **4**—Danielle Sprecher, "Well-Dressed Men: From Montague Burton to Topman," in *Moses, Mods and Mr. Fish: The Menswear Revolution,* ed. Elizabeth Selby (London: Jewish Museum, 2016), 79–86. **5**—John T. Molloy, *Dress for Success* (New York: Warner Books, 1975), 45. **6**—The zoot suit, first worn for the most part by black and Hispanic Americans, including Malcolm X, was a flamboyant sartorial expression that in some cases attracted racist white assailants, such as the 1943 assaults in Los Angeles that came to be dubbed the Zoot Suit Riots. **7**—Breward, *Suit*, 146. **8**—*Sapeurs* are members of La Sape, or Société des Ambianceurs et des Personnes Élégantes, translated literally as "Society of Ambiance-Makers and Elegant People."

SUNSCREEN **1**—Beginning in the mid-1940s, the cream was marketed as Piz Buin, after the mountain on which Franz Greiter received his sunburn. **2**—With an eye to reaching the same lucrative demographic, in 2015 Nivea created a doll made of a UV-sensitive material that reddens in the sun if sunscreen is not applied, an effective marketing gimmick to teach children about the importance of wearing such products.**3**—Antonio Tovar-Sánchez et al., "Sunscreen Products as Emerging Pollutants to Coastal Waters," *PLOS One* 8, no. 6 (June 5, 2013): 1.

SURGICAL MASK **1**—Nathan L. Belkin, "The Evolution of the Surgical Mask: Filtering Efficiency Versus Effectiveness," *Infection Control and Hospital Epidemiology* 18, no. 1 (January 1997): 49. **2**—Ibid., 49. **3**—Park Jong Woo quoted in Emilia Petrarca, "This Man Might Be the Kanye West of Seoul Fashion Week," *W*, October 19, 2016.

SWATCH **1**—Nicholas Foulkes, "How Swatch Saved the Swiss Watchmaking Industry," *Telegraph* (London), July 2, 2010. **2**—"Swatch Group History (yesterday)," Company History, swatch.com. **3**—Jonathan Glancey, "Retrotech: The Art on Your Sleeve," *Independent* (London), March 27, 1993, 39. **4**—Silke Koltrowitz, "Swatch to Launch Smartwatch Operating System by 2018," *Business of Fashion*, March 16, 2017.

TABI BOOT **1**—Woody Hochswender, "Thierry Mugler: Nuts, Bolts and Sequins," *New York Times,* March 18, 1989, 32. **2**—Martin Margiela quoted in Geert Bruloot, *Footprint: The Tracks of Shoes in Fashion* (Tielt, Belgium: Lannoo, 2015), 149. **3**—Ibid. **4**—Linda Loppa, interview with The Museum of Modern Art, New York, June 26, 2017. **5**—Margiela quoted in Bruloot, *Footprint*, 149.

TATTOO **1**—See Rene Friedman, "New Tattoos from Ancient Egypt: Defining Marks of Culture," 11–36, in *Ancient Ink: The Archaeology of Tattooing*, ed. Lars Krutak and Aaron Deter-Wolf (Seattle: University of Washington Press, 2018); and W. Mark Gustafson, "Inscripta in Fronte: Penal Tattooing in Late Antiquity," *Classical Antiquity* 16, no. 1 (1997): 79–105. **2**—Lyle Tuttle quoted in George James, "From Back Alleys to Beauty Queens," *New York Times*, July 29, 2001. **3**—Ed Hardy is extensively published in his own right; see his *Tattootime* series for further reading. **4**—Michael Rees, "From Outsider to Established—Explaining the Current Popularity and Acceptability of Tattooing," *Historical Social Research/ Historische Sozialforschung* 41, no. 3 (2016): 160. **5**—Aurora Alemdral, "At 100, She Keeps A Philippine Tattoo Tradition Alive," *New York Times*, May 15, 2017. See also the work of Dr. Lars Krutak, a prolific and incisive anthropologist of global tattoo cultures. **6**—As Rees writes in "From Outsider to Established," "The exotic rituals of cultural outsiders, once the preserve of publications such as *National Geographic*, are now readily available for all through popular media forms such as the Internet and television" (166).

TEVA SANDAL **1**—Mike Koshmrl, "River Guides Reporting Gnarly Cases of Foot Rot," *Jackson Hole News and Guide*, August 24, 2016. **2**—See Jonathan Walford, "Shoes," in *The Berg Companion to Fashion*, ed. Valerie Steele (Oxford, U.K.: Bloomsbury Academic, 2010) and Doran H. Ross, "Footwear," in *Berg Encyclopedia of World Dress and Fashion: Africa*, ed. Joanne B. Eicher and Doran H. Ross (Oxford, U.K.: Berg, 2010), 113–19. **3**—Orna Ben-Meir, "The Israeli Shoe: Biblical Sandals and Native Israeli Identity," in *Jews and Shoes*, ed. Edna Nahshon (Oxford, U.K.: Berg, 2008), 77–90. **4**—Leeann Duggan, "Crunchy Footwear Is Happening, Whether We Like It or Not," *Refinery 29*, April 14, 2014. **5**—Laird Borrelli-Persson, "Why Is Fashion Falling for the Pretty/Ugly Shoe All Over Again," *Vogue,* June 14, 2016.

TIE **1**—The scarflike steinkirk was worn looped through the buttonhole of a man's jacket, while the rigidly folded muslin stock of the cravat was wrapped tightly around the neck. **2**—The name "four-in-hand" may derive from the Four-in-Hand Club, a London gentlemen's club where members knotted their ties. It is also suggested that the name comes from the tie's resembling the reins of the four-horse carriages driven by members of the English aristocracy. **3**—"The Bold Look," *Esquire,* April 1948, 78.

TIGHTS **1**—In the United States, the term *panty hose* is often used exclusively for sheer iterations of the garment. **2**—This iteration, known as fully-fashioned stockings, resulted from the addition of a drive mechanism that allowed for extremely fast production that knitted the garment flat, requiring the two sides to be united by a single seam. **3**—This notion was captured in a headline in *Life* magazine: "Women hope new yarn will halve their stocking bill without loss of glamor"; see "Nylon," *Life*, June 10, 1940, 61. **4**—Ibid. **5**—Belle-Sharmeer advertisement, *Vogue*, May 1, 1942, 16. An advertisement for Armand leg make-up declared it was "pretty and patriotic" and "more glamorous than sheerest silk or nylon stockings"; see *Life*, August 17, 1942, 6. **6**—Glen Raven Panti-Legs advertisement, *Vogue,* November 1, 1964, 43. **7**—Danskin advertisement, *Vogue*, August 15, 1968, C3.

TRACKSUIT **1**—A decade later, the combination of cellulose triacetate and polyester gave birth to the lightweight nylon shell suit on whose surface a riot of colors danced (but the fabric quickly became a public safety concern due to its flammability). **2**—Tracksuits remain prevalent in sports but are now canvases for corporate branding, national identity, and designer collaborations (for example, Stella McCartney's designs for Team GB at the London 2012 Olympic Games). **3**—See Mary Whowell, "Male Sex Work: Exploring Regulation in England and Wales," *Journal of Law and Society* 37, no. 1 (2010): 125–44. **4**—Madonna and Paris Hilton were converts to the Juicy Couture brand, as was Britney Spears, who memorably outfitted her wedding party in white and pink Juicy Couture velour in 2001; Mariah Carey wore her suit with skyscraper heels.

TRENCH COAT **1**—Jane Tynan, "Military Dress and Men's Outdoor Leisurewear: Burberry's Trench Coat in First World War Britain," *Journal of Design History*, 24, no. 2 (2011): 146. **2**—Ibid., 149–50.

TURTLENECK **1**—"Fashion: Turtle-Neck Sweaters Enter the Race for Spring Smartness," *Vogue*, April 1, 1925, 94. **2**—"In Vogue for Men: Turtleneck Sweaters, Inside and Out," *Vogue*, November 1, 1963, 82. **3**—"Best Dressed for 1963," *Life*, January 11, 1963, 38. **4**—Troy Patterson, "On Clothing: Can the Turtleneck Ever Be Cool Again?," *New York Times Magazine,* December 30, 2015, 14. **5**—Dennis R. Jenkins, *Dressing for Altitude: U.S. Aviation Pressure Suits—Wiley Post to Space Shuttle* (Washington, D.C.: National Aeronautics and Space Administration, 2012). **6**—"Turtlenecks Come in from the Cold," *Life*, November 10, 1967, 113. **7**—Walter Isaacson, *Steve Jobs* (New York: Simon & Schuster, 2011), quoted in Alex Heath, "Why Steve Jobs Wore Turtlenecks," *Cult of Mac*, October 11, 2011. **8**—Hana Tajima,

"T = Turtleneck," May 26, 2016, Hana Tajima (blog), http://hanatajima.com/blog/2016/5/26/t-turtleneck.

UNISEX PROJECT   **1**—Rudi Gernreich quoted in Peggy Moffitt, *The Rudi Gernreich Book* (New York: Rizzoli, 1991), 25.   **2**—Ibid., 19.   **3**—"Rudi Gernreich Makes Some Modest Proposals: Fashion for 1970," *Life*, January 9, 1970, 117.   **4**—Ibid.   **5**—Valerie Cumming, C. W. Cunnington, and P. E. Cunnington, eds., *The Dictionary of Fashion History* (Oxford, U.K.: Berg, 2010), 215.   **6**—Gernreich quoted in Moffit, *The Rudi Gernreich Book*, 28.   **7**—Julie Byrne, "Gernreich Bares His Soul on the Future of Fashion," *Los Angeles Times,* January 22, 1970, 63.

WHITE T-SHIRT   **1**—Statistics show that 95 percent of Americans wear T-shirts and 89 percent of them put one on at least once a week. Furthermore, nine in every ten own at least one T-shirt they refuse to throw away because of sentimental attachment. As *Vogue* summed it up, "Its very plainness, after all, leaves room for self invention, the root of the American dream." See Laird Borrelli-Persson, "A Brief History of the White T-Shirt," *Vogue,* May 20, 2015.   **2**—Nancy Szokan, "The Fashion Industry Tries to Take Responsibility for Its Pollution," *Washington Post*, June 30, 2016.   **3**—Shaun Cole, *The Story of Men's Underwear* (New York: Parkstone, 2009), 15.   **4**—Ibid.   **5**—For more on the global implications of cotton products, see Pietra Rivoli, *The Travels of a T-Shirt in a Global Economy: An Economist Examines the Markets, Power and Politics of the World Trade* (New York: Wiley, 2005), 63.   **6**—The *Oxford English Dictionary* traces *T-shirt*'s first appearance in print to F. Scott Fitzgerald's 1920 novel *This Side of Paradise*, in which it is included on a boarding school packing list.   **7**—See Cole, *The Story of Men's Underwear*, 62, where he quotes fashion historians Richard Martin and Valerie Steele.   **8**—It embodies what author Jeremy Seabrook terms the "mutability of progress," the post-modern, postindustrial anxiety and despair over the devaluation of labor, materials, and human life. See Seabrook, *The Song of the Shirt: The High Price of Cheap Garments, from Blackburn to Bangladesh* (London: Hurst, 2015), 1.

WONDERBRA   **1**—Chris Vanderwees, "Wonderbra," in *The Cultural Encyclopedia of the Breast*, ed. Merril D. Smith (New York: Rowman & Littlefield, 2014), 270.   **2**—For a succinct summation of the "Bra Wars," see Susanna Hailstone, "The Wonderbra—How Thinking Big Ensured the Survival of the Fittest," a report for TBWA and the Institute of Practitioners in Advertising, London, 1994.   **3**—See Angela Smith, "From Girl Power to Lady Power: Postfeminism and Ladette to Lady," in Claire Nally and Angela Smith, eds., *Naked Exhibitionism: Gendered Performance and Public Exposure* (London: I. B. Tauris, 2013), 137–64. The term "ladette" is thought to have been coined by the men's magazine *FHM* in 1994. In Britain, it is largely associated with young working-class women.   **4**—Wendy A. Burns-Ardolino, "Reading Woman: Displacing the Foundations of Femininity," *Hypatia* 18, no. 3 (Autumn 2003): 51.

WRAP DRESS   **1**—Diane von Furstenberg quoted in Jerry Bowles, "Diane von Furstenberg: Life at the Top," *Vogue*, July 1, 1976, 141.   **2**—Von Furstenberg quoted in "40 Years Later, Diane von Furstenberg's Wrap Dress Still Wears Well," *NPR,* October 24, 2014.   **3**—For more on the Taxi dress, see Richard Martin, *Charles James* (New York: Thames and Hudson, 1997); for more on the Pop-Over dress, see Kohle Yohannan, *Claire McCardell: Redefining Modernism* (New York: Abrams, 1998).

Y-3   **1**—Yohji Yamamoto quoted in Sarah Mower, "Fashion: Tank Girl," *Vogue,* April 1, 2003, 204.   **2**—Sarah Mower, "Vogue View: Most Valuable Player," *Vogue,* November 1, 2002, 301.   **3**—Ibid., 300.   **4**—Yamamoto quoted in Holly Shackleton, "There Are No Rules: How Yohji Yamamoto Is Taking Y-3 to the Next Level," *ID*, June 1, 2016.   **5**—Cathy Horyn, "Critic's Notebook: Designers, Forget Vreeland. Look at Your Own World," *New York Times*, December 24, 2002, B8.   **6**—Yamamoto quoted in Allyson Shiffman, "Ten Years of Y-3," *Last Magazine,* December 30, 2013.

YOGA PANTS   **1**—Andrea Jain, *Selling Yoga: From Counterculture to Pop Culture* (New York: Oxford University Press, 2014), 41.   **2**—Penelope Green, "Modern Yoga: Om to the Beat," *New York Times*, May 15, 1998.   **3**—Robert Sullivan, "Strike a Pose," *Vogue*, August 2002, 136.   **4**—Ruth La Ferla, "Yoga Wear, Not Yoga, Is the Mantra," *New York Times*, December 15, 2002.

YSL TOUCHE ÉCLAT   **1**—Terry de Gunzburg, e-mail interview with The Museum of Modern Art, New York, December 7, 2016.   **2**—For an overview of the history of cosmetics, see Brian Moeran and Lise Skov, "Cosmetics and Skin Care," in *Berg Encyclopedia of World Dress and Fashion: West Europe*, ed. Skov (Oxford, U.K.: Berg, 2010), 420–25.   **3**—Ibid.

PROTOTYPE DESIGNERS

Bolt Threads & Stella McCartney —Shift Dress

Wei Hung Chen —Premaman

Liz Ciokajlo with Maurizio Montalti —
Moon Boot

Revital Cohen and Tuur Van Balen —
Diamond Engagement Ring

Nana Kwaku Duah II, Tewobaabihene —
Kente Cloth

Anne van Galen —Trench Coat

i-am-chen —Pencil Skirt

Pia Interlandi —Little Black Dress

Kerby Jean-Raymond of Pyer Moss —
Space Age

Lucy Jones —Tights

Salim Al Kadi —Keffiyeh

Ryohei Kawanishi —Guayabera

Asher Levine —Biker Jacket

MagnaReady —Oxford-Cloth Button-Down Shirt

Richard Malone —Jumpsuit

Modern Meadow —Graphic T-Shirt

Richard Nicholl and XO —Slip Dress

Miguel Mesa Posada —Harem Pants

Laduma Ngxokolo —Aran Sweater

Mary Ping —Birkin Bag

Francesco Risso, Marni —Mao Jacket

**John A. Rogers, Rogers Research Lab,
Northwestern University** —Fitbit

Sartists —Chinos

Somarta —Tights

Unmade —Breton Shirt

Verbal + Yoon, AMBUSH —Cartier Love Bracelet

Zhijun Wang —Surgical Mask

Brandon Wen and Laura Zwanziger —
Body Meets Dress—Dress Meets Body

LENDERS TO THE EXHIBITION

adidas Archive
Alpargatas SA
Anderson & Sheppard
Anouschka-Paris
Jacob Arabo
Giorgio Armani Archive
Liz Baca
Valarie Benning Barney
The Bata Shoe Museum
Catherine B Paris
Manolo Blahnik
Blueman
Carlo Brandelli Collection
Ulla Olsenius Brautigam, Olofdaughters
    of Sweden and Olsson Clogs
Brooklyn Museum
The Brooks Brothers Archives
Thom Browne
Burberry Heritage Archive
Cartier Collection
Hussein Chalayan
Chanel
Jimmy Choo
Converse Archive
Cooper Hewitt, Smithsonian Design Museum,
    Smithsonian Institution
Daniel "Dez" Day
Dapper Dan of Harlem
Design Museum Helsinki
The Robert and Penny Fox Historic Costume
    Collection at Drexel University
The Museum at the Fashion Institute
    of Technology
The FIDM Museum at the Fashion Institute
    of Design & Merchandising, Los Angeles
Fred Perry
Diane von Furstenberg
Sanjay Garg
Glen Raven, Inc.
W. L. Gore & Associates Archives
Tom Gruat
Hanesbrands, Inc.
Samuel P. Harn Museum of Art, University
    of Florida
Laura McLaws Helms
Hodinkee
Indianapolis Museum of Art
Norma Kamali
Donna Karan Archive
Kashmir Loom Co. Pvt Ltd.
Malika V. Kashyap
Miyake Design Studio
Kelis
Kobe Fashion Museum
Todd Kramer
Collection of The Kyoto Costume Institute
Lacoste
Collection Lafayette Anticipations—Fonds de
    dotation Famille Moulin, Paris
Ralph Lauren Corporation
Leather Archives & Museum
Bruce Lee, LLC

Leeds Museums and Galleries
Sonja de Lennart
Levi Strauss & Co. Archives
Jason Ling
Lions Gate Entertainment Corp
Linda Loppa
Los Angeles County Museum of Art
Christian Louboutin
Lululemon
E. Marinella Srl
The Metropolitan Museum of Art
Mikimoto
ModeMuseum Provincie Antwerpen
Moncler SpA
Ann and Mike Moore
MAK–Austrian Museum of Applied Arts/
    Contemporary Art, Vienna
Museum of Applied Arts and Sciences, Sydney
Museum of Chinese in America, New York
    (MoCA)
Museum of the City of New York
The National Museum of Ireland
New Era
The Department of Nike Archives
Orcival
Patagonia
People for the Ethical Treatment of Animals
    (PETA)
Phelan
Philadelphia Museum of Art
Collection of Phoenix Art Museum
Prada
PVH Corp. Archives
Raw Mango
Ray-Ban
Rick Owens
Rogers Research Lab, Simpson-Querrey
    Institute, Northwestern University
Schott, NYC
Shrimpton Couture
Rabbi Jodie Siff
Amanda Dolan & Megan Colby of Spark Pretty
Stolper Wilson Collection London
Swatch Ltd.
Tecnica Group SpA
Teva
Tiffany & Co.
Victoria & Albert Museum, London
Mark Walsh Leslie Chin, Vintage Luxury
Vlisco
Collection Louis Vuitton
Vivienne Westwood
Wilton Historical Society
Woolrich
Yohji Yamamoto Inc.
Association pour le Rayonnement de l'Oeuvre
    de Monsieur Yves Saint Laurent (AROYSL)

ACKNOWLEDGMENTS

The exhibition and book *Items—Is Fashion Modern?* were complex projects that could never have been realized without the expertise, hard work, and good will of many people. Personally and on behalf of The Museum of Modern Art, we thank the designers, manufacturers, institutions, collectors, companies, and archives that have so generously helped us, freely sharing their knowledge and loaning us their possessions. Additionally, we must thank the visionary companies and designers who accepted our invitation to reimagine several of the items in the exhibition. All of these various contributors may be found in our list of lenders to the exhibition (p. 283). The generosity of our sponsors, Hyundai Card and WGSN, made this endeavor possible.

It would be impossible fully to convey our appreciation for our Advisory Council (see p. 282). They answered our questions, asked great ones of their own, coached, connected, and counseled us. We are also enormously grateful for the collegiality of our counterparts at The Jewish Museum and at The Metropolitan Museum of Art's Costume Institute who showed us their preparation methods for fashion exhibitions. Colleagues Glenn Adamson, Leah Dickerman, Pamela Golbin, Mayank Kaul, Thomas Lax, Ann Temkin, and Claire Wilcox offered their wisdom at crucial moments.

In May 2016 we kicked off our research in earnest with a two-day public program at the Museum, and we remain deeply indebted to the speakers who participated: Omoyemi Akerele, Grace Ali, Carmen Artigas, Maxine Bédat, Mickey Boardman, David Godlis, Malu Halasa, Kim Hastreiter, Tinker Hatfield, Sofia Hedman, Kerby Jean-Raymond, Kabuki, Michael Kane, Harold Koda, Joan Kron, Hala Malak, Penny Martin, Serge Martynov, Dan Mathews, Alphonso D. McClendon, Emma McClendon, DeRay Mckesson, Aimee Mullins, Hari Nef, Troy Patterson, Mary Ping, Valerie Steele, Hana Tajima, Sean Trainor, Maholo Uchida, Leslie Vosshall, and Sara Ziff.

The curatorial team gave the exhibition its spine and its soul. Stephanie Kramer, Project Research Assistant—an accomplished educator and scholar with hands-on understanding of the fashion industry—oversaw the exhibition's related online course, contributed numerous insightful essays to this catalogue, and participated in shaping the checklist, as did year-long intern Anna Burckhardt, a fashion scholar, who also secured hundreds of image permissions. Kristina Parsons, Project Curatorial Assistant, was masterfully in control of logistics for the exhibition. *Items* attracted a wonderful cohort of interns: Margot Drayson, Alice Gong, Oliver Graney, and Maria McLintock. Xaviera Kouvara, Research Assistant in the Department of Research and Development, helped us organize Fashion Is Kale, the symposium that accompanied the exhibition.

Our book could only have achieved a fraction of its ambitions without our colleagues in Publications. We offer sincere thanks to Christopher Hudson, Publisher, for supporting the book from its conception; to our editor, Rebecca Roberts, who tirelessly oversaw a devoted editorial team and shaped our texts with grace and insight; to Hannah Kim, Production Manager, who was supremely patient and unflappable; and to Marc Sapir, Production Director, Chul Kim, Associate Publisher, and Don McMahon, Editorial Director, who offered invaluable guidance. We must also thank Stephanie Emerson, Emily Hall, Tanya Heinrich, Libby Hruska, and Maria Marchenkova, all of whom contributed to the editing of this volume. The book was elegantly designed by Natasha Chandani and Lana Cavar of Clanada, aided by Narcisa Vukojevic's illustrations. The catalogue benefited greatly from the essays contributed by two esteemed colleagues, Luke Baker, formerly Curatorial Assistant, and Jennifer Tobias, Librarian at MoMA. Sarah Rafson of Point Line Projects and her team, as well as independent researcher Marguerite Dabaie, aided the gargantuan task of image permissions. Finally, we are hugely indebted to Nancy Diehl, Director of the Costume Studies Program at New York University, who served as peer reviewer for the great majority of the catalogue's entries; Otto von Busch at Parsons The New School, who provided incisive and constructive remarks on the catalogue's introductory essay; Malika V. Kashyap, who provided a precious review of the entries on the salwar kameez and sari; Lars Krutak, who generously reviewed the entry on tattoos; and Zahra Billoo, Director of the Council on American-Islamic Relations, who kindly reviewed the entry on the hijab.

While we could fill a book with the names of those who helped us on this journey, the following people made extraordinary contributions to our research: Roxx 2Spirit; Pam Alabaster and her colleagues at Revlon; Rachel Anderson; Zara Atelj and her colleagues at Vlisco; Valarie Benning Barney; Paola Bay; Marisa Beard; Claire Bergkamp; Siobhan Bohnacker; Ralph Borland; Janie Bryant; Rabbi Melissa Buyer; Hussein Chalayan; Joseph Bryce; Rta Kapur Chishti; Duncan Clarke; Jemal Creary at Alamy; Anja Aronowsky Cronberg; John Cronce and Matthew Waller at Jockey; Franca Dantes; Howard Davis; Anna Daw; Jelani Day; Sylvia and Eleonora DeLennart; Paul Dillinger; Aitor Eguia; Julie Eilber; Ivette Feliciano; Joyce Fung; Lisa Gabor; Bobbito Garcia; Sanjay Garg; Kevin Gippert, Dana Gordon, and Sarah Zimmer at Getty Images; Michael Govan; Hugo Gozenbach; Charlotte Hagan; Ed Hardy; Tinker Hatfield; Martin Herde; Maura Horton; Deborah Hughes; Allison Ingham at Condé Nast; Wendy Israel at Hearst; Alex Jackson; James Jebbia; Clara Jeon; Laurene Powell Jobs; Dylan Jones; Nick Jones; Jenna Joselit; Marisa Kakoulas; Amanda Kasper; Kelis; Lulu Kennedy; DJ Clark Kente; Gabriella Khorasanee; Sandeep Khosla; Bruce Kilgore; Nick and Charlotte Knight; Nozomi Kobayashi; Lars Krutak; Maximilian Lang; Shannon Lee and Rafael Iniguez Jr., and their team at the Bruce Lee Archive; Sharon Lee; Mel Leverich and her colleagues at the Leather Archives and Museum; Reina Lewis; Jesse Leyva; Amanda López; Shaz Madani, Danielle Pender, and the team at *Riposte*; John Maeda; Phyllis Magidson at the Museum of the City of New York; Hala Malak; Dan Mathews and Karla Waples at PETA; Mike McCabe; Matilda McQuaid, Caitlin Condell, Kira Eng-Wilmot, and their colleagues at the Cooper Hewitt, Smithsonian Design Museum; John Merchant; Alexandra Midal; Margot Mifflin; Florence Muller; Freya Murray and her colleagues at the Google Cultural Institute; Michelle Myles; Mireille Nagourney; Rie Nii; Jane Nisselson; Hannah O'Leary; Bukola Olofinlade; Ulla Olsenius and her daughter Anna Lena; Cristian Panaite; Tracey Panek; Rajshree Pathy; Lauren Downing Peters; Suzanne Peterson and Ada Hopkins at the Bata Shoe Museum; Maria Popova; Srinivas Pokkunuru; Alice Rawsthorn; Laura Regensdorf; Aline Rezende; Chris Richards; Bibi Russell; Nadia and Rajeeb Samdani; Steven Sammut at Rex/Shutterstock; Michael Sanders; Rajshree and Samvit Sarabhai; Clare Sauro and Monica Stevens Smyth; Peter Saville; Sarah Scaturro; Karuna Scheinfeld; Sandy Schreier; Ajanta Sen; Suzanne Shapiro; Yael Shenberger; Rabbi Jodi Siff; Soumaya Slim; Galia Solomonoff; Samuel Spitzer; Nancy Talcott; Stephanie Tamez; Bernadette Thompson; Tracy Timmins; Maholo Uchida; Anuradha Vakil; Silvia Ventosa Muñoz; Diane Wendt; Louis Westphalen; Demetria White; Amy Williams; and Shaway Yeh.

Many of our outstanding colleagues at the Museum contributed importantly to the *Items* project. In the Department of Exhibition Administration and Planning, we thank the indefatigable Ramona Bannayan, Senior Deputy Director, Exhibitions and Collections; Erik Patton, Director, Exhibition Planning and Administration; and Rachel Kim, our rock of an exhibition manager, who oversaw logistics, contracts, and budgets and somehow maintained an aura of calm, as did stellar Registrars Jennifer Wolfe and Regan Hillman and conservators Lynda Zycherman and Megan Randall.

Betty Fisher, Senior Exhibition Manager, was a constant friend and partner and designed the entire exhibition, leading the outstanding carpentry and operations crew to produce a great installation. Their work was buttressed by the oversight of Mack Cole-Edelsack, Senior

Exhibition Manager, and Michele Arms, Assistant Production Manager. The look of the exhibition also greatly benefited from our conversations with designer Randall Peacock and his assistant, Marland Backus. In the Audio Visual Department, Aaron Harrow, AV Design Manager, Mike Gibbons, AV Exhibitions Foreperson, and Travis Kray, AV Technician, deserve special thanks. Tom Krueger led the incomparable art-handling squad, which also included preparators Eric Araujo, David Dawson, Elizabeth Riggle, and A&D's cherished Pamela Popeson. We cannot fathom how Maria Marchenkova did it, but she edited all our labels for the galleries. And, as usual, Peter Perez made impeccable frames. We were supremely fortunate to have the expert help of master dresser Tae Smith and her great team (Christina Ewald, Whitney Hanscom, Noelle Kichura, Virginia Theerman, and Friese Undine). They began as outside consultants and ended up as family. The same can be said for information designers Giorgia Lupi and Gabriele Rossi, who, with the support of Cara Smyth and Frank Zambrelli of Glasgow Caledonian New York College's Fair Fashion Center, rendered the past, present, and future of the fashion system in the glorious visualization with which the exhibition ended.

In MoMA's Department of Graphic Design, we thank Ingrid Chou, Associate Creative Director, and Claire Corey, Production Manager. Elle Kim, Senior Art Director, and Kevin Ballon, Graphic Designer, together not only created the graphics for the exhibition but provided invaluable contributions to the book's cover design. Thanks, also, to Rebecca Stokes, Director of Digital Initiatives and External Affairs; Cortney Cleveland, Digital Marketing Manager; Victor Samra, Digital Media Marketing Manager; Wendy Olson, Department Manager, Marketing; and Lama Makarem, Project Marketing Coordinator, for the crucial advertising, marketing, and social media efforts made on behalf of the exhibition.

Our colleagues in the Education Department spent countless hours helping to conceptualize and execute programming for *Items*, including the aforementioned Fashion Is Kale symposium, the Artists Experiment—for which Emily Spivack served as Artist-in-Residence—and the audio guide. One cannot underestimate the contributions of Wendy Woon, Director of Education; Pablo Helguera, Director, Adult and Academic Programs; Jess van Nostrand, Assistant Director, Exhibition Programs and Gallery Initiatives; Jenna Madison, Assistant Director, Interpretation, Research and Digital Learning; Sarah Kennedy, Assistant Director, Learning Programs and Partnerships; Adelia Gregory, Associate Educator, Public Programs and Gallery Initiatives; and Alexis Gonzalez, Public Programs Fellow. Special thanks go to Sara Bodinson, Director, Interpretation, Research and Digital Learning, and Kelly Cannon, Associate Educator, Interpretation, Research and Digital Learning, who, along with MoMA Digital colleagues Eva Kozanecka, Digital Producer, and outside consultants Karen Kedmey and Sean Yetter produced the free Massive Open Online Course (MOOC) that accompanied the show.

MoMA Publicist Meg Montgoris coordinated the exhibition's media coverage with exceptional grace. In Development, Bobby Kean, Associate Director, Exhibition Funding, and Jessica Smith, Development Officer, worked hard to underwrite this ambitious project, while Nancy Adelson, Deputy General Counsel, and Alexis Sandler, Associate General Counsel, adroitly handled the many legal aspects of this endeavor, from contracts to image-rights issues.

In our own department, we wish to thank Martino Stierli, Philip Johnson Chief Curator of Architecture and Design, who supported the project without wavering; Juliet Kinchin, Curator; Sean Anderson, Associate Curator; Emma Presler, Department Manager; Paul Galloway, Collection Specialist; Bret Taboada, former Assistant to the Chief Curator; Sam Fox, former Department Assistant, and Nadine Dosa, our brilliant Department Assistant and a key member of the *Items* team. We are also grateful to Amber Sasse and Kristina Mompoint at MoMA PS1, for allowing us to go on planning retreats there in the summer of 2016.

We are thankful to the Museum's Board of Trustees, and in particular, to Ronald S. Lauder, Honorary Chairman; Robert B. Menschel, Chairman Emeritus; Agnes Gund, President Emerita; Donald B. Marron, President Emeritus; Jerry I. Speyer, Chairman; Leon D. Black, Co-chairman; and Marie-Josée Kravis, President, for their passionate support of the Museum's curators. We also greatly appreciate the unflagging support of Peter Reed, Senior Deputy Director, Curatorial Affairs, and James Gara, Chief Operating Officer.

Finally, we would not have had the unmitigated pleasure and privilege of putting this show together had it not been for the vision and leadership of MoMA's Director, Glenn D. Lowry. Little did he, or we, foresee the outcome when, some years back, he encouragingly asked, "What if your list of garments that changed the world became an exhibition?" *Items—Is Fashion Modern?* is the answer to that question.

Last but not least, we thank two of the best-dressed people we know, Larry and Austin, for putting up with it all.

Paola Antonelli and Michelle Millar Fisher
The Museum of Modern Art, New York
August 2017